Kyoto's Gion Festival

Bloomsbury Shinto Studies

Series editor: Fabio Rambelli

The Shinto tradition is an essential component of Japanese religious culture. In addition to indigenous elements, it contains aspects mediated from Buddhism, Daoism, Confucianism, and, in more recent times, Western religious culture as well—plus, various forms of hybridization among all of these different traditions. Despite its cultural and historical importance, Shinto studies have failed to attract wide attention also because of the lingering effects of uses of aspects of Shinto for the ultranationalistic propaganda of Japan during WW II. The Series makes available to a broad audience a number of important texts that help to dispel the widespread misconception that Shinto is intrinsically related to Japanese nationalism, and at the same time promote further research and understanding of what is still an underdeveloped field.

The God Susanoo and Korea in Japan's Cultural Memory
David Weiss

Mountain Mandalas: Shugendo in Kyushu
Allan G. Grapard

The Origin of Modern Shinto in Japan: The Vanquished Gods of Izumo
Yijiang Zhong

Overseas Shinto Shrines
Karli Shimizu

Religion, Power and the Rise of Shinto in Early Modern Japan
Edited by Stefan Köck, Brigitte Pickl-Kolaczia and Bernhard Scheid

The Sea and the Sacred in Japan
Edited by Fabio Rambelli

Shinto, Nature and Ideology in Contemporary Japan
Aike P. Rots

A Social History of the Ise Shrines
Mark Teeuwen and John Breen

Kyoto's Gion Festival

A Social History

Mark Teeuwen

BLOOMSBURY ACADEMIC
LONDON • NEW YORK • OXFORD • NEW DELHI • SYDNEY

BLOOMSBURY ACADEMIC
Bloomsbury Publishing Plc
50 Bedford Square, London, WC1B 3DP, UK
1385 Broadway, New York, NY 10018, USA
29 Earlsfort Terrace, Dublin 2, Ireland

BLOOMSBURY, BLOOMSBURY ACADEMIC and the Diana logo are trademarks
of Bloomsbury Publishing Plc

First published in Great Britain 2023
This paperback edition published 2024

Series design by Dani Leigh

Cover image: *Rakuchû rakugaizu byôbu (Rekihaku kôhon)* © National Museum
of Japanese History

A catalogue record for this book is available from the British Library.

A catalog record for this book is available from the Library of Congress.

ISBN: HB: 978-1-3502-2992-1
PB: 978-1-3502-2996-9
ePDF: 978-1-3502-2994-5
eBook: 978-1-3502-2993-8

Series: Bloomsbury Shinto Studies

Typeset by Deanta Global Publishing Services, Chennai, India

To find out more about our authors and books visit www.bloomsbury.com
and sign up for our newsletters

Contents

Preface

Between 1989 and 1991, I spent eighteen months as a 'research student' at the private Shinto university Kōgakkan Daigaku in Ise. This was entirely due to the late Mayumi Tsunetada (1923–2019), whom I had encountered in the Netherlands through an interpreting job a year or two earlier. At the time, Mayumi-sensei was a senior priest at Yasaka Shrine in Kyoto, while also lecturing at Kōgakkan. He not only kept a keen eye on my behaviour but also gave me the opportunity to work at various shrines. In 1989, I spent a near-sleepless week at Yasaka Shrine as a trainee, doing all kinds of chores during the busy period around New Year. I recall that the *hakui* I was to wear offered little protection against the winter weather; this made our visits to a nearby bathhouse feel like sheer bliss. In 1991, before returning home, I attended the Gion festival. I vividly remember witnessing Mayumi-sensei riding a white horse in impressive priestly garb. Since that day, the Gion festival has been on my mind as a topic that, some day, I will need to study in earnest.

The chance to do just that came in 2018, when I had the opportunity to study at the Institute for Research in Humanities (Jinbun Kagaku Kenkyūjo) at Kyoto University as a research fellow for six months. My gratitude is due to Professor Takagi Hiroshi, who encouraged and guided me during my stay. I used my time to collect materials, meet participants from various corners of the festival and discuss my countless questions with scholars. I also signed up as a volunteer via the NPO Miyakogusa and worked at the Ōfune-hoko meetinghouse during *yoiyama*. My tasks were wrapping *chimaki* in plastic foil (a remarkably difficult craft), selling amulets and the like at *yoiyama*, and working the shoe shelves in the meetinghouse. The rewards were much camaraderie with fellow volunteers, and an invitation to a very alcoholic post-festival party in the meetinghouse. Thanks to Professor Yagi Tōru of Bukkyō University, I was introduced to Ōshima Hiroki of the nearby Ayagasa-hoko float, where I was allowed to attend *kippu-iri* and other float rites and had my first experience of wrapping *chimaki*.

The late Takeuchi Kōhei, a retired Yasaka priest whom I had first met in 1989, took me under his wing and introduced me to a range of central festival leaders. Among others, I met and interviewed Imanishi Tomoo, president of the Purity Association, and Yoshikawa Tadao, secretary-general of the Sanwaka *mikoshi* association, who kindly invited me to several *mikoshi*-related events. Murakami Tadayoshi, formerly of the Kyoto City Division for the Preservation of Cultural Properties, made time not only to talk to me but also to introduce me to the staff of the Floats Association office, where I was allowed access to the unpublished records that feature prominently in Chapter 5 of this book. I had two occasions to visit Mayumi-sensei in his Osaka home; he allowed me to steal various books from his upstairs library. Festival experts Satō Hirotaka, Saitō Hideki, Kikuchi Akira, Kobayashi Takao, Itō Setsuko and Nishiyama Tsuyoshi generously shared their work and their thoughts with me on multiple occasions. Ōta Tōru of Yūhisai Kōdōkan told me about his experiences as the father of a Naginata-hoko *chigo* and broadened my horizon by introducing me to both Kitano Tenmangū and Shimogamo Shrine, as well as to many aspects of Kyoto culture more generally.

Matthew Stavros created the maps for this book, and Miyake Tōru, Nishiyama Tsuyoshi, Satō Hirotaka, Matthew McKelway and John Breen helped me in different ways to procure some of the images. My gratitude is due to the very helpful staff of the Kyoto City Library of Historical Documents (Kyōto Rekishi Shiryōkan), the Kyoto Institute, Library and Archives (Rekisaikan), the Museum of Kyoto (Kyōto Bunka Hakubutsukan), the National Museum of Japanese History (Kokuritsu Rekishi Minzoku Hakubutsukan), the Suntory Museum of Art in Tokyo, the Ritsumeikan University Art Research Center, the International Research Center for Japanese Studies (Nichibunken) and the National Institute of Japanese Literature (Kokubungaku Kenkyū Shiryōkan).

Numerous other people have brightened my stay in Kyoto. Rather than burdening the reader with personal minutiae, let me finish by regretting the fact that the Covid-19 pandemic prevented me from returning to Kyoto after 2018. No doubt, more time and perhaps new discoveries would have made this book richer and more accurate. Sadly, it was not to be.

Explanatory notes

Dates prior to the introduction of the Gregorian calendar on New Year's Day of 1873 are given according to the lunisolar calendar that was in use at the time. To give an example, the name Gion is first mentioned in a diary entry dated 23.i6.920. This refers to the twentieth year of the Engi era, intercalary sixth month, twenty-third day, which corresponds to 9 August 920 according to the Gregorian calendar. Gregorian equivalents are generally one or even two months later than lunisolar dates. This explains why the traditional dates of the festival, on the seventh and the fourteenth of the sixth month, were eventually (after some back and forth) converted to 17 and 24 July from 1877 onwards. In some cases, dates at the end of the lunisolar year cross over into the following year according to the Gregorian calendar. I have preferred to stick to the Japanese year because this reflects the understanding of time that is relevant to the material. In case of a longer postponement, for example, it was regarded as crucial that the festival was performed before the last day of the year – in lunisolar terms.

Entries from court diaries (including *Teishin kōki*, the source of the date 23.i6.920) can be found in different printed compilations, including online databases. Particular handy (though not entirely complete) is the *Kokiroku* full-text database (wwwap.hi.u-tokyo.ac.jp/ships), created and made available by the Historiographical Institute of Tokyo University. On paper, *Dainippon kokiroku* (compiled by the same institute) is the most comprehensive collection. Since diaries are ordered chronologically, I give the dates of entries rather than page numbers in a particular printed version.

Personal names are given in the Japanese order, with the family name first. Many persons are referred to by a variety of names and titles in the sources; where a particular name is in common use in modern handbooks, I have adopted that name for easy reference.

A number of conventional period names are used in the text. For easy reference, their dates are listed here:

Nara	710–794
Heian	794–1185
Kamakura	1185–1333

Muromachi	1336–1573
Sengoku	1467–1568
Edo	1600–1867
Bakumatsu	1853–1867
Meiji	1868–1912
Taishō	1912–26
Shōwa	1926–89

The Nara and Heian periods are at times referred to as the 'ancient' or 'classical' period; Kamakura, Muromachi and Sengoku as the 'medieval' period; Edo as the 'early modern' period and Meiji and beyond as the 'modern' period.

Finally, I include here a full list of the *mikoshi* and floats that participate in the Gion festival. The numbers refer to Map 1 on p. 2. As the reader will soon find out, this list applies to the present festival, although it has changed little from the sixteenth century onwards. Some floats were known under different names in earlier periods; unless there is a point to make, I have referred to them by the names listed here.

Mikoshi
Before Meiji:
Ōmiya (carrying the deity Gozu Tennō)
Shōshōi (Harime or Harisainyo)
Hachiōji (Hachiōji)

After Meiji:
Naka-goza (carrying the deity Susanoo)
Higashi-goza (Kushi-inada-hime)
Nishi-goza (Yahashira no Mikogami)

Floats
The numbers refer to the locations indicated in Map 1 (see p. 2).

First parade (17 July; before 1877, the seventh day of the sixth month):
Hoko: Hōka-hoko (17); Tsuki-hoko (18); Kikusui-hoko (19); Kanko-hoko (20); Naginata-hoko (22); Niwatori-hoko (27); Iwato-yama (33); Fune-hoko (30)

Yama: Arare Tenjin-yama (11); Yamabushi-yama (12); Urade-yama (13); Tōrō-yama (15); Kakkyo-yama (16); Mōsō-yama (21); Ashikari-yama (23); Hakuga-yama (24); Abura Tenjin-yama (28); Tokusa-yama (29); Hakurakuten-yama (31); Taishi-yama (32); Hōshō-yama (34)
Kasa: Shijō Kasa-hoko (14); Ayagasa-hoko (26)

Second parade (24 July; before 1877, the fourteenth day of the sixth month):
Hoko: Taka-yama (1); Kita Kannon-yama (7); Minami Kannon-yama (10); Ōfune-hoko (25)
Yama: En no Gyōja-yama (2); Suzuka-yama (3); Hachiman-yama (4); Kuronushi-yama (5); Jōmyō-yama (6); Koi-yama (8); Hashi Benkei-yama (9); Hotei-yama (currently lost)

Illustrations

Maps

Figures

Introduction

If Japan has a proverbial *matsuri*, it must be Kyoto's Gion festival. This festival is remarkable for many reasons. It is among the oldest and the largest, although the Aoi (or Kamo) festival in the same city is even more ancient and Tokyo's Sanja festival rivals it in visitor numbers. Many festivals offer more spectacle and excitement; in its present form, the Gion festival is in fact rather subdued, more elegant than 'wild'. Yet Gion stands out for its high status, its long, almost unbroken history going back more than a millennium, and not least its influence on other festivals in Japan. Festivals of what I will call the Gion type spread throughout Japan in the medieval and early modern periods, and it is no exaggeration to state that this type became the defining *matsuri* format. Studying the history of the Gion festival will allow us to reveal many aspects of the proliferation of other similar festivals throughout Japan.

The Gion festival revolves around the notion that for the duration of the festival, the three deities who usually reside in Yasaka Shrine, on the eastern outskirts of Kyoto, take up residence in the centre of the city. There they are installed in a temporary site called the *otabisho*, the destination of the gods' 'journey' (*tabi*) from shrine to city. The gods are transported there in three *mikoshi*, elaborately decorated palanquins carried on the shoulders of large groups of men. They stay in their city quarters for a week, arriving on 17 July and returning on the 24th. Departing in the afternoon, the *mikoshi* circle the city by different routes, arriving at their destination late at night. The *mikoshi* weigh well over 2 tons, and they are carried over a distance of more than 10 kilometres. At token points along the route, the men put on rowdy shows of strength by thrusting the *mikoshi* up into the air, while onlookers cheer them on. The *otabisho*, which is located on Shijō Street, serves as a souvenir shop (Otabi Kyoto) during the rest of the year. While the *mikoshi* are stationed there, the street-facing wall is folded aside. The space in front of the *mikoshi* is filled with altar tables carrying food offerings, wooden tablets announcing the names of sponsors and donors, and rows of candles lit by people offering prayers.

On the days that the gods are moved, parades of large floats (*yamahoko junkō*) take place in the morning. The first parade, on the seventeenth, features twenty-

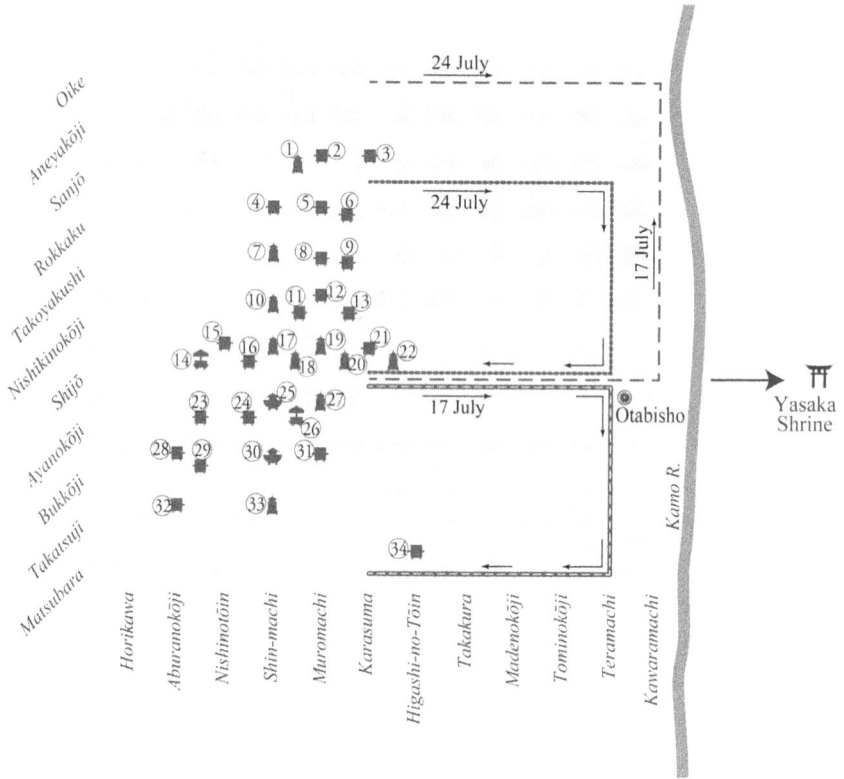

Map 1 The modern Gion festival: Float streets, the *otabisho* and Yasaka Shrine. The numbers refer to the list of floats on pp. xi–xii. The present route of the float parades (indicated by dashes in the map) is the result of reforms in 1955 and 1977. The older route (indicated by dots and a dotted line) remained largely unchanged since 1500 at the latest. Until 1873, the parades were held on the seventh and fourteenth days of the sixth month. Created by Matthew Stavros.

three floats, while the second, on the twenty-fourth, has eleven. In front of large crowds, the floats are pulled along a route of about 3 kilometres along the broad avenues of Shijō, Kawaramachi and Oike Street. Each float is accompanied by large groups of men in traditional formal garb, who walk with obvious authority; others, in simpler costumes, physically handle the floats by pulling, pushing, shouting and gesturing. The floats pass by the *otabisho* but do not cross the Kamo River to approach Yasaka Shrine. Their order is partly set, and partly determined by a lot-drawing ceremony performed on 2 July at City Hall. Not far into the parade, each float stops to present its lot to officials with ceremonial flourish.

The floats come in different shapes. Most spectacular are the *hoko* ('halberds'), large carts weighing 8–12 tons, built around a central pole (*shingi*) that reaches a height of up to 25 metres from the ground. Two *hoko* are decked out to represent

Figure 1 The Naka-goza *mikoshi* returns to Yasaka Shrine on 24 July 2015. Photograph by Miyake Tōru.

Figure 2 The first float parade, 17 July 2014. Naginata-hoko is turning the corner at the front, followed by Urade-yama, Ashikari-yama and Mōsō-yama. The tall Kanko-hoko is approaching in the distance. Photograph by Miyake Tōru.

ships.[1] All *hoko* carry groups of musicians seated on an elevated platform, playing flutes, hand-cymbals and small drums; each float has its own repertoire of rhythmic pieces. The *hoko* are moved by large teams of pullers, manning two ropes. The wheels don't turn, so the corners in the route provide an opportunity for the pullers to display their manoeuvring skills. More numerous than the *hoko* are floats called *yama* ('hills'). These are decorated platforms which typically display dolls that depict famous scenes, taken from Japanese or Chinese lore and literature. Until recently some of the *yama* were carried on people's shoulders, but in the 1960s and 1970s they all acquired wheels. Finally, the first parade has two 'parasols' (*kasa*), fitted on modest box-like carts. These are pulled along the parade route, accompanied by musicians and dancers. All floats, large or small, are decorated with exquisite materials; particularly famous are the Gobelin tapestries hung from many of them, some of which are antique Chinese, Korean, Persian and even European imports handed down since the Edo period.

The floats are based in a cluster of 'streets' (*chō*), concentrated in an area of Kyoto known as Shimogyō, the Lower City. Some of these streets have retained their traditional form, dominated by low, terraced houses, many with shop fronts. Others consist mainly of apartment blocks, interspersed with a few private houses. Some are no longer residential areas and contain only high-rise office blocks. Each of these streets has a street meetinghouse (*kaisho*) where the float materials are kept, and where the float organizers convene. The floats are managed and funded by 'preservation associations' (*hozonkai*), which in some streets consist of local residents but may also include members who live elsewhere; some are dominated by employees of companies based in the street. Each street has its own ritual traditions, and the annual exertions and excitement of the festival offer the participants a sense of local pride and belonging.

Around this framework of float parades and *mikoshi* processions, numerous smaller rituals stretch out the festival from the beginning of July until the last day of that month. The *mikoshi* are ritually cleansed on 10 July (*mikoshi arai*). Rites involving water and fire last deep into the night, and an elaborate 'lantern parade' (*omukae chōchin*) follows one of the *mikoshi* to the Shijō Bridge over the Kamo River. Late at night on 15 July, the gods are moved from the shrine into the *mikoshi*; they are returned to the shrine in a similar fashion on 24 July. For most common Kyotoites and other visitors who are not directly involved in the festival, the days before the parades (*yoi-yama*, *yoiyoi-yama* and *yoiyoiyoi-yama*, *yoi* meaning 'eve') are the main highlight. In the evenings of these days the floats and their treasures are displayed to the public. As the summer heat disperses after sundown, large crowds of viewers roam the float streets to listen to the float musicians, buy float amulets and

Figure 3 The bustle along Shijō street during *yoiyoi-yama* (15 July 2015). Tsuki-hoko is visible on the right. Photograph by Miyake Tōru.

souvenirs, eat and drink at street stalls or simply enjoy the bustle. There are rituals connected to the setting up, the first pulling and the disassembly of the floats, while others relate to the handling of the sacred figurines that they contain. One *hoko* and both *kasa* have 'divine children' (*chigo*), who sit in or accompany these floats;[2] their transformation from primary school boys into sacred figures involves further ritual cycles. The official end of the Gion festival is on 31 July (*nagoshi matsuri*), when participants and the general public are invited to pass through a ring of bamboo grass at Yasaka Shrine and receive amulets that protect against illness.

The key feature that defines 'Gion type' festivals is the combination of *mikoshi* palanquins and a float parade. Surveys show that across Japan, some 1,500 festivals follow this general pattern, including some festivals that have recently been discontinued.[3] Implicit in this format is a decentralized structure involving many distinct groups of participants. The shrine priests, the float groups and the *mikoshi* bearers are at the festival's centre, but even they have limited influence on the proceedings. At arm's length, but arguably even more influential, are the festival's patrons and sponsors, who often include local authorities, businesses and politicians, and in the past rulers, warlords and merchants of various descriptions. In the course of their history, festivals wax and wane as such agents rise to dominance, elbow past competitors, suffer setbacks and are replaced by newcomers. The Gion festival is unique in that at least some of these dynamics are documented. Although the historical record is riddled with gaps, it allows us to trace the outlines of its history from the tenth century until today at a level of detail that no other festival can match.

The aims of this book

Why study *matsuri* festivals, and why now? One reason for writing this book is that *matsuri* have emerged as one of the central symbols of Japanese culture and heritage in recent years. This trend gathered pace in the late 1970s, when festivals across the country were designated as Important Intangible Cultural Properties under the revised Law for the Protection of Cultural Properties (1975). In 2009, it culminated in the inscription of the Gion festival's float parades in UNESCO's List of Intangible Cultural Heritage of Humanity.[4] To point up the value of these festivals, the UNESCO website stresses that 'they involve the collaborative efforts of various sections of the community and as a traditional practice are an important aspect of the cultural identity of participants'.[5] This sentence, which flowed from the pen of heritage officials from the Japanese Agency for Cultural Affairs, aptly sums up the current understanding of festivals and their function in society: they enact 'traditions' that maintain the 'cultural identity' of communities.

It is characteristic for the rhetoric of heritage to celebrate ancient, changeless tradition rather than remember actual history. Festivals, it appears, have become caught up in this discourse of nostalgia, and they now serve as the most striking arenas for nostalgic re-enactment in all corners of Japan. This is a recent development. One festival researcher remembers the 1970s as a turning point. From that decade on, he notes, every festival he investigated suddenly began to grow larger, more popular and more extravagant by the year. He observes that this was a great change from the 1950s and 1960s, when festivals were seen as 'mouldy lumps of dust, left over from the past': boorish, noisy and dirty, out of tune with modern times, a stage for ignorant louts or, even worse, small-time criminals.[6]

The current discourse on festivals as tradition invites us to regard their survival as a matter of course. Without these traditions, after all, the community would lose its cultural identity, so it is only natural that their continuation has always been a matter of the highest priority. This assumption, however, is far from the lived reality of those who organize and carry out the Gion festival. In my interaction with them, many expressed a sense of precariousness even in this era of active city and state involvement. Participants struggle to solve issues of economy, social change, access to public space and much else. That precariousness was much more pronounced at the many moments of crisis that punctuate the festival's history, most obviously during two periods when it could not be staged at all (1467–1500 and 1943–7). As a large and costly event that has to be created anew every year, the Gion festival (like any festival) is and has always been on the verge of crisis. The festival has not only survived; people have gone to great lengths to revive it multiple times. Its resilience cannot be readily accepted as a natural state of affairs. Few festivals, after all, have such long lives. The Gion festival's longevity should amaze us and inspire us to question how this decidedly unnatural state of affairs has come about. My agenda, then, is to strip away the illusion that 'tradition' has carried this festival through troubled waters for over a millennium, and that we can trust this same force to keep it going into the future. In my view, the festival is not testimony to such an elusive force but, rather, to the actions of a string of historical actors who, by some miracle, have 'caught the ball' every time it was dropped. My simple question is: How was this possible?

On a theoretical level, Olivier Morin (2016) has addressed the question of the transmission of 'tradition' from a position of maximum abstraction. Morin is interested in stability of cultural transmission. He uses the term 'tradition' to refer to practices that have spread beyond their original context and that have achieved some degree of stability across time and space. His definition of the term does not include 'practices [that] are only thought to be ancient because they serve as tokens of worship or identity symbols, though they date from yesterday or the day before'[7] – which, as he rightly points out, is another central meaning of 'tradition'. In other words, he is not interested in traditionalists' inventions of ancient historical origins for recent practices that are sacred to their community identities. Rather, he asks to what degree stable cultural transmission over time is theoretically possible, and under what conditions.

Morin identifies two key challenges to the transmission of any practice, idea or other cultural element. He calls them the Wear-and-Tear Problem and the Flop Problem. The first refers to the difficulty of transmitting information correctly over time; small changes in every link of a transmission chain will soon corrupt the message (or practice) beyond recognition, as in a game of Chinese whispers (more commonly known in the United States as 'telephone'). There are, however, mechanisms that limit the damage. Widely practised 'traditions' are transmitted many times and through countless channels, helping actors to correct accidental mistakes. Likewise, incomplete transmissions can often be reconstructed or reinvented, allowing the tradition to continue or be revived in a form that may not be identical, but that is nonetheless recognized as a continuation of a past practice. A greater challenge than 'wear and tear', Morin argues, is the often ignored and less studied Flop Problem. Tradition has long been ascribed to a natural compulsion in humans to imitate their fellows and abide by established social norms (Morin refers to Herder, among others, as an early propagator of this idea). This raises the question why cultural practices change at all, in defiance of allegedly 'compulsive' imitation. It is a palpable fact that only very few cultural practices are 'successful' enough to catch on, spread and endure. The main problem is not that they are corrupted in transmission, although that, too, is unavoidable; rather, their ability to engage actors fades away. It is when people lose interest that traditions 'flop'.

This book is not concerned with cultural epidemiology (the discipline that Morin identifies with) but with the concrete history of the Gion festival as one of Japan's most influential festivals. Where Morin seeks to find universal rules that govern cultural transmission by circumventing the serendipities of local contexts, this book concerns itself with exactly those contexts. By following this festival through history, this study confirms Morin's suggestion that the question of wear and tear, which has dominated transmission studies, can be circumvented quite easily by drawing on living memory, extant documents or the surviving traditions of neighbouring communities. Questions of engagement and relevance under new circumstances, on the other hand, are of paramount importance. At no point in history was it physically impossible to revive the festival; the more pertinent question was always whether there were enough reasons to do so for a large enough section of actors.

A fundamental problem with studies that approach the transmission of 'tradition' as a game of Chinese whispers is the underlying assumption that an unbroken chain of transmitters is necessary. The game naturally ends when the cake is brought out, and the whispered words are no longer transmitted. It will be played again, however, by other groups of people, who will take the idea and fashion it to fit their own setting. What is transmitted is not the whispered words but the idea of whispering words. This idea is never interesting to one group of people for a long period of time; but others will find it attractive at some other time, and try it again. Groups of participants will form and disperse, but as long as the attraction exists, the 'tradition' will keep being reinvented. The crux of the matter is the question whether interest and attraction survive historical moments of radical social change.

In their search for universal laws, scholars of cultural transmission ignore the fact that the actors who perform, control, define or make a living out of attractive practices are frequently exchanged. Typically, this happens in a moment of crisis; often it spells the end of the transmission and the practice. Not many practices survive the demise of a cultural setting, the burning down of central assets necessary to their performance, the disappearance of established networks of patronage and sponsorship, changes in economic structures that put central actors out of business or the emergence of new value systems that undermine the prestige of a practice, or even frame it as an outdated remnant of 'the bad old days'. In some cases, however, new groups of people take over and redesign a practice in a manner that fits its new social, economic or political context. At such moments, the 'transmission chain' is broken; but the practice rises from the ashes to see another day. Only very few practices pull this off multiple times; the Gion festival has been one such rare exception. The festival came close to flopping at numerous junctures, but every time this happened, it has been reinvented by people whose agendas differed from those of their predecessors.

It is this process of a practice changing hands that John Breen and I examined in a previous book in this same series about the history of the Ise Shrines.[8] As an ancient site of imperial worship and, later, as a particularly popular pilgrimage hub, Ise is the most prominent and authoritative shrine complex in the country, with a documented history of thirteen centuries. At first sight, it appears to be an obvious example of a 'stable' cultural practice of ritual and worship. A second look, however, reveals a succession of crises, caused by the demise of central groups of agents and their replacement by others. Again and again, new stakeholders took over the baton, redeveloped the site with the help of new support networks, funding mechanisms, significations and narratives, infrastructures, ritual (and non-ritual) services and more. Looking back on this history, there is indeed stability, particularly on the surface; but this stability has merely served as a lasting canvas on which changing groups have drawn up one radical innovation after another. To describe this continual process in terms of 'wear and tear' is to miss the point entirely.

Festivals are even more precarious in nature than shrines, because they have to be recreated every year. Like shrines, however, they represent 'divine capital' that has the potential to remain attractive to participants, patrons and investors of many kinds. The aim of this volume is similar to that of *A Social History of the Ise Shrines*: to trace the social dynamics that have kept the festival going in the face of incessant fundamental changes and occasional disasters, by pinning down the actors who made this possible.

Festivals as public events: Avoiding the 'religion versus politics' trap

The current definition of the Gion festival as a 'tradition' that expresses communal cultural identity competes with another perspective that stresses the festival's religious meaning. Not only the shrine priesthood but also many other participants stress 'faith' (*shinkō*) as the 'true meaning' (*hongi*) of the festival – though usually without specifying what that faith entails in more concrete terms. The demise of faith in the face of political manipulation of the festival, including adaptations to 'improve' it as a tourism resource, has been seen as an imminent threat to the festival's authenticity. In 1963, for example, the newspaper *Kyōto shinbun* published articles with such titles as 'Tourism or faith?' and 'Between show and faith', debating whether the festival was a 'ritual for the gods' (*shinji*) or an 'event' (*gyōji*) that supported Kyoto's position as a city of international tourism.[9] Yasaka Shrine's head priest has pointed out that this discussion can be traced back to the pre-war period.[10] The notion that faith rather than spectacle forms the essence of the festival has since resurfaced at times of national crisis, notably after the tsunami and nuclear meltdown in 2011, and during the Covid-19 pandemic in 2020–1.[11] In many float streets, the felt need to stress the festival's inner essence as a ritual for the gods has inspired new ritual practices, not only at such times of prayer but also under more normal circumstances, as Christoph Brumann has documented.[12]

Faith also plays a role in the discourse of tradition and cultural identity but mostly as a matter of the past. According to the official description of the festival as UNESCO Intangible Cultural Heritage (2009), the festival floats were '*originally* intended to summon the Plague Deity', but '*today* showcase the creative spirit and artistry of the float-building districts and provide entertainment for the entire city' (emphasis added). This narrative reflects a common understanding of the history of festivals, as events that started as religious 'rituals for the gods' but in the modern era morphed into secular celebrations of culture, or as mere entertainment. It reflects a common notion of a pious past that may have lost its religious functionality, but that continues to enrich traditional culture. This narrative is wrong about the present, because it downplays the explicit emphasis on faith, and also about the past, because it ignores the many aspects of the festival that did not involve faith.

To avoid falling into a false dichotomy between the religious and the political, I follow Don Handelman in approaching the festival simply as a 'public event', rather than a 'religious ritual that has turned secular' or a 'secular ceremony with religious elements'. In his book *Models and Mirrors: Towards an Anthropology of Public Events* (1990), Handelman analyses events of a particular significance that occur in the public sphere, without assuming that these events must or can be categorized as religious or secular. This approach has several advantages. It helps us avoid condemning political, commercial or playful aspects of what we (randomly and anachronistically) choose to label as religious as signs of decline or inauthentic corruption. It also opens our eyes to the fact that questions of power and commerce can be as essential, or more essential, for the festival's design and resilience as ideas about religious meaning.

Handelman not only liberates us from the paradigm of religious versus secular but also proposes a different set of categories as tools to analyse public events.[13] He starts his book with three images that serve to illustrate different 'modes of apprehending the lived-in world through public events'. The first shows a royal entry into sixteenth-century Antwerp, the second a Sinhalese Buddhist exorcist performing a healing ritual and the third a playful scene of Halloween fun in Newfoundland. These vignettes, Handelman proposes, represent the three modes that 'index' public events of different kinds. Handelman is interested in the mechanics of public events, the ways in which they acquire the 'capacity to make something happen'. He assumes that public events are designed to communicate a message that must be 'cognitively graspable, but also emotionally livable' if the event is to retain its value to the people who invest in its staging. The three modes help us identify what it is that specific public events are trying to 'make happen'. Depending on what public events seek to communicate, they require different 'logics of meta-design'. Recognizing the modes and designs of public events allows us to identify the logic that structures them.

The three modes of public events do different kinds of work. In Handelman's terms, which I sometimes find counterintuitive, the first, exemplified by the royal entry, 'mirrors' or 'presents' an ideal that the main patrons or agents behind the public event want to communicate. The event's main aim is not to bring about a change but, rather, to present an already existing reality to the observers: it serves as a mirror, for example of the king's power in the example from Antwerp, or of the Communist order in the march of the Great October Socialist Revolution in Moscow's Red Square. The mirroring event not only reflects but also sustains, or even creates, the power that it presents. The second mode, in contrast, follows a certain 'model' – a set procedure, to be performed in a predetermined order – with the aim to make a change. The Sinhalese exorcist in the vignette wants to change the sick client into a healthy one. The *chisungu* initiation of prospective brides in Zambia transforms Bemba girls into women ready to become wives. These procedures do not merely reflect an already existing reality but are designed to transform that reality. Finally, the third mode, illustrated by the playful Halloween in Newfoundland, can be described as ludic or carnivalesque. It temporarily breaks the order of normality through play and, by exposing implicit norms, makes them acutely visible. This is a kind of 'presenting' with a twist, and Handelman calls it 're-presentation'. In brief, then, we can label Handelman's three modes as mirror, model and play.

The meta-designs of these three modes have different characteristics. 'Events that mirror' make declarations or enunciations in a regimented and standardized format, without contradictions or paradoxes; the only tension involved occurs at the interface between the event and society outside of it. 'Events that model' create a schematic microcosm of the lived-in world and perform operations on that microcosm in order to create a change in a goal-oriented manner. Sometimes this involves playing with fire, and there is always tension because things can go badly wrong. Finally, 're-presenting events' play with inversion but ultimately end in a reversion that reaffirms the status quo. Events in this mode are often loosely organized and potentially unstable, though the temporary chaos that they cause is seldom allowed to escalate out of control.

It should be stressed that Handelman sees these modes not as mutually exclusive, and rather visualizes them as the extremities of a triangular field, with most events located somewhere in the middle. He also points out that events change over time, and that elements in one mode can be 'nested' within events that are predominantly composed in another mode. The result is a structure of overlapping modes and designs that reflect not only the festival's present but also its past.

Handelman's field of modes is simple and yet rich in nuances. It leads us to think about what the festival's patrons and participants were trying to achieve at different stages of its history, and gives us tools to deduce the festival's 'work' from its format, rather than from explicit statements by participants or patrons about their intentions. This is all the more valuable because such statements are rare. In the eleven centuries of its history, the Gion festival has 'flopped' (in Morin's terms) and changed 'mode' (in Handelman's terms) on multiple occasions. The leading questions in my investigation of this festival's history are why new people stepped in after every collapse, and how the festival's meta-design changed repeatedly under new circumstances. Both Morin's notion of the constant danger of 'flopping' and Handelman's theory of modes and meta-designs serve to put us on the trail of the festival's social history – that is, the history of the ever-changing networks of participants, patrons and other social groups who reinvented the festival whenever its political, economic and social setting was transformed.

Ultimately, my aim is to provide an overview of the historical development of this best-documented of all Japanese festivals through a critical reading of primary and secondary sources, while applying these analytical tools to the available material. The merit of a *longue-durée* history is that it forces us to abandon essentializing notions of inherent meaning and function. As Scott Schnell has pointed out in his history of the Fukagawa festival, historical awareness prevents the observer from reducing a festival to a conservative, static re-enactment of an ancient status quo.[14] By focusing on moments of radical innovation in the post-Meiji development of the Fukagawa festival, Schnell brings out its role as a site where power is performed, negotiated and challenged, or even as an instrument of sociopolitical change. The history of the Gion festival gives us many excellent examples of this same dynamic over an even longer timeframe.

In this book, I will follow the festivals' history as closely as I can manage up to the end of the Occupation period in 1952. The festival's post-war history is no less fascinating as that of early periods, but it is covered in some detail elsewhere and must remain beyond the scope of this book.[15] We will leave the festival at a point in time when its present structures were already fully visible and recognizable. Rather than repeating other works dealing with those structures in their contemporary guise, I will reserve space to study the very different dynamics of earlier periods in more detail.

Such a task is made easier by the painstaking work of many Japanese historians, whose work forms the main body of sources on which I draw. There are several archives of primary sources that allow us to catch glimpses of the festival in different periods. The main ones are diaries of court nobles for the earliest centuries, and collections of documents preserved and published by Yasaka Shrine for the medieval and Edo periods. There are very few depictions of the festival before the sixteenth century, but from that point onwards the historian is spoiled with a large number of paintings and prints, some of such high quality that they have been designated as National Treasures. Written sources multiply from the eighteenth century onwards. Classical and medieval sources made (mostly fleeting) mention of the festival through the eyes of the court nobility, the shogunate or the shrine; but from the mid-Edo period onwards, we gain access to other perspectives. The festival is lauded in guidebooks for visitors, street communities noted down their local procedures, peddlers sold cheap printed sheets that announced or reviewed fringe events, and visitors wrote about their impressions in their diaries. From the Meiji period onwards the festival was featured in the newspapers, where debates about its value – and the disruption it caused to traffic and business – flamed up. With the arrival of state subsidies in the 1920s, the festival was documented and regulated in new ways that created yet another category of sources. In my discussion of this last period, I will draw primarily on unpublished records of the Floats Association.

Especially before the Edo period, a lack of sources makes detailed study of the history of most festivals very difficult. While there is more to go on for historians of the Gion festival, the historical record remains patchy, not only for early periods but even for the recent past. We have few sources about the activities of many groups of participants, from the pariah guards and cleaners who led the *mikoshi* processions to the caretakers of the *otabisho*. There is a lot of material about the float parades, but less on the *mikoshi* processions, and almost nothing on goings-on at the *otabisho*. The festival archive may appear large, but it is riddled with holes, and often it has nothing to say about the questions that interest me most. Resisting the temptation to fill in those holes with conjecture is an exercise that I have not always mastered. The painful truth is that there is much we will never know; I see pointing out what we don't know as an important task in what follows.

1

900–1200

The politics of divine wrath

The Gion festival was the product of a time of upheaval. Already when it first emerged, in the latter half of the tenth century, it was many things at once: a desperate measure against disease, a splendid display of cultural and economic power, a showcase for elite authority and an arena for protest and agitation. The tenth century was a time of profound political and economic change; Kyoto was the place where that change was created, and from where it washed over the country. The factional infighting, the splendour of the winners and the despair of the losers, and the transformation of imaginations of the suprahuman realm are all on vivid display in the early Gion festival. This chapter will shed light on the social, political and religious dynamics that determined the festival's shape in the first phase of its development. First, however, we must briefly set the scene.

The setting: Kyoto and its politics

Until the late medieval period, Kyoto was the only 'city' in the Japanese islands. It was founded in 794 by Emperor Kanmu (r. 781–806) as a replacement of the earlier capitals of Nara (710–84) and Nagaoka (785–94). Modelled on the much larger Tang capital of Chang'an, Kyoto (at the time named Heiankyō, or simply Miyako) was planned as a city of large, straight avenues and square blocks of housing, covering an equally square area of about 4.4 by 5.2 kilometres. In theory, it was to occupy almost all of the plain between the Katsura and Kamo Rivers, hemmed in by steep hills on three sides while opening up to the south. A wide boulevard entered the city from the south, running in a straight line to the southern gate of the Imperial Palace on the northern edge of the city. This

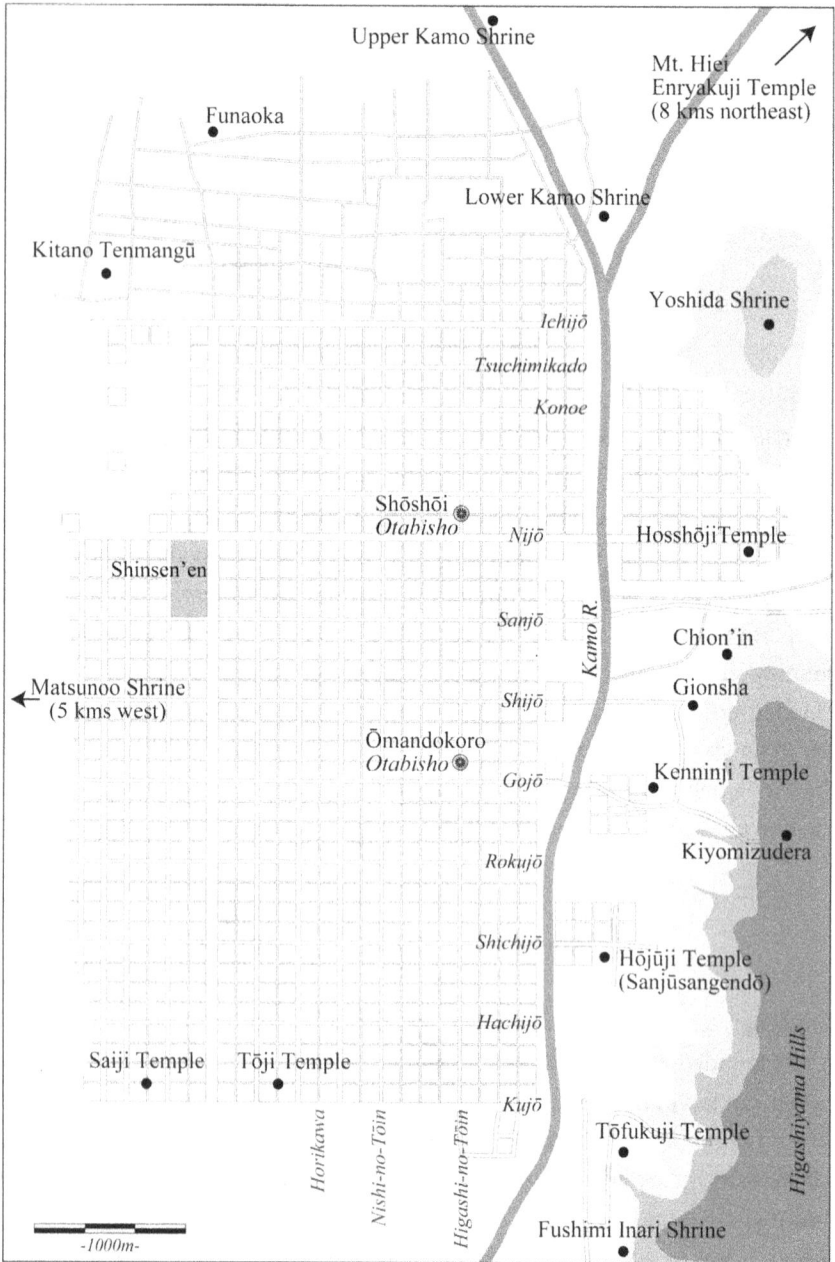

Map 2 Kyoto in the eleventh century. Created by Matthew Stavros.

boulevard crossed with straight avenues, running from east to west, which were numbered from one, on the city's northern edge, to nine in the south.

Some 7,000 officials held positions within the imperial bureaucracy; they formed the core of the official city. Adding their families, house servants and workers of various kinds, the population of ninth-century Kyoto was perhaps in the order of a hundred thousand inhabitants.[1] Plots within the blocks carved out by Kyoto's oversized roads were assigned to officials on the basis of rank, while many areas in the vicinity of the palace were dominated by dormitories for corvée workers from the provinces. Two official markets for the exchange of products were located on Shichijō, the 'seventh avenue' in the southern half of the city. Right on the city's southern edge were the only two temples of Kyoto's original design, named simply the 'Eastern' (Tōji) and 'Western Temple' (Saiji). While the north was dominated by the court, the south was the domain of people connected with these markets and temples. Places beyond the city boundaries were used to deposit the remains of the dead and dump other sources of pollution. The area east of the Kamo River, where Gion would be founded two centuries later, was one such place.

Kyoto's original design was never completely realized, and over the first centuries of the city's existence it gradually became more concentrated, smaller and more diverse. The western half of the city proved swampy and flood-prone, and most of this area was soon transformed into farmland or brush. The western market atrophied, while new communities of artisans and traders emerged further east along Shichijō, where the eastern market had been, and in the area between the third and fourth avenues, Sanjō and Shijō. The system of assigning plots based on court rank became a dead letter, and especially in the southern half of the city people made their own arrangements, narrowing the streets and abandoning plots on the inside of blocks that lacked street frontage.

Many of these changes were related to political developments that occurred in the ninth and tenth centuries. In Kanmu's time, when Kyoto was founded, candidates from different lineage backgrounds had competed for positions within the imperial ministries of the court. In the course of the ninth century, however, the Fujiwara, ancient allies of the imperial line and suppliers of imperial consorts, came to dominate the court as imperial 'regents' (sesshō and kanpaku), sharing out court appointments among themselves and their supporters almost at will. Their dominance soon undermined the economic foundation of the court bureaucracy.

In the eighth and ninth centuries, the imperial apparatus had registered the population in its provinces, allocated public land to commoner households at regular intervals and collected taxes (including produce, corvée labour and military service) from those households in return. These taxes provided the court bureaucracy with products and manpower. In the tenth century, however, this system was abandoned. Instead, so-called custodial governors (*zuryō*) were given an almost free hand in extracting taxes from their assigned provinces by whatever means they preferred. After a set amount was paid to the court treasury, any excess takings were theirs to keep. The power to appoint such governors rested with a Fujiwara elite, who formalized their decisions through their control of the court bureaucracy while channelling much of the revenues into their own network. The eleventh century, moreover, saw the rise of an entirely new method for people of power to secure income from land: the commended estate (*shōen*). Under this system, public lands were granted complete or partial freedom from taxation (often through the offices of a custodial governor) and exploited by a chain of managers, proprietors and guarantors, who all held rights to income from the tax-exempt lands. Again, Fujiwara leaders held the largest portfolio of *shōen* estates as their proprietors, guarantors or both.

These changes transformed the city. Classical Kyoto had been designed around the Imperial Palace, surrounded by court ministries and offices that were crowded into the walled palace compound that occupied the northernmost precinct of the city. Now that political and economic power was leaking to the Fujiwara and their clients, the palace compound lost much of its relevance. Whenever the palace burned down (and this happened fourteen times between 960 and 1082 alone), the emperor and his staff were reduced to temporary lodgings – often in the villas of Fujiwara leaders. By the thirteenth century, temporary lodgings had become a permanent solution and the original palace was no longer rebuilt. In the process, Kyoto had changed from an orderly stage for the emperor and his officials into a chaotic city of rivalling networks, dominated by the Fujiwara regents at first but soon fragmenting further as the city's politics grew even more opaque.

Temples played a large role in this transfer of power. By moving the capital to Kyoto, Kanmu had taken the court away from the immediate vicinity of the grand temples of Nara. This created new opportunities for temples around Kyoto. In the course of the ninth century, the rapidly expanding Tendai temple complex on Mt Hiei (granted the imperial name of Enryakuji in 823) to the north-east of the capital and the older Tōji on the city's southern edge emerged as the main purveyors of Buddhist court rites. Such rites were at the very core of the court's ideology of rule. In a setting where droughts and floods, failed harvests, famines, epidemics, fires and social unrest were regular occurrences, the emperor served not only as the ruler of the realm of human affairs but also as the guarantor of harmony in the suprahuman domain of the gods and spirits. It was these suprahuman entities that caused the calamities that so often struck the land; and only the court possessed the authority and the means to identify the causes of disorder, determine the measures that might prevent or stop it, and stage the grand rites necessary for that purpose. Enryakuji and Tōji competed for the patronage of the court both with each other and with the temples of Nara (notably Kōfukuji and Tōdaiji). That patronage typically took the form of the allotment of economic resources and monastic appointments, as well as the privilege of performing both regular ceremonies and ad hoc rites in response to particular crises. Such ceremonies and rites involved rich court offerings that were an important source of income for the officiating temple. Sometimes, temples were rewarded with land rights and estates.

The large temple complexes functioned as integrated components of the court apparatus. The Fujiwara maintained particularly close ties with Enryakuji and Kōfukuji. At the former, they held the authority to appoint the head abbot (*zasu*), and the Fujiwara leaders often selected one of their own. Positions within the court bureaucracy and within the temple complexes were fought over by the same, or at least overlapping factions. The Fujiwara regents not only sought to control existing temple complexes but also founded their own temples. These Fujiwara temples held portfolios of land rights as proprietors and guarantors of estates, and they served as nodes of networks of clients and service people, ranging from farmers and skilled workers to leaders of armed men.[2] The estates and their service people provided the regents who owned them with both economic and military clout.

Temple complexes like Enryakuji were very active in expanding their own reach. Enryakuji developed ways to enlarge its portfolio of tax-exempt estates, held by different temple halls and cloisters on the mountain. Often, small branch temples (*betsuin*) were founded on such estates to administer them. Enryakuji defined the farmers, fishermen, workers and traders who lived on its estates as 'service people of the deities' (*jinin*) and extracted produce and labour from them, while offering them its protection in return. This model of making contributions to Enryakuji (or its subsidiary Hie Shrines, at the eastern foot of Mt Hiei) as *jinin* in exchange for protection spread far beyond the confines of the temple's estates. As we shall see in Chapter 2, it would be adopted by many Kyoto merchants in subsequent centuries, allowing Enryakuji to become the most powerful institution of the capital.

Enryakuji also expanded its network of temples and shrines into the city of Kyoto; and this is where we finally arrive at Gion. The Gionsha ('Gion Shrine'), which would be renamed Yasaka Shrine in 1868, had been founded in the late ninth or early tenth century and was incorporated in Enryakuji's network as one of its *betsuin* in the 970s. The Gion festival was therefore conducted under the aegis of the temple complex on Mt Hiei, while also enjoying patronage from the court. This put the festival in the frontline of struggles between Enryakuji and its clients on one hand, and various factions based at the court on the other – a situation that was rendered even more murky by the many overlaps between temple and court factions, and by the ever-changing landscape of alliances and rivalries between and within those factions.

With the collapse of the old imperial order, its formalized policies for controlling the suprahuman realm were also forced to change. The classical court drew not only on Buddhism but also on imperial worship of the 'gods of heaven and earth' (*jingi*) as a means to render its authority visible.[3] This entailed the performance of a wide range of rituals aiming to secure good harvests and protect the nation, the capital and the palace from disease, floods, fires and other calamities. The signature rite of the *jingi* cult (performed multiple times a year, and most grandly as part of the *kinensai* spring ritual in prayer for a good harvest) was the distribution of imperial offerings to shrines across the land – or, to be more precise, to local leaders who, in their turn, derived their authority from their leadership in worshipping the deities of those shrines.

By the tenth century, however, the *jingi* cult had been reduced to a less national, more regional format. Local leaders from distant provinces were excluded from positions within the court bureaucracy. As a result, their deities fell out of the purview of *jingi* ritual. Instead, the court patronized a much shorter list of shrines within its heartlands, the Kyoto and Nara area; the number stopped at twenty-two in the first half of the eleventh century. The Gionsha was among the last to join this list. With the exception of Ise, the twenty-two 'shrines' were in fact all dominated by temples where monks performed court-sponsored Buddhist rituals to pacify the shrine deities.[4] The Gionsha and its festival arose from such rituals. Its deities, as we shall see, were of a new type, quite unrelated to the gods of the *jingi* cult. In the volatile factional battles of the tenth and eleventh centuries, which often involved claims that opponents suffered punishment from deities or spirits for transgressions they had allegedly committed, novel types of divine beings took centre-stage and eroded the prestige of the old gods of classical court mytho-history. As we shall soon see, the Gionsha deities were typical examples of such fearsome deities.

The situation became even more volatile in the late eleventh century, when emperors followed the example of the Fujiwara regents by founding their own temples and using those temples as political, economic and also military bases, now used to undermine Fujiwara power. This marked the start of the period of 'cloistered rule' (*insei*), whose beginning is usually dated to 1086, the year Emperor Shirakawa (1053–1129) abdicated and built a new power base as retired (or 'cloistered') emperor. The temple Hosshōji (founded in 1077) in eastern Kyoto served as Shirakawa's headquarters. From this majestic complex, the retired emperor's staff created and coordinated an expanding network of richly endowed imperial temples.[5] Shirakawa's strategy was emulated by subsequent emperors. By the mid-twelfth century, the simmering tension between Fujiwara regents and retired emperors escalated as both parties began to employ the help of warrior groups. This opened the door to the participation of warriors in Kyoto politics, triggering a full-scale war in the 1180s and leading to the founding of the first shogunate, in Kamakura, in 1192. By that time, however, the first heyday of the Gion festival had already passed.

The beginnings of the Gion goryōe and Kyoto politics

To unravel the early history of the Gion festival, we have only a few fragmentary sources to guide us. To make matters worse, even these fragments invite reservations; most survive only in the form of quotations embedded in texts that were compiled centuries later. The tales they tell have likely been skewed to reflect the interests of the medieval writers who 'quoted' them, and some may well be outright falsifications. As a result of this paucity of reliable sources, there is no consensus about many aspects of Gion's early history. It is likely that important turns of events have been lost to us forever.

The now standard name *Gion matsuri* became current only in the twentieth century. For most of its history, the festival was known as the Gion *goryōe*; the short form *Gion'e* remained in regular use well into the post-war period. A *goryōe* was a Buddhist 'gathering' (*e*) for the placation of vengeful spirits who were believed to spread illness or cause other calamities (*goryō*). Sources on *goryōe* are surprisingly few, considering the fact that such ritual attempts to quell epidemics appear to have been fairly common. One reason for this lack of sources may be their informal nature, placing them beyond the sphere of official court ceremonial. The eighth, ninth and tenth centuries were an age of pestilence in Japan.[6] Increased contacts with the continent, combined with the founding of imperial capitals as centres of national administration, gave microbes unprecedented opportunities to multiply and spread. Frequent movement of people between the provinces and the capital, for court duties, labour or war, made matters worse. Smallpox, measles, mumps, dysentery and what the sources call the 'coughing sickness' were particularly rampant. Epidemics were blamed on deities, demons or spirits (*ekijin, ekiki, kimi*) that invaded the land and the city from the outside – typically from a foreign realm beyond the capital, beyond the sea or even beyond the world of the living.

Preventing such outbreaks and controlling the spirits that caused them was seen as a central task of the imperial court. Calamities unleashed by angry spirits or deities were often blamed on prominent members of the court nobility, and claiming credit for appeasing such spirits was a much-used strategy to gain political power. The politics of disease were an extremely serious matter. Because the authority to apportion blame for calamities constituted a powerful weapon of factional infighting within the court, references to divine wrath (*tatari*) are numerous in court records and diaries of nobles from the tenth century onwards.[7]

Between the lines, moreover, one can catch glimpses of another dimension of the fear of the demons and spirits of disease: they provided commoners with an avenue for protest and resistance. There are numerous cases of riotous groups of commoners invading the capital in the company of an angry deity, pressing their grievances in a manner that was not easily dismissed. In 945, for example, 'hundreds of people carrying three *mikoshi*' approached the city from the west, singing and dancing so wildly that 'even the hills moved'.[8] At Yamazaki, a port on the Yodo River south-west of Kyoto, a large crowd from the city joined them. There the gods took possession of a woman. In an oracle, the gods expressed their wish to proceed to the nearby temple-shrine complex of Iwashimizu Hachimangū rather than entering Kyoto – no doubt, to the relief of the court.[9] Such gods who were carried around by singing and dancing groups of commoners were sometimes referred to as *shitara-gami*, '*shitara* deities'. Although the meaning of *shitara* is unknown, the very existence of such a term suggests that this incident was not unique.

Court ritualists used various ritual measures to protect the capital, and within it the imperial compound, against *ekijin* spirits of disease. At regular intervals these spirits were chased away, halted or placated with offerings at the four corners of the city and the palace. Twice a year court priests of the Urabe lineage performed a rite called 'roadside feasting' (*michiae*), feeding the spirits at the city's and palace's borders to disencourage them from entering. Experts on Yin-Yang divination performed similar rituals (*tsuina, taina*) with the aim of dispelling the 'dirty, evil gods of illness who are lurking in the villages' beyond the borders of the realm.[10] Alternatively, rites were addressed not to the spirits of illness themselves but to gods who guarded the city boundaries. The prayer recited during *michiae*, as recorded in the tenth century, called upon three named gods of the crossroads, beseeching them to protect the city from 'violent and hateful spirits from the underworld'.[11] According to court chronicles, the underworld was the domain of the goddess Izanami, who had died in labour and turned into a corpse teeming with maggots. Angered by her impertinent brother and husband Izanagi, Izanami had sworn to kill 'a thousand people' every day.[12]

In the heated political atmosphere of the court, spirits of disease took on a new and more concrete form in the late ninth century. The idea spread that rather than unnamed demons who assault the city from some other realm, these spirits were the ghosts of victims of power struggles at court: nobles and even members of the imperial house who had been exiled, who had died dismal deaths in evil places far from the city, and whose wrathful spirits (*goryō*) were now returning to seek revenge. This particular threat required new countermeasures, in the form of a new ritual format. It was this new form of ritual that came to be called *goryōe*.[13]

The court chronicle *Nihon sandai jitsuroku* (901) includes a description of a classical *goryōe*, performed on the twentieth day of the fifth month of 863 in the Shinsen'en palace garden.[14] Here, six angry spirits, all of named courtiers who had fallen victim to court intrigues, were presented with offerings and placated by monks who recited sutras and lectured on their contents. Court musicians played their instruments, court attendants and specialists from China and Korea danced, and various kinds of performers displayed their arts. The Shinsen'en, normally a place where the court nobility gathered for seasonal ceremonies and games, was on this occasion opened to commoners, who flocked to its grounds to enjoy the spectacle.

The author of this chronicle entry notes that the grand ceremony of 863 was inspired by similar rituals staged by commoners both in the capital and in the provinces beyond. Every summer or autumn, people would hold *goryōe* where 'buddhas are revered and sutras recited, songs and dances are performed, dressed-up youngsters shoot arrows, strongmen wrestle or show their skills at horseback archery and horse racing, and all kinds of performers compete in their arts'. An 865 entry in the same chronicle announces a ban on 'private gatherings under the name of *goryōe*' that featured military displays such as horseraces and archery, but exempting innocent groups of 'children at play'.[15] This suggests that the primary reason for this ban was a fear of popular unrest that might trigger violence.

Although the 863 *goryōe* had no obvious relation to the later Gion festival, there is a thin thread that suggests a link. The 865 ban was issued on the fourteenth day of the sixth month – the day on which the Gion *goryōe* would be held more than a century later. The mid-sixth month coincided with the end of the rainy season. In the heat of summer, stagnant pools of water and flood-contaminated wells caused illness to sweep through the city. The Gion *goryōe*, then, drew on a tradition of staging rites at this ominous time of year. Though not a direct successor of the court *goryōe* of 863, the Gion *goryōe* drew on the private performances that the court had tried to ban in 865.

Gion and its deities

The name Gion appears in the historical record for the first time in 920, in a short entry in the diary of the imperial regent Fujiwara no Tadahira: 'To dispel the coughing sickness, offerings will be made and horseraces held at Gion.'[16] Gion referred to an area east of the Kamo River, between that river's shifting riverbed and the hills of Higashiyama, in an area called Yasaka, 'eight (or: many) slopes'. It was close to one of the city's main charnel grounds, where impure persons scraped together a living by dealing with the pollution of death. The name is a translation of Jetavana, the 'Park of Prince Jeta' – a property in India that a wealthy disciple of the Buddha had bought from this prince and donated as a suitable place to found a monastery. How this rather dismal location in Yasaka acquired such a celebratory name, extant records do not tell.

Tadahira's 920 diary entry implies that Gion was already an established cultic centre at this time. For the site's history before that date, we can only rely on medieval shrine records, compiled more than four centuries later. *Shake jōjō kiroku* (compiled *c.* 1323) carries an entry recording that the Gionsha was founded in 876 by a monk called Ennyo, from the temple of Jōjūji in Kashiwara, south-west of Nara.[17] In the following year, 877, an epidemic ravaged the land, killing nobles and commoners alike. Divination revealed that the cause was a curse from a deity who dwelt to the south-east of the palace. Inspectors were sent to both Ise and Inari, but they found no evidence of such a curse; it then turned out that the source of the epidemic was Gion. When imperial messengers brought gifts to the Gion deities, the sickness disappeared instantaneously. Impressed with this feat, the imperial regent Fujiwara no Mototsune then donated multiple buildings from his own residence and founded a shrine at Gion. None of the details of this account are backed up by other sources, but the notion that Gion originated as a small shrine in the late ninth century is not unreasonable.[18]

A court edict gave official status to the Gionsha in 935, which meant that it was now included in the list of temples and shrines that received imperial offerings whenever a crisis occurred.[19] This edict included a brief description of the complex, which consisted of a temple hall containing images of a Yakushi triad (Bhaiṣajaguru, the buddha of medicine) and a shrine that likewise accommodated three images, named as Tenjin, Harime and Hachiōji.[20] The names vary in different sources, but it would appear that these gods were thought of as emanations of Yakushi and his two helpers, in the guise of exotic gods who were associated with illnesses that invaded the realm from distant places.

The names used to refer to Gion's buildings vary among sources. The temple is called Gionji or Kankeiji, while the shrine goes under the names of Gionsha, Tenjindō or Kanjin'in.[21] The terms 'temple' and 'shrine' are, in fact, rather misleading in this context. The Gion complex was not a combination of Buddhist temple and a Shinto shrine, staffed by monks and priests respectively. Rather, it functioned as a so-called *miyadera*, a Buddhist temple enshrining deities to whom the monks directed rites of pacification. These monks, sometimes referred to as 'shrine monks' (*shasō*), were mostly recruited from a single family lineage (the Ki lineage), suggesting that they had wives and sons and stood somewhere between monastic and lay status. *Miyadera*, or 'temples that focus on a shrine', constituted a category of their own. In court documents such institutions could be listed either as a temple or as a shrine, depending on the context.

Tenjin, meaning 'Heavenly Deity' or 'Deva', was a generic name for various kinds of deities, often associated with lightning and disease, and including *goryō*. The most prominent of the three *mikoshi* that had approached Kyoto in 945 was also identified as the vehicle of a Tenjin, in this case specified as Daijizai Tenjin, the spirit of Sugawara no Michizane – a courtier who had been exiled to a humiliating post in Kyushu, died there in 903, and whose ghost returned to Kyoto where he took gruesome revenge on the Imperial Palace.[22] To pacify this spirit, a shrine (or, more accurately, a *miyadera*) was dedicated to Michizane in 947: Kitano Tenmangū. The Tenjin of Gion was not associated with the spirit of a particular individual, but its deities displayed similar characteristics. Harime, sometimes called Harisainyo, is not known from any other context; the element *hari* may derive from a word used in Buddhist scriptures for 'crystal'. The Hachiōji ('eight princes') are the sons of Tenjin and Harime. Deities, and also buddhas, were often imagined as kings or generals, directing an band of foot soldiers to execute their orders; Gion's princes must have served a similar role.

None of these deities occur in any known Chinese or Japanese sources. The earliest explicit discussion about their identity can be found in the diary of a courtier called Nakahara Moromoto (1109–75), two centuries after Gionsha's founding. In 1147, Moromoto's superior asked him about the identity of Gion's Tenjin. Moromoto replied that since this deity has the head of an ox (*gozu*), he might well be the spirit of the Chinese primordial emperor and sage Shennong, the famous inventor of both agriculture and medicine – but, he admitted, there were other theories as well. Moromoto clearly thought of Tenjin as having an ox head, just like Shennong.[23] Likewise, a court chronicle mentions that in the following year (1148), a fire at Gion damaged the feet of a statue of 'Gozu Tennō', the Ox-Headed Deva King.[24] Another five decades later, the Shingon compendium *Kakuzenshō* explains that Gion's Gozu Tennō is an emanation of Yakushi, and therefore identical to Shennong, who appeared in China as a manifestation of Yakushi.[25]

Gion's Tenjin may have been known as Gozu Tennō from the start, or acquired his ox head at a later date. *Asabashō*, a large Tendai compendium of ritual procedures and deity images from the thirteenth century, refers to a tale about an exotic king who appealed to Kannon during an epidemic. In response, the Eleven-Headed Kannon transformed into 'Bishamon with Eleven Ox Heads', who again transformed into 'the Great Deva King with Eleven Ox Heads' (*Jūichizu Gozu Makatennō*); these frightening manifestations vowed to protect the country against disease and suffering.[26] *Asabashō* quotes this tale from a now-lost tenth-century text, so this passage may imply that an ox-headed deity associated with epidemics was a part of the Tendai repertoire already at that time. Alternatively, it can explain why Tenjin acquired its ox head by the twelfth century at the latest. Either way, the early Gionsha must have accommodated an exotic and powerful deity who guarded the city against foreign diseases, accompanied by attendants or perhaps, as in later sources, by his consort and sons.

The oldest extant sources on the deities enshrined at the Gionsha are occasional reports about damage caused by fires. In 1070, a fire destroyed not only four of the shrine's eight Hachiōji statues but also images of Daishōgun (the Great General) and Jadokukeshin (the God of Snake Poison). These are calendrical deities, associated with Yin-Yang divination and the calculation of inauspicious dates and directions. Such deities were believed to move to different corners of the compass at specific dates, casting curses on those who failed to avoid the directions where they resided at any point in time. Calendrical deities were further associated with celestial bodies, including stars, planets and comets: Daishōgun was clearly visible in the night sky as Venus, and Jadokukeshin appeared as a comet of devastating power called Keito (in Sanskrit, Ketu).[27] Illness was often explained as a result of breaches of calendrical and directional taboos. Again, it is not possible to pin down when these calendrical deities appeared at Gion, but it is worth noting that they were present there already many decades before Gion's Tenjin was first referred to as Gozu Tennō.

However this may be, the Gionsha and its Tenjin must have been in place by the early tenth century at the latest, and they rose to some prominence by the middle of that same century. The Gion festival, in its earliest form, originated when *goryōe* rituals came to be performed there regularly. Different sources, all too late to be trustworthy, cite various dates in the early 970s as the start of regular *goryōe* at Gion.[28] From this decade onwards, the court annually sent offerings and sponsored horseraces and Gagaku music and dances (*azuma asobi*) at the Gionsha as a measure against disease.

The year 974 was particularly significant. It was in this year that the Gionsha fell under the control of Enryakuji, the Tendai temple complex of Mt Hiei.[29] It would remain a part of the Enryakuji 'empire' (though in different ways) until the late sixteenth century. As such, it shared a common fate with other shrines in the city, including the aforementioned Kitano Tenmangū and the much older Matsunoo Shrine (today's Matsuo Taisha), and also the Hie Shrines (Hiyoshi Taisha) at the eastern foot of Mt Hiei. As we shall see later, Gionsha went on to serve as an advanced outpost of Enryakuji on the city's eastern rim throughout the medieval period. This is also reflected in some striking parallels between the Hie Shrines and the Gionsha; Hie, for example, also had a shrine dedicated to the 'eight princes' (Hachiōji).[30]

The *mikoshi* procession and the *otabisho*

In the 970s, the Gion *goryōe* may have developed from a ritual of interim offerings at the Gionsha into festival that included a *mikoshi* procession that took the deities into the city. Again, there are no contemporary documents to date this development with any confidence. What we do know is that by the late fourteenth or early fifteenth century, the founding of Gion's first *otabisho* was said to have occurred in 974, the same year that the Gionsha passed into Enryakuji's hands.[31] The 974 dating is confirmed indirectly by the fact that in 975, court offerings were presented to the Gionsha on the fifteenth day of the sixth month. Until the festival's modern rescheduling according to the Gregorian calendar (in 1873), the *mikoshi* were carried to the *otabisho* on the seventh day of the sixth month, and back to the Gionsha on the fourteenth.[32] Presumably, the 975 offerings, in thanks for Emperor En'yū's recovery from illness, were timed to ride on the climax of the *goryōe* on the previous day.

The founding legend of the *otabisho* first appears in a medieval document that is tentatively dated to *c.* 1431.[33] This document claims that late in the fifth month of 974, Gion's deities pronounced in an oracle that they wished to proceed to the city, where the residence of a certain Sukemasa (comprising a city block along Takatsuji and Higashi-no-Tōin Streets) should be turned into their *otabisho* or 'travel residence'. There was a fox altar (*kitsunezuka*) on Sukemasa's property, and when the Gionsha shrine monks went to check this site they found that a spider's thread led from this altar all the way to the Gionsha deity hall. The monks consulted the court about this, and it was decided that Sukemasa's property would henceforth serve as the Gionsha's *otabisho*, while Sukemasa and his descendants would be its priests. 'This', the document concludes, 'was the beginning of the festival (*sairei*).'[34] This event became a celebrated milestone in the legendary history of the festival. To this day, the *mikoshi* procession is headed by a group of men who carry 'divine treasures', including a lacquered board inscribed with the 974 imperial edict announcing the establishment of the *otabisho* and giving orders to move the Gion gods to this *otabisho* every year.

The 1431 document that serves as our source refers to a conflict over the priestship of the *otabisho*, pitting Sukemasa's descendants against the Gionsha monks. The Sukemasa legend, then, represents a rare transmission of the *otabisho* priests. Seta Katsuya points out that the historical record is heavily skewed towards the Gionsha and its perspective on the festival, rendering the community around the *otabisho* invisible. Yet that community must have played a central role in the proceedings. Who formed this community, and what were the social and economic dynamics that shaped the *otabisho* rituals? In the fifteenth century Sukemasa's lineage eventually lost its battle for control of the *otabisho*, which became a mere outpost of the Gionsha. Sukemasa's tale reminds us that before that time, the *otabisho* was a separate shrine with its own priestly lineage. If the creation of this *otabisho* marked the start of the Gion festival, that lineage and the community it served must have been crucial agents in that development. Yet in surviving documents, selected by Gionsha monks, the *otabisho* priests are almost entirely absent.

The idea of moving deities from a permanent shrine to a designated *otabisho* and back on a set date was a procedure typical of *goryōe*.[35] Older festivals, including the Kamo (or Aoi) festival in the north of the capital, had neither *mikoshi* nor *otabisho*. The Kamo festival built on the idea that the gods were invited from their more permanent abode in the hills to the shrine for the duration of the festival; one might say that in this festival, the shrine itself served as an *otabisho*. In the case of the Gion *goryōe*, the gods were permanently accommodated in the Gionsha at the foot of the Higashiyama hills, and brought into the city only during the festival period. There, they were entertained by the *otabisho* priests. It appears likely that these priests, rather than their counterparts at the Gionsha, may once have been the main celebrants of the festival.

Perhaps even this interpretation represents a Gionsha-centred reconceptualization of the *goryōe* as it might have been conceived in its earliest form. Fukuhara Toshio suggests that the *otabisho* priests may have had a different understanding. He points out that Heian-period sources almost never mention the *mikoshi* procession on the seventh; diarists were exclusively interested in the procession from the *otabisho* to the Gionsha of the fourteenth, and the term *goryōe* referred only to the festivities on that day. The same applied to other early *goryōe* in and around Kyoto. According to Fukuhara, this suggests that the gods of disease were thought to manifest themselves at the *otabisho*, during rites performed by *otabisho* priests and shrine maidens. They were then carried across the city boundaries to polluted sites on its outskirts, such as the Gionsha, where they were left in the care of Gozu Tennō.[36] The evidence Fukuhara adduces remains circumstantial. At the very least, however, the festival was likely interpreted differently by different actors, and perhaps the lasting lack of interest in the procession on the seventh hints at the lingering influence of older ritual patterns.

Fukuhara's hypothesis is strengthened by the fact that a similar pattern is documented for a *goryōe* that took place at Funaoka Hill, on the north-western outskirts of Kyoto, in 994.[37] Like Gion, Funaoka was an area where corpses were deposited. In this year an epidemic afflicted the city. In response, carpenters from the court's Timber Office (*mokuryō*) constructed two *mikoshi*. These were carried to Funaoka Hill, where monks recited sutras and preached, accompanied by musicians. Crowds from the city flocked to Funaoka, where offerings (*heihaku*) were presented. Finally, the *mikoshi* were carried over the hill and flushed away towards Naniwa Bay, where Kyoto's rivers enter the sea. Although the source is too terse to be clear, one imagines that the *mikoshi*, carrying the spirits of sickness, were sent down the river in the hope that the pestilence would never return. Alternatively, *heihaku* might refer to objects that attracted and contained the spirits, which were then set adrift towards the sea. In this procedure, the *mikoshi* arrived empty and were 'loaded' with pestilence spirits at Funaoka. The removal, or return, of the *mikoshi* was naturally the most important and elaborate part of this ritual procedure.

In the case of the Gion festival, too, the term *goryōe* was used specifically for the day of the deities' return from the *otabisho*. Yet from the perspective of the Gionsha, the festival assumed a different meaning – stressing the blessings of the Gion deities, led by Gozu Tennō, as protectors against the nameless spirits of illness. Tenjin, the heavenly lord of disease who dwelt at Gion, a place of pollution beyond the river, was placated and carried into the heart of the city so that he may keep lesser spirits at bay. This conception differed both from the *goryōe* at Funaoka and from the older offerings to the 'gods who guard the crossroads' in the ritual of *michiae*. The character of Tenjin and his family gave the *mikoshi* procession a whiff of danger. Court nobles noted in their diaries that they avoided the roads where the *mikoshi* would pass and abstained from eating fish until the *mikoshi* had returned to the Gionsha.[38] Not only the gods but also the revellers evoked unease: barely controlled violence was a hallmark of all *goryōe* festivals.

The new type of *goryōe*, involving *mikoshi* and an *otabisho*, was not unique to Gion. Developments that resembled the *goryōe* of Gion can be seen at Fushimi Inari Shrine on Gion's southern flank and Matsunoo Shrine west of Kyoto. Being further removed from the court, and therefore less attractive to noble sightseers and diarists, these *goryōe* are even more sparsely documented than Gion's, but it appears that at least at Fushimi Inari, a villa within the city limits that was originally the property of a 'big man' (*chōja*) was donated to the shrine as its first *otabisho*. In the same manner as Gion, the Fushimi Inari *otabisho* had its own priests (*kannushi*) who passed down the priestship within a lineage based 'in the village of Shichijō' and confirmed by the shrine. Although this *otabisho* first appears in the sources in 1167, we can be certain that Fushimi Inari staged a festival involving a *mikoshi* procession, presumably to this *otabisho*, by 1040 at the latest.[39]

Fushimi Inari was closely linked to the Tōji Temple, while it appears that Matsunoo served as the tutelary shrine of Tōji's western neighbour Saiji. Based on these links with Kyoto's two main temples, Okada Shōji suggests that the two *goryōe* of these shrines may well have been (among) the oldest.[40] If that is indeed the case, the reference to a 'fox altar' at the Gion *otabisho* might even suggest that the Gion *otabisho* was inspired by a similar set-up at Fushimi Inari. If the first *otabisho* priest Sukemasa was a worshipper of Inari (and it bears repeating that we only have a fifteenth-century source to suggest such a supposition), he may have imported this festival format to Gion. Similar developments also occurred at other *goryōe* in the city, from Matsunoo to Kitano, Imamiya and Izumoji.[41]

While the *otabisho* of Fushimi Inari was located within the traders' district around Shichijō, Sukemasa's *otabisho* was located on the southern end of a similar traders' community around the fourth avenue, Shijō (at the intersection of Takatsuji and Higashi-no-Tōin Streets, about 2 kilometres from the Gionsha and 1 kilometre to the south-west of today's *otabisho*). This location can perhaps give us some indication of the emerging festival's social context. What little we know about the establishment of the *otabisho*, and with it the *mikoshi* procession, suggests that a rising class of successful traders played a central role even in this early phase of its history. Sukemasa, like the owner of the Fushimi Inari *otabisho*, is described as a 'big man' (*chōja*). The Gionsha *otabisho* in his residence took the *mikoshi* away from the court-dominated north, in a south-eastern direction. Almost all our sources view the festival from the perspective of the court and the shrine, and they stress the involvement of the court as the Gion festival's dominant patron and protector. It is only between the lines that we can glimpse the ways in which patronage from Kyoto's self-made men, like Sukemasa, shaped Gion worship as a festival of commoners.

Several episodes suggest that a struggle was taking place between commoners (or their overlords) and the court over control of the Gion festival already in its earliest form. In 999, a performer of some fame who was popularly known as 'Boneless' (Mukotsu) appeared in front of the Gionsha on the fourteenth day of the sixth month, the *goryōe* day when the *mikoshi* were carried up to the shrine.[42] Mukotsu brought a homemade contraption that our source calls a *mura* – in this case clearly not a 'village' but perhaps rather something resembling a grassy hill (cf. *kusamura*).[43] Fujiwara no Michinaga (966–1028), the dominant strongman at court, was offended by this because Mukotsu's *mura* reminded him of an object called *hyō* (a 'marker') that was used in the imperial Rite of Great Tasting (*daijōe*). According to one description, such a *hyō* (or *hyō no yama*) consisted of a 'hill', topped by a tree decorated with phoenixes, 'five-coloured clouds' and images of the sun and moon; in front of the tree were figures of Chinese immortals and of the propitious mythical beast *qirin* (J. *kirin*, now of beer fame). Such *hyō* were large; one source says twenty pullers were needed to move it.[44] Mukotsu's version must have been much smaller and simpler, but even so, Michinaga was 'startled' and ordered for Mukotsu to be arrested. Mukotsu's *mura*, it seems, struck Michinaga as an appropriation of a symbol of court authority. Mukotsu had already fled, however, and could not be caught. Even worse, Michinaga's interference apparently enraged Gion's Tenjin. Tenjin caused priests to fall off the worshipping stage, and then took possession of a 'servant' (*genin*), through whom he gave an oracle. That same night a fire broke out in the palace, reducing the entire court compound to ashes.

Mukotsu's *mura* is sometimes mentioned as a possible ancestor of the later *yama* floats, but there is a large time gap. Centuries would pass before such floats appeared in the Gion festival. More intriguing are the social dynamics that this episode reflects. Presumably, some sponsor paid Mukotsu to stage this performance, maybe as a special prayer to avert the plague that was affecting the city at this time, to express thanks for having survived a spate of illness, or to further some worldly ambition. Considering Michinaga's reaction, Mukotsu's sponsor was hardly Michinaga's friend. It is striking that the court chronicle reporting this incident implies that the sponsor had Tenjin on his side.

A somewhat similar incident occurred in 1013. In this year the *mikoshi* make their first appearance in an entry in the diary of Fujiwara no Sanesuke (957–1046), *Shōyūki*. Sanesuke was a specialist of ceremony (*yūsoku kojitsu*) and the head of a Fujiwara branch that regarded Michinaga as a rival. Sanesuke's point in mentioning the *mikoshi* was to record another instance of Tenjin's anger. On the day of the *goryōe*, the *mikoshi* were followed by 'an open cart carrying *sangaku* performers'. Michinaga ordered court guards (*zōnin*) to put a stop to this. Michinaga's guards blocked the procession and tore up the performers' costumes. According to Sanesuke, the *mikoshi* bearers and other witnesses were convinced that there would be a divine retaliation; and indeed, soon an icy rain started to fall, accompanied by thunder and lightning. Again, Michinaga's attempt to stop commoners from taking up prominent space in a *goryōe* procession was met with divine wrath.

It is tempting to speculate about the circumstances that produced such incidents. Michinaga, as the hegemon of the time, had many enemies. Enryakuji, in particular, was a wasps' nest, and Michinaga was a prominent party in the never-ending factional struggles on Mt Hiei. In 1013 he was planning the construction of his own temple, Hōjōji, causing some to fear that this would upset the balance of power. When Michinaga fell ill in 1012, Sanesuke reported rumours that his disease had been caused by a curse from Mt Hiei's Mountain King, the deity Sannō. This was only the first of multiple incidents of divine wrath directed against Michinaga – who overcame them all and held on to the reins of power until his death in 1028.[45]

Since the Gionsha was an outpost of Enryakuji, one may surmise that Michinaga's scuffles with the Gion festival were part of his struggles with (sections of) Enryakuji. It is possible, too, that strongmen like Sukemasa were somehow aligned with Enryakuji in a relationship similar to that of the *jinin* mentioned earlier, trading contributions to these temples for protection. Either way, these events help us imagine how the Gion festival may at times have functioned as a catalyst, causing the fault lines of politics to surface in the wake of the *mikoshi*.

Embellishing the Gion *goryōe* procession

In the course of the eleventh and twelfth centuries, the day of the return of the *mikoshi* grew into one of the largest spectacles of the capital. It was rivalled only by the Inari festival, which celebrated the return of its *mikoshi* in a similar manner. The excitement is expressed in a very lively manner in *Nenjū gyōji emaki*, an illustrated scroll from the late twelfth century that has survived in the form of copies from the early Edo period. The scroll depicts large crowds along the street where the procession passes, including women, children and nobles in ox-drawn carriages. The three *mikoshi* of Tenjin, Harime and Hachiōji are preceded by a wide variety of performers: a troupe of *dengaku* dancers (on which more will be said later); four riders on prancing horses; a child carrying a large bamboo stick with paper streamers (*gohei*); two *miko* shrine maidens on horseback, one carrying a decorated parasol; an *ō-no-mai* dancer[46] carrying a halberd; a troupe of *shishi-mai* lion dancers; and four more men with halberds. The *mikoshi* are followed by another *dengaku* troupe, a group of men performing the *sei-no-o* dance,[47] and five Gionsha monks on horses. The final frame shows the dismantling of a temporary altar at the place where the routes of the three *mikoshi* converged, and where they made a brief stop to receive offerings (*rekke no tsuji*). This was the prime spot for viewers to gather and watch the spectacle, and for persons of power to exhibit their patronage.[48]

We know from other sources that this is not a complete picture of the procession. Strikingly, the most celebrated spectacle is missing: tens of elaborately dressed-up youngsters on horseback called *uma no osa* ('horse chiefs') or *mechō no warawa* ('horse chief youngsters'), each led by two grooms holding the reins, and accompanied by a retinue of up to twenty colourful attendants. An *uma no osa* does feature in another section of *Nenjū gyōji emaki*; perhaps the artist simply wanted to avoid duplication, or scenes in this scroll have been scrambled in the surviving Edo copyings, which in fact have been found to contain other mistakes. Such *uma no osa* were provided by court nobles on orders of the reigning emperor, a retired emperor or imperial spouses. The young men were typically sons of those nobles' retainers. Most were junior staff (*kodoneri*) of the

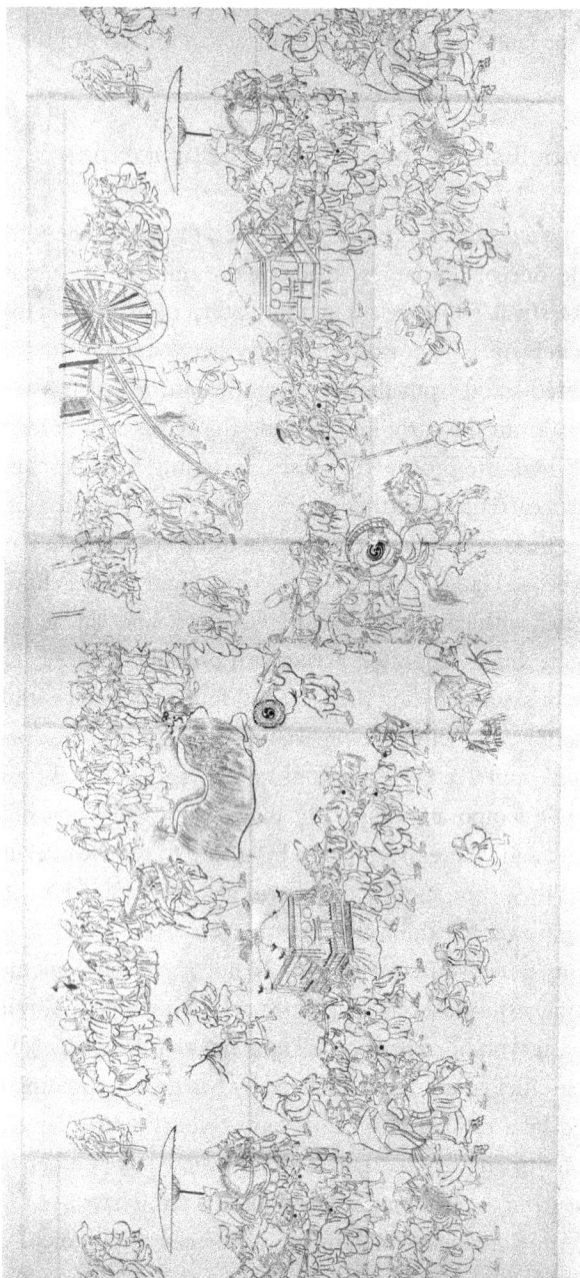

Figure 4 *Nenjū gyōji emaki*: The *mikoshi* procession on its return to the Gionsha. A lion dance and musicians are visible in front of the first *mikoshi*; it is followed by a *miko* maiden riding a horse. National Diet Library digital collection.

kurōdo-dokoro, the private offices of the emperor or of a retired emperor. The *kodoneri*, who lived in designated blocks, vied among each other to cut the most striking figure.[49] Nobles focused on the *uma no osa* in their diaries because they were involved in the provision of them in some way or other. In *Makura no sōshi* (The Pillow Book, *c.* 1001), Sei Shōnagon mentioned '*uma no osa* at a *goryōe*' in her list of 'things that please'.[50] *Uma no osa* were also a feature of other festivals in the capital (notably the Inari festival) and present another example of the prominence of horses in such events.

Members of the court also sponsored some of the *dengaku* troupes. *Dengaku* or 'paddy dances' were closely associated with the Gion *goryōe*. Such dances were originally a rural accompaniment to the planting of rice but developed into the most popular form of entertainment in the course of the late Heian and Kamakura periods.[51] *Dengaku* involved colourful, often outrageous, costumes and wild dancing to rhythmical music, typically performed on different kinds of drums, small bronze cymbals, *sasara* whisks and flutes. In the Kyoto region it is mentioned for the first time in 998. The entry is terse but suggestive of the nature of *dengaku* crowds. On the tenth day of the fourth month, the day of

Figure 5 *Nenjū gyōji emaki*: *Dengaku* dancing in front of the Gionsha gate. Men playing flutes, drums and *sasara* whisks accompany a dancer holding a small drum. National Diet Library digital collection.

the Matsunoo festival, a crowd from the river port of Yamazaki was dancing *dengaku*. Soon, the situation became chaotic. 'Fighting ensued between commoners (*zōnin*) and many in the capital suffered damage. People set fire to that port, burning down some thirty buildings there.'[52] Whether this dancing was connected to the Matsunoo festival remains unclear. The entry shows, however, that the *dengaku* crowd was angry, that the dancers were seen as a threat, that the situation triggered a riot and that the people of Yamazaki paid a high price. Similar *dengaku* protests, at times leading to violence, recurred at regular intervals in the ensuing century.

A disturbing *dengaku* craze occurred in the fifth and sixth months of 1096, when the so-called Great Dengaku put the whole city on hold. *Chūyūki*, the diary of Fujiwara no Munetada (1062–1141), gives a detailed account of this episode. Munetada found the entire episode unsettling. On the thirteenth day of the seventh month, he wrote:

> Since the fifth month until today, everyone, high or low, has been dancing *dengaku*. People have been gathering at Iwashimizu or Kamo, Matsunoo or Gion, filling the streets with the noise of drums and flutes. Tens of thousands have joined, claiming that [the dancing] pleases the gods. Some receive oracles in their dreams, and there are also those who make up oracles on the spot; people love spirit talk and will go through water and fire when they hear of such things.

During the Gion *goryōe* of this year, crowds of low-ranking court guards (*aozamurai*), court retainers and servants, and commoners filled the streets day and night. Nobody could control the dancers now that the gods of Gion were at their *otabisho*. Munetada suggested that 'malevolent rumours' (*yōgen*) may have set this ominous craze into motion. He hinted at a possible connection with the postponement of the Matsunoo festival earlier that year, due to a death pollution that had arisen at Sumiyoshi Shrine (in today's Osaka) and spread from there to Kyoto. A month later (12.7.1096), retired emperor Shirakawa had *dengaku* dances performed within the palace itself, reportedly at the request of his teenage son, Emperor Horikawa. The dancing was led by prominent figures within Shirakawa's faction.[53] Others, too, were alarmed by this outbreak of wild dancing; the court scholar Ōe no Masafusa (1041–1111) ascribed it to 'the workings of a fox spirit'.[54]

These events are sometimes interpreted as commoner protests in a time of great hardship.[55] They also coincided with troubles within the court, where the hegemony of the Fujiwara regents was under increasing strain. Retired emperor Shirakawa seized upon the *dengaku* craze to further his own political agenda by orchestrating elite *dengaku* performances at his palace. In this manner, he demonstrated his supremacy over the Fujiwara-dominated regime, which – according to his enemies – had unleashed the apparent anger of the gods. This incident is a perfect illustration of the ambiguous character of *dengaku* as an integral part of *goryōe* festivals. The dancing vacillated between, on one hand, wild rioting in the shadow of the gods with an undertone of resistance to the rulers of the day, and, on the other, an elite art performed by court nobles or professional troupes as a means to cement elite power.

The appointment of merchants as 'chiefs of horses'

In 1156, a conflict over the imperial succession – or, more accurately, over the division of power between different court factions – escalated into military action, with 600 warriors attacking and burning down the Shirakawa palace where retired emperor Sutoku (1119–64) was residing. Sutoku was exiled and ended up as another vengeful spirit; the victor was his younger brother, Emperor Go-Shirakawa (1127–92). This incident, known as the Hōgen disturbance, launched the career of one of Go-Shirakawa's warriors, Taira no Kiyomori (1118–81), who soon rose to the position of Kyoto's hegemon. This entry of warriors into court politics was a first step on the way to the Genpei war of 1180–5 and the subsequent founding of the Kamakura shogunate in 1192.

The ensuing decline of the court nobility had a direct impact also on the Gion festival. As tensions within the court heightened, court sponsorship dwindled away. The number of *uma no osa* had topped at more than a hundred in the time of retired emperor Shirakawa (around 1100); when hostilities escalated in the 1170s and 1180s it dropped rapidly. According to shrine and court sources, Emperor Go-Shirakawa found a new way to 'increase Tenjin's powers' and 'add to the grandeur of the festival' as the festival began to decline. In 1157, he dispatched three 'sickle-shaped halberds' (*kamahoko*) to the Gionsha, ordering that they be assigned to wealthy persons within the city to signal that they had been given the obligation, or the honour, of providing funding for that year's procession.[56] Perhaps these three halberds were linked to the three *mikoshi*. This obligation was termed *bajōyaku*, 'the duty to serve as chiefs of horses (*bajō*, or *uma no kami*)'.

According to the surviving sources (the court chronicle *Hyakurenshō* and the Gionsha record *Shake jōjō kiroku*), the *bajōyaku* halberds were bestowed on the Gionsha by the emperor. This, however, is yet another example of imaginative spindoctoring. In actual fact, the *bajōyaku* was not new, nor did it originate as a pious imperial policy. The main actors behind the development of this system were not the emperor and the shrine but, rather, Enryakuji and the *otabisho*. Enryakuji had obtained imperial sanction to levy *bajōyaku* for a festival of the Hie Shrines called Kosatsuki-e ('the festival of the fifth month') already in 1138, during the reign of Emperor Sutoku. Hie had two main festival events: a *mikoshi* procession in the fourth month that developed into today's Sannō festival and the Kosatsuki-e which revolved around horseraces in the fifth month. As its name indicates, the *bajōyaku* originated in the context of this horseracing festival (which disappeared in the fifteenth century). It was already an established practice at Enryakuji to raise money from merchants in connection with specified festivals at this time.[57] In 1157, Go-Shirakawa extended this sanction to the Gionsha; Fushimi Inari received the same favour not much later. Rather than actively creating a new method to ensure the continuation of court ceremonies in difficult times, Go-Shirakawa was merely sanctioning private financial arrangements between temples, shrines and merchants that were already well established.

Little is known about the concrete functioning of the *bajōyaku* before the late fourteenth century. We have no idea who selected the 'chiefs of horses', what kind of persons were eligible or how the proceeds were used. Anecdotal evidence suggests that the 'wealthy persons' who were assigned the *bajōyaku* halberds may have belonged to the class of 'big men' represented by Sukemasa one and a half-century earlier. Among the few who are mentioned by name, not all appear to have had any obvious connection with the festivals or the shrines that they now had the duty to fund. Not all chiefs of horses, in other words, were *jinin* of the Gionsha or any other Enryakuji branch.

Understandably, some of those who were saddled with this duty put up determined resistance. In 1157, the year that Go-Shirakawa sanctioned the Gion *bajōyaku*, the duty was assigned to a mid-range retainer and official of nobility status, probably in the employ of a retired emperor or regent. It appears unlikely that such a person would be a *jinin* of either Enryakuji or the Gionsha. In 1179, fighting broke out between the Gionsha and nearby Kiyomizudera when the *bajōyaku* fell to a man who lived within the Kiyomizudera precinct.[58] This man, who ran a business transporting goods, did not appreciate the prestige or the opportunities that this obligation might bring. In spite of the fact that he did hold the status of a Gionsha *jinin*, he resented the costs enough to appeal to Kiyomizudera for support and incite a violent protest. Both temple buildings and people's houses in the area went up in flames. At Hie, too, the *bajōyaku* for the Kosatsuki-e festival (which was much more costly than that of the Gion festival) was at times assigned to non-*jinin*, while Fushimi Inari claimed the right to select its *bajō* among all who lived in its 'territory' (*shikichi*) south of Gojō (today's Matsubara Street), including inhabitants who were *jinin* of the Gionsha.[59] These episodes suggest that almost anyone might be chosen as the year's holder of the *bajōyaku* halberds.

Even less clear is the question who did the choosing. Based on surviving documents drafted after the *bajōyaku* system had been reinstated in a new format in the late fourteenth century, Seta Katsuya proposes that at least initially, the *otabisho* priests – Sukemasa's descendants – may have had a leading role in the allocation of the *bajōyaku* halberds for the Gion festival. Seta highlights the role of the community around the *otabisho*, which as we have seen is almost invisible in the surviving shrine records. He invites us to consider what the festival may have meant to the commoners who invited the Gionsha deities into their community, and who year after year invested their efforts and economic resources in the festival in the shadow of the court and the shrine.

The influence of such commoners is clear from another striking development. A second *otabisho* was founded in the Upper City at an unknown date on land donated in 1136.[60] This *otabisho* was located near a famous well called Shōshōi ('the well of the junior general'), some 2 kilometres north of the first *otabisho* (now known as the Ōmandokoro or 'Great Office' *otabisho*). It served as the destination of the *mikoshi* of Tenjin's wife, Harime or Harisainyo. A shrine hall was built here in 1234; according to the court chronicle *Hyakurenshō*, 'locals' (*zaichinin*) were the driving force behind its construction and embellishment.[61] Based on this admittedly meagre evidence, Seta proposes that Gion's two *otabisho* functioned as places where locals congregated and performed community rituals linked to the Gion *mikoshi*, perhaps even in a manner that resembled 'shrine guilds' (*miyaza*).[62]

The term *miyaza*, mentioned in this context by Seta, needs some explanation. Although the word itself is of modern coinage, the concept is used to designate a particular format of shrine festivals that has been characteristic of the Kansai area and western Japan from the medieval period onwards. Typically, *miyaza* members formed a select circle of prominent family heads who enjoyed special privileges in village life. In many cases, these same people controlled local economic resources, while also serving as a permanent members of the group that organized the village festival. Every year, the *miyaza* members decided who would take the responsibility to coordinate and fund the festival as that year's *tōya* or 'head'.

Miyaza are typically associated with the semi-autonomous village communities (*sōson*) that arose in the fourteenth century. The *otabisho* communities of Kyoto two centuries earlier had little in common with such villages, but even so, one might argue that there are some structural similarities. *Miyaza* created ritual events by and for the village community, in which priests (if there were any) played a minor role. It is at least possible that the *otabisho* served a similar function as a stage for merchant rituals that were semi-independent from the Gionsha priesthood, and also from the court and (later) the shogunate as the Gionsha's official patrons. The *bajōyaku* system, where members of a merchant elite took turns shouldering the responsibility for and the costs of the embellishment of the *mikoshi* procession, resembles the *miyaza* system of rotating *tōya*. If the *bajōyaku* did indeed function in this manner (and it must be stressed that the evidence is circumstantial at best), the merchants of *otabisho* communities had a much more active role in the Gion festival than surviving court and shrine documents suggest.

Summing up

In its first phase, the Gion festival was already a complicated event with multiple actors, who had as many agendas. It reflected a variety of ideas and beliefs, and it depended on investment from a range of stakeholders with different interests.

On the institutional side, there was the Gionsha and its temple, Kankeiji; the *otabisho*, run by their own priests as separate shrines; and the Tendai complex of Enryakuji on Mt Hiei, which governed the Gion complex as one of its many branches in the city. The Gionsha owned shrine lands in and beyond Kyoto, where its shrine monks were free to extract income and labour from the inhabitants and exercise judicial control over them as 'service people' (*jinin*), meaning that their taxes and corvée duties were payable to the shrine. The *otabisho* also stood on shrine-owned land, but at least some of the rents and duties of the inhabitants of these blocks were due to the *otabisho* priests. The *otabisho*, the Gionsha and Mt Hiei stood in a hierarchical relation to each other; ultimately, they were all subject to the authority of the Tendai abbot.

Then there was the court, which staged rituals at selected temples and shrines both annually and ad hoc, in response to particular incidents. The Gionsha appeared on this list already in the 940s and 950s, before the Gion festival began. Severe epidemics in the 990s inspired further investments in the Gionsha and its *goryōe*; with this, the Gion festival earned its permanent place on Kyoto's ritual calendar.[63] These investments took the form of institutionalized patronage. On the fifteenth day of the sixth month, a day after the return of the *mikoshi*, court emissaries carried offerings to the shrine with imperial prayers. As at other similar shrines in the city, the court staged grand horseraces and dispatched court dancers to entertain the gods.[64] On these occasions the Gionsha received considerable amounts of rice, oil, beans and other grains, as well as silver, paper, silk, robes and such ritual accessories as incense and candle wax.[65] Individual court nobles, too, visited the shrine on this day to present their personal offerings and prayers. Most court diarists referred only to these events on the fifteenth, which were called *rinjisai* or 'interim rites', while ignoring the *mikoshi* processions.

There was, in fact, a sense among higher-ranked court nobles that those processions were best avoided. After an incident in 1085, when the main consort of Emperor Shirakawa died soon after the Gion festival, it became customary practice for the emperor to keep his distance from the *mikoshi* and take a ritual bath (*oyudono misogi*) in order to protect the imperial body from the impurity that the festival stirred up. According to *Chōshūki*, the consort's death was attributed to the fact that the emperor had been staying in the southern half of the city at the time of the *mikoshi* processions. The *rinjisai* on the fifteenth day was a 'public ritual' (*kansai*) that allowed direct, official court involvement in the festival, while also signalling a ritually significant distancing of the emperor from the potential dangers of the *mikoshi* processions and 'private' worship of the Gion deities at the *otabisho*. At the same time, however, adorning the *mikoshi* procession was an important task of selected nobles, who were expected to provide horses, riders, dancers and more to the accompanying parade. At times, as we have seen, 'private' additions to this parade (like Mukotsu's *mura* in 999 and the *sangaku* cart in 1013) were forcibly stopped as illicit intrusions into a court event.

The Gion festival depended on court patronage and sanction, but that patronage only touched a few selected sections of the festival. Rather than a court ceremony, the festival as a whole was the product of a coalition between the inhabitants of the city blocks where the first and (later) second *otabisho* were located, the *otabisho* priests, the Gionsha priesthood and, further in the background, Enryakuji. Tensions remained between the 'private' and 'public' (i.e. court-initiated) aspects of this and other *goryōe* in the city. Gomi Fumihiko has argued that while the court preferred to worship and pacify pestilence deities outside of the city boundaries, the growing population of urban commoners felt the need to invite those deities into their own neighbourhoods as protectors against rampant disease and other misfortunes.⁶⁶ The pattern of permanent shrines accommodating such deities on the city outskirts combined with *otabisho* within the city itself can then be understood as an uneasy compromise.

A change occurred in the way the court related to the festival in 1124. By this time, the balance of power had shifted from the emperor to the retired emperors, a shift that had been further stimulated by stricter isolation of the emperor from the *goryōe* deities. In this year, the main responsibility for funding and organizing *uma no osa* for the *mikoshi* processions was transferred from the private offices of the emperor and retired emperor to court nobles, retainers and military guards (*hokumen*).⁶⁷ These changes paved the way for the gradual devolvement of the duty to sponsor *uma no osa* from court nobles and retainers to merchants from 1157 onwards.⁶⁸ This laid the foundation for a new funding system that would keep the festival going after the medieval marginalization of the court in Kyoto life in subsequent centuries.

The Gion *goryōe* was not a stand-alone event but formed part of a succession of similar festivals in different parts of the capital. All these *goryōe* followed a similar format, with multiple deities carried from shrines outside the city, or on its outskirts, to one or more *otabisho* within the city limits and back again. The festivals of Matsunoo and Fushimi Inari took place in the fourth month, followed by the Imamiya festival in the fifth month, the Gion festival in the sixth month and Kitano Tenmangū's festival in the eighth month. By the twelfth century, this succession of similar festivals had come to be seen as a set sequence that should not be disturbed. In 1167, for example, the festival of Fushimi Inari was postponed to the fifth month because an instance of ritual impurity had forced the Matsunoo festival to be delayed.⁶⁹ The coming and going of numerous *mikoshi* was almost merging into a single, protracted ritual procedure, where a disturbance in one segment had to be resolved before the next could be initiated. This notion of a set sequence continued to affect Kyoto's various *goryōe* into the medieval period.

From the perspective of the court, the message conveyed by the Gion *goryōe* in its early stage of development was that the emperor was taking responsibility for the well-being of the people as the main patron and sponsor of ritual procedures that ward off sickness. In Handelman's terms, the festival was a combination of events that 'model' (i.e. effect a change) and events that 'mirror' (i.e. visualize and present power relations). 'Modelling' procedures at the Gionsha and the *otabisho* called upon the pestilence deity Gozu Tennō and his entourage to exorcise disease. The emperors and retired emperors staged impressive displays that served to claim credit for this grand rite of exorcism as part of the court's mission to pacify heaven and earth. The extravagantly clad horsemen (*uma no osa*) who accompanied the *mikoshi* transformed the modelling power of the processions into a mirroring visualization of court authority.

The staging of spectacles like dances and horseraces on such occasions is often interpreted in terms of their 'modelling' (i.e. transforming) effect on the invoked deities: the gods are placated, soothed or even induced to change their behaviour.[70] Just as important would have been the ability of these performances to attract crowds of viewers, so that the imperial message of presenting authority might reach a broad audience. When commoners emulated court spectacles by staging their own spectacles at sites of imperial display, the court, if sufficiently provoked, treated this as an illegal assumption of imperial privilege and reacted with violence. As the *dengaku* crazes demonstrated, people were all too ready to use 'spirit talk' for their own purposes, unleashing chaos that threatened the authority of the court and the temples associated with it. Modelling events typically involve a sense of danger; after all, the exorcist is engaging with entities that are ultimately beyond his or her control. Mirroring events, on the other hand, are regimented performances that present a status quo of power relations to the viewers. Court involvement with such modelling events as the *mikoshi* processions and mass *dengaku* dancing sought to transform the unstable powers of exorcism into a mirror of stable authority – while also trying to maintain a safe distance.

In the second half of the twelfth century, however, that status quo was rapidly undermined as conflicts between retired emperors and Fujiwara regents escalated, leading to war and, eventually, the founding of the first shogunate. As an event that depended on court patronage, the Gion festival began to 'flop' in the sense of Morin. First the Fujiwara regents and not much later also the retired emperors lost both the motivation and the ability to make the kinds of investments in the festival that had created the large displays of the eleventh and early twelfth centuries. As we know, however, the festival survived; this was possible only because new groups of agents took over. Prominent among those agents were representatives of the new regime, notably the Muromachi shoguns, who likewise used the festival as a stage to visualize their power. Equally important were the merchants who already participated actively in the festival by way of the *otabisho* communities. Commoners like them stepped in to shoulder the costs of the procession from the second half of the twelfth century onwards. In the process, the Gion festival underwent a complete transformation, most visibly by the replacement of the aristocratic *uma no osa* by a parade of *yama* and *hoko* floats.

2

1200–1467

Between temple overlord and shogun

The Kamakura period: Temples and their merchant networks

The thirteenth century was marked by the founding of the Kamakura shogunate, its entry into Kyoto politics and the gradual erosion of court authority. Established structures of political and economic power within the city, however, were not easily undermined. As long as the shogunate was based in distant Kamakura, its impact on daily life in Kyoto was limited. The fall of the Kamakura shogunate (1185–1333) and the founding of the Muromachi shogunate (1336–1573) ended what remained of the court's residual autonomy. In contrast to their Kamakura predecessors, the Muromachi shoguns took up residence in Kyoto and assumed direct control over the city. Enryakuji, too, suffered a loss of influence – although as we shall see, the monastic establishment of Mt Hiei continued to make determined and often violent efforts to retain its grip on the capital, using the Gion festival as one of its weapons. In its first phase, the festival had thrived as a public event in which the Fujiwara imperial regents, the retired emperors, the monks of Enryakuji and the Gionsha and *otabisho* communities vied for attention. In its second phase, the Muromachi shoguns and other warrior leaders pushed many of these actors into the shadows and succeeded in turning the limelight on themselves.

The most decisive factor behind the festival's transformation, however, was not the new political regime but rather the emergence of a market economy, which created new opportunities for an elite of commoner merchants. Traders and artisans had always been an integral part of Kyoto society, but in the first centuries of Kyoto's existence they had conducted their business mostly as purveyors of goods in the service of emperors, court nobles and temples. Bound to an overlord in the manner of classical service households, they conducted their trades primarily as salaried servants, with little opportunity to pursue their own profits in an open marketplace. The appearance of figures like Sukemasa suggests, however, that by the end of the first millennium this did not prevent some traders, at least, to accumulate significant capital and make their own investments.

In the thirteenth century, an influx of Song dynasty coins transformed the economic environment and helped merchants to develop stable networks of commerce built around this new medium of exchange.[1] These merchants, too, needed the protection of an overlord. Until the end of the fourteenth century, merchants under Enryakuji's protection were exempt from taxation from both the court and the shogunate on the grounds that they owed their taxes and other duties exclusively to this temple as its *jinin* ('service people'). Enryakuji, or one of its many component cloisters on Mt Hiei or in the city, also held full judicial powers over its *jinin*. It was the temple overlord, not the emperor or the shogun, who held the authority to arrest and punish its *jinin*. When a *jinin* was killed or wounded by shogunal retainers, his temple might take violent action to protest against this as a breach of its sphere of autonomy. Enryakuji offered its *jinin* economic benefits by enforcing monopolies for their products or monopsonies for their raw materials, and by exempting their merchandise and provisions from tolls at Enryakuji's numerous tollgates, which littered the trade routes into Kyoto. Temple overlords also used their armed men to assist *jinin* merchants in conflicts with debtors, routinely confiscating debtors' possessions, dismantling their houses and selling the timber. Independent merchants had no way to compete with the members of *jinin* 'guilds' (*za*) and were soon set upon by temple goons. Performing services for and paying regular contributions to an overlord was the only road to success in early medieval Kyoto.

The first guilds of this kind appear in the sources in the twelfth century. Suzanne Gay (2001), who has studied the practices of moneylenders in medieval Kyoto, describes how early 'service guilds' were joined by or transformed into more autonomous 'trade guilds' in the course of the Kamakura period. 'Service guilds' supplied their overlords with specified goods or services and were rewarded for this with privileges and protection. In contrast, the members of 'trade guilds' simply paid fees to their overlord and in return gained their permission to conduct a particular branch of business. Service guilds were concentrated in particular neighbourhoods, while the members of trade guilds were typically spread out across a wider area. Members of trade guilds often peddled their wares in the city streets rather than running a shop. Both types of guilds depended on the protection of powerful overlords; the difference lay in guild members' relationship with those overlords, with the members of trade guilds enjoying more autonomy but perhaps less assistance. There were guilds for most common trades, from procuring foodstuffs like salt and fish to various processes within the world of textiles (sourcing and transporting hemp, weaving, dyeing), and sake brewing. Women were actively engaged in some guilds, both as producers and as traders or peddlers. Sake brewers played a particularly central role in the Kyoto economy, because they doubled as financiers and were involved in everything from pawning and moneylending to accountancy for court nobles and warrior leaders.

Enryakuji was an active player in the field of merchant overlordship. Eighty per cent of Kyoto's brewers-*cum*-financiers, whose guild dominated the city, looked to Enryakuji for protection. As *jinin* of Enryakuji's Hie Shrines, these merchants paid a share of their earnings to the complex via this shrine. In return, they had the backing of Enryakuji's footmen both in conflicts with noisome debtors and in struggles with the shogunal authorities or the imperial court. The elite among these financiers held temple ranks and carried Buddhist names. Enryakuji not only skimmed off their profits but also depended on them as a channel for moneylending and other investments. Enryakuji's branches in Kyoto, notably the Gionsha and Kitano Tenmangū, oversaw guilds in the same manner; taken together, the 'Enryakuji empire' controlled and derived income from a large proportion of all trading that was conducted within the capital.

The Gionsha was strategically located to serve as the overlord and protector of guilds. By the early fourteenth century it was the home base of a number of guilds to do with textiles and clothing, a lumber guild, a clam guild, a kettle guild and a guild dealing in fruit and sweets. Some of these Gionsha guilds were of the 'service' type, while others were newer 'trade guilds'. There were, for example, two guilds of cotton merchants, one of each type. The older service guild consisted of merchants who lived within Gion's territory. They contributed to the Gion festival by presenting offerings to the *mikoshi* along the route.[2] In addition to this ritual practice, they paid a fee to receive tablets that proved their *jinin* status; these tablets had to be renewed every third year. In contrast, the sixty-four members of the newer trade guild lived spread around the city. They paid a substantial fee of membership to the shrine every year, but did not participate in the festival.[3] The service guild, then, was more closely integrated in the Gionsha's network, while the trade guild held a more peripheral position, almost as 'buyers' of Gionsha privileges.

Two of the Gionsha's guilds performed specific functions in the Gion festival's proceedings. The members of the lumber guild (*kiya-za* or *zaimoku-za*) were known as the Horikawa *jinin*, and sometimes labelled as the Gionsha's oldest, 'original' *jinin*. The Horikawa stream that runs parallel to the western bank of the Kamo River had allegedly been donated to the Gionsha as early as 879, which implies the lumber merchants who lived and worked along this stream were placed under the shrine's authority even before the Gion festival originated. From an unknown date (no later than the mid-fifteenth century), they were responsible for the construction of a temporary bridge across the Kamo River, to be used only by the *mikoshi* on their way to and from the *otabisho*. The guild of clam sellers was based in Imamiya in modern-day Osaka. They were not only Gionsha *jinin* but also exclusive suppliers of the imperial court (*kugonin*), and they enjoyed a monopoly on the Kyoto trade in *hamaguri* clams, shrimp and crabs. In return for Gionsha protection, they served as bearers of one of the three *mikoshi* – the Ōmiya palanquin of Gozu Tennō.[4]

In addition to its financial power as a guild overlord, Enryakuji was also in a strong position militarily. The temple made active use of its expertise in manipulating suprahuman forces or divine violence, in its countless conflicts over lands, positions, trading rights, patronage and more. A favourite tactic, with roots in the late tenth century and used with increasing frequency from the twelfth century onwards, consisted of carrying the powerful gods who resided in Enryakuji's shrines (notably the Gionsha and Kitano Tenmangū) to their enemies in their *mikoshi*.[5] Accompanying these *mikoshi* were armed monks, lay temple retainers (*kunin*), and *jinin*. The threat of divine retribution from the gods made it more difficult to prevent Enryakuji's forces from harassing their enemies and pressuring figures of authority. In 1104, for example, Retired Emperor Shirakawa honoured a monk from Enryakuji's rival Onjōji. In protest, Enryakuji monks flocked to the Gionsha, where they joined up with city-dwelling *jinin* of the Gion and Hie Shrines. On New Year's Day of 1105 the Enryakuji forces carried the *mikoshi* of the Gionsha to the palace, where the gods were abandoned to exude menace until the Onjōji appointment was revoked.[6]

Later in the twelfth century, it became common practice to carry the seven *mikoshi* of the Hie Shrines on the eastern side of Mt Hiei all the way over or around the mountain, instead of (or in addition to) bringing out the *mikoshi* of the Gionsha. The first time this happened was in 1123. In an attempt to put pressure on the court in a conflict over an estate, Enryakuji's 'mountain monks' descended Mt Hiei's western slope towards the city, carrying the seven *mikoshi* of Hie. Warriors dispatched by the court rushed to stop them from crossing the Kamo River, forcing the armed monks to abandon the *mikoshi* on the riverbank. Most of the monks fled to the Gionsha, which soon became the stage of a pitched battle. The court chronicle *Hyakurenshō* reports that many lost their lives inside the main sanctuary, which was defiled by blood and death pollution. Shirakawa had the *mikoshi* repaired and returned to Hie two months later,[7] while the defiled hall had to be torn down and rebuilt to avoid angering the gods. After these dramatic events the Gionsha was even more tightly integrated in the Enryakuji empire – formally as a branch temple of the Yokawa section of the mountain, and more informally as a fortified strongpoint for the entire complex on the outskirts of Kyoto.

As we have already seen, the Gionsha was located near one of Kyoto's main charnel grounds, an area dominated not only by temples but also by the slums of the city poor. Known as 'people of the riverbanks' (*kawara no mono*), 'people of the slope' (*saka no mono*; this refers to the ascending road from the Kamo River up to Kiyomizudera), or, more enigmatically, as 'dog *jinin*' (*inu jinin*), many of these slum dwellers sought the protection of the Gionsha and Enryakuji.[8] In addition to handling the dead in the city, they dealt with the removal of different kinds of pollution, produced bows, bowstrings, arrows and leather goods, and served as the 'hounds' of their masters by harassing competing temples and shrines, dunning the debtors of guild merchants and moneylenders, and also by joining the Hie and Gion *mikoshi* whenever they were brought out in a conflict. They were instantly recognizable by the white cloth they used to cover their faces. During the Gion festival, these *jinin* prepared the route of the *mikoshi* by clearing away all impurities (in particular, the carcasses of Kyoto's countless street dogs) and accompanying the gods on their way to the *otabisho* as armed guards. The Gionsha and its dog *jinin* were an essential economic and military asset for Enryakuji, and helped cement its position as the overlord of many of the city's richest merchants. Their presence enhanced the importance of the Gionsha to Enryakuji and contributed to Gion's status as an Enryakuji base on Kyoto's doorstep.

As the warriors of the Muromachi shogunate took control over the city, however, Enryakuji's position of dominance was gradually undermined. The Kamakura shogunate increased its influence in Kyoto and the western half of Japan after a failed court attempt to crush Kamakura in 1221 (the Jōkyū war). After this coup had been defeated with alarming ease, shogunal offices were established at Rokuhara, a site not far south of the Gionsha that had already been used as the main seat of warrior power in the capital by Taira no Kiyomori, half a century earlier. Soon, this office assumed the responsibility for security in Kyoto, as well as taking care of communications between the court and the shogunate. Yet in confrontations with the *jinin* of Enryakuji, the Rokuhara officials struggled to gain the upper hand. In 1229, for example, a Rokuhara retainer cut down a Hie *jinin* in spite of express orders to refrain from violence; in the aftermath of this incident, violent Enryakuji protests could only be prevented by exiling the responsible Rokuhara official.[9] Although the powers of the Rokuhara office gradually increased, it was never in a position to challenge large temples like Enryakuji.

The 1330s brought another change of regime to Kyoto. First, Emperor Go-Daigo (1288–1339) won the throne thanks to the support of the Kamakura general Ashikaga Takauji (1305–58), who turned his back on the Kamakura shogunate and threw his weight behind Go-Daigo instead. After Kamakura's fall in 1333, Go-Daigo pushed for a full-blown restoration of classical imperial rule. Soon, however, Takauji became disenchanted with Go-Daigo's project. In 1336 he rebelled, forcing Go-Daigo to flee first to Mt Hiei, and later the same year to Yoshino south of Nara. This was the start of more than six decades of intermittent warfare between the 'Northern' court in Kyoto, under the control of a dynasty of Ashikaga shoguns and their allies, and the 'Southern' court that operated from a guerrilla base in the hills of Yoshino.

The situation remained chaotic until the end of the century. In Kyoto, the years 1351 and 1352 were particularly dramatic. Briefly, the Southern court gained the upper hand as Takauji's brother Tadayoshi (1337–92) changed sides, sowing division in the Ashikaga camp. For five months (from 11.1351 until 3.1352), Kyoto came under Southern rule. The Northern forces then reconquered Kyoto, only to be dislodged once again a year later, in the sixth month of 1353.[10] These struggles also affected the Gionsha, which became the scene of power struggles between priests who supported the Southern cause and a rivalling faction of the priesthood that was loyal to Takauji. The leaders of that faction joined Takauji when he withdrew from the capital and on many occasions offered prayers to the Gion deities for victory in his many battles.[11] The situation did not stabilize until 1355. From this time onwards Kyoto remained safe from Southern forces, although the Southern court continued its struggle in other parts of the country and finally agreed to a permanent settlement only in 1392.

These changes in the festival's political and economic environment triggered the most radical transformation of the festival in its long history: the demise of the court-sponsored *uma no osa* and their replacement by parades of floats organized by merchants. In this chapter, I will sketch the effects of these changes on the direct environment of the Gionsha and then explore the new forms of display that emerged as a result.

Upper Kamo Shrine

Mt. Hiei
Enryakuji Temple
(8 kms northeast)

Funaoka

Upper Goryō Shrine

Shōkokuji
Temple

Lower Kamo Shrine

Muromachi
Palace

Kitano Tenmangū

Kitabatake

Yoshida Shrine

Ichijō

Nishijin

Imperial
Palace

UPPER CITY

Konoe

Lower Goryō Shrine

Shōshōi
Otabisho

Nijō

HosshōjiTemple

Nanzenji Temple

Sanjō

Chion'in

Kamo R.

Matsunoo Shrine
(5 kms west)

Shijō

Gionsha

Ōmandokoro
Otabisho

Gojō

Kenninji Temple

LOWER CITY

Kiyomizudera

Rokujō

Rokuhara

Shichijō

Hōjūji Temple
(Sanjūsangendō)

Hachijō

Tōji Temple

Horikawa

Nishi-no-Tōin

Higushi-no-Tōin

Kujō

Tōfukuji Temple

Higashiyama Hills

-1000m-

Fushimi Inari Shrine

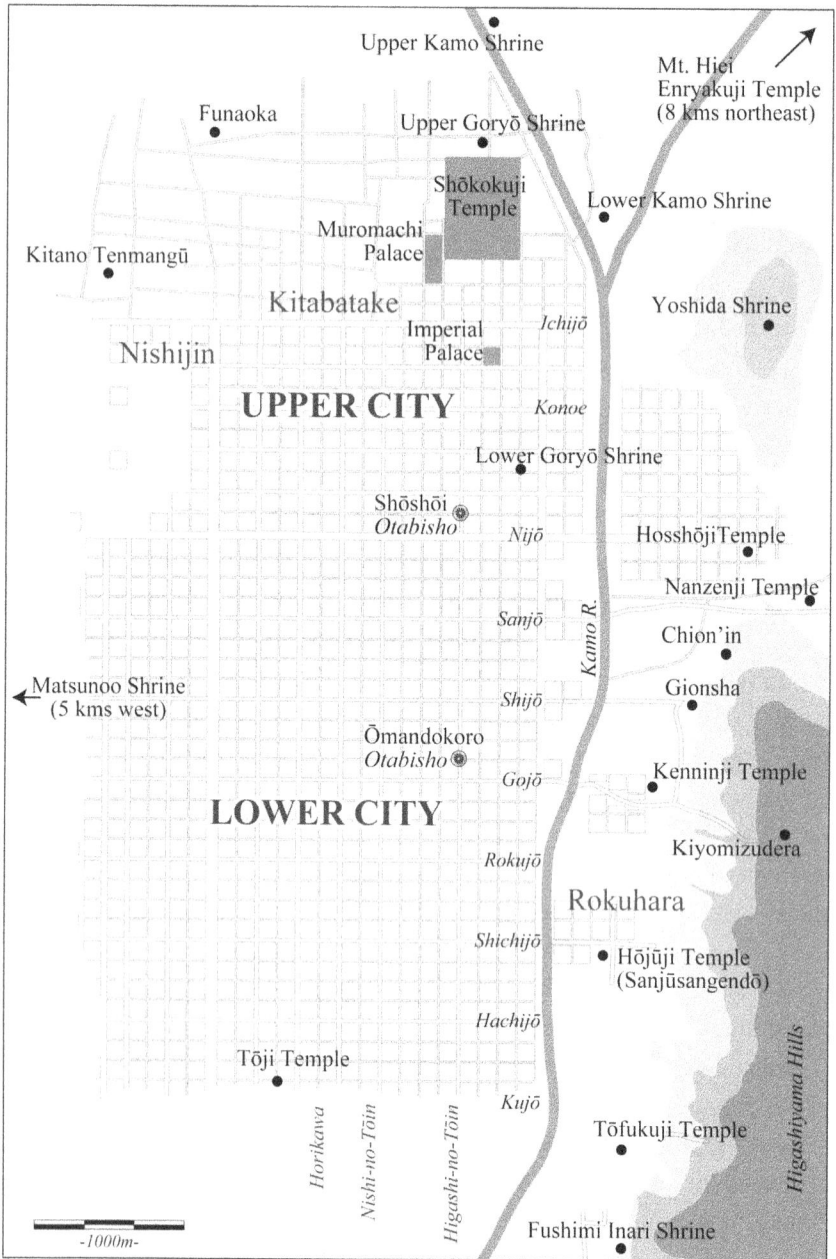

Map 3 Kyoto in the fifteenth century. Created by Matthew Stavros.

The Ashikaga shoguns challenge Enryakuji

On the day of the *goryōe* in 1355, shogun Ashikaga Takauji had a viewing pavilion (*sajiki*) set up at the crossing of Sanjō and Karasuma Streets. Fourteen yards long, this temporary structure was designed to accommodate the shogun, his son and designated successor Yoshiakira (1330–67), his main wife, and another eight of his children. While watching the *mikoshi* processions pass by on their way back to the Gionsha, the shogunal family enjoyed a vegetarian meal in honour of the occasion, though fish was added to make their repast somewhat less ascetic.[12]

The practice of viewing festival processions from *sajiki* pavilions was not in itself a novelty; court nobles, including retired emperors, had done so already in late Heian period.[13] Even so, the fact that this first-ever shogunal viewing occurred in the year that Takauji finally resumed relatively stable control over Kyoto is hardly a coincidence. Shogunal viewings were not just designed for the enjoyment of the shogun and his inner circle. They were also a political statement, addressed directly to the many kinds of people who were involved in the Gion festival, from Enryakuji's abbot to the *jinin* merchants of Enryakuji's guilds.

Loosening Enryakuji's grip on Kyoto life was one of the main objectives of shogunal policy, particularly in the first half of the Muromachi period. The strategies employed to pursue this goal had a direct impact on the Gionsha and its festival, because they hit at its central actors. Three such strategies stand out. First, the Ashikaga shoguns founded and sponsored a new network of Zen temples and favoured these at the expense of older, more threatening monastic powers like Enryakuji and Kōfukuji. The Gionsha was caught up in the often violent protests that this policy provoked. Second, measures were taken to bring the Gionsha itself under the shogunate's control by weakening the line of command that tied the shrine to Mt Hiei. After all, this shrine served as Enryakuji's most effective vanguard base in the capital. Third, the shogunate sought to undermine the position of Enryakuji as the overlord of the merchant *jinin* and their guilds. From the viewpoint of Kyoto's merchants, these policies transformed their role in the Gion festival. Before these changes took place, the festival had been an event where they confirmed their identity as Enryakuji *jinin*. Afterwards, it became a performance where they sought to establish a relation with the shogun in his viewing pavilion.

Enryakuji demonstrated vehemently against shogunal attempts to grant privileges to new Zen temples and enhance their status. Enryakuji argued that its rituals guaranteed 'the safety of the state', while Zen offended the gods.[14] In the 1340s and 1360s, incidents involving the shogunal Zen temples of Tenryūji and Nanzenji escalated into full-blown military attacks, pitting Enryakuji and the Gionsha against the shogunate. These conflicts, which occurred in the early years of the new shogunate, served to sharpen the shogunate's determination to confront Enryakuji.

In 1368 and 1369, Enryakuji monks carried the *mikoshi* of Hie and Gion into the city to protest against privileges granted to Nanzenji.[15] This shogunal temple had earlier been given permission to set up a tollgate, which armed monks from Onjōji tore down in 1367. The shogunate retaliated by demolishing some of Onjōji's own tollgates. In response, Onjōji allied itself with a range of other temples that also felt threatened by the shogunal support of Zen, including Enryakuji. The matter ended badly for Nanzenji. Nanzenji's abbot was sent into exile and the temple's ornate Southern Gate was demolished. Clearly, the shogun had been forced to make concessions. However, there were also signs that shogunal attempts to weaken Enryakuji's control over the Gionsha were already having some effect. In spite of dire threats from Enryakuji, the Gionsha monks had stubbornly refused to unleash Gion's 'dog *jinin*' on Nanzenji.[16] Clearly, there were now forces within the Gionsha that sought to rebalance their dependence on Enryakuji by compromising with the shogunal government.

The *mikoshi* of both the Gionsha and the Hie Shrines were badly damaged in the Nanzenji conflict. Enryakuji insisted that the shogunate should pay for their replacement, but the shogun resisted by prevaricating. The whole affair was a perfect illustration of the precarious position of the Gionsha on the frontline between the shogunate and Mt Hiei. As a result, the Gionsha lacked *mikoshi* for a decade at least, and possibly even until the early 1390s.[17] This had a profound effect on the Gion festival for decades to come. In 1370 and 1376, one diarist notes that although there were no *mikoshi* processions, 'halberds from different parts of the city' (1370), or 'halberds and decorated *yama* floats from the Lower City' (1376), were paraded on the days of the festival. As we shall see in more detail later, these events heralded profound changes in the structure of the Gion festival. After 1380, however, the festival went into a real crisis from which it recovered only when the *mikoshi* returned more than a decade later.[18]

It was in this time of instability and low activity that the Gionsha – and, with it, the Gion festival – was forced to recalibrate its position between Enryakuji and the shogunate. To understand the effects of this crisis, we need to take a closer look at the structure of the Gionsha and its management. The Gionsha hierarchy consisted of four levels. As we have already noted, its overlord was the Tendai *zasu*, the abbot of Enryakuji, while the running of the shrine was overseen by another Hiei official called the *mokudai* (supervisor). Below these mountain overlords were the shrine monks (*shasō*), who worked for a number of semi-autonomous Gionsha cloisters (*bō*) and were mostly recruited from the Ki lineage. The Enryakuji abbot appointed a manager (*shigyō*) from among these shrine monks. Under this manager's supervision, other such monks staffed the shrine office (*mandokoro*) as its first, second and down to seventh scriveners (*kumon*). Below the shrine monks were lay shrine retainers (*kunin*), who in turn oversaw the *jinin* and 'dog *jinin*'.[19] The shrine held land rights over much of the area east of the Kamo River (stretching from Sanjō to Gojō), as well as the *jinin* blocks of lumber workers along the Horikawa River just across the Kamo, the two *otabisho* and some other minor properties in the city; there were also a few rural estates.[20] Many of these possessions had by the late-Kamakura period been transformed into Enryakuji branch shrines or temple lands, and these no longer generated income for the Gionsha and its cloisters. The areas in front of the southern and western gates, however, largely remained in the shrine's hands, and the rents that its occupiers (some of them *jinin* brewers or other types of merchants) paid to the Gionsha provided much of its income.

As long as the Tendai abbot was in control of the appointment of the Gionsha manager, Enryakuji retained full authority over the shrine. On numerous occasions, Enryakuji used its power to extract extra funds from the shrine, or to employ the forces of the Gionsha for its own campaigns. Ashikaga Takauji, the founder of the Muromachi shogunate, challenged Enryakuji's control over its Kyoto shrines already when he first entered the city in 1333. Takauji introduced the novel position of shogunal 'prayer masters' (*oshi*), not only at the Gionsha but also at other important Enryakuji strongholds (e.g., Kitano Tenmangū).[21] At the Gionsha, this *oshi*'s main task was offering rituals and prayers to the Gion deities in Takauji's name, mostly for peace in the realm or victory in battles against 'rebels'. The position of shogunal *oshi* at the Gionsha became hereditary in subsequent generations and soon proved to offer a springboard to shogunal dominance over the Gionsha as a whole.

In the early 1350s, when Mt Hiei was thrown into chaos as Kyoto repeatedly changed hands between the Northern and Southern courts, it became clear that these shogun-appointed *oshi* were perfectly positioned to compete for the office of Gionsha manager. The Ashikaga shoguns granted lands to their *oshi* to cover the costs of their prayers and offerings, and also placed their *oshi* in charge of shrine repairs – a task that placed levies raised to fund such repairs under the *oshi*'s control. In the early 1380s, shogun Ashikaga Yoshimitsu (1358–

1408) transferred the ownership of the areas in front of Gionsha's southern and western gates to his *oshi*. Then, in 1385, he installed his *oshi*, a Gionsha priest called Kenshin (dates unknown), as Gionsha's manager, while decreeing that this office henceforth was to remain in Kenshin's lineage. In this manner he cut out the Tendai abbot and undermined Enryakuji's control over the Gionsha as a base for its activities in Kyoto. Kenshin's lineage would go on to dominate the Gionsha from their cloister headquarters, the Hōjuin, until 1872.

Yoshimitsu chipped away at Enryakuji's influence also in other ways. In the early 1390s, he extended the jurisdiction of the shogunate to include the *jinin* merchants in the city, and he began to collect annual taxes from them. This was a revolutionary change in the political and economic structure of the city. Neither the court nor the Kamakura shogunate had exercised judicial powers over the *jinin* of Kyoto's large temples, nor raised taxes from them. In 1393, Yoshimitsu issued a series of laws, one of which decreed that *jinin* 'shall lose their special privileges and will be taxed as are others'.[22] These new laws did not remove the time-honoured right of temple overlords to tax their *jinin*, but they did put an end to those overlords' power to grant their clients full exemption from taxation by others. Now that the merchants in Enryakuji-controlled guilds no longer could use their *jinin* status to avoid shogunal taxation (as well as its jurisdiction and right to punish), the benefits of Enryakuji overlordship were much diminished.

These developments occurred simultaneously with the institutionalization of shogunal viewings as an annual ritual.[23] Takauji's son and successor Yoshiakira watched the Gion parades in 1364 and 1367; Yoshimitsu did the same in 1374, 1376, 1378 and 1380, when the festival lacked *mikoshi*. In 1378, he was accompanied in his pavilion by the Noh (*sarugaku*) actors and playwrights Kan'ami (1333–84) and his son Zeami (*c*. 1363–*c*. 1443). Yoshimitsu, who was eighteen years old at the time, in fact shared both his mat and his food with the young Zeami, who was likely also his boy lover.[24] This episode is often adduced as a telling sign of Yoshimitsu's predilection for Noh, and as a key moment of the 'process whereby the patronage of both *sarugaku* (Noh) and *dengaku* troupes was largely shifted from religious institutions to warrior leaders'.[25] This shift in patronage would also have a striking impact on the Gion festival, where the merchants who sponsored the emerging parade of floats vied for the shogun's favour by focusing on scenes and themes from Noh plays. The Gion festival, too, was beginning to lean towards the warrior regime and changing its appearance as a result.

A striking string of events that occurred in 1364 illustrates the shifting forces of gravity between Enryakuji, the shogunate and *jinin* merchants.[26] In this year

Enryakuji tried to stop the *mikoshi* from leaving the Gionsha in order to exert pressure on the court and the shogunate in an ongoing dispute. The shogunate refused to budge and forced the Gionsha to stage the procession against Enryakuji's will. Predictably, this led to violence. One of the *mikoshi* was attacked on its way to the Shōshōi *otabisho*, leaving one dead. The *jinin* who carried this *mikoshi* fled, leaving Gozu Tennō's wife Harisainyo stranded. Retainers of the shogunate were now ordered to replace the *jinin* and move the *mikoshi* to its destination. A week later, when the *mikoshi* began its return journey to the Gionsha, it was targeted once more, again with lethal effect. This time, shogunal retainers and merchants donned harnesses and managed to bring the *mikoshi* home to the Gionsha without further mishap. Assuming that the attackers were sent by Enryakuji, we here see the merchants (our source uses the term 'storehouse forces', *dosō-zei*) cooperating actively with the shogunate's Board of Retainers (*samuraidokoro*), in spite of their status as *jinin*.

As we have already seen, the festival entered a prolonged slump in the 1380s and 1390s. Yoshimitsu did not return to his viewing pavilion until 1399; when he finally did, his presence gave the festival a decisive boost. The shogunal viewings soon became an annual event, solidly integrated in the ceremonial calendar of the Muromachi shogunate. Unless circumstances prevented the shogun from attending (mostly because he was in mourning and therefore in a state of ritual impurity), he would be there to grant the festival participants the honour of subjecting their efforts to his gaze. It was under these circumstances that the parades of floats emerged and grew to such proportions that they outshone the *mikoshi* processions. When the shogun was absent, this could lead to a much reduced parade. The years 1401 and 1402 are good examples of this. In 1401, the parade consisted only of 'one small halberd', and in 1402 there was no parade at all – 'perhaps due to the absence of the shogun', as the diarist who recorded this noted with obvious regret.[27] In 1422, on the other hand, a different diarist described the parade of *hoko* and *yama* floats as 'beautiful beyond words' in spite of the shogun's absence, reminding us that while the shogun was important, there were also other audiences worth impressing.[28]

Yoshimitsu's practice of annual Gion parade viewings was continued by his successors Yoshimochi (1395–1423) and Yoshinori (1429–41) until Yoshinori's murder in 1441; it was then revived by Yoshimasa (1449–73) in 1457 and continued until the Ōnin war of 1467–77 put a stop to the Gion festival altogether. During this period, the viewing ritual became steadily more elaborate. Takauji's viewing in 1355 had almost had the character of a family outing, with a meal not much more elaborate than a bento (*warigo*) picnic. In contrast, fifteenth-century viewings involved impressive displays of power, introducing a new, military parade to the festival as the shogun proceeded to his steadily expanding pavilion, while the austere lunch of the early viewings evolved into a sumptuous banquet. Manuals of shogunal ceremony compiled during Yoshimasa's rule proscribe the performance of Noh plays after the first parade on the seventh day, contributing further to the influence of Noh on the design of the merchants' floats.[29] Those floats came to reflect shogunal culture; there was a striking absence of Buddhist themes, scenes about Gozu Tennō and his entourage, or merchant concerns. In this sense too, the new Gion festival that emerged in the late fourteenth and early fifteenth centuries was genuinely new. Not only did it feature new forms of display and performance; it was carried by a new set of actors, giving place of prominence to the merchants and the military elite. The new parade of floats served to visualize their agenda and their authority on the streets of the capital.

In the course of the fourteenth and fifteenth centuries, the Gion festival was transformed beyond recognition. The Gion parades and processions of, say, the 1450s had little in common with the *goryōe* described in the previous chapter. In the following two sections, we will investigate this process of transformation from two perspectives: the emergence of a new funding system, and the novel forms that the festival took as the classical *goryōe* procession, with its *uma no osa* horseriders and *dengaku* dance troupes, was gradually replaced by the float parades of late medieval times.

A new system of funding: The 'chiefs of horses'

To trace the development of the festival's new economic structure, we need to return to the decades when the power balance between court and shogunate was slowly tipping in the latter's favour: the early days of the Kamakura shogunate.

In 1230–1, the realm was struck by an extraordinarily severe famine, caused by a cold summer followed by a hot and dry one. Troubles broke out across the country and revenues from court estates were much reduced. As survivors streamed into the capital, the stench of death disturbed even the nobles in the Upper City; soon, disease invaded their mansions.[30] In response the court issued a new legal code (*Kangi shinsei*), aiming to restore order. This code set out with six articles related to the worship of temples and shrines, followed by twelve articles banning 'extravagance' (*kasa*), sixteen on court procedures and eight on policing. This code has been compared to the more common *tokusei* decrees ('[restoring] virtuous rule'), which were issued by both the emperor and the shogun in times of crisis. Such decrees often included bureaucratic and judicial reforms, but always started with measures directed at the realm of the divine, seeking to soothe the apparent anger of the gods by restoring the land rights and buildings of temples and shrines and renewing the patronage of rituals that had lapsed in recent times. In this case, however, the emphasis was more on curbing excessive consumption than on embellishing services to the gods.

As we saw in the previous chapter, in 1157 Emperor Go-Shirakawa had sanctioned the practice of calling on the resources of 'big men' in the city to ensure that the Gion *mikoshi* processions were conducted in style. Every year, one or a few rich merchants were selected to hold the '*bajōyaku* halberds' and serve as 'chiefs of horses' (*bajō*), a title that was now understood to refer to the expensively decked-out *uma no osa*. In the crisis of 1231, however, the court called for moderation. One of the articles in the *Kangi shinsei* law code berated the 'extravagance' on display in the festivals of Fushimi Inari, Hie and Gion. The *uma no osa* and their grooms must dress more modestly. The practice of decorating the halberds and the divine treasures carried in *mikoshi* processions with precious fabrics must cease. The banquets held by the *jinin* before and after festivals must be abolished, and the large numbers of priests, servants and armed men in the processions must be reduced. The 'wealthy persons of low status' who served as chiefs of horses were singled out as particularly deplorable, because their example taught 'villagers to admire extravagance'.

Kangi shinsei is a telling witness of the court's attitude towards these festivals in the Kamakura period. The first six articles in this code sought to restore order in the human realm by displaying the court's dedication to the gods. Yet it would appear that the efforts of commoners, even when sanctioned by the court, were looked upon with ambiguity. Their displays in Kyoto's festival processions added to the power of the deities, but could also be interpreted as a sign of chaos, undermining the status order, wasting valuable resources and perhaps even causing divine wrath. After all, the *mikoshi* often brought violence to the streets, and tension between different groups regularly resulted in bloody fights and even deaths. Displays that failed to 'mirror' court power in an effective manner, as was increasingly the case due to the decline of court patronage, could easily be perceived as sources of disorder. Conversely, the condemnation of festival extravagance in 1231 indicates that even in these terrible times, merchants agreed to inject their funds in the Gion procession (though we cannot know whether they did so eagerly or reluctantly).

By the late-Kamakura period, however, it appears that the *bajōyaku* was no longer welcomed by Kyoto's men of wealth. It became a common occurrence for those who were selected as chiefs of horses to put up a fight to deflect the cost, causing delays that disrupted the festival.[31] The situation worsened further in the 1320s, the final decade of the Kamakura period, when the *bajōyaku* system fell victim to the ambitions of Emperor Go-Daigo. Go-Daigo hoped to restore direct imperial rule, without shogun or regent. To achieve this, he sought to confiscate lands that over the centuries had been transformed into privately taxed estates. For the same reason, the control of 'private' trade by overlords like Enryakuji needed to be broken. In 1323, the first year of his rule, Go-Daigo issued a decree banning temples and shrines from extracting levies from their *jinin*; in 1324, this was followed by a ban against the *bajōyaku*.[32] This proved to be the end of the *bajōyaku* system at Fushimi Inari, which instead began to raise contributions from all who lived in its territory south of Gojō (today's Matsubara Street). Enryakuji, in contrast, fought back and would eventually succeed in restoring the *bajōyaku* in a different form.

The Gion *bajōyaku* was reinstated in 1343, a few years after Go-Daigo's flight to Yoshino. Unsurprisingly, the merchant who was selected in 1343 as that year's chief of horses refused to pay until he was forced, and as a result the festival was delayed until the twenty-seventh day of the twelfth month.[33] This merchant carried a pseudo-monastic name that identifies him as an Enryakuji agent.[34] He belonged to a group called the *karakura jinin*, a guild that presented the Hie Shrines with 'continental saddles' (*karakura*) in exchange for protection of its business, which may well have revolved around sake brewing and moneylending. After the 1343 festival had finally been carried out, the *karakura jinin* appealed to Enryakuji that the members of this guild might henceforth be exempted from the *bajōyaku*. Similar conflicts, delays and appeals for exemption became a regular occurrence in succeeding decades.

Matters settled down in the 1380s when the *bajōyaku* system was reformed – or, more likely, reintroduced in a new format after having gone defunct for a number of years. The practice of appointing individual persons of wealth as chiefs of horses was now given up. Instead, the *bajōyaku* halberds became the permanent responsibility of a group of leading merchant houses known as the '*bajō* association' (*bajō isshū*). This association consisted of the largest moneylenders and financiers in the city, most of whom maintained close ties with Enryakuji either as *jinin* or as *kunin* – lay retainers of Enryakuji who used monastic names and held temple ranks.[35] There were now not three but twelve or thirteen *bajō* halberds, one for each member of the association. Rather than paying the *bajōyaku* themselves, these members collected contributions from tens or even hundreds of lesser *jinin* businesses, ranging from sake brewers and miso manufacturers to bathhouse keepers; these were referred to collectively as the *gōriki* ('donating') *jinin*. The *bajō* association collected funds not only for the Gion festival but also for the Kosatsuki-e festival of the Hie Shrines. Under the new system there was only one *bajōyaku* levy that was shared between the Hie and Gion Shrines, with Hie consistently receiving a much larger share.

As we have seen earlier, it was in this same decade that shogun Yoshimitsu succeeded in setting up his *oshi*, Kenshin, as the manager of the Gionsha, loosening Enryakuji's grip on the shrine. The restructuring of the *bajōyaku*, too, was closely linked to Yoshimitsu's measures to undermine Enryakuji's power in Kyoto. In 1386, Yoshimitsu issued a law limiting the powers of *jinin* of Hie and other shrines to crack down on tardy debtors. This law was one of a long series of attempts to stop *jinin* violence in the city and bring conflicts between lenders and borrowers into the purview of the shogunal court.[36] It is likely that the *bajō* association originated at this time not only as a way to raise funds for the Hie and Gion festivals but also as a structure that allowed the shogunate to keep a check on the dealings of Enryakuji-related moneylenders and merchants.

As we have already seen, Yoshimitsu took the next step in 1393, when he extended shogunal taxes to Enryakuji *jinin*, who earlier had claimed exemptions. These taxes were collected not by the shogunate itself but by a designated group of selected merchants or financiers; this group's membership list was almost identical to that of the *bajō* association.[37] Starting in 1393, these financiers annually collected 6,000 *kanmon* to fund the shogunal office in the city (*mandokoro*), as well as about 2,100 *kanmon* for the funding of the Kosatsuki-e at Hie and the Gion festival procession – the *bajōyaku*. One *kanmon* was roughly the equivalent of one *koku* (*c*. 180 litres) of rice, or a year's rations. Out of these 2,100 *kanmon*, 300 were set aside for the Gion festival. The members of the *bajō* association must have collected more than this, since membership was a coveted asset that itself became an object of trade, suggesting that it generated considerable income.

More information becomes available about the functioning of the *bajōyaku* system after this date. A collection of 368 documents relating to the *bajōyaku* between 1397 and 1502 has been preserved at the cloister of the Gionsha manager (*shigyō*), the Hōjuin.[38] This complex, located right next to the Gionsha, was the home base of Kenshin, Yoshimitsu's *oshi* and manager, and of his successors. A document dated 1409 reveals that each of the thirteen *bajōyaku* halberds was associated with an office-holder or a group within the hierarchy of the Gionsha.[39] The first halberd belonged to the Tendai *zasu*; the second to the manager (Kenshin's Hōjuin). The third was owned by the senior scrivener (*kumon*) in charge of the Gionsha office (*mandokoro*); the sixth and seventh by the priests of the Ōmandokoro and Shōshōi *otabisho*; the ninth and tenth by the supervisor (*mokudai*); and so forth.

It is possible that these halberds were in some manner associated with the Gionsha gods. In 1220, the Gionsha experienced one of its periodical fires; an official record notes the loss of the shrine's 'thirteen deity bodies' – likely Gozu Tennō, his wife Harisainyo, their eight princes (Hachiōji), Daishōgun, Jadokukeshin and one final deity whose identity is unknown.[40] Maybe the thirteen halberds served to visualize these thirteen deities, supplementing and partly overlapping with the three *mikoshi* that they accompanied? If so, no source found this connection worthy of recording. What our sources do reveal is that the halberds ranged from very elaborate to comparatively modest, with the first halberd sporting as many as twelve decorative 'hangings' (*kakemono*) and the thirteenth only two. The first and second halberds were each accompanied by two horses (*jinme*) and the tenth by just one. The sum of 300 *kanmon* collected by the *bajō* association was delivered to the Gionsha a few days before *mikoshi* were due to leave for the *otabisho*.

The Hōjuin archives include detailed (though never comprehensive) budgets for use of the *bajōyaku* takings for the years 1423 and 1431.[41] The 1423 budget reveals that a portion from the *bajōyaku*'s 300 *kanmon* was distributed among the persons responsible for the halberds, ranging from 14.8 *kanmon* for the first halberd down to just 0.6 *kanmon* for the thirteenth. Additional expenses were used to cover the costs of hiring troupes of lion-dancers and performers of *kagura* and *dengaku*, and to pay for offerings as well as food and drink served at festival banquets.[42] The 1431 budget, which is more complete, shows that the total outlay amounted to less than half of the 300 *kanmon*; the remaining half may have been distributed among the halberds' 'owners', or ended up in the coffers of the Hōjuin.[43] This shows that while in name the *bajōyaku* paid for 'horses' and other contributions to the festival, most of the collected taxes served as a source of income for a range of individuals (and their groups) connected to the shrine. The same was true for the portion of the *bajōyaku* that was intended for the Kosatsuki-e festival at the Hie Shrines. Budgets from the 1460s show that the bulk of this sum, which at that time amounted to about a thousand *kanmon*, was paid to semi-military 'protectors' (*gego*, *katōdo*) within the Enryakuji community, while only a small proportion served to cover the costs of the ritual proceedings.[44]

Seta offers an explanation why the 1431 budget for the Gion *bajōyaku* was compiled with such special care and filed away. As part of his scheme to strengthen Kenshin's position at the Gionsha, in 1397 Ashikaga Yoshimitsu had taken the priestship over the Ōmandokoro *otabisho* away from the Sukemasa lineage of *otabisho* priests and transferred it to Kenshin's Hōjuin. In 1432, the Ōmandokoro priests appealed to the new shogun, Yoshinori, to have the Ōmandokoro priestship returned to them, and won.[45] Among the paperwork submitted in connection with this lawsuit is a list of the entitlements that accrued to the *otabisho* priests: rent from the inhabitants of the *otabisho* block, levies on three guilds engaged in various branches of the textile business, a levy on sellers of used goods and 150 *kanmon* out of the *bajōyaku*. This implies that before 1397, these entitlements had been part and parcel of the *otabisho* priestship – and now, thirty-five years later, they were restored.[46]

Although this victory proved short-lived,[47] this outcome serves as a telling witness of the tenacious hold of the *otabisho* communities on the Gion festival. In 1432, the *bajōyaku*, raised by merchants from fellow merchants, was once again shared by the Gionsha and the *otabisho* priests, with each receiving half of the takings. The Gionsha used a portion of their 150 *kanmon* to add lustre to the *mikoshi* procession. What the *otabisho* priests did with their half is not recorded in any surviving documents. It seems likely that they used at least a portion of this sum to run the *otabisho* shrine and its rituals, of which we know nothing at all.

The fact that the Kosatsuki-e and the Gion processions were funded conjointly, by the same *bajōyaku* levy, served to keep the Gion festival within the grasp of Enryakuji. This remained unchanged even after the Ashikaga shoguns had succeeded in weakening Enryakuji's control over the Gionsha in the 1380s and 1390s. Whenever there was a problem with the *bajōyaku*, the Kosatsuki-e had to be postponed, and Enryakuji would not allow the Gion festival to go ahead before the Kosatsuki-e. The 300 *kanmon* destined for Gion would not be paid until the much larger sum for the Kosatsuki-e had been distributed among its Hie and Enryakuji stakeholders. Enryakuji would force the processions of the Gion *mikoshi* to be cancelled until after the Kosatsuki-e had been successfully performed.

Enryakuji could put a stop to the Gion *mikoshi* also for other reasons. In 1415, Mt Hiei was embroiled in a conflict with the military governor (*shugo*) of Ōmi province (a man called Rokkaku Mitsutaka) and demanded his exile. To put pressure behind this demand, Enryakuji effectively sabotaged the Gion processions. 'This morning', a diarist wrote, 'Mt Hiei sent down armed monks (*akusō*) to Gion. They stole the phoenixes from the roofs of the *mikoshi* and took them with them up the mountain. As a result, the processions cannot go ahead.'[48] This conflict ended in a settlement, allowing the festival to be arranged in the beginning of the seventh month – without the governor being exiled. The 'halberds (*hoko*) prepared by the locals', however, had already been paraded as usual on the normal dates in the sixth month, independently of the cancelled *mikoshi* procession. Enryakuji, it would seem, had direct control only over the *mikoshi*. This circumstance may explain the development of a parade of floats that was staged separately from the *mikoshi* processions.

The shogunate retained the power to enforce settlements like this one in 1415 while the political situation was reasonably stable. For a while, Enryakuji made no more attempts to manipulate the Gion festival. This changed in the 1440s, when the shogunate was rapidly disintegrating. In this period, Kyoto's merchant houses fell victim to frequent rural uprisings (*tsuchi ikki*), with armies of farmers invading the city from the surrounding countryside with the demand that their debts to city merchants be cancelled. As a result the collection of both the *bajōyaku* and shogunal taxes stalled. In response, Enryakuji repeated its stance that the Gion *mikoshi* would be stopped unless the *bajōyaku* for the Kosatsuki-e was paid in full. The temple threatened to launch a full attack on the Gionsha if this demand was not heeded – a turn of events that demonstrates the success of the shogunate in weakening Enryakuji's hold over the Gionsha. Such an attack was in the end prevented, but only after lengthy negotiations that lasted far into the autumn, or even the winter. In 1449, 1452, 1456, 1458, 1462 and 1463, the festival was postponed until the end of the twelfth month; in 1458, both the Hie Kosatsuki-e and the Gion processions were finally staged in a much abbreviated form on the final day of the year, the thirtieth day of the twelfth month.[49] The terse diary entry that is our only source for this year appears to imply that the *mikoshi* left the Gionsha on the thirtieth and returned late at night on the same day. It is worth noting that even under such circumstances, performing some semblance of the festival before the year ran out was deemed crucial – although no sources help us to pin down by whom, or why.

Although the parades of floats had been performed independently of the *mikoshi* processions both in the 1370s–80s and in 1415, Enryakuji now applied pressure to cancel also the parades whenever the *mikoshi* were stopped. Kawauchi Masayoshi, the most prolific historian of the late-medieval Gion festival, argues that the main reason for this change of strategy was economic: Enryakuji demanded that the merchants who put up these floats made contributions to the *mikoshi*, while cutting down on the costs of their floats.[50] It is easy to imagine, however, that other considerations may also have played a role, even if they are not reflected in extant documents. Cancellation of the Gion festival robbed the shogun of the opportunity to perform his annual public viewing of the Gion parade. Stopping the *mikoshi* was an effective political tool that not only caused embarrassment but also undermined the shogunate's ability to 'mirror' and display its authority. If the parades went ahead, the absence of the *mikoshi* alone failed to sabotage such viewings, undermining Enryakuji's negotiating position. The rushed end-of-year processions of the 1450s and 1460s were a telling sign of the shogunate's decline and a portent of the disastrous collapse that would soon follow.

The development of the float parade

From the late fourteenth century onwards, the Gion festival consisted of two parts: the processions of the three *mikoshi* and the parades of floats. The appearance of the latter marks the beginning of the festival's second phase of development. As we saw in Chapter 1, in the first phase court nobles and, to a lesser degree, also commoners had embellished the *mikoshi* processions with *uma no osa*, *dengaku* dances and other arts. In the fourteenth century the *mikoshi* processions gradually became less extravagant, while floats sponsored by merchant guilds as well as the shogun came to be paraded separately from the *mikoshi*, at a different hour and by a different route.[51] When exactly this change occurred remains unclear, but there is no doubt that this was an epoch-making transformation that would have an impact on festival culture throughout Japan. The new format, combining a *mikoshi* procession with a parade, would later spread as the 'Gion model' of festivals, copied across the Japanese islands from the fifteenth century onwards. How did the Gion parades emerge, and what was their original function?

Yamaji Kōzō, a historian of folk arts, proposes that the float parades must be distinguished from the *mikoshi* processions as separate events with different roots. Yamaji argues that while the *mikoshi* processions were organized by the Gionsha under the auspices of the court and the shogunate, the float parades emerged organically from folk beliefs about spirits of disease. The floats, mainly of the *yama* and *hoko* types, were paraded through the Lower City to attract and gather up such spirits, cleansing the streets at the beginning of the annual season of illness as the rainy period gave way to the heat of high summer. The rich decorations of the floats, together with the music and dancing that accompanied the *hoko* in particular, were designed to please the spirits and 'catch' them. Yamaji proposes that 'originally', the floats would have been burned or thrown into the

Kamo River to dispose of the caught spirits. By historical times, however, the floats had become so elaborate and valuable that such radical measures were replaced by the rapid disassembly of the *yama* and *hoko* after the end of each parade.[52]

Yamaji argues that the medieval Gion festival was a combination of two ritual procedures that were performed by different social groups, that had different origins and that were based on different sets of beliefs: the *goryōe*, staged by the Gionsha priests since classical times and paid for by the *bajōyaku*, and what Yamaji calls the *matsuri*, performed and funded mainly by commoners in the city (*machishū*) at their own initiative. The *goryōe* followed court protocol dating from the late Heian period and reflected faith in the powers of Gozu Tennō and his entourage to avert illness. In contrast, the *matsuri* ignored the Gionsha and its deities, and also the *otabisho*. Rather, the parade resembled the 'folk' *goryōe* that took place at Funaoka Hill in 994 (see p. 29), in that it sought to ensnare malevolent spirits with a combination of decorated contraptions, music and dance, and then obliterate or disperse them. As a combination of these two disparate practices, Yamaji maintains, the medieval Gion festival was an amalgam of two radically different responses to the seasonal illnesses that plagued the Lower City.

Yamaji's hypothesis is appealing in its clarity, but needs to be tested against the admittedly limited sources on the emergence of the Gion parades. In the light of what we have already learned about the *otabisho* and the *bajōyaku*, his dichotomy between rituals staged by 'the shrine' and by 'the community of believers' (*shinkōsha shūdan*) in the city ignores many entanglements. If the *otabisho*, as argued by Seta Katsuya, functioned as centres of merchant communities and were their main conduit of participation in the festival, this means that the *mikoshi* processions always were a ritual in which commoners (or, more accurately, *jinin* merchants) played a central role. Also, the *hoko* floats of the parade cannot be separated completely from the *hoko* halberds that identified the merchants who coordinated the collection of the *bajōyaku* levy. Goshima Kuniharu detects a pattern in which the parades grew when the *mikoshi* processions were cancelled, while they shrunk when the processions went ahead.[53] This, he argues, shows that these two events were funded by the same class of people – Kyoto's guild merchants – and that the latter diverted the funds collected for the processions to the parades when Enryakuji stopped the former. In turn, this demonstrates that the festival was valued by these merchants, that they begrudged and resisted Enryakuji's frequent interference with the *mikoshi* and that they possessed the wherewithal to give substance to that resistance by developing the parades as alternative events.

Yamaji builds his argument on an interpretation of the floats as a means to dispel disease spirits. He does not adduce any evidence for this interpretation, but Kawauchi Masayoshi offers at least a hint that appears to point in the same direction. In the eighth month of 1471, a few years after the Ōnin war had put a stop to the Gion festival, a measles-like illness spread among the so-called Eastern army – the shogunal forces that were holed up in the north of the city. According to a court noble's diary, the locals (*jigenin*) sought to 'see off' (*okuru*) the illness by staging an extravagant display of 'spectacles and *yama* floats'.[54] The circumstances are extraordinary and the source is late, but if this one-line diary entry reflects an older practice, it may constitute the only evidence to support Yamaji's thesis.[55]

Yet, even if we accept this diary note as evidence in support of Yamaji's understanding of the floats, it is difficult to imagine that the new float parades of the fourteenth and fifteenth centuries were expressions of a 'folk belief' that had survived, latently, since the tenth century. Can one assume the existence of a folk belief without any evidence of communal events that expressed such a belief? While folklorists in the tradition of Yanagita Kunio (1875–1962, the father of Japanese folklore studies) have tended to accept such assumptions, historians are more sceptical. Kawauchi Masayoshi leads the historical study of the medieval Gion festival. While being critical of undocumented speculation about the ideas or beliefs that may have inspired the performances recorded in the sources, he offers no alternative interpretations. Most surviving sources stem from the brushes of elite diarists, who were more interested in the movements of the shogun than in the doings of commoners. Adhering too closely to those sources results in a narrative that overemphasizes the role of the shogun and plays down the (admittedly unknowable) initiatives and concerns of other groups. Is there a middle way? What can we say about the early history of the float parades, based on the limited historical evidence that we have at our disposal?

Prominent among the earliest floats were contraptions called *hoko*, 'halberds'. Perhaps we can take this as a hint that halberds stood at the beginning of the evolution of the extravagant floats of later times. Halberds were distributed to merchants as emblems of their divine duty to raise the *bajōyaku* levy. This practice drew on a long tradition of using halberds (a weapon that was popular in the prehistoric Yayoi period but had long since been replaced by spears, arrows and swords in actual battle) to signal authority.[56] Halberds already featured in the Gion *goryōe* procession as depicted in the twelfth-century *Nenjū gyōji emaki*, as we saw in Chapter 1. These halberds do not look particularly impressive, however. They appear to be about 3 metres long, decorated only with a small banner and carried by persons in unimpressive garb. Such halberds were also a part of other festival processions. A guard shouldering a decorated halberd can be seen, for example, in a Kamakura-period illustrated scroll of the Kamo festival (*Kamo matsuri ekotoba*, 1274).[57] As the 1231 *Kangi shinsei* testifies, the halberds of chiefs of horses (*bajō*) were lavishly decorated already at that time, to the point that they outshone the *uma no osa* that these chiefs were expected to fund. When the *bajōyaku* was restored in the 1380s, the twelve or thirteen halberds of that time were linked both to the members of the *bajō* association and to a person or group within the priestly hierarchy of the Gionsha and Enryakuji, and their decorations were strictly prescribed.

In 1321, the diary of retired emperor Hanazono (1297–1348) describes a performance of 'halberd groups' (*hokoshū*) from the Gion *goryōe* in the palace courtyard. Two halberds, each accompanied by such a 'group', were joined by two drummers on horseback and an *uma no osa*. This performance took place after the *goryōe* had finished and was carried out by court nobles, who were rewarded for their efforts with gifts of robes.[58] Two years later (on 14.6.1323), the same diarist describes how a number of halberd groups veered off from the procession in order to perform in the presence of the retired emperor.[59] These *hokoshū* were likely groups of drummers and dancers, one of whom carried a decorated pole topped with a halberd blade. They not only accompanied the *mikoshi* but also made their own way through the city streets. This suggests that the *hokoshū* halberds were unrelated to the halberds of the *bajō* association. As they roamed the city, the *hokoshū* could be as unruly as the *dengaku* groups had been in the past. In 1332, armed members of a halberd group committed a killing while they were dancing their way through the streets. The warrior authorities in the city responded with an order that 'halberd [groups] of the Gion *goryōe* must abstain from carrying weapons'.[60]

These halberd groups may well have been a Gion invention, although we cannot be certain. There are references to halberds as the main attraction of the Fushimi Inari procession in 1340, while another diary entry notes that in 1391, the *mikoshi* of Kitano Tenmangū was followed by the 'halberds of the various neighbourhoods' (*hoho no onhoko*). If halberd groups did indeed originate in the Gion festival, they soon spread to Kyoto's other *goryōe* festivals.[61] No fourteenth-century illustrations reveal what these halberds looked like. They are often imagined to have been similar to the 'blade halberds' (*kenboko*) that still accompany the *mikoshi* of many festivals in and around Kyoto.[62] *Kenboko* are long poles, up to 7 metres long, topped with a metal blade and small bells. They are carried by one man who while walking makes the thin blade at the top of the pole sway and bend to the sound of the jingling bells. Honda Ken'ichi suggests that these blade halberds, which can be traced back to the early sixteenth century, may derive from the halberds that became part of *goryōe* of the Upper and Lower Goryō Shrines in northern Kyoto in the fifteenth century.[63] Those, in turn, may well have drawn on the halberds that emerged yet another century earlier at Gion, Fushimi Inari and Kitano Hachimangū.

However this may be, these halberds and halberd groups appear to have gradually replaced the *uma no osa* and *dengaku* dancers of the previous period. In diaries, *dengaku* groups are last mentioned in 1349 and *uma no osa* in 1351,[64] so they overlapped with halberds for about three decades before disappearing, perhaps in the wake of the 1351–2 crisis that saw Kyoto change hands repeatedly between the Northern and Southern courts. By the mid-fourteenth century, a combination of *mikoshi* with multiple halberds, each accompanied by drums, flutes and gaudily dressed dancers, had become the new standard for festivals in the Kyoto region. The diaries refer to these displays with new terms: *furyū* or *hayashimono*, both meaning something like 'artful spectacles'.

While most communities in Japan had only one or two festivals, or indeed none at all, medieval Kyoto was a festival hothouse where competition between neighbouring festivals was fierce. The switch from *uma no osa* to halberd groups occurred not only at Gion but at many other sites across Kyoto, as lesser events emulated the new patterns established by the prestigious groups that participated in the city's largest festivals. One-upmanship was an aspect also of the halberd groups that participated in the same festival, as it had been among the sponsors of *uma no osa* earlier. As the halberds became steadily grander, inevitably this led to accidents. In 1376, for example, 'a high and large halberd toppled, killing an aged nun'.[65] As the limits of halberd upsizing were reached and breached, other novelties appeared.

Among these novelties were contraptions called *yama*, 'hills'. If we exclude Mukotsu's *mura* described in the previous chapter, *yama* get their first mention in 1345. The court diary *Moromori ki* notes that due to rain on the seventh, '*yama* and other contraptions' (*yama ika no tsukurimono*) were paraded through the streets on the eighth, the day after the *mikoshi* processions.[66] One imagines decorated floats that would normally parade through the streets before the *mikoshi* processions on the seventh and the fourteenth, though not when it rained (as it often did). Another new addition were 'parasols' (*kasa*), similar to halberds but with a cloth canopy at the top rather than a blade. Perhaps they were somewhat similar to the flower-topped parasols still in use today at the Yasuraibana festival of Genbu Shrine in northern Kyoto.[67] These parasols were sometimes referred to as 'parasol halberds' (*kasahoko*). They could also feature on *yama*, some of which were described as *yamagasa*, 'hill parasols'.[68] A diary entry from 1422, finally, mentions a 'ship' as part of the parade on the fourteenth of the sixth month. Presumably, this was another form of large-scale *tsukurimono*; perhaps a distant ancestor of today's Fune-hoko or Ōfune-hoko.[69]

A description of the Gion festival in the early fifteenth century can be found in *Sekiso ōrai*, a two-volume work on letter writing by the court scholar Ichijō Kanera (1402–81). *Sekiso ōrai* takes the form of a long sample letter (*ōrai*) that describes both ceremonial and quotidian events through the year, while explaining elegant epistolary phrases and offering additional examples of their literary usage. This work, which was likely completed in the 1420s, suggests to aspiring writers of formal letters that they should emulate the following pattern when describing the Gion festival:

> This year, the Gion *goryōe* was particularly splendid. The *shizume* halberds from Yamazaki, the halberd with the parasolled white herons from the *ōdoneri* [guild], the dancing halberds from various places, the parasols and carts of various houses, the decorated *yama*, the *yatsubachi* drummers, the *kusemai* dancers, and the efforts of the locals must surely have pleased the gods. There are rumours that in the evening, the Shirakawa halberd will enter the city.

The term '*shizume* halberds' was used already in the same 1345 *Moromori ki* entry that told of the postponement of the *yama* parade because of rainy weather.[70] An earlier textbook of letter writing, *Shinsatsu ōrai* (written by the monk Sogan in 1367) talks of '*shizume* halberds from various places', suggesting that there were a number of them. *Shizume* means 'pacifying', but whether these halberds were meant to pacify the gods or the crowds is unclear. *Sekiso ōrai* indicates the reading *shizume* in a gloss to the character 定 (*sadame*), perhaps indicating that these halberds were 'fixed' or 'regulated'. Already in 1345, these halberds were regarded as indispensable; while the '*yama* and other contraptions' were postponed due to rain, the *shizume* halberds were paraded as usual, on the same day as the *mikoshi*.

Yamaji proposes that in contrast to the postponed *yama*, these halberds must have accompanied the *mikoshi* procession, and he wonders whether the term *shizume-hoko* refers to the twelve or thirteen halberds of the *bajōyaku*. In his analysis, this would place them in the category of shrine rituals, while the '*yama* and other contraptions' constituted the *matsuri* of the 'community of believers'.[71] However, *Sekiso ōrai* locates at least one of the *shizume-hoko* in Yamazaki, Kyoto's harbour on the Yodo River and the base of a guild of oil merchants who conducted their trade as *jinin* of Iwashimizu Hachimangū. Also, the *shizume-hoko* disappeared from the sources after 1424, while the *bajōyaku* survived until 1470.[72] Perhaps the *bajōyaku* levy no longer required halberds – or, equally likely, the term *shizume-hoko* might refer to another type of halberds, sponsored by guilds like the Yamazaki oil merchants.

The 'halberd of the parasolled herons' (*kasasagi-hoko*) is mentioned for the first time in 1365. *Moromori ki* deplores its absence from that year's parade, implying that it was already a well-established ingredient of the festival at that time.[73] This halberd was accompanied by a troupe of dancers, dressed as white herons that carry miniature parasols ringed with small paper streamers on their heads. *Sekiso ōrai* attributes this float to the *ōdoneri* guild, which, in spite of its name, consisted not of senior court staff (*ōdoneri*) but of silk weavers and merchants based in Nishijin in the Upper City. A later diarist, however, writes that 'the *kasasagi-hoko* of Kitabatake' was followed by a separate '*hoko* of the *ōdoneri* [guild]' (in 1436), so it is at least possible that the author of *Sekiso ōrai* confused these two floats.[74] Kitabatake, an area north of Ichijō Street (today's Imadegawa) and east of Nishijin, was home to a community of so-called *shōmoji*, professional musicians, dancers and play actors of outcast status who had formed their own guilds. Whether these *shōmoji* participated with their own float, or (perhaps more likely) were hired by the merchants of Nishijin to add lustre to their *ōdoneri* float, remains unclear.[75]

Only one visual image of the fifteenth-century parade is known today. Tokyo's National Museum holds a set of Edo-period copies of six images from two six-panel screens that were once in the possession of the Tokugawa shoguns; sadly, the original screens have since been lost to fire.[76] It is generally known as *Tsukinami sairei zu*, 'Images of festivals in respective months'; the Gion festival must have been included to evoke the atmosphere of Kyoto's summer. The first two surviving images show the shogunal headquarters at Sanjōbōmon, which were used by Ashikaga Yoshimochi and Yoshinori until the latter moved to Muromachi in late 1431.[77] The copies are said to retain characteristics of fifteenth-century Tosa-school paintings. The imagery of the Gion parade on these screens differs from that of the Kyoto screens of the sixteenth century in many details.

The fifth and sixth panels of one of these two screens depict scenes from the float parade. The fifth screen shows a square *yama* wrapped in decorative fabric and carrying a pine-topped hill. Such float hills were made of plaited bamboo strips, covered with cloth. At the foot of the hill, a Chinese-looking man and a younger companion point at a crane. No such *yama* existed after the Ōnin war. Behind this float, an armed man carrying a fan calls and gestures to a line of men in various states of undress who are pulling a rope, no doubt attached to a larger *hoko* that is not in the frame. A party of ferocious-looking men, many of them carrying *naginata* glaives and dressed in anything from a mere loincloth to full armour, follow behind the *yama*; whether they are accompanying this *yama* or form the vanguard of the approaching *hoko* is hard to tell. Also visible are two dancers wearing costumes of parasolled herons, so perhaps the men are pulling the *kasasagi* float.[78]

To the right of the *yama*, a comically dressed man rides an ox. On his head he wears an outrageously large *kanmuri* hat. A stick across his shoulders spreads out the arms of his noble garb, and a duck-like bird is perched on one of his sleeves. The rider holds a ridiculously oversized ritual baton (*shaku*), completing his *sokutai*-style ritual garb. Called the 'ox-rider' (*ushi no nori*), this figure can also be seen in two other later depictions, where he is followed by a crowd of laughing onlookers. The ox-rider appears to have moved through Kyoto's streets on the day of the *mikoshi*'s return, entertaining onlookers with a bit of parodical fun.[79] The Gion festival contains few ludic elements; this seems to be an exception, mocking, subverting and, ultimately, perhaps reconfirming the authority of Kyoto's nobility in the mode that Handelman calls 're-presenting' play.

The sixth panel shows the swaying *shingi* poles of two huge halberds, the front half of the 'ship halberd' (Fune-hoko) and two decorated *kasa* parasols. Izumi Mari argues that a decoration of near the top of one of the halberd poles identifies it as the *katsurao* or *katsuraotoko* ('Man in the Moon') halberd, named after a figure from Chinese lore;[80] if so, this is perhaps a medieval ancestor of the Tsuki-hoko ('moon *hoko*') of later times. Of one of the halberds only the pole can be seen up in the sky, but the other is depicted in its entirety. Supported by huge wheels, the balustraded deck is crowded with musicians and maybe a few dancers. The roof is covered in exotic panther skins; the pole rises up from the roof's centre. A crowd of people carrying glaives and long leafy branches surround the halberd and the parasols. Where the men in the fifth panel are all dressed differently and all have exaggerated facial features, the crowd on this sixth panel is a mass of identically dressed figures. Perhaps their main role in the image is to look small, adding perspective to the height of the soaring halberds.

Returning to *Sekiso ōrai*, we encounter a few more contributions to the parade that were important enough to be singled out by the author: *yatsubachi* drummers and *kusemai* dancers. The *yatsubachi* were young boys carrying small drums called *kakko*, attached with a string around their neck. *Kakko* had two drumheads on either side of a cylindrical body and were played with small drumsticks. Combinations of song, dance and *kakko* rhythms became popular in the Kamakura period. *Kusemai* was a new type of dance closely related to the new genre of the shoguns' favourite art of Noh (*sarugaku nō*). At least in some of its many forms, it involved chanting and even storytelling. In the 1360s, the shoguns Ashikaga Yoshiakira and Yoshimitsu sponsored '*kusemai* carts' as part of the parades, and there is frequent mention of professional dancers (often female) called *gaga*, literally 'songs of celebration', who presumably performed such songs on the *kusemai* carts as they moved along the parade route. When the shogun was in mourning, the parades lacked such carts. Also, it became an established practice for *gaga* dancers to be received at the shogunal headquarters after the Gion parades. This practice continued long after the *kusemai* carts had disappeared from the parades in the early fifteenth century.[81] Both the *yatsubachi* and the *kusemai* were common elements of numerous festivals and ritual celebrations in this period; their appearance in the Gion festival reflected that popularity.

How the halberds, parasols and *yama* of Gion may have looked at different stages of their development, we cannot tell. Court diaries mention merely that the parades featured '*yama* and *hoko*', '*yama* and *kasa*', or even just 'displays' (*furyū*).[82] It appears likely that there was a gradual process of enlargement, leading from halberds that were carried by one man to wheeled cart structures similar to, though still smaller than, the *hoko* of today.

Yamaji has proposed that the *hoko* that we know from sixteenth-century illustrations (and that are similar to those still in use today) emerged as a combination of *kusemai* carts and *hoko* halberds. These *hoko*, after all, are carts with giant wheels, and they include a stage where a young boy performs *kakko* drumming and dancing. As Yamaji himself admits, however, it is difficult to tally a possible fusion of carts and *hoko* with the scarce data on the development of the parades. The *kusemai* carts seem to have disappeared from Kyoto's Gion parade well before the *hoko* groups developed into wheeled *hoko* floats. In surviving images (none related to the Gion festival), *kusemai* carts look structurally very different from the later *hoko*. Also, it is difficult to imagine a smooth transition from the *kusemai* of professional *gaga* women to the much simpler *kakko* dances performed by merchant children on the *hoko* decks.[83] Perhaps the *hoko* floats developed independently, with the *kakko* dancers (as well as the musicians who accompanied them) moving from the street to an elevated stage within the *hoko* at some unknown point in this process. There is no diary entry expressing shocked delight at the sight of the first-ever wheeled *hoko* float.

The parade described in *Sekiso ōrai* was structurally different from the early modern and modern float parades in that it was more fluid and varied, both in its forms of expression and in the social groups that participated in it. None of the three floats mentioned in *Sekiso ōrai*, the *shizume*, *kasasagi* and Shirakawa halberds, survived beyond the fifteenth century. Various 'places' and 'houses' participated in the parades with smaller floats that did not (yet) have fixed names. This suggests that their *hoko* and *yama* did not necessarily participate every year, or that they were redesigned at the fancy of their owners. Who these 'places' and 'houses' refer to is not specified. The main attractions of the parades (the named halberds) were associated with guilds of merchants rather than 'streets', as would become the case from the sixteenth century onwards. Perhaps the terms 'places' and 'houses' can be interpreted as occupational units. Last on *Sekiso ōrai*'s list are the nameless 'efforts' (literally, 'duties', *shoyaku*) of 'locals' (*zaichi*). The term 'locals' may be interpreted as a reference to the inhabitants of Gionsha's territory in Lower Kyoto, whose contributions would initially have been less impressive and more fluctuating. In the early fifteenth century, it would appear, the Gion festival served as a stage both for the members of occupational guilds in and beyond the Gionsha territory and for other 'locals'.[84]

This social landscape of different participants is reflected in a comical play (Kyōgen) called *Kuji zainin*, 'The sinner [who drew the wrong] lot'. In this play, the 'head' of a group that participates in the Gion parade with a *yama* float assembles the group's members to discuss the upcoming festival. At their meeting, he proposes various ideas. His servant, in typical Kyōgen fashion called Tarō-kaja, exposes his master's ignorance time and again by pointing out that his suggestions are less than original. Some of his ideas, Tarō-kaja points out, are already used 'every year' by certain streets; others were tried out last year but failed to impress, making a laughing stock of the *yama* group that had put up such a miserable show. In the end Tarō-kaja comes up with his own proposal, which wins the support of the assembled group members. Their *yama* will depict a scene where a demon chases a sinner up and down the *yama* hill at the entrance to the realm of the dead. The roles in this sketch will be shared out by drawing lots. As luck would have it, the master ends up with the role of the sinner and Tarō-kaja with that of the demon – giving him a much-appreciated opportunity to give his master a good beating in view of the entire city.[85]

This play is often brought up as additional evidence that in the fifteenth century, *yama* were redesigned regularly – although Tarō-kaja also mentions that many designs were repeated by the same groups every year. Although the play is an entirely fictional farce, written down (in various versions) long after such a practice of redesigning *yama* had ceased to exist, this is perhaps not entirely unreasonable. Goshima Kuniharu has pointed out that at least in the earliest known versions of the play, the members of Tarō-kaja's *yama* group were presented as living in different parts of Kyoto, rather than all in the same street.[86] Since this circumstance is irrelevant to the plot of the play, it is all the more likely that it reflects an actual social reality.

Kuji zainin also shows that *yama* designs were completely unrelated to the gods of the Gionsha, whose *mikoshi* they were supposed to accompany. Even the theme of epidemics and illness was completely absent. Instead, they referred to episodes from Chinese or Japanese tales and legends, often taken from Noh tales. I will return to these designs in more detail in Chapter 3.

The emergence of regional Gion festivals

The Gion festival would not be of such great interest if it weren't for the fact that copies of it proliferated throughout Japan. It was because of this widespread copying that *mikoshi* processions and float parades became a prominent feature of festivals in most parts of Japan. This process of proliferation began in the fourteenth century and picked up speed in the fifteenth.

Ōtsuka Katsumi (2001) divides the early dissemination of Gion-type festivals to other regions into three phases. The first, which likely started already in twelfth century, began with the founding of small Gion Shrines on lands that were donated to or acquired by the Gionsha. In 1098, four estates in Tanba, Ōmi and Bingo provinces were awarded to the Gionsha in thanks for the recovery from illness of Emperor Horikawa. Shrines dedicated to Gozu Tennō were erected on all these estates, and it appears likely that some much simplified form of the Gion *goryōe* became established there soon afterwards, although the earliest sources on such performances date from the fourteenth century. The Gionsha acquired more estates in the twelfth and thirteenth centuries, and at least on some of them, small 'Tennō' Shrines served as the stages for miniature Gion festivals. A 1275 land register of the Horie estate in Etchū province, for example, includes ricefields labelled as 'fields for the maintenance of the Tennō [Shrine]' and 'fields of the deity association', set aside for the funding of shrine events on the seventh and fourteenth days of the sixth month – the dates of the Gion festival.

These local performances, which served to tie distant Gionsha lands to their overlord, had little impact beyond the estate borders. More important in spreading the Gion festival format was the conscious transplanting of the festival by warrior leaders who sought to adorn their headquarters in the provinces with cultural practices from the capital. Already in the twelfth century, the so-called Ōshū Fujiwara in northern Honshu designed their capital Hiraizumi to resemble Kyoto; this included the founding of a Gionsha and the annual performance of a Gion festival in the sixth month. More lasting was the impact of Gion Shrines founded in the towns of Kamakura, Nara and Yamaguchi in the thirteenth and fourteenth centuries. Kamakura gained its own Gionsha already in the 1080s, but the earliest evidence that a Gion festival was performed there dates from the early Muromachi period, when this town served as the seat of the Kamakura *kubō*, the Ashikaga governor in charge of eastern and northern Japan. A Kamakura ritual calendar (*Kamakura nenjū gyōji*, 1456) mentions that *mikoshi* from the town's main shrines, including the Kamakura Gionsha, assembled at the quarters of the *kubō* on the seventh day of the sixth month. On the fourteenth, the *kubō* viewed a parade of Gion floats (including 'ships') and dances from a pavilion.

In fifteenth-century Nara, villages belonging to the Tōdaiji Temple there took turns organizing and funding a Gion parade that included *yama* with scenes from Noh plays, *kasahoko* halberds and carts that carried musicians and dancers (*maiguruma*). Here too, the parade passed pavilions, which in this case accommodated members of the Furuichi warrior house as well as prominent monks from the Tōdaiji and Kōfukuji temple complexes.

Yamaguchi, finally, was a garrison town in Suō province, founded by the Ōuchi warrior house in 1360. The Ōuchi controlled up to six provinces in western Honshu and northern Kyushu from their Yamaguchi stronghold, and they ranked among the most influential warlords within the Muromachi shogunate. Yamaguchi acquired its own Gionsha in 1369, and it is likely that this shrine served as the stage for some form of Gion festival from around the same time. By the late fifteenth century, the festival sported a parade of three *hoko* floats (one of which was called the Naginata-hoko), followed by a *mikoshi* procession to an *otabisho*. The parade was viewed by the Ōuchi daimyo from a pavilion outside one of his residences. A later account (from 1583) also mentions *kasahoko* halberds and heron dancers (*sagi mai*). Clearly, the Yamaguchi festival was designed with Kyoto's parade in mind. It is also a good example of the role of politics in the dissemination of Gion-type festivals. Yamaguchi was less prone to urban epidemics of the kind that Kyoto experienced at regular intervals. Rather than as a countermeasure to illness, the festival was imported to this seat of power as a stage for the display of Ōuchi authority. Arguably, its centre of gravity was not the small Gionsha shrine, or the even less memorable *otabisho*, but the Ōuchi pavilion.

The third phase saw the spread of Gion-inspired events to smaller towns and even villages – a phenomenon that was particularly conspicuous in the wider sphere around Yamaguchi and its Ōuchi lords, from Aki and Iwami in western Honshu to Buzen and Hizen in northern Kyushu. In many cases, the links that tied these local festivals to the Gion festival in Kyoto are unclear, and some may well draw on (Gozu) Tennō festivals that must be regarded as independent traditions, such as those of Hakata (today's Fukuoka) and Tsuyama in Ise province. Many of these festivals, however, took place on the same dates as Kyoto's Gion festival, and they may have been influenced by it in more subtle ways.

This early dissemination of Gion-style festivals formed the basis for the spread of festivals featuring float parades in the new towns that emerged throughout Japan in the sixteenth and seventeenth centuries. When Edo-period castle towns, market towns and harbour towns developed their own festivals, these tended to follow the format of *mikoshi* processions and float parades that was first developed in Kyoto.[87] However, in contrast to the regional Gion festivals of medieval times, these new festivals no longer used the Gion floats as their model.[88] The result was a dazzling range of different float forms with striking regional characteristics. As towns and neighbourhoods competed to put up the best show, they primarily looked to local examples for inspiration. The float parades of Edo's new Kanda festival, in particular, inspired similar parades in castle towns around the country, from where they spread to smaller market and harbour towns in the same domain.

Gozu Tennō

While the Gion floats carried no relation to the gods that were carried in the *mikoshi*, it is worth noting that those gods, too, were taking on new guises. There are few sources that can give us a clear image of the nature of the gods enshrined at the Gionsha before the Kamakura period. We saw that the names of Tenjin, Harime and Hachiōji appeared already in tenth-century documents, soon after the Gionsha was founded. A twelfth-century source described Tenjin as a deity with the head of an ox, and a statue lost to fire in 1148 was named Gozu Tennō, the Ox-Headed Deva King. The three deities of Gion clearly consisted of a main male deity, his female consort and their eight sons. Beyond that, no further details about these deities can be gleaned from Heian-period sources. It was in the thirteenth and fourteenth centuries that the central myth of this divine family was worked out and disseminated. To what degree this myth already existed in the Heian period must remain an open question.

The tale of Gozu Tennō and his family makes its first appearance in *Shaku Nihongi*, a work by Urabe (Yoshida) court priests.[89] This collection of transmissions about the *Nihon shoki* (720) was compiled by Urabe Kanekata (dates unknown) in the latter half of the thirteenth century. It was an in-house document for use within the Urabe lineage, which positioned itself as experts on the *jingi* and *jingi*-related court rituals. In that capacity, they gave advice on the protocol of court ceremonies and ritual countermeasures in response to calamities. The Urabe also lectured to high-ranking court nobles (notably the Ichijō house) on such classical texts as the *Nihon shoki* (Chronicles of Japan, 720). The *Shaku Nihongi* was part of the trove of exclusive knowledge that constituted the working capital of the Urabe.

It is in a note to a *Nihon shoki* passage about the deity Susanoo (or Haya-Susanoo) that *Shaku Nihongi* brings up Gozu Tennō. Susanoo, the brother of the sun goddess Amaterasu, caused his sister to retire to a cave by a series of defiling acts. This plunged the world into darkness, and the gods of Heaven assembled in front of Amaterasu's cave to lure her back into the world. After they had succeeded in this, Susanoo was punished and banished from Heaven. Susanoo now roamed the earth, wearing a broad hat and a coat of woven straw to ward off the never-ceasing rain. In the evenings he asked the gods for lodgings, but everywhere he was refused; ever since, *Nihon shoki* notes, there has been a taboo on entering other people's houses in such gear.[90]

To link this tale to the circumstances of Kyoto, Urabe Kanekata referred to a tale about Gozu Tennō, allegedly recorded in a centuries-old gazetteer (*fudoki*) of Bingo province, which is no longer extant. This legend tells of a deity called Mutō; that same name occurs as 'another name for Gozu Tennō' in an entry about 'Gion' in *Iroha jiruishō*, a Kamakura-period dictionary. Mutō in the Bingo gazetteer, however, was enshrined in Enokuma, a shrine not far from modern Okayama.

Bingo no kuni fudoki says:
Enokuma no Kuni-tsu-yashiro
Mutō no Kami of the northern sea travelled south to court the daughter of the god of the southern sea. Night fell while he was on the road. In that place, there were two brothers called Somin Shōrai. The elder brother was poor, while the younger brother was so rich that he owned a hundred storehouses. Yet the younger brother denied Mutō shelter, while the elder brother invited him in. The elder brother offered Mutō a seat of millet straw and a meal of cooked millet.

Mutō left this place and returned many years later with his eight sons. He asked [the elder brother]: 'I want to strike back against [the younger] Shōrai. Are any of your children in his house?' Somin Shōrai replied that his daughter had married into his brother's household. Mutō told him: 'Make sure that your daughter carries a ring of straw on her hip'. That same night, Mutō killed all the people in that household, saving only the daughter of the elder brother.

Mutō said: 'I am Haya-Susanoo no Kami. In years to come, whenever there will be an illness, all who announce that they are your descendants and carry a ring of straw on their hip will be saved.'

In *Shaku Nihongi*, this passage is linked to the tale of Susanoo's roaming, offering information about Susano/Mutō's fate after his banishment from heaven. Kanekata goes on to quote his father, Urabe Kanefumi (dates unknown), who transported this Bingo tale to Kyoto itself. Mutō, Kanefumi stated, is none other than Gozu Tennō, and this legend is an account of the origin of the Gionsha and the Gion festival. The deities of the three *mikoshi* are Mutō Tenjin/Susanoo, his wife Kushi-inada-hime, and his second wife, the daughter of the god of the southern sea. During the *goryōe*, he added, millet must be presented to the gods in their *mikoshi* at the crossing of Shijō and Kyōgoku Streets, in memory of Somin Shōrai's hospitality. Also, since ancient times it has been said that there is a hole beneath the floor of the Gion shrine hall that leads to the dragon palace. Perhaps, Kanefumi speculated, the god of the northern sea travelled to the daughter of the god of the southern sea by this route.

The Bingo gazetteer allegedly quoted in *Shaku Nihongi* is likely apocryphal; the linguistic form of the quoted passage effectively rules out a date in the early eighth century, when this set of provincial gazetteers was compiled.[91] Rather than an authentic remnant of an ancient tale, this legend emerged in the context of what Itō Masayoshi (1980) has called the 'medieval *Nihongi*' – an expansive body of texts that present new myths and legends about the gods, disguised as quotations from the *Nihongi* (i.e. *Nihon shoki*). Others, notably Yamamoto Hiroko (1998) and Saitō Hideki (2006), have further expanded Itō's concept. They propose to read texts like the *Shaku Nihongi* as samples of a fluid 'medieval mythology' (*chūsei shinwa*). That mythology built on classical texts about the Age of the Gods, including *Nihon shoki*, in a strikingly free manner, seeking to adapt the narratives of the authoritative canon of the classical court to the needs of a different age.

The myth of Gozu Tennō/Mutō Tenjin and Somin Shōrai was not an Urabe invention; it must have circulated in some form by the thirteenth century at the

Figure 6 Gozu Tennō, as depicted in *Zōho shoshū butsuzō zui* (Images of the buddhas of all sects, expanded version, 1792), volume 3. Gozu Tennō is here identified as Gion Daimyōjin or Susanoo, residing in Yasaka. He is listed as the twenty-fourth of the thirty deities who offer protection on the corresponding days of the month (*sanjū banjin*). Hidenobu Tosa / Wikimedia Commons.

latest. Perhaps it was already presented as a quote from the Bingo gazetteer when Urabe Kanefumi learned of it; this appears all the more likely because the reference to distant Enokuma remains unexplained in Kanefumi's interpretation of the tale. Kanefumi's association of Gozu Tennō with Susanoo, however, is not attested in any other sources of this period and does fit the profile of an Urabe innovation because it finds a basis for a contemporary myth in the *Nihon shoki*. Many centuries later, Kanefumi's association offered an opening for the 'Shintoization' of the Gionsha, and in 1868, Susanoo, Kushi-inada-hime and Susanoo's eight children (rather than his 'second wife', as Kanefumi would have it) replaced Gozu Tennō, Harisainyo and Hachiōji as the kami of the shrine under its new name of Yasaka Jinja.

A more elaborate version of the Somin Shōrai myth can be found in a text that, in contrast to the *Shaku Nihongi*, may be connected to the Gionsha. This text carries the impressive title 'Collection of the golden raven and the jade hare, containing the inner transmissions of the essence of Yin and Yang, preserved in the containers [of the gods of heaven and earth], as passed down in the three countries [of India, China, and Japan]' (*Sankoku sōden onmyō kankatsu hoki naiden kin'u gyokuto shū*). I will refer to it as *Hoki naiden*. The legend of Gozu Tennō starts off this work, which offers an encyclopaedic overview of calendrical and astrological knowledge. *Hoki naiden* is loosely based on an astrological sutra titled 'Sutra on the methods to determine auspicious and inauspicious days and times of day based on the twenty-eight lunar mansions and the seven celestial bodies, as taught by the Buddha Mañjuśrī and the immortals' (*Monjushiri bosatsu oyobi shosen shosetsu kikkyō jinichi zen'aku sukuyō kyō*). *Hoki naiden* reorganizes this sutra around the tale of Gozu Tennō and expands its scope to include Japanese practices and taboos associated with Yin-Yang divination. *Hoki naiden* was ascribed to the famous Yin-Yang diviner Abe no Seimei (921–1005); this is clearly a fictional attribution. Most scholars agree that this text must have originated in the fourteenth century. Some hold that *Hoki naiden* was written by a Gionsha priest, while others believe the author to have been a Shingon priest, or a specialist of Yin-Yang divination without a Gionsha connection.[92]

In *Hoki naiden*, Gozu Tennō appears as a king from northern India. A lapis lazuli bird sent by the Heavenly Sovereign (Tentei) reveals to him the existence of Harisainyo, the third daughter of the Dragon King Sagara, whose palace is located in the southern seas. Gozu Tennō departs, accompanied by a large retinue, to ask for her hand. When night falls, he seeks lodging in the palace of the demon king Kotan Daiō, but he is abused at the gate and turned away. One of Kotan's slave girls leads Gozu Tennō to Somin Shōrai, who is poor but nevertheless accommodates him and even gives him a meal of millet. Somin also lends Gozu Tennō his boat, which takes him to the dragon palace. There he marries Harisainyo, and they have eight sons.

Kotan fears that Gozu Tennō will attack him when he returns, and he asks a diviner to find the best way of defence. The diviner advises Kotan to have a thousand monks recite great spells and appeal to Taizanfukun, the lord of Mt Taishan (in China) who judges the dead. This is sound advice but one of the monks falls asleep, leaving a breach in Kotan's defences. Gozu Tennō's footmen enter through this gap and kill Kotan with all his companions – except for the slave girl, who is spared thanks to an amulet that Gozu Tennō has made for her, carrying the formula *kyūkyū nyoritsuryō*.[93] Gozu Tennō cuts Kotan's corpse into five parts and teaches Somin Shōrai to pacify these by means of five rites on five calendar dates (*gosekku*); the foodstuffs offered on those days correspond to Kotan's body parts.[94] He also teaches Somin a secret spell (*niroku himon*, the 'spell of two plus six [characters]'): 'All this is a rite to subdue Kotan.'[95] Gozu Tennō announces that the cold and hot illnesses that will affect the people in generations to come are all caused by beings from his retinue; only those who observe the five rites correctly and have faith in Gozu Tennō's spell will be saved. Since the year 999, *Hoki naiden* concludes, pacification rites for Kotan have been performed every year at the Gionsha throughout the sixth month. These rites, needless to say, include the Gion *goryōe*.

In his discussion of this first chapter of *Hoki naiden*, Murayama Shūichi proposes that this account was a ceremonial text that was recited in front of

Gozu Tennō's image by the Gionsha monks as part of rituals.[96] While recounting the origins of Gozu Tennō's worship, it also served to explain the rationale and underline the importance of a range of ritual practices: the *gosekku* offerings, the chanting of the secret spell, the offering of millet, and the distribution and use of amulets. When Gozu Tennō overpowers the great spells chanted by an assembly of monks and their Taizanfukun rites, this tells the audience that the rituals of Gozu Tennō prevail even over such powerful practices.[97] Millet was indeed offered to the *mikoshi* on the day of the *goryōe* until the early Edo period.[98]

Hoki naiden consists of two parts. The first deals with 'origins' (focusing on the Gozu Tennō legends), while the second part focuses on divination, notably propitious and unpropitious calendar days and the movements of calendrical deities. Gozu Tennō, Harisainyo and Somin Shōrai are here associated with the propitious calendar deities Tendōshin, Toshitokushin and Tentokushin; the eight sons of Gozu Tennō and Harisainyo with the Eight Generals led by the baleful Daishōgun (Great General); and Kotan with the evil Konjin (the Deity of Gold), who was said to kill seven relatives of any person who offended him.[99] The direction of Tendōshin is most propitious of all; *Hoki naiden* notes that after childbirth, the placenta must be buried in this direction. These calendrical deities are associated with celestial bodies (stars, planets or comets), whose movements can be seen in the night sky. Gozu Tennō is identified as Tengyōshō, the Star of Heavenly Punishment, who commands over all stars in the heavens. Tengyōshō, *Hoki naiden* explains, responds to people's sincere faith by descending to our Sahā world under the name of Gozu Tennō in order to bring salvation to all.[100]

From the Muromachi period onwards, variants on the myth of Gozu Tennō and Somin Shōrai appear in a widening range of sources. The most well-known example is *Shintōshū*, a fourteenth-century collections of legends about fifty different deities, likely transmitted among storytellers based at Agui, a community located in the Upper City with links to Mt Hiei. It would appear that in the course of that same century, the tale of Somin Shōrai – of which the provenance remains unknown – constituted a central myth of the Gionsha deities.

These myths must have contributed to the dissemination of Gion Shrines beyond Kyoto, and as we have just seen, they served to explain certain rites at the Gionsha, including the Gion *goryōe*. Yet, it must be said that within the performances that defined the festival, the Gionsha gods remain strikingly anonymous. Amulets invoking Somin Shōrai predate the Gion *goryōe* by centuries; the earliest example has been found at the site of Nagaoka-kyō, the ill-fated capital that was abandoned for Kyoto in 794.[101] *Chimaki* amulets distributed by float communities came to be labelled with the spell, 'We are descendants of Somin Shōrai' (*Somin Shōrai no shison nari*), but as far as we know this practice began first in the Edo period. The festival was never a re-enactment of the Gozu Tennō myth; rather, the myth was used to add colour to the festival at a late stage of its development.

Summing up

It was in the Muromachi period that the Gion festival took on the structure that I have earlier described as the 'Gion type': a combination of *mikoshi* processions with parades of floats. The emergence of these float parades signalled the rise of new groups of participants. Court nobles continued to sponsor the embellishment of the *mikoshi* processions until the middle of the fourteenth century; as late as 1439, the diarist Madenokōji Tokifusa lamented that 'it appears that in recent times, there are no orders to procure *uma no osa* anymore'.[102] Yet already in the Kamakura period, the processions depended on the *bajōyaku* levy, paid by commoner merchants. The *bajōyaku* is of interest because it reveals the new social structures behind the processions. Payment of this levy was enforced by Enryakuji and the shogunate. The *bajōyaku* tied the Gion festival to Hie's Kosatsuki-e and gave Enryakuji occasion to interfere in the Gion processions. The shogunate put its might behind the *bajōyaku* because it depended on the same group of merchants for the collection of another, larger levy that funded the shogunal office in the city. Meanwhile, the imperial court and the retired emperors who had been so dominant in the festival's first phase receded into the background.

This was not, perhaps, an example of a tradition 'flopping' in Morin's terms, although there were prolonged periods when the processions could not go ahead (notably in the 1380s) and when the Gion festival came close to fading away. There is clear evidence of what Morin calls 'wear and tear', as the procession was reduced to a much less impressive spectacle. Yet, rather than causing the festival to die, the decline of one set of patrons and participants allowed others to redesign it for their own purposes. As we have seen, Enryakuji had many uses for both the *bajōyaku* levy and the *mikoshi*; also, the festival fortified Enryakuji's position as the overlord of guilds of *jinin* merchants. The Muromachi shoguns, especially from Yoshimitsu onwards, pushed back against Enryakuji and other temple complexes in order to expand their own sphere of authority. By staging elaborately ritualized shogunal viewings and ceremonial events linked to the Gion festival, they absorbed the prestige that emperors, regents and retired emperors had bestowed on it in earlier centuries. They established new connections both with the *jinin* merchants and with the priesthood of the Gionsha, and followed the same strategy at other shrines that were part of Enryakuji's Kyoto network. In the process, shogunal culture – symbolized by Noh and *kusemai* dancing – made its mark on festivals around Kyoto, inspiring new forms of display that were performed by the city's commoners to please the shogun as he watched them from his pavilion along the route.

Those new forms of display were not added to the *mikoshi* processions but performed separately, as parades of diverse and rapidly evolving floats. It appears that these parades came into their own in the late fourteenth century and grew into the 'main events' of the festival after the slump of the 1380s. The people behind the parade floats are difficult to pin down. The most prominent floats, it appears, were organized by merchant guilds based in various parts of the city, rather than the 'streets' that ran the floats from the sixteenth century onwards. About the role of the two *otabisho* and their priests we know almost nothing, although there are many hints that they served important functions, both in the parades on the seventh and fourteenth days and during the week-long stay of the *mikoshi* at their *otabisho* shrines.

What meanings were attributed to the proceedings of the festival by the many different actors involved, including those who merely watched them from the side of the street or gathered in the hope of receiving blessings? We have seen that the Gion gods were the subject of new legends that reflected new practices. However, those legends are not in any way reflected in the float parades – and hardly in the *mikoshi* processions, either. While folklorists and ethnologists explain the *hoko* halberds, and also the *yama* 'hills' and *kasa* parasols, as 'spirit-catchers' (*yorishiro*) designed to cleanse the city of disease, there is little evidence in contemporary sources to confirm this interpretation. Because this view has been adopted by the Floats Association (*Yamahoko rengōkai*) in the post-war years, and currently serves as the official line on the meaning of the floats, it is worth subjecting it to some closer scrutiny here.

The theory that festival floats are designed to function as 'spirit-catchers' was first launched by the folklorist Orikuchi Shinobu (1887–1953) in an article titled *Higeko no hanashi* ('The tale of the *higeko*'), published in two parts in 1915 and 1916.[103] *Higeko* are strips of bamboo sprouting like a fountain from the top of a type of floats that is used in certain festivals in the larger Osaka area, for example, the Kokawa festival. Orikuchi argued that floats in this area represented an early model that shed light on ancient folk beliefs. Reinterpreting *mikoshi* festivals, he argued that basket-like objects attached to the tops of Kokawa float poles (in his view, the ancient prototype of the *higeko*) had originally been designed to attract gods and spirits, who were then transported to the local shrine. In Orikuchi's view, the understanding that the gods permanently reside in shrines and visit *otabisho* during shrine festivals was a later refashioning of an older belief, which saw the gods as beings that dwell beyond the realm of humans and are 'invited' to receive human worship at regular intervals. Orikuchi created the terms *yorishiro* (a medium that holds a god or spirit) and *ogishiro* (a medium that invites or attracts gods or spirits) in the context of this new theory.

Orikuchi was influenced by the work of Yanagita Kunio (1875–1962), who had already written about the gods as beings who visit communities from their dwelling places in other realms. Orikuchi's concepts *yorishiro* and *ogishiro*, however, differed from Yanagita's *kamishiro* (an object that holds a *kami* deity) and *yorimashi* (the seat of a god or spirit) in the sense that they add a new dimension of movement, played out in festivals. Yanagita's terms were static, referring to the objects that hold or represent deities in ritual settings. In contrast, Orikuchi's neologisms were designed to fit a narrative where such objects attracted or 'caught' gods and spirits in one place, in order to move them to another place where they could be worshipped, placated or temporarily settled.

Fukuhara (2016) points out that there is no evidence that the *higeko* baskets which play a central role in Orikuchi's argument ever existed. He reads Orikuchi's *yorishiro* theory as an attempt to liberate the gods from the stale ideology of the period's nationalized Shrine Shinto. For Orikuchi, the 'real' realm of the gods was to be found in nature, or in ancient folk beliefs, rather than in the closed-off halls of state-run shrines. Fukuhara proposes that rather than *higeko*-type decorations, the soaring poles of floats might be regarded as symbols of the presence of divine spirits. Floats, then, are moving 'pillars' (*hashira*) – a device so common in early Japanese ritual that it even served as the grammatical counter for gods.

Even this, however, remains speculative because no pre-modern source makes mention of such an interpretation of the meaning of floats. In fact, there is a striking absence of discussion of the design or the function of any of the floats, or of the routes taken by the two processions and parades, in the entire body of extant sources. This stands in marked contrast to the rich doctrinal explorations into, for example, the nature of Mountain King (Sannō) who protects the Mt Hiei in the guises of the gods of Hie, as laid out in the encyclopaedic *Keiran shūyōshū* ('Collected leaves from hazy valleys', compiled between 1311 and 1348) and other doctrinal works. Likewise, the thirteenth and fourteenth centuries saw the development of a large esoteric literature about the Ise Shrines, imbuing every detail of the shrine buildings with cosmic and salvific meanings.[104] Nothing similar was written about the Gionsha, the *otabisho*, the *mikoshi* or the floats. As we have seen, the themes of the *yama* floats, which carry more explicit narrative content than the *hoko*, have no obvious relevance for the supposed aim of the festival – subduing the roaming spirits of disease. In Handelman's terminology, the 'modelling' purpose of the festival – exorcizing the demons of disease – became less visible, as elements of 'mirroring' – presenting social hierarchies – proliferated.

Clearly, the festival was not designed by a single mastermind who was playing with a coherent symbolic scheme. Rather, it was shaped by the ambitions and creativity of different groups of people of different social status, with diverging interests, ideas and faiths. Perhaps it was this chaotic multitude of meanings and functions that helped the festival survive what was arguably its greatest crisis: the long war that started in 1467 and that came close to destroying Kyoto once and for all.

1467–1582

Revival in an age of war

After almost six decades of intermittent warfare with the Southern court, the Muromachi shogunate finally won full control over the country in 1392. However, it knew only a few decades of stability. This second shogunate was from the start an unstable construction, in which the shogun headed a volatile coalition of semi-autonomous warlords. In 1441 one such warlord assassinated the sixth shogun, Yoshinori, and the Muromachi order fragmented. Both the shogunal house itself and many of its central allies were caught up in a vortex of destructive conflicts, while lesser warriors in the provinces made good use of the opportunities that the escalating chaos at the centre placed within their grasp.

Matters came to a head in 1467, when the so-called Ōnin war turned Kyoto into a battleground. Two armies of more than a hundred thousand soldiers each divided the city among them. Northern Kyoto was in the hands of the so-called Eastern army, led by the shogunal deputy (*kanrei*) Hosokawa Katsumoto (1430– 73), while the Lower City was occupied by the Western army, a shifting coalition led by Katsumoto's son-in-law, Yamana Sōzen (1404–73). The immediate issue was a series of succession disputes. Most importantly, the two armies backed two candidates for the post of shogun. Soon, however, the fighting gained its own momentum. Already in the summer of 1467 the Western army gained the upper hand, forcing the Eastern army to ensconce itself in a cramped stronghold in the north of the city. Small groups of soldiers from both camps made frequent forays into the streets, systematically setting strategic places on fire. Fighting was fierce until 1473, when the original commanders of the two armies both died. After 1473 a military stalemate limited the options for effective action. For four more years the two camps eyeballed each other from their respective fortified

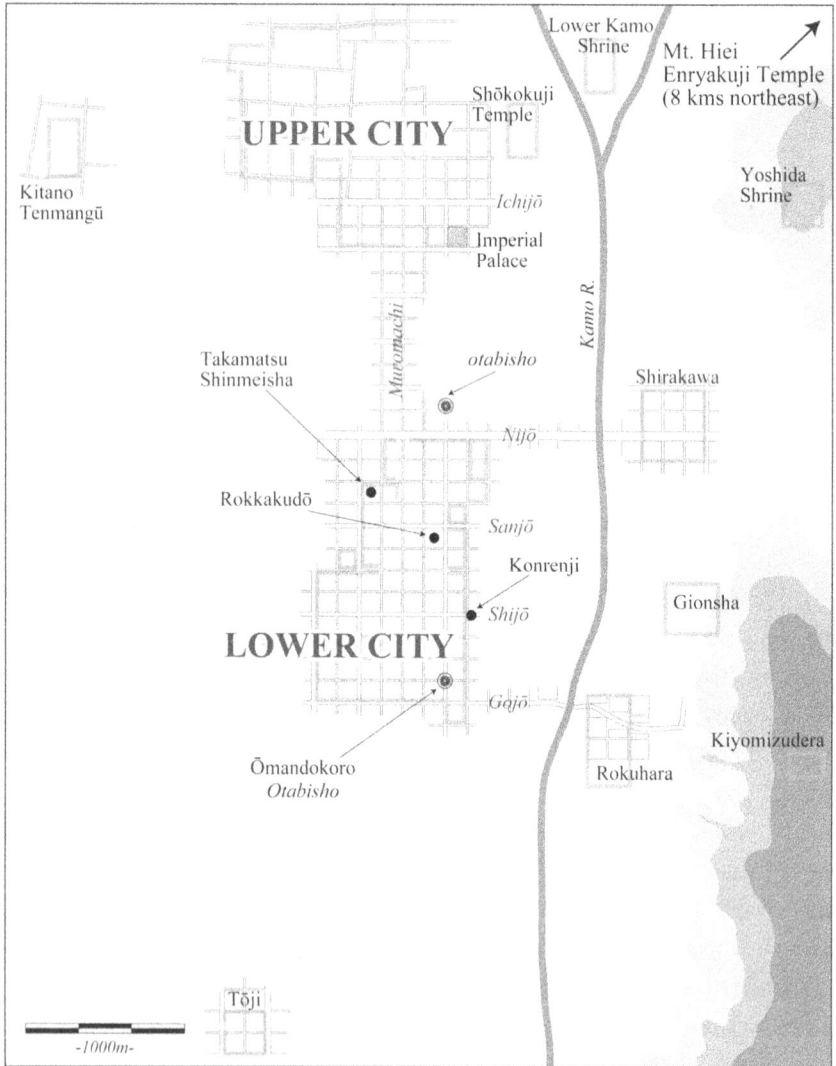

Upper City labels: Lower Kamo Shrine, Shōkokuji Temple, Mt. Hiei Enryakuji Temple (8 kms northeast), UPPER CITY, Kitano Tenmangū, Yoshida Shrine, *Ichijō*, Imperial Palace, *Muromachi*, Takamatsu Shinmeisha, *otabisho*, *Kamo R.*, Shirakawa, *Nijō*, Rokkakudō, *Sanjō*, Konrenji, *Shijō*, Gionsha, LOWER CITY, *Gojō*, Kiyomizudera, Ōmandokoro *Otabisho*, Rokuhara, Tōji, -*1000m*-

Map 4 Kyoto after the Ōnin war. Created by Matthew Stavros.

positions, limiting themselves to occasional sallies. By then, what had begun as a military campaign had long since degenerated into anarchy.

In 1477 the remaining troops finally decided that other battlefields promised better returns, and the two armies dispersed. The war had solved nothing, but Kyoto was forever transformed. The capital had been reduced to two village-sized neighbourhoods: the Lower City, between Sanjō and Gojō, and the Upper City, north of Ichijō. Linked only by Muromachi Street, each of these neighbourhoods consisted of condensed mazes of barricaded streets, fortified with wooden palisades and manned gates. The city's mansions, palaces, villas, temples and shrines had all been looted and burned at least once, and in many cases multiple times.

Spates of fighting, arson, looting and even all-out warfare continued to plague Kyoto for a century after 1467. Military activity flared up in 1493–4, 1507–8, 1527–36, 1549–53 and 1565–8.[1] Ever-changing configurations of warlords stood for much of the action, but other groups also joined the fray. Commoners formed militias (*ikki*) to defend their interests and staged violent protests against levies and taxes. Rural communities around Kyoto invaded the city almost annually, armed with pikes and torches. They demanded that their debts to city merchants be cancelled and confiscated lands returned. Hokke (Lotus, Nichiren) and Ikkō (Pure Land) temples presided over well-organized congregations of lay adherents both in the city and in the surrounding countryside. These temple networks challenged the authority of established powers, including Enryakuji and the shogunate, while also entering into shifting alliances with them when this appeared opportune. The Hokke and Ikkō movements each had their periods of success and even dominance within the city, but they soon suffered heavy defeats, were temporarily expelled from the city and eventually returned in more subdued forms. Warlords, commoner militias, temple networks and established monastic powers like Enryakuji clashed at regular intervals. The city burned time and again, although there were lulls of peace and spates of rebuilding.

In 1568 the warlord Oda Nobunaga (1534–82) entered Kyoto and finally brought an end to the worst of the fighting. His entry is often seen as the beginning of a new phase of the long war, turning the tide from fragmentation to unification. In 1573 Nobunaga expelled the Muromachi shogunate from Kyoto by defeating the last shogun, Ashikaga Yoshiaki (1537–97), and forcing him into exile; in this operation, the northern half of the city was once again reduced to ashes. Nobunaga started Kyoto's reconstruction in the last decade of his life, but it was left to his successor, Toyotomi Hideyoshi (1537–98), to lay the foundations for early modern Kyoto – and, indeed, for a new, reunified Japan. All in all, the century that passed between 1467 and 1568 transformed both Japan and Kyoto beyond recognition, physically as well as socially.

Needless to say, these dramatic events also disrupted and transformed the Gion festival. The festival was last performed in 1466. Efforts to revive it started in the 1490s and finally succeeded in 1500. Until 1571 the situation remained volatile, and the festival was often postponed and reduced, though never again cancelled.[2] Fundamental to the festival's fate in these chaotic years were the fortunes and misfortunes of the institutions on which it depended: the Gionsha and, towering above it, Enryakuji.

The Gionsha was among the first victims of the fighting. The main hall burned down in the second month of 1466, and the outbreak of the war precluded any attempts at rebuilding it. Only the 'deity bodies' (*shintai*) were saved, ending up 'somewhere near Gojō' in the Lower City.[3] Decades would pass before a new main hall could be erected; it was finally inaugurated in the eleventh month of 1492. The new Gionsha included a modest booth located at the side of the new main hall, where begging monks wielding ladles with long handles collected coins for the restoration of the *otabisho* and the *mikoshi*.[4] Their efforts laid the foundation for the revival efforts in that same decade.

The Gionsha's old overlord, Enryakuji, was a central military agent already during the Ōnin war. Enryakuji controlled the only route from the stronghold of the Eastern army to the outside world: from the Upper City, via Mt Hiei, to the port of Sakamoto on the western shore of Lake Biwa. The Eastern army had access to necessary provisions only as long as Enryakuji allowed Eastern soldiers and purveyors to pass through its territory. The mountain's armed men were no match for the warlord forces that constituted the Western army, but for a long time Mt Hiei's natural defences saved Enryakuji from the fate of the Gionsha. Yet the temple complex proved unable to prevent warlords from confiscating many of the lands that had made Mt Hiei so rich. Cut off from its economic base, the mountain grew weaker year by year, and visitors reported that many of the Hiei temples were in a state of advanced decay.

Then, in 1499, the warlord and kingmaker Hosokawa Masamoto (1466–1507) attacked troops stationed on the mountain. Those troops supported the fugitive ex-shogun Yoshiki (1466–1523), and Masamoto was determined to forestall Yoshiki's plans to retake Kyoto. Almost all structures on Mt Hiei were torched. Also lost to fire were the Hie *mikoshi*, which had been carried up to the mountain in the hope that their presence would deter the fighters.[5] When the Gion festival was restored in 1500, Mt Hiei lay in ruins.

Disaster struck even more cruelly after Nobunaga entered Kyoto in 1568. As the wars of unification intensified, Mt Hiei regularly housed entire armies. In a situation where Nobunaga felt that his control over Kyoto was under threat, he decided to destroy the mountain once and for all. In the ninth month of 1571 Nobunaga's fleet landed in Sakamoto. His troops burned the Hie Shrines, proceeded up the mountain from the rear, massacred thousands and torched every building. Remaining temple lands were shared out among Nobunaga's main allies. It was Toyotomi Hideyoshi who in 1584 finally granted permission and pledged support for the gradual rebuilding of Enryakuji – a process that was completed only in the 1660s. These dramatic events ended the glory days of Mt Hiei. In its revived form, the mountain was no longer the economic and military giant that had once cast its shadow over every corner of Kyoto life.

The 'streets' of Lower Kyoto

Who restored the Gion festival in 1500, and why? This question is of particular interest because it is directly related to the festival's contemporary identity and signification. The Gion festival was disrupted again during the Second World War, and in the late 1940s its revival seemed as impossible as it had appeared in 1500. The revival process in the years 1947–52 included the creation of a new narrative designed to give meaning to the festival in a completely new setting. This narrative presented the Gion float parades as symbols of the 'power of the people', expressing the emergent self-emancipation of the 'masses' (in this case, the townspeople) in a feudal age. This notion was based on a particular interpretation of events from the early 1500s – a desperate time that Kyotoites associated with the circumstances of the immediate post-war.

Drawing on the research of the Marxist historian Hayashiya Tatsusaburō (1914–98),[6] members of the History Section of the Kyoto Association of Scientists for Democracy created teaching materials for schools, including a 1953 picture show (*kami shibai*). This show, printed in the form of a booklet with pictures and narration text, represented the revived float parade of the early 1500s as a demand for peace, directed by the 'people of the streets' (*machishū*, *chōshū*) against the military elite.[7] The story pits the *machishū* commoners against the shogun, claiming that in 1533, these people defied a shogunal ban in their determination to parade their floats through the streets. In the narrative of the picture show, the *machishū* used the parade as a powerful demonstration of their unity and as an artistic protest against the warlords' cynical and bloody despotism.

Later, a large-scale feature film titled *Gion matsuri*, produced with generous public subsidies to celebrate Kyoto Prefecture's centenary in 1968, re-enforced this reading of events. The notion that the Gion festival is a monument of *machishū* culture persists as the most widely accepted current understanding of its value. During my fieldwork in 2018, for example, a journalist started his interview by asking me about my impression of the festival 'as an expression of the vigour of the *machishū*'; he titled the resulting article 'Telling the world about the festival of the *machishū*'.[8] In the post-war period, the historical moment of the Gion festival's revival in the early 1500s inspired a new foundation legend that clearly continues to dominate the festival's modern signification. According to that legend, the festival, and especially the float parades organized by the commoners of Lower Kyoto, were, and still are, an expression of the autonomy, resilience, unity and creativity of the 'people of the streets'.

This vision, however, suitable though it was to the new democratic Japan of the post-war years, does not stand up to a dispassionate analysis of the available sources from the years around 1500. This has been demonstrated in great detail by Kawauchi Masayoshi, the leading specialist on the history of the Gion festival in the Sengoku period.[9] Kawauchi's main objection to the *machishū* narrative is that it suppresses the leadership of other agents in the revival of the festival. Where scholars in Hayashiya's tradition stress the agency of the *machishū*, Kawauchi focuses on the involvement of figures of power within the Muromachi shogunate and their struggles with Enryakuji. In his reading, the 1500 revival was the result of high politics, and he makes little room for the contributions of Kyoto's commoners.

There is no doubt that Kawauchi's works offer a myth-crunching correction to an overly romantic fantasy of pre-modern 'people's power'. Kawauchi clings closely to sources that are without exception written (or drawn) by members of the court or warrior elite. While this strategy avoids ungrounded speculation, it also runs the risk of ignoring undocumented commoner initiative and involvement. As we have seen in the previous chapters, commoner merchants played a central role already before the Ōnin war. As the *uma no osa* sponsored by the court nobility gave way to the floats and different kinds of *furyū* 'spectacles' organized by merchant guilds, the festival became a showcase of commoner wealth, put on display within the context of the Enryakuji empire of *jinin* guilds and viewed – but not funded – by the Muromachi shoguns. In 1500, too, the festival depended on a combination of commoner and shogunal interests, with the commoners paying the bill and doing the work, while the shogunate used its military dominance to make the festival possible and basked in its glory. Our task is not only to reconstruct the shogunate's efforts but also to imagine the unrecorded motivations, exertions and struggles of the commoners who were the ultimate carriers of the festival.

Who were those commoners, and what kind of communities did they form in the post-Ōnin era? As we have seen, before the devastation of the late fifteenth century Kyoto's merchants conducted their business in symbiosis with the monastic communities that were their overlords and protectors. Some guilds, in particular those of the older 'service guild' type, were concentrated in particular areas or streets, while the members of others, notably those of the newer 'trade guild' type, were spread around the city and even beyond its boundaries. The merchants who created and organized the floats of the pre-Ōnin parades were part of complicated networks that centred not so much on the streets where they conducted their business, as on their dynamic relationship with their fellow guild members and their temple overlord, who offered them protection, monopolies and opportunities in return for regular tribute. They were, in other words, more *jinin* than *machishū*. Ashikaga Yoshimitsu inserted the shogunate into these networks when he started raising his own taxes from *jinin* merchants in the 1390s. The medieval Gion festival was shaped by the resulting tension between temple, guild and shogun. The communities behind the Gion floats of that era consisted of guild fellows rather than street neighbours, and by their efforts guild members sought to appeal both to the shogun in his viewing pavilion and to their temple overlord, Enryakuji.

These structures collapsed during the century of chaos and violence that began with the Ōnin war. If the festival had been a mechanism to maintain such structures, it would have 'flopped' and disappeared with them – but once again, it was found that the festival could serve new purposes also under the radically changed circumstances of the sixteenth century. The revival in 1500 would not have been possible without the determined engagement and decisive action of Hosokawa Masamoto. However, it was not Masamoto who performed or paid for the festival; that was the task of the commoners who populated the Lower City. Unless they saw some purpose in this expensive enterprise, it would indeed have flopped. Moreover, the festival continued to flourish after Masamoto's death in 1507. This shows that once the festival had been kick-started, the commoner 'streets' (*chō*) of Lower Kyoto were interested in keeping it going – albeit with constant input from Masamoto's successors.

From guild to 'street'

The most striking aspect of this new, revived Gion festival was its successful transition from a guild- to a street-based festival. To understand this transition, we need to investigate the emergence of these streets as social, political and economic units.

Hayashiya (1950) was among the first to delve into the history of the terms *chō* and *chōnin* ('*chō* people') in Muromachi-period documents. In such warrior documents *chō* (or, in an alternative reading, *machi*) can refer either to a store with a shopfront or to a street. Depending on the context, *chōnin* was used in different meanings. Sometimes the word referred to any 'guild merchant who manages his own store', while in other contexts, it signified a 'local leader of a *chō* street'. In the latter meaning, the word was used to refer to representatives of localities with special responsibilities, notably collecting levies from all the street's inhabitants as intermediaries between the warrior authorities and individual house owners, or capturing and holding thieves so that officials could arrest and jail them. The people referred to by warriors as *chōnin* in these documents were called 'aldermen' (*oyakata*) by their fellows, highlighting their function as local leaders.

Goshima Kuniharu argues that it was in the context of festivals that streets first developed into units of governance that required *chōnin* or *oyakata* leaders.[10] Already in 1320, contributions to the Fushimi Inari festival were raised 'by street' (*chōbetsu*) within the territory (*shikichi*) associated with Fushimi Inari Shrine – south of Gojō (i.e. Matsubara) Street. In the Gionsha territory, north of Gojō, festival funds were raised by means of the *bajōyaku* levy, which was not organized by street but rather through guild-based structures. However, Goshima points out that some festival-related costs were in fact raised by street even here. In 1397, for example, a troupe of lion dancers stated that they customarily received contributions of 500 coppers (*mon*) per street to fund their 'duty to the gods'.[11] A rudimentary framework of street-based organization, then, must have been in place already in the fourteenth century. Shogunal levies on commoner owners of city properties (*jiguchi-sen*, *munabechi-sen*), to be collected by the street leader or representative (*chōnin*), strengthened such early street structures further. Yet their importance could not be compared to the networks of guilds and their overlords. In places where guild members were concentrated in particular neighbourhoods, those networks had sometimes created street-based communities, but more often guilds brought together merchants who ran businesses in different parts of the city.

During the Ōnin war and the chaotic decades that followed, guild merchants fled the city, overlord temples went up in flames and shoguns were forced to abandon the city into the hands of rival warlords. The commoners who chose to stay survived by building ramparts (*kakoi*) and heavy gates. Guard duties at these defensive works rotated among neighbours. Tightly contained areas consisting of a few streets now served as the main social units, with their own leaders, duties and rules. Hayashiya picks up names of such units of neighbours as they occur in contemporary sources: Ichijō-Muromachi *shū* (the people who lived within the fortified area around the intersection of Muromachi and Ichijō Streets), Nijō-Muromachi *shū*, Gion *shū* and so on.[12] As a collective designation for commoner merchants of such gated *chō* (or *machi*), he adopted the term *machishū* or *chōshū*, 'street people'. In fact, this word is rarely used in historical documents. More current are terms like *chōnin*, referring to the leaders of particular *chō*, or the collective *jigenin*, 'local commoners', and later scholars have pointed out that Hayashiya's term *machishū* is, for the most part, an anachronistic construct.[13] In substance, however, his main argument retains much of its value. As larger structures built around guilds and temple overlords crumbled, neighbourhood ties increased in importance as Kyoto's remaining commoners were forced to depend on their neighbours more than ever before.

It was in the decade around 1500 that Kyoto finally began to show clear signs of reconstruction after the ravages of the Ōnin war. Hayashima Daisuke argues that *chō* coordinated not only their defences against external enemies but also the restoration and maintenance of public spaces within the city as empty lots were rebuilt and repopulated. *Chō* streets, after all, shared wells and latrines as well as ramparts and gates.[14]

Hayashiya shows that festivals and communal celebrations were another pillar of *chō* organization. Such festivities also fostered the development of broader structures of cooperation between neighbouring *chō*. In the Upper City, summer street dancing (*furyū odori*) became so popular in the early 1500s that the shogunate felt compelled to restrict it in 1506, and again in 1544. In the context of this summer festival, streets cooperated in larger groups, such as 'the four streets of the Tachiuri neighbourhood'. These networks would later serve other purposes as well. In the Lower City, the Gion festival with its large parades had a similar effect of promoting grassroots cooperation and coordination. Rather than a mere *expression* of social integration, festivals of this kind functioned as concrete occasions to *create* new organizational structures.

All this does not mean that the horizon of commoners in the 1500s was limited to their immediate neighbours. Even if streets became more important as units of cooperation, people were still involved in wider networks of family, business and faith. Most relevant in that latter category was the proliferation of Hokke (Lotus, Nichiren) temples in Lower Kyoto. Supporting these temples were groups of lay adherents with a strong institutional structure. The lay congregations of the Hokke temples formed the basis for the so-called Lotus leagues (*hokke ikki*), urban militias that, for a time, dominated the Lower City.

Between 1527 and 1536 there was no shogunal administration in Kyoto, as two rivals fought over the shogunal title from temporary quarters to the east and west of the city, in Ōmi and Sakai. In this power vacuum the Lotus leagues ran vigilante patrols, organized the city's defence against raids from the countryside, challenged guild overlords and warlords, and carried out their own raids. The Lotus leagues soon became embroiled in conflicts between the larger players of the age. In the summer of 1536, they came under massive assault from Mt Hiei. Thousands were killed and most of Lower Kyoto was, once again, burned to the ground. None of the twenty-one Hokke temples that had been at the core of the movement were left unscathed.[15]

The Lotus temples evacuated to Sakai, but they left an important legacy in the form of a much more self-reliant and powerful structure of 'streets' associations' (*chōgumi*), of which there were five in Lower Kyoto. These associations allowed the inhabitants of clusters of streets to coordinate their resistance to outsiders. In times of crisis, the leaders of the streets and the streets' associations of Lower Kyoto met at the Rokkakudō Temple. They bargained collectively with warrior authorities and temple overlords, and when necessary hired their own mercenary forces. The *chōgumi* took on a more definite form after the arrival of Oda Nobunaga in 1568, who developed them further for his own purposes, but they originated in the chaotic 1530s, when the Lower City first had to manage itself through a shogun-less decade, and then was forced to rebuild after the devastating fire of 1536. These developments lifted commoner networks to another level of institutionalized cooperation, both among neighbours in individual streets and, more widely, through streets' associations and interlinking temple groups.

The emergence of street communities and streets' associations coincided with the decline of older networks of power. Guilds and overlords became increasingly irrelevant to commoners' daily struggle for survival in Kyoto's embattled streets. Enryakuji, which had been the spider in Kyoto's web of *jinin* merchants, proved in 1536 that it remained a powerful foe, but in subsequent decades it gradually lost its military and financial muscle, its power to enforce guild monopolies, its lands and its tollgates. Twice, in 1499 and 1571, Mt Hiei was razed to the ground. When the Gion festival was revived in 1500, the social landscape had already changed beyond recognition; and in the decades after 1500, the pace of change remained relentless. The old format, with *jinin* merchants displaying the riches that their participation in the Enryakuji empire had brought them in front of the shogun, was no longer viable. The *bajō* association had failed to survive the Ōnin war, and the *bajōyaku* levy, which had symbolized Enryakuji's power over the Gion festival, was no longer collected after 1470. Now that the structures of medieval Kyoto were all but destroyed, the only logical outcome was for the festival to 'flop'. That was indeed the fate of festivals that were closely linked to the Gion *goryōe*, including Hie's Kosatsuki-e and the *goryōe* of Fushimi Inari.

Yet that is not what happened with the Gion festival. Who decided that the festival still had value, and what was in it for all the different groups of actors – from Hosokawa Masamoto to the commoner inhabitants of Kyoto's streets?

The new Gion festival of the sixteenth century

To answer this question, we must begin with the festival's critical infrastructure. As we have seen already, the Gionsha was finally restored in 1492, thanks to the efforts of mendicant monks and nuns who specialized in fundraising (*kanjin*), a favourite method of funding both religious and public projects in medieval times. Such mendicants collected contributions from the general public for the rebuilding of destroyed bridges, roads, wells and temples and shrines across the country.[16] The lowlier among them were little more than beggars who roamed the countryside, carrying official papers to show that (part of) the donations they gathered would go to specific holy sites, while some of the karmic merit would reflect back on the givers. Others were organized groups, based at temples and maintaining mutually beneficial relations with court and warrior leaders.

Gionsha records give the honour for resurrecting the shrine to 'the Jikkoku mendicants' – the begging monks I already mentioned earlier. *Jikkoku* ('ten kinds of grain') refers to the ascetic practice of abstinence from eating any kind of grain, which was often associated with *kanjin* practitioners. In addition to soliciting contributions with long-handled ladles, the Gionsha mendicants also put on dances (*manzai*) to attract people's attention. They acted with shogunal sanction and must have been well established; by the mid-sixteenth century, they ran their own quarters (*honganbō*) at the Gionsha.[17]

In 1496 the Jikkoku mendicants finished the rebuilding the Ōmandokoro *otabisho*.[18] With the gods back at the Gionsha, and at least one *otabisho* restored, it now became possible to consider reviving the festival itself. In this same year, two shogunal officers (*bugyōnin*) dispatched a shogunal order to the Gionsha manager, informing him that the shogun, Ashikaga Yoshizumi (1481–1511), had instructed the leader of the mendicants, Jikkoku Enjitsu and the priest of the Ōmandokoro *otabisho*, Miyachiyo, to raise funds and make arrangements for the restoration of the three *mikoshi*. The Gionsha manager was ordered to cooperate with these efforts and exert himself for a speedy revival of the festival.[19]

Yoshizumi had become shogun in 1493 as the result of a coup against the previous shogun, Yoshiki (1466–1523). This coup was instigated by the shogunal deputy (*kanrei*) Hosokawa Masamoto. Masamoto defeated Yoshiki in battle, paraded him through Kyoto, imprisoned him in the Hosokawa temple of Ryōanji (now famous for its Zen garden), burned down the compounds of Yoshiki's allies and installed the twelve-year-old Yoshizumi as Yoshiki's successor.[20] This coup, known as the Meiō incident, is often identified as the beginning of half a century of 'Hosokawa rule' (1493–1549), a period when Ashikaga shoguns were reduced to puppets of their Hosokawa deputies. The order to restart the Gion festival was issued as Masamoto was consolidating his position in Kyoto – a position that he had won in battle only a few years earlier in the most significant military turnaround since the Ōnin war.

The urgency with which Masamoto pursued the matter became clear in the following year, 1497. By this time it was obvious that the replacement of the *mikoshi* would not be possible without many more years of *kanjin* fundraising. In the fifth month, Yoshizumi (or, more realistically, Masamoto) issued orders that the gods should be moved to their *otabisho* with the help of *sakaki* branches, until the *mikoshi* were finally ready. This not only broke with ritual precedent but also threatened the connections between the Gionsha and the communities linked to the *mikoshi*. More importantly, such a procedure deprived Enryakuji of its long-established strategy of stopping the Gion festival by hijacking the *mikoshi*. What the shogun and his deputy were proposing was not merely a pragmatic adaptation of a ritual to the circumstances; they were throwing a hefty rock into the Gion pond of social and economic relations.

Enryakuji reacted by reminding the Gionsha manager that the Kosatsuki-e ritual of the Hie Shrines had to be revived prior to the Gion festival. If the Gionsha were to disobey Enryakuji in this matter, the monastic assembly of Mt Hiei warned, it would suffer severe repercussions.[21] The Kosatsuki-e had, in fact, been performed for the last time in 1470. As noted, the *bajōyaku* was no longer collected after this year, depriving Enryakuji of yet another source of income.[22] Enryakuji's insistence on the primacy of the Kosatsuki-e was cemented by the fact that the *bajōyaku* funded both the Kosatsuki-e and the Gion *mikoshi* processions, with most of the proceeds going to semi-military groups linked to the Hie Shrines. To Enryakuji, the shogunal desire to revive the Gion festival created a unique opportunity to press for the restoration of both the *bajōyaku* levy and the Kosatsuki-e festival. As had happened on many occasions in the 1440s and 1450s, Enryakuji carried the day also in 1497. To

Masamoto, this was an unpleasant reminder of the fact that his control over Kyoto was still circumscribed by the medieval prerogatives of older powers – notably Enryakuji on Mt Hiei. The Gion festival now became the ultimate symbol of those limitations.

Masamoto lost his patience with Enryakuji in 1499. He suspected that the temple was implicated in Ashikaga Yoshiki's plans to invade Kyoto and win back the shogunate. To prevent this, Masamoto sent troops up the mountain and reduced it to rubble. As a result, the Gion festival could finally be restored without Enryakuji interference in the following year, 1500. Some of that year's correspondence between shogunal officers and the manager of the Gionsha has survived in the shrine archives. On the first day of the sixth month, the officers sent a reply to the Gionsha manager's renewed protest against the use of *sakaki* branches as a replacement of the still unfinished *mikoshi*:

> Any disruption of services to the gods is unacceptable. Multiple times, we have sent orders to carry out the festival even if precedent must be set aside. With this strict order we now command your shrine to make the resumption of services to the gods your priority, even if the festival of the Hie Shrines will be delayed.[23] Any troublemakers who try to stir up mischief in this regard will be punished immediately.[24]

Now that the shrine was once again faced with the same stern order as in 1497, it turned out that miraculously, the *mikoshi* were ready for use after all, and the festival could finally go ahead.

This first Gion festival in a generation was by necessity a sober affair, also because the time for preparations, in a half-rebuilt city, was so short. The court noble Kujō Hisatsune (1469–1530) noted in his diary that many of his peers set up pavilions along the route. Hisatsune, for whom this was the first Gion festival in his lifetime, was not impressed by the parade, and he reports that according to an older acquaintance, 'the spectacles (*furyū*) on offer amounted not even to one tenth of what they were before'.[25] Another noble, Konoe Masaie (1444–1505), counted twenty-five *yama* and one *hoko* on the seventh. In contrast to Hisatsune, Masaie was old enough to recall the pre-Ōnin parade. He wrote that the floats of 1500 were disappointingly plain and could not be compared to the ones he remembered from his youth.[26] The weather failed to cooperate, too: heavy rain did great damage to the floats and spoilt their decorations. On the fourteenth, Masaie saw ten *yama* floats; the unceasing rain made them look all the more drab.[27]

It was during the second (returning) *mikoshi* procession that the dangers of enforcing performance of the Gion festival in a city on edge manifested themselves. On the fourteenth, Hisatsune wrote:

> Rain. Today is the *goryōe*. Fighting broke out and continued for many hours. Tens of people sustained wounds or were killed in the rioting; the exact number is not known. The *mikoshi* were abandoned *en route*.[28]

The *mikoshi* and their gods spent the night ditched at an unidentified site and finally returned to the Gionsha on the following day. We can only speculate whether Enryakuji agents may have provoked this skirmish. Fights had long been an integral part of the *mikoshi* processions and arguably, there was no real need for provocateurs to set fists, swords and arrows flying – but then again, such a brawl would have provided Enryakuji with perfect cover for spiteful sabotage.

In 1500 there was no official shogunal viewing; instead of the youthful shogun, it was his deputy, Masamoto himself, who inspected the parade. The fact that Masamoto's gaze was the very purpose of the parade is expressed unambiguously in a diary entry for the following year, 1501: 'The *yama* began their parade after Lord Hosokawa [Masamoto] had entered his pavilion.'[29] Five years later, in 1506, the Gionsha once again held back its *mikoshi* in response to threats from Enryakuji, which was already recovering from the 1499 assault. Rather than entering into a violent confrontation with Enryakuji, Masamoto forced through a different solution. The *mikoshi* were allowed to absent themselves, but the float parade went ahead on the customary dates, simply 'for the sake of Lord Hosokawa's viewing'.[30]

The diarists whose brief notes are our only contemporary sources clearly viewed the revival of the Gion festival as an initiative of the new hegemon, Hosokawa Masamoto. They focus on Masamoto's defiance of Enryakuji and on his viewing of the parade. In fact, the very reason why the Gion festival drew the attention of these court diarists was that it offered such a telling illustration of Masamoto's dominance. Although the diarists make no mention of this, it is striking that a revival of the classical *rinjisai*, with its court offerings and Gagaku dances on the day after the *mikoshi*'s return, was never on Masamoto's agenda, although a much reduced version of it had survived into the 1460s. Promoting imperial prestige was not part of Masamoto's plan. Perhaps the diarists' sceptical tone reflects their ambiguous feelings about this. Either way, it is clear that in their view, the float parade was restored simply because Masamoto had decided that he had some use for it.

While this is not incorrect, it is hardly the whole story. The affairs of commoners from the streets of Lower Kyoto remain all but invisible in court diaries, and it is easy to forget that it was these commoners who recreated the floats, albeit on Masamoto's orders. If the people of Lower Kyoto had stubbornly resisted the duty of reinventing the floats, as well as the dances, *hayashi* music and other 'spectacles' that gave them life, Masamoto could hardly have forced them to do so. Even in 1500 Masamoto did not offer any funding, either for the restoration of the *mikoshi* or for the float parades. Unless the people who now had the opportunity to rebuild their floats agreed that the revival of the festival was a matter of some urgency, Masamoto's words would likely have fallen on rocky ground.

Despite the dearth of sources, there is some evidence of such a popular sense of urgency. In the summer of 1494, one year after Masamoto's coup, Kyoto was hit by a heatwave, rampant illness and an upsurge of violent crime and arson. On the sixth day of the seventh month a fire spread from some place along Shijō Street through much of the Lower City. In spite of the drought and the known presence of a gang of arsonists, there were rumours that this string of disasters was ultimately caused by the deities of the Gionsha. Kujō Hisatsune noted in his diary that a *miko* medium had uttered an oracle during a *yudate* ritual at the Takamatsu Shinmeisha Shrine, revealing that the Gion deities were punishing the city in anger. In yet another oracle, this time delivered at the Gionsha itself, the Gion deities allegedly complained that even after 'thirty-three years' the festival was still not revived and warned that the fires would not stop until this happened. In response to these oracles, Hisatsune writes, locals flocked to the Gionsha to beseech the deities with displays of various *furyū* spectacles (most likely, *furyū odori* music and dancing around *kasa* parasols) on the seventh and fourteenth days of the eighth month.[31] Clearly, those days were chosen to hint at the long-abandoned Gion festival, which should have taken place two months earlier.

These events in 1494 can be interpreted as a spontaneous revival of the festival, not at the initiative of the shogunate, but of the Gionsha and the commoners of Lower Kyoto. The 1494 festival was inspired by a well-founded fear of divine wrath, triggered by that year's calamitous fires and rampant disease. There were no *mikoshi*, and no floats either. Instead of staging a parade, people sought to soothe the angry deities with dances at the newly restored Gionsha. Hayashima argues that this bottom-up revival occurred in the context of a renewed interest in *goryōe*-type rites, at a time when Kyoto was finally beginning to recover. In Upper Kyoto, the Goryō festival (associated with the Upper Goryō Shrine, and likewise featuring dancing around *kasa* in the seventh month) was restarted only a few years later, in 1498.[32]

The 1494 rumours and events around the Gionsha must have caught Masamoto's attention. Masamoto, too, had good reason to be concerned about the never-ending cycle of fires, crimes and epidemics, described by Hisatsune as suprahuman tokens of divine wrath (*kaii*). Reviving the Gion festival must have served the triple purpose of fighting the 'curse' that appeared to hold the city back, allaying the fears that instigated popular dancing in the streets, and displaying shogunal power in a manner that, for once, also addressed commoner concerns. For the savvy merchants of Lower Kyoto, the parades must have been attractive not only as much-needed measures to exorcize divine wrath but also as opportunities to strengthen communal solidarity and cooperation, while also serving to establish good relations with the warrior leadership of the day. When Masamoto set the wheels in motion, the people of Lower Kyoto responded; this alone indicates that they saw this expensive undertaking as a worthwhile venture.

The Gion festival after Hosokawa Masamoto: More instability

The period of relative peace created by Masamoto's dominance did not last long. In 1507 Masamoto was murdered by a kinsman while taking a bath in his own Kyoto residence; a year later, his protégé Yoshizumi fled the city and Yoshiki returned as the new shogun, appointing Hosokawa Takakuni (1484–1531) as his *kanrei* deputy.[33] This change of guard emboldened Enryakuji, and already in 1508 the Gion festival had to be postponed until the end of the ninth month. Things went downhill after that. Postponements were to remain a common occurrence until Oda Nobunaga's destruction of Mt Hiei in 1571. In 1511 the delay even carried over to the next year, so that in 1512, the festival was staged twice. The festival of 1511 was held on 23.5.1512, 'on orders of the shogun [Yoshiki]';[34] the 1512 version began just two weeks later, on the correct dates.

Under these precarious circumstances, staging the Gion parade became a matter of political prestige for the shogunal regime. The festival was now part of the annual round of warrior ceremonies, and its successful performance served as proof of the shogun's control over the city. By this measure shogunal control left much to be desired. Shogunal viewings, even with much less pomp than in the pre-Ōnin years, proved difficult to realize as consecutive shoguns were time and again forced to flee the city. In 1521 Hosokawa Masakuni

(1484–1531) forced Yoshiki out of Kyoto and replaced him with the ten-year-old Yoshiharu (1511–50). In the following year (1522), Yoshiharu was ill during his first Gion festival, which for once was carried out on its regular dates. Masakuni staged a special show on the twenty-seventh, ordering the Gion floats of both parades to be assembled for the second time in that year and be paraded past Yoshiharu's residence, where the new shogun put himself on display in a pavilion. One diarist tersely noted: 'Gion'e today, ordered so the shogun (*buke*) can view it.'[35] Masakuni and Yoshiharu were dislodged from Kyoto in 1527, inaugurating another lengthy period of instability. After the special event of 1522 there was to be only one final shogunal viewing, by Ashikaga Yoshiteru (1536–65) in 1548.

An incident in 1533 inspired Hayashiya's notion that the Gion parades served as a *machishū* statement of emancipation. The importance of this incident to modern understandings of the Gion festival demands that we take a closer look at this turbulent year. The year 1533 fell in the period of shogunal absence that had begun with Yoshiharu's flight from Kyoto in 1527. The city was once again verging on anarchy. Yoshiharu was holed up in Azuchi in Ōmi province, while his deputy Hosokawa Harumoto was in Osaka to fight the Ikkō (Amida) leagues, which had ensconced themselves there after the fall of their previous stronghold in Yamashina near Kyoto the year before. The Hokke leagues, which dominated Kyoto at this time, had suffered heavy losses in Yamashina. Now many of the Hokke members had joined Harumoto in Osaka, so that in the summer of 1533, Kyoto's streets were all but empty.

In the middle of this crisis, Yoshiharu's officials in Kyoto ordered the *shigyō* manager of the Gionsha to stage the Gion festival 'even if the Hie festival is cancelled, in accord with our orders as issued in 1500 and 1506'.[36] However, on the sixth day of the sixth month of 1533, one day before the festival's start, a counter-order arrived at the Gionsha: the festival must be postponed 'because of objections from Mt Hiei'. On this day, Enryakuji delegations had arrived both at the Gionsha and at Yoshiharu's Azuchi headquarters, threatening to attack the Gionsha if the festival was not called off immediately. Yoshiharu was in no position to counter this threat and acknowledged defeat by ordering cancellation.

According to the diary of the Gionsha manager, the following morning brought a delegation of 'monthly representatives' (*gachi gyōji*) from sixty-six *chō* streets in Lower Kyoto to the Gionsha office. They were accompanied by liaison officers (*fureguchi*) and watchmen (*zōshiki*) of the shogunal Board of Retainers in the city.[37] The mention of 'monthly representatives' is of great interest, because it implies that at this time, the responsibility for the floats lay with streets, and that these streets had a formalized organization with a system of rotating duties. The *zōshiki* watchmen, who provided security during the parades, must have joined the representatives on this day mainly to prevent trouble in their confrontation with the Gionsha and witness the result of their petition – or perhaps, the *fureguchi* and *zōshiki* just refer to a category of street inhabitants who also happened to work for the Board of Retainers.[38]

According to the diary of the Gionsha manager, the street representatives argued that the parade of floats should be carried out on that same day, the seventh, even if the 'deity rituals' (*shinji*) – that is, the *mikoshi* processions – were cancelled. The floats must have been standing ready in their streets already, and the streets had spent time and money on their assembly. Although the outcome of this petition is not recorded, it seems likely that the street representatives' plea was not heard. In the end, the festival was postponed to the eighth month. At that time, the '*chōnin* of Lower Kyoto' again asked to be relieved of the duty to set up the floats of the first parade a second time. However, the shogunate concluded that the floats were essential to the festival proceedings and informed the Gionsha manager of its decision. The streets, depleted of many of their young men due to the Osaka campaign, were to reassemble their floats and carry out the parade as usual.[39]

Were Hayashiya and the Kyoto Association of Scientists for Democracy correct in interpreting these events as an expression of a burgeoning commoner autonomy, or even as a response to the tyranny of warlords? A more realistic reading is that the inhabitants of the float streets involved in the first parade asked to be allowed to go ahead with the parade on the regular date because they hoped to avoid the costs of having to assemble them once again later in the year. The idea that they were protesting against warlords' bloodthirst is at odds with the fact that many men from Lower Kyoto were with Harumoto at this very time, fighting the Ikkō headquarters in Osaka. The notion that the parade might go ahead in spite of the cancellation of the *mikoshi* processions was not new; this is exactly what had happened in 1522. The difference between 1522 and 1533 was that Enryakuji was now in a stronger position, while the shogun could not even enter the city. Therefore Enryakuji got its way, and both the *mikoshi* processions and the float parades were postponed.

Yet, Hayashiya makes an important point when he stresses the agency of what he calls the *machishū* in this incident. The Gionsha manager's report on the street representatives' petition is the first time the term *gachi gyōji* occurs in the historical record. The *chō* streets, the *chōgumi* streets' associations and the system of rotating representatives were now part of the bearing structure of

Kyoto society. The 1530s saw the replacement of the old network of Enryakuji-connected *jinin* guilds by commoner leagues and militias linked to a new network of Hokke temples. The festival was now carried by street communities that organized themselves partly through the *chōgumi*, and partly through the Hokke network.

One imagines that this must have left the Gionsha in a difficult position. Many of the Gionsha 'parishioners' now pledged allegiance to a group of temples that opposed Enryakuji, and that in 1536 fell victim to a massacre carried out primarily by forces from Mt Hiei. What did the Gion festival mean to the commoners of Lower Kyoto under these circumstances? Did they see the float parades as a supplement to the *mikoshi* processions, or did they feel estranged from the Gionsha as a part of the Enryakuji complex? How did the *otabisho* fit into this new setting? Was the festival still about the Gionsha deities at all, or was it more about relations between the *machishū* and their shifting military masters? We must wonder, but there are no answers to any of these questions.

At least, however, this period finally offers a few excellent sources on the floats themselves, their names and themes, and even details of their design. While not contributing much to solving these more fundamental issues, these sources at least provide us with a clear idea what the float parades looked like, and what stories they told.

Reconstructing the float parades

As we have seen, the 1500 revival of the Gion festival was the result of determined action by Hosokawa Masamoto, the military hegemon of this time. The actual work was done by officials of the Board of Retainers (*samuraidokoro*) in Kyoto, in particular by its head (*kaikō*), a man called Matsuda Yorisuke, and another official by the name of Iio Kiyofusa, whose responsibilities included relations with the Gionsha. These two men set about collecting information about the festival as it had been performed before the Ōnin war. They compiled lists of floats and their locations, perhaps updating them as the parades developed in the years after 1500. These lists, together with some information about the *mikoshi* processions, were later collected in a document titled *Gion'e yamahoko no koto* (On the Gion festival floats).[40]

This compound document ends with record of the order of the floats that made up the parades of 1500, as decided by way of drawing lots. At the end of this final list, Yorisuke and Kiyofusa note: 'These *yama* and *hoko* floats [of the second parade] have been paraded without any alterations from the time of the [Gion festival's] revival until 1507.' In 1507 the hegemon Hosokawa Masamoto was murdered, and under the new shogun, Ashikaga Yoshiki, the festival rapidly fell into disarray. The years 1500–7 represented a brief period of stability, and in subsequent decades, the festival performances of these years continued to be looked upon as a model.[41] The mention of the year 1507 in *Gion'e yamahoko no koto* creates some uncertainty about the status of the lists that make up this document. Were some of these lists drawn up in 1500 and others in 1507? Do some of these lists record memories about pre-Ōnin floats, or must they be read as notes or ideas for the revived parades of 1500 – or even for another year between 1500 and 1507? This document contains many contradictions that are not easily explained.

Gion'e yamahoko no koto consists of four main parts. The first (list 1) prescribes the routes of the *mikoshi* to the two *otabisho* on the seventh day and back on the fourteenth – the first extant record to do so.[42] The *mikoshi* processions, we read, were to be headed by a contingent of *inu jinin* shrine guards and 'patrons offering their various prayers'. Then came lion dancers, representatives from the Gionsha (*shanin*), one or more *miko* in palanquins, and *kannushi* priests from the *otabisho* on horseback. Behind the *mikoshi*, officials and footmen from the Board of Retainers held up the rear.

List 2 is an 'inventory of floats' (*hoku no shidai*) that featured in the parades before the Ōnin war as recalled by a certain Shin'emon, identified as an elderly official at the Board of Retainers. Shin'emon placed the sixteen floats and one *hayashimono* (a group of musicians and dancers) that he could remember along Shijō, Ayanokōji, and Gojōbōmon (i.e. Bukkōji) Streets. This implies that he imagined these streets to have been the organizers and caretakers of these floats – an understanding that appears as an anachronism in the light of the guild-based nature of most floats before Ōnin. Many of the floats in this list lack names; some names appear to have been added at a later date. With the exception of one 'ship float' (Ōfune-hoko), all floats in Shin'emon's list belong to the first parade, held on the seventh day.

List 3, titled *Gion'e yamahoku no shidai* (Inventory of the Gion'e floats), is a similar list of floats and their streets, labelled as a reconstruction of the situation 'before Ōnin'. It names thirty-one floats and one *hayashimono* for the parade on the seventh, and twenty-eight for the fourteenth – a total of no less than fifty-nine floats plus one *hayashimono*. On closer inspection, the list appears erratic. Some floats recur twice (Mōsō-yama), or even thrice (Ashikari-yama), with different street names. Not all locations are precise enough to place them on a map, and some floats lack street names altogether. Yet it is clear that this list presents a wider geographical spread than we know from the Edo period, including places further east, west and north. Some floats occur in different locations compared to Edo-period sources. There is no note as to who compiled this list, but the differences with Shin'emon's list are striking.

The confusion increases further when we reach list 4, which details the sequence of the first and the second parades in 1500. This list is titled 'Settling the order of Gion'e floats by drawing lots'.[43] In an attached note, Yorisuke explains: 'After the recent revival, there was a conflict among representatives of the *chō* streets (*chōnin*) about the order of the floats, so [it was decided] to draw lots. One or two days before [each parade] the *chōnin* gathered at my residence to draw lots in the presence of *zōshiki* staff.'[44] This is the first reference to the practice of settling the sequence of floats in this manner – a practice that continues to this day.

This list has twenty-seven elements for the first parade (one *hoko*, two *hayashimono* and twenty-four *yama*) and ten *yama* for the second parade. The numbers correspond almost perfectly with those that Konoe Masaie noted in his diary in 1500, but the floats listed deviate from those in the first three lists of *Gion'e yamahoko no koto*. Some of the lot-drawing floats of 1500 do not appear in those lists at all (Hakurakuten-yama, Urade-yama, Michitsukuri-yama, Hakuga-yama and Hotei-yama).[45] Others are listed twice (Hōka-yama, Yamabushi-yama and Tenjin-yama[46]). Many floats are called *hoko* (or *hoku*, which may just be a shortened form of that word) in one list and *yama* in another; in 1500, in fact, Naginata-hoko was the only *hoko*-type float. Some of these discrepancies reflect the fact that the newly revived parades were still a work in progress; but some of the listed entries look suspiciously like anachronisms, added at some point in time after 1500.

How are we to interpret these four different lists? Clearly, it is unlikely that lists 2 and 3 offer an accurate description of the Gion parades before Ōnin, or even in 1500. List 4 displays much continuity with the parades as we know them from the Edo period, but also this list is puzzling in many of its details. In lists 2 and 3, some float names and even locations were perhaps meant merely as proposed candidates for the revived parades, rather than as an attempt at historical reconstruction. Some of the floats mentioned in these lists may have participated in the parades only once or twice, or they may reflect inaccurate recollections, hesitantly suggested by elderly informants.

The picture, then, remains hazy. What we do have, however, are the names of a large number of floats, real or not. At the very least, those names give us

Figure 7 Hashi Benkei-yama. *Gion'e saiki*, National Institute of Japanese Literature.

Figure 8 Jōmyō-yama. *Gion'e saiki*, National Institute of Japanese Literature.

an indication of the themes that were deemed suitable as float designs. These themes can be grouped in a small number of categories: floats inspired by warrior lore, Noh, Chinese literature and Japanese court culture, as well as floats designed around divine figures, sometimes with a special connection to the float street. I will here survey these different categories of floats, while referring to the eighteenth-century *Gion'e saiki* (A detailed record of the Gion festival, 1757) as our oldest source on the narrative content of the float themes.

A fair number of floats displayed episodes from Minamoto lore. There are tales about legendary warriors and other valiant figures, many of them playing on the *Tale of the Heike* and related epic literature. The Ashikaga lineage identified itself as a branch of the Minamoto, so tales of Minamoto heroism reflected directly on the shogun and indeed on most of the warrior elite. Hashi Benkei-yama shows the soldier monk Benkei, balancing on the railing of Gojō Bridge in high *geta* clogs and bringing down his sword on the young Minamoto no Yoshitsune. Benkei is defeated, realizes that he has found a worthy master and becomes Yoshitsune's loyal retainer. Jōmyō-yama shows two warrior monks from Mt Hiei, Jōmyō and Ichirai, in a scene from a battle at Ujigawa Bridge that marked the rise of the Minamoto clan. The float shows Ichirai making a somersault off the railing of the bridge while supporting himself with one hand on Jōmyō's helmet. Jōmyō coolly grunts "scuse me" (*ashū sōrō*) – a stoic remark considered even more impressive than Ichirai's athleticism. This float was therefore called not Ichirai-yama but Jōmyō-yama, or even Ashū sōrō-yama (the 'scuse-me float).

A number of other floats in this genre feature in lists 3 and 4: another one about Benkei (Benkei Koromogawa-yama), and also floats featuring the warrior heroes Nasu no Yoichi, Izumi no Shōjirō and Asahina Yoshihide. A more romantic float focused on the tragedy of Kogō no Tsubone, a consort of Emperor Takakura who was forced into hiding by Taira no Kiyomori. Jingū Kōgō, the empress who (according to classical court histories, notably the *Nihon shoki*) sailed to Korea and forced the Korean king to pay tribute to Japan, featured on three floats. Ship-shaped floats depicting Jingū Kōgō's expedition concluded the first and second parades. Urade-yama shows Jingū Kōgō with a fishing rod, catching an *ayu* sweetfish and thereby predicting that the Korean expedition will bring victory. After her return, Jingū Kōgō gave birth to Emperor Ōnin, deified as the Great Bodhisattva Hachiman – who, in turn, was the tutelary protector of the Minamoto lineage; this must have made her story an attractive topic for float designs. List 3 mentions a Hachiman-yama (or Yawata-yama) not only in the second parade, as today, but also in the first.

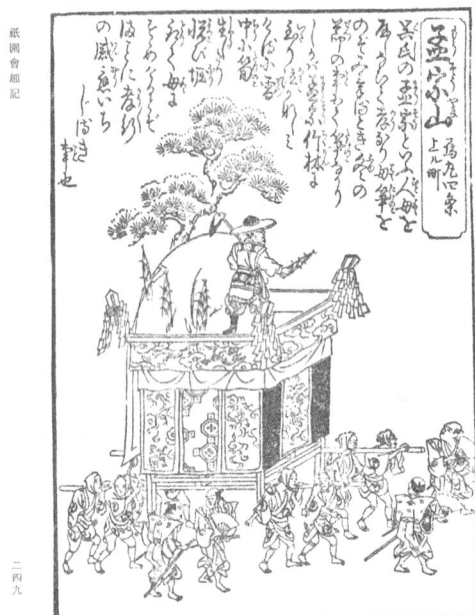

Figure 9 Mōsō-yama. *Gion'e saiki*, National Institute of Japanese Literature.

Some of these tales were put on the stage as Noh plays; this was the case with both Hashi Benkei and Kogō no Tsubone. Noh was a prominent source of float concepts. Ashikari-yama, for example, was based on a Zeami play about a rich Kyotoite who has fallen on hard times. This man arranges for his wife to serve in a noble household and leaves for the countryside, where he makes a humble living cutting and selling reeds. The play is about the couple's longing for each other and their eventual reunion. Other float names that refer to Noh plays are Ukaibune-yama ('the boat of the cormorant fisher'), which was likely based on another piece by Zeami (*Ukai*, 'The cormorant fisher'), and Tenko-yama ('The drum from heaven'), inspired by a tragic piece about a young drummer who died trying to save his instrument and later appeared as a ghost to play it one last time.

A third prominent category draws on scenes from Chinese classical lore. Kanko-hoko refers to a tale about Lord Mengchang of Qi, one of the Four Lords of China's Warring States period as described in Sima Qian's Records of the Grand Historian (*Shiji*). Mengchang managed to escape from the king of Qin, Qi's enemy, thanks to one of his soldiers, who imitated the morning cries of a rooster. Those cries tricked the border guards into opening the gates at the last moment, and Mengchang lived to fight another day. Mōsō-yama illustrates a tale from the Yuan period, taken from the work Twenty-four Exemplars of Filial Piety (*Ershisi xiao*). In the middle of winter, Mōsō (Mengzang) goes looking for fresh bamboo shoots for his aging mother. Of course, there are none; but some appear miraculously as Mengzang's tears hit the snowy ground. Most famous, perhaps, is Tōrō-yama (Kamakiri-yama), which features a mechanical mantis that moves as the float's wheels turn. It is based on a story about the sage Zhuangzi, who once encountered such a mantis on the road. As Zhuangzi's carriage approached, the mantis raised its arms to fight off the towering wheels. Zhuangzi admired the insect's spirit and carefully steered around it. Kikusui-hoko, Niwatori-hoko, Koi-yama, Tsuki-hoko and Hakurakuten-yama also take their subject matter from Chinese literature.

A fourth group of floats evoke the atmosphere of the classical court by featuring famous poets. Hōshō-yama, earlier known as Hana Nusubito-yama or 'the flower thief float', shows the poet Hirai no Hōshō, who risked his life by sneaking into the palace grounds to steal a branch of plum blossoms for his beloved lady. Hakuga-yama, earlier known as Kotowari-yama or 'the broken *koto* float', shows Hakuga breaking his *koto* when his friend fails to recognize the melodies that he is so expertly performing. Other floats featuring famous poets were Saigyō-yama, Kuronushi-yama (Ōtomo no Kuronushi) and Taka-yama (Ariwara no Narihira). Only one float referred to Japanese mythology: Iwato-yama ('the Rock-Cave float') displayed the gods Amaterasu and Izanagi.

Finally, most of the remaining floats carried divine or semi-divine figures, sometimes chosen because they were enshrined in the street that staged the float. Arare Tenjin-yama is not a reference to the 'Tenjin' of the Gionsha, but honours such a street deity. A finger-sized Tenjin statue fell from heaven in an unseasonal hailstorm that miraculously extinguished a fire that otherwise might have developed into a calamitous conflagration. In the same category is the Hachiman-yama of the second parade, which shows the god of the Hachiman Shrine in that street. Other floats enshrined Kannon (Yōryū-yama, named after the healing Yōryū or 'Willow' Kannon, and Fudaraku-yama, named after Kannon's celestial dwelling on Mt Potalaka), Jizō, Idaten (Skandha, who features here as a companion of Kannon) and Hotei. Human figures of semi-divine status are installed on En no Gyōja-yama, featuring the legendary founder of Shugendō, and on Taishi-yama, which shows Shōtoku Taishi taking an axe to a tree in order to provide timber for the building of Shitennōji Temple in Naniwa (Osaka).

There are only a few floats that fail to fit into these five categories. The Naginata-hoko drew less on a catchy narrative than on the power of its defining

Figure 10 Kasa-hoko (*kokiyako*). *Gion'e saiki*, National Institute of Japanese Literature.

symbol: the glaive blade that tops its soaring pole. Various tales were told about this blade, its maker and warriors who performed warlike feats with it, so this float, too, reflected warrior culture. Hōka-hoko was named after a category of street performers (*hōka*) and perhaps featured some of their acts at an early stage of its development. A few streets had only a *kasa* parasol and concentrated their efforts on dances and other displays of skill. An act called *kokiyako* is listed as a *hayashimono*; its location suggests that this may have been the ancestor of today's Ayagasa-hoko or Shijō Kasa-hoko, known for their stick-twirling dances (*bōfuri*), performed around such a simple parasol.[47]

In short, the lists of float names in *Gion'e yamahoko no koto* reveal that the float parades were filled with sophisticated references to elite culture, ranging from tales of Minamoto (Ashikaga) valour and the sensibilities of court poets to Chinese anecdotes of heroism and wisdom. Strikingly absent are the gods of the Gionsha, concerns about epidemics or reflections of popular movements such as the Hokke leagues.

Pictorial renderings of the Gion festival

Float names offer valuable hints concerning the subject matter of the floats, but they do not allow us to visualize them. Fortunately, the Gion festival quite abruptly became a theme in painting from the mid-sixteenth century onwards. Members of the warrior elite commissioned Tosa- and Kano-school painters to create extravagant pairs of six-panelled screens that offer views of the city of Kyoto from a bird's-eye perspective (*rakuchū rakugaizu byōbu*). These screens show exquisite details of Kyoto's palaces, temples, shrines, streets, bridges and, not least, inhabitants from all walks of life, interspersed with billowing clouds of gold. In western Kyoto the headquarters of the shogun and the Hosokawa stand out, while the eastern section is dominated by the Imperial Palace in the north and the Gionsha and its festival in the south. Many of these Kyoto screens also allude to the seasons, with one screen showing the western half of the city in autumn and winter and the other the eastern half in spring and summer. In this context, the Gion festival served as the ultimate symbol of summer on the right-hand screen, offering a striking contrast to the snowy Golden Pavilion on the left.

In his study of these screens, Matthew McKelway points out that many were in the possession of provincial warlords far away from Kyoto. For this reason, the screens are often interpreted as 'pictorial symbols of the center made for the periphery'. On closer inspection, however, the details depicted on the Kyoto screens 'chart sociopolitical networks and physical changes within the capital that spoke more to the interests of those within the city than of those outside'.[48] McKelway argues that the screens show a city under reconstruction in an age when it was redesigned multiple times by a succession of conquerors. The screens show no signs of violence, destruction, poverty or disease, all of which were rife in sixteenth-century Kyoto. Instead, they present bustling images of peace and

Figure 11 The *mikoshi* crossing the Kamo River. *Rakuchū rakugaizu byōbu*, *Rekihaku-A*. National Museum of Japanese History.

prosperity in a cityscape that is dominated by the construction projects of the new rulers – who, in real life, rarely were able to stay in their splendid-looking palaces for long.

Among the earliest and best preserved of the Kyoto screens are the so-called Rekihaku-A[49] and Uesugi versions. The Rekihaku-A version is generally regarded as the oldest, dating perhaps to the late 1530s or 1540s.[50] Near the uppermost rim of the screen that shows eastern Kyoto we find the 'Gion hall' (*Gion-dono*), where nothing special appears to be going on. A bit further down (i.e. west) from the Gionsha, the three *mikoshi* can be seen crossing the Kamo riverbed over a temporary bridge, consisting of no more than some planking laid out in the riverbed next to the much higher permanent bridge. The *mikoshi*, each carried by a mere ten men in white clothing, are accompanied by armed guards; one of the guards is chasing away two naughty-looking boys. In a doorway nearby, a man kneels with folded hands as the *mikoshi* pass.

Meanwhile six floats are shown parading along Shijō, Higashi-no-Tōin and Gojō (Matsubara) Streets. In actual life, the parade would have been long finished by the time the *mikoshi* reached the river, so the juxtaposition of procession and parade is an artistic sleight of hand. The parade is led by another group of men

Figure 12 Tōrō-yama. *Rekihaku-A*, National Museum of Japanese History.

in armour, carrying bows and swords. This group is followed by the Naginata-hoko, pulled by men in white; this scene features on the cover of this book. The pullers are urged forward by a leader who is gesturing with a red fan. On the platform halfway up the float, two musicians are playing a small *kakko* drum and a flute, while people in the corners hold red *gohei* wands out towards the street. The body of the float (which looks much higher than in the pre-Ōnin *Tsukinami sairei zu* discussed in the previous chapter) is covered with colourful fabrics, some of which show golden dragons against a red background. The parade continues with Hakuga-yama, the moon-topped Tsuki-hoko, the particularly high Hōka-hoko and Tōrō-yama. This last *yama* sports a large mantis that stands on top of a carriage. The carriage, carried on two poles by four men, looks like a regular two-wheeled ox-drawn carriage of the type used by Kyoto's nobility. The sixth float, perhaps the Fune-hoko, is no longer visible in what appears to be a clumsily repaired section of this screen.

The head of the parade is just approaching the Ōmandokoro *otabisho*, but there are no signs of ritual activity there. There is no crowd to watch the parade go by, nor are there any viewing pavilions; people are going about their usual business just a street away. The juxtaposition of procession and parade, the selection of a few representative floats, the obviously insufficient numbers of pullers and other participants in the parades, and the complete absence of throngs of viewers can all be explained as technical solutions to the problem of space on a screen that is primarily about the city of Kyoto rather than the Gion festival. The function of the Gion floats in this context is primarily to add summer-like colour to the scenery of the city.

The Uesugi pair of screens is named after the famous warlord Uesugi Kenshin (1530–78). The painter has been identified as Kano Eitoku (1543–90). Kenshin received these screens from Oda Nobunaga in 1574, six years after Nobunaga entered the city. McKelway (following Seta Katsuya) argues that they were likely commissioned a decade earlier by shogun Ashikaga Yoshiteru (1536–65). Details suggest that these screens were designed as a present from Yoshiteru to Kenshin.[51] Their history, then, is entangled in warlord diplomacy. While on the Rekihaku-A screens Kyoto has an improvised and almost bucolic look, the Uesugi screens give a much more urbanized, permanent and crowded impression. The streets that were relatively quiet on the Rekihaku-A screens are now filled with people. It is as though in the intervening decades Kyoto has been transformed from a collection of scattered neighbourhoods interspersed with fields, temples, shrines and villas into an uninterrupted sea of rooftops.

Again, we see the Gionsha at the top, the *mikoshi* crossing the Kamo River, and further down (west) the seventh-day parade proceeding along Shijō Street. The Naginata-hoko is followed by Tōrō-yama, a *kasa* parasol with *bōfuri* dancers (the *kakiyako*?), Kanko-hoko, Hakurakuten-yama, Niwatori-hoko, Iwato-yama and finally Fune-hoko. Naginata-hoko and Tōrō-yama have just turned right (south) into Kyōgoku (Teramachi) Street, while Fune-hoko at the bottom (west) has yet to enter Shijō from Machi (Shinmachi) Street. On the platforms of the *hoko* we can make out youngsters wearing large red wigs (*shaguma*) of the kind that were often used by both warriors and street performers at this time. They are joined by musicians and people pointing *gohei* towards the street from the platforms' corners; here, the *gohei* are white.

Among the *yama*, Iwato-yama is not carried but pulled with ropes in the manner of the *hoko*. In future decades, more *yama* would become too large to carry and developed into towering structures similar to *hoko* (for example, Kannon-yama and Taka-yama). Iwato-yama would evolve further into a *hoko*-like structure in the Edo period. The main figures of this float are Amaterasu, hidden in the Rock-Cave of Heaven, and Izanagi holding something that looks like a fishing rod, which according to *Gione saiki* represents the spear with which he created the first island in the primordial sea, Onogorojima. Naginata-hoko and Tōrō-yama, which are depicted on both the Rekihaku-A and Uesugi screens, display subtle changes. They seem to have increased in size, and the Naginata-hoko platform accommodates more people. Tōrō-yama has acquired a box-like structure that surrounds Zhuangzi's carriage, making it look much grander, and the green mantis of the Rekihaku-A screen is now brown. While the Uesugi screens differ from the older Rekihaku-A pair in many such details, they are all but identical in their overall conception. They show that by this time, the format of this type of Kyoto screens and the role of the Gion floats in their design were being standardized.

Radically different, though, is another pair of six-panel screens known as the Suntory version (*Santorii-bon*), named after the Suntory Museum of Art in Tokyo where they are currently kept. This pair, dated to the second half of the sixteenth century, consists of two screens of a slightly smaller size. The left-hand screen shows the Hie Sannō festival in Sakamoto, while its right-hand companion is dedicated to the Gion festival. In contrast to the Kyoto screens, which simply included a few memorable scenes from the Gion festival to evoke a summer atmosphere, the Suntory version focuses squarely on the Hie and Gion festivals. This allowed the painter, tentatively identified as Tosa Mitsumochi (*c.* 1496–*c.* 1569), to design the screen around the festivals and include many more details.

The combination of Hie and Gion is striking in light of the many conflicts in this period over the priority of Hie's Kosatsuki-e festival. Were these screens meant as a reminder of Enryakuji's claim on the Gion festival, in a time when Mt Hiei was fighting for survival? Was this pair of screens commissioned by a patron with close links to Enryakuji? Although some have argued along these lines, other scholars have recently presented a different reading.[52] Kamei Wakana points out that the Hie screen makes little effort to depict the actual festival in any detail. It shows the *mikoshi* on boats, heading out onto Lake Biwa to receive offerings there; but the *mikoshi* appear to be heading not to the place of offerings but rather to a stately pine tree at nearby Karasaki.[53] This tree played a central role in Hie legend as the place where the deity of its largest shrine, Ōmiya, first revealed itself. Kamei, however, proposes that it may also refer to the shogun, who was often referred as the *daiju* or 'grand tree'.

Shogun Yoshiharu fled from Kyoto in 1527 and moved the shogunal headquarters to nearby Azuchi in 1532–4. Azuchi offers a view across Lake Biwa to Hie and Karasaki. In 1536 Yoshiharu had to flee Kyoto again; he installed himself in the town of Sakamoto, where the Hie Shrines are located. In the following decade, Yoshiharu was repeatedly forced to retreat to Sakamoto. It was here that in 1546, he passed on the position of shogun to his young son, Yoshiteru (1536–65). In short, Yoshiharu's tenure as shogun was divided between Azuchi, Kyoto and Sakamoto/Hie. Kamei proposes that the Suntory pair of Hie-Gion screens reflects Yoshiharu's life and was most likely made for his private use.

In 1548 the political situation was (temporarily) safe enough for Yoshiharu to take Yoshiteru to Kyoto. This visit was timed to coincide with the Gion festival, and Yoshiharu and the young Yoshiteru viewed the parade on the fourteenth from the temple of Konrenji (also known as Shijō Dōjō) together with Kyoto's hegemon at this time, Hosokawa Harumoto.[54] This turned out to be the very last shogunal viewing of the Gion festival.[55] It happened in a short window of détente; Harumoto would soon become Yoshiharu's and Yoshiteru's enemy once again. The Suntory Gion screen depicts Konrenji in great detail, though it does not show the shogunal viewing itself.

These circumstances support the theory that this pair of screens was commissioned by Yoshiharu or maybe Yoshiteru. It is conceivable that Yoshiharu ordered these screens to tie his nomadic life together; or perhaps Yoshiteru had them made as a tribute to his father.[56] Either way, it appears likely that these screens were not intended to illustrate Enryakuji's ambitions to control the Gion festival but, rather, to cast a flatteringly festive light over the disturbing reality of the rapidly collapsing authority of the last Muromachi shoguns.

The result was a screen that reveals Tosa Mitsumochi's intimate knowledge about the Gion festival in its every detail. Shijō and Sanjō Streets run from across the screen from left to right, dominating the scene. All highlights of the festival are represented here as though they occurred simultaneously: the *mikoshi* procession along Sanjō, and both float parades along (and around) Shijō. On Sanjō, the three *mikoshi* are returning to the Gionsha on the shoulders of large groups of men who are loosely wrapped in white cloth. Armed *inu jinin* lead the way, and more men with pikes and longbows, some in full armour, swarm around the procession on all sides. Two youngsters, seated on a dark and a light horse, ride in front of the first *mikoshi*, each wearing a sculpted horsehead on his chest. People sit or stand along the road, folding their hands with solemn expressions.

The return of the *mikoshi* occurs on the fourteenth, but the scene on Shijō takes us back to the seventh. Here we see sixteen floats parading eastwards. The head of the parade, led by the Naginata-hoko, has already turned south and west, entering Gojō (Matsubara) Street. The floats are easily recognizable, although most are only partially visible among the billowing clouds of gold. The *yama*, in particular, appear to be a bit larger than on the Uesugi screen. The timeframe of this screen becomes even more multidimensional when we turn to the right-hand (western) edge, where six *yama* floats are in the process of being assembled

Figure 13 Jōmyō-yama and Hashi Benkei-yama getting ready to depart. *Hie Sannō Gion saireizu byōbu*, Suntory Museum of Art.

for the second parade. Two men are adding the finishing touches to Jōmyō-yama; Hashi Benkei-yama, in the neighbouring street, appears to be ready to move. Meanwhile, Hachiman-yama (here depicted as having *hoko*-like wheels) and En no Gyōja-yama are moving in different directions in order to allow other floats to pass, in accord with the year's order as decided by lots. In other words, the first parade is in full swing, while at the same time the second parade is getting ready to depart at any moment. A week's action has been condensed into a single scene.

In contrast to the Rekihaku-A and Uesugi screens, the Suntory version makes space for lots on onlookers. Along Shijō, in front of the Niwatori-hoko, a large area is occupied by a group of solemn-looking warriors, all gazing westwards to watch the approaching floats. Commoners can be seen seated in storefronts that have been emptied for the occasion, in the entries of alleyways, and on the roofs, or standing in groups along the route. Some find shade under parasols in the summer heat. In contrast to the *mikoshi* procession, no one appears to be praying while viewing the parade. People are happily enjoying the display and, we imagine, the music, the dancing and the general bustle.

There are more depictions of the Gion festival from this period, but they add little to the image conveyed by the three screens discussed here. For the first time in the festival's history, we gain a concrete and detailed understanding of its spectacle through these pictorial renderings, especially when we combine them

with the names given in the lists in *Gion'e yamahoko no koto*. As important as
those details is the screens' testimony to the status of the festival in the conception
of warrior authority in these chaotic times. The Kyoto screens do not show any
other festival scenes – neither at Kamo, Kitano or Matsunoo, nor at any of the city's
grand temples. Other than the Gion processions and parades, the only festival-
like scenes on these screens are groups of gaudily dressed commoners dancing
in a circle in the Upper City – the *furyū odori* that set Kyoto alight at the time of
Obon in the seventh month.[57] This is yet another indication of the fact that the
revival of the Gion festival, and of the parades in particular, was intimately tied up
with the restoration of Ashikaga control over Kyoto and, indeed, the wider realm.

At the same time, the crowds of people depicted on these screens remind us
that extant sources reveal very little about commoner perspectives on the festival,
be it the street communities that created the new floats, the *mikoshi* bearers or
the worshippers and onlookers who filled the streets. In this respect, a 1561
letter by the Jesuit Gaspar Vilela is more helpful than the diaries of court nobles
or even the Gionsha managers. Vilela was building up a Christian community in
Lower Kyoto at this time, and he saw the festival as an event owned and run by
the commoners among whom he was working:

> In Miyako they celebrate in the month of August the festival of Gion (*Guivon*).
> . . . First of all they portion out among the streets and craftsmen all the
> representations which are to be carried in the procession. On the morning
> of the day, people form up in a sort of procession, which is led by fifteen or
> more triumphal carriages covered with silk and other costly trappings. These
> carriages, which are fitted with very high masts, carry many children who sing
> and play on drums and flutes. Each carriage is drawn by some thirty or forty
> men, and behind it process the craftsmen, to whom it belongs, with their badges
> of office. They all carry their weapons – lances, pikes and *naginata*, a type of
> weapon which has the blade of a broadsword fitted to the shaft of a lance. And in
> this way the carriages, accompanied by the craftsmen and people to whom they
> belong, pass by. After these there follow carriages of armed men; these vehicles
> [the *yama*] are decorated with depictions of ancient events and with other very
> fine things, and throughout the whole morning they pass in due order in front of
> the temple of the idol in whose honour the festival is held [that is, the *otabisho*].
> This is how they spend the morning.
>
> In the afternoon a large number of people carry out of the temple a very big
> palanquin in which travels the idol. Those who carry it pretend that they can
> hardly bear the weight because, they say, they are carrying their god. Along
> with this one they carry out another palanquin which they declare contains the

mistress of the idol. And as they proceed along, there comes another palanquin about a musket shot away and this, they say, carries the idol's wife. And when the men who are carrying this last palanquin see the approach of the palanquins of the idol and his mistress, they begin to run hither and thither, thus giving the onlookers to understand that the wife is extremely angry. At this point the people start to grieve and weep to see her in such straits. Some join up with one of the palanquins while others with the other two, and then they all go together to the temple of the idol, where the procession comes to an end.[58]

The floats, Vilela stresses, are 'owned' by the people of these streets, and the armed men accompanying the floats are 'craftsmen' (*oficiaes*) who proudly display their 'badges of office' (*devisa*). The military rulers are not present at all. Vilela recognizes the parade as an event that may be compared to church processions. As a missionary, he stresses the religious aspects of the festival and manages to make it sound like a painfully misguided display of silly idolatry.

The revived Gion festival: Mirror and model

The revival of the Gion festival is always dated to 1500, when both the *mikoshi* processions and the float parades were restored on orders of Hosokawa Masamoto. The first post-Ōnin festival, however, occurred six years earlier, in 1494. In that year, people gathered at the Gionsha and staged *furyū* displays in response to rumours that the massive fire that destroyed most of the Lower City in that year was a token of divine wrath. This *furyū*, as we have seen, would likely have consisted of costumed dancing in neighbourhood-based groups (*furyū odori*).

Perhaps we can discern a distant echo here of the dancing crazes of earlier ages: the *shitara-gami* of the tenth century and the *dengaku* of the eleventh. While these dances undoubtedly had an element of show, they were also a response to desperate circumstances. The dancers sought to placate the gods and express their anxiety and anger in ways that at times triggered rioting. The dancing retained elements of what Handelman has called an 'event that models' – in this case, an attempt to change a bad situation by following an established procedure or mode of behaviour in a public space. The goal of such an event is not to mirror established structures of power but to deal with a crisis by transformative action. As was the case with the *shitara-gami* and *dengaku* dancing, this kind of event forces the authorities of the age to react and take control. Such a reaction inspired

the patronage of the Gion festival in its earliest phase; it must have played a role
also in Masamoto's initiatives to revive the festival in 1497 and 1500.

While the *mikoshi* processions may be said to retain the unpredictable and
potentially violent characteristics of a transformative 'event that models' (as
became clear in 1500, when the first attempted procession ended with multiple
deaths), the parades had all the hallmarks of an 'event that mirrors'. The floats
that constituted the parades made no reference to the crises and fears of the
age. Their relation with the gods of the Gionsha, who took centre stage in the
mikoshi processions hours later, is entirely obscure.[59] Rather than functioning
as an ingredient in a *goryōe* ritual designed to exorcize demonic forces, the float
parade paid homage to warrior, court and merchant culture. More in particular,
a striking number of floats (notably among the *yama*) presented episodes
of Minamoto lore that reflected directly on the Ashikaga lineage and the
shogunate. In this sense, Vilela's description of the floats as 'triumphal carriages'
(*carros triumfantes*) was right on the mark. At least during Masamoto's reign,
the parades' main purpose was to offer a stage for Masamoto and his puppet
shogun, Ashikaga Yoshizumi, to display themselves in front of the people of
Kyoto and beyond, and to perform their authority as legitimate rulers. These
parades were mirroring events, designed to present or visualize power, and
thereby strengthen it.

As Handelman notes, mirroring events are marked by the 'visibility of
symbols', a 'relative plenitude of orderliness' and a predilection for 'morality play
with a set of striking, allegorical messages'. Their internal dynamic, he writes, is
'one of simple addition (or subtraction) of signs that magnify (or reduce) the
accumulation and embellishment of the occasion'.[60] The Gion festival was no
Soviet-style military parade, but it certainly followed a similar logic of design.
The floats symbolized the military and cultural prowess of the shogunate and
the imperial court, while offering merchants a chance to write themselves into
that story. The parades' dynamic followed a logic of accumulation: a repetitive,
orderly stacking of allegories as one float followed another. The allegories
pointed towards military valour, loyalty, self-sacrifice, courtly aesthetics and
transcendent sources of power – all displayed by the city's commoners as they
passed by the pavilions of their rulers in an well-ordered, regimented fashion.

The floats were poor in ludic elements; this was no carnival. The Kyōgen play
described in the previous chapter, which was recorded and likely also performed
in the post-Ōnin years, derived its humour from the very seriousness of the
parade as the Kyoto audience knew it in real life. Some contemporary depictions,
including the Suntory screen, show the parodic 'riding ox' (*ushi no nori*), but

with this single exception there is a striking absence of comedy. This further confirms that the parades followed the meta-design of an 'event that mirrors'. Presenting power, after all, is no laughing matter.

Yet we must perhaps be careful not to over-interpret our sources, which are all of an elite nature. The diary entries that inform us about the actual performances of the festival were written by outsiders, who merely saw what happened in front of their pavilions. The lists of *Gion'e yamahoko no koto* tell us nothing at all about what may have been going on in the streets where the floats were now based. The screens, too, were made by outsiders for outsiders; no 'locals' were involved, and the screens themselves were likely mirroring devices, designed to impress visitors to shogunal or warlord headquarters. The *hayashi* rhythms and dancing stressed by Vilela remain abstract in the static mediums of text and image, and we get no sense of what occurred before and after the parades, in the streets themselves, at the two *otabisho* or even at the Gionsha. Perhaps the festival was less regimented than warrior documents and idealized paintings suggest. If so, the merriment has been lost to history.

4

1582–1864

Urban blossoming

When the reign of Toyotomi Hideyoshi began in 1582, peace returned to Kyoto. In contrast to Oda Nobunaga, Hideyoshi spent much time in the city, using Kyoto as his main base between 1586 and 1591. In the course of those five years the city was redesigned, enlarged and set on track for a century of spectacular growth. Kyoto served not only as the seat of the imperial court but also as a major centre of production and trade, as a cultural hub of learning and performance arts, and as the undisputed heart of Japan's temple networks. In the last decades of the sixteenth century the city grew from well under a hundred thousand to perhaps as many as four hundred thousand inhabitants.[1]

Hideyoshi initiated numerous grand building projects and reordered the city to fit his own needs. The Upper City was expanded westwards by the construction of a moated castle named Jurakutei, which was soon surrounded by daimyo compounds on one side and barracks on the other. The whole of Kyoto was enclosed within an earthen wall (*sōgamae, odoi*) that was part embankment and part rampart, protecting the city from both floods and enemies. The city could now only be entered through a limited number of guarded gates in this earthen wall. Smaller temples scattered around the city were uprooted and ordered to move to allocated plots along the Kamo River embankment. Relocation was also the fate of neighbourhoods that found themselves in the way of one of these building projects. Hideyoshi's Kyoto was laid out along the lines of a late medieval castle town (*jōkamachi*), with clearly separated districts for warriors, nobles, commoners and temples, all strategically arranged.[2] The main differences with other castle towns were the presence of the imperial court and its nobility in the eastern half of the Upper City, and the clusters of large temples and shrines on both sides of the Kamo River and along the Upper City's northern rim.

In 1592 Hideyoshi left the Jurakutei to his adopted son Hidetsugu and moved his own residence to a new castle, in Fushimi south of the city. Only three years

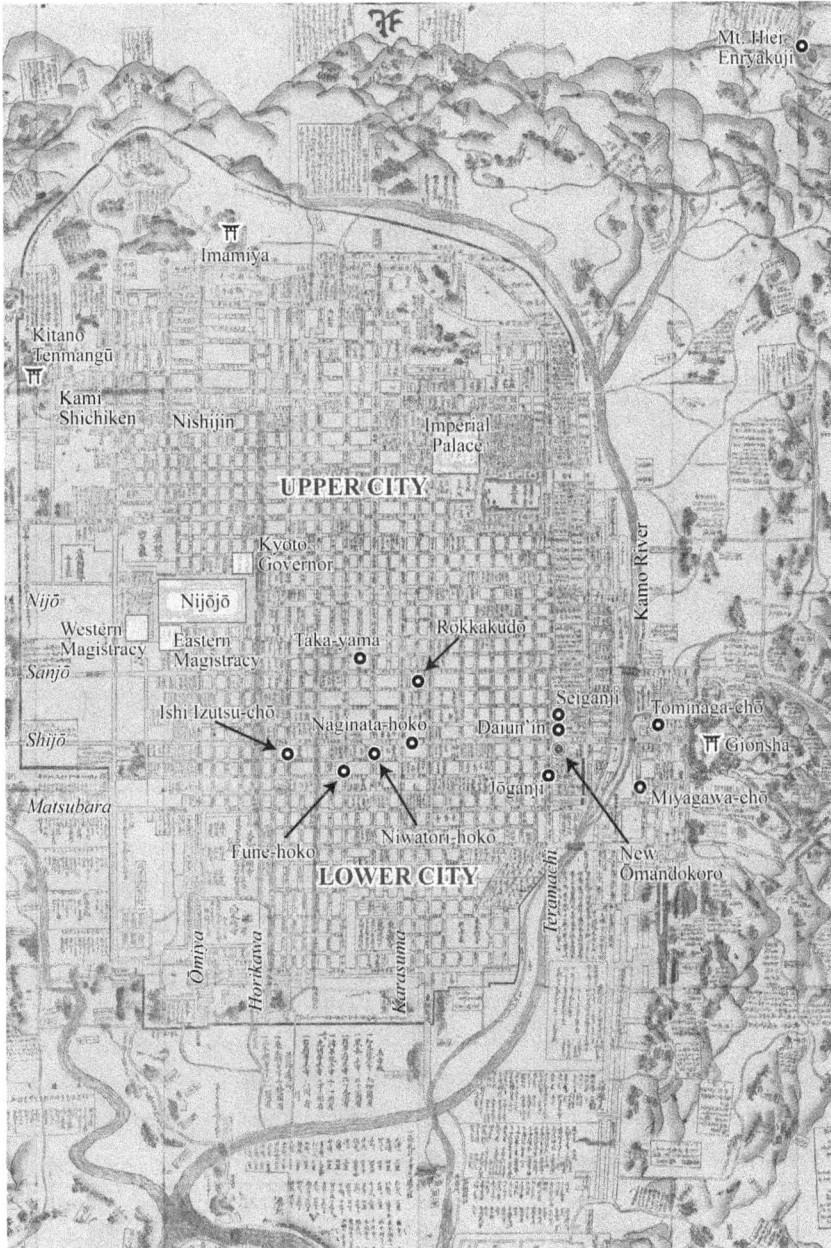

Map 5 Kyoto in the seventeenth century. *Kyōto ezu* (1686), National Diet Library digital collection.

later, Hideyoshi fell out with Hidetsugu and had the Jurakutei pulled down. Most of the Kyoto warrior district was now relocated from the Upper City to Fushimi. After Hideyoshi's death in 1598, the gravity of warrior politics moved away from Kyoto. Hideyoshi's new heir, his son Hideyori, ensconced himself in Osaka until the fall of Osaka castle in 1614, while Tokugawa Ieyasu built Edo as the grand seat of the new shogunate. In the process, Kyoto retained its emperor but lost its shogun. The city was now a definite number two among Japan's 'three cities' (*santo*): shogunal Edo, imperial Kyoto and the merchant capital of Osaka. Over time, Osaka would outgrow Kyoto in both size and commercial activity.

The presence of the court and some of the largest temples of the realm fed a thriving industry of luxury goods and highly skilled crafts. This enabled Kyoto's merchants to build up local and national networks of trade. The imperial court also created a need for close warrior supervision. Nobunaga and Hideyoshi installed trusted retainers in Kyoto who inherited the Muromachi-period title of *shoshidai*, 'representatives of the Board of Retainers' – I will call them Kyoto governors. These men were in charge of both military and civilian matters. They mediated between the court and the shogunate, intervened in conflicts between temples, organized building projects, collected taxes and levies and exercised judicial powers over both warriors and commoners, though not over the court nobility.

In 1603 Tokugawa Ieyasu completed a new shogunal compound in the north-western corner of the Lower City, called the Nijōjō Palace. Although the Nijōjō saw little use from the second half of the seventeenth century onwards, this area became the centre of Kyoto's warrior administration. In 1668, responsibility for the administration of Kyoto was permanently delegated to two city magistrates (*machi bugyō*) who acted under the supervision of the Kyoto governor. The governor's office and barracks for its warrior staff were located on the northern flank of the Nijōjō, while the two divisions of the Kyoto magistracy, each with a staff of seventy warrior officials (*yoriki* and *dōshin*), occupied nearby plots on the western and southern side of this palace.

The new warrior authorities incorporated, rather than replaced, the medieval 'police force': the watchmen of medieval Kyoto. Known as the 'four *zōshiki* guilds' (*shiza zōshiki*,[3] carrying the family names Ogino, Matsuo, Igarashi and Matsumura), these watchmen were gradually transformed into magistracy footmen. We have already seen that in 1500, the *zōshiki* were in charge of security during the Gion festival, forming a conspicuous element of the *mikoshi* parades and keeping order during the drawing of lots. They retained these roles also in the Edo period. In addition, they had various guard duties both at the court and the imperial temples, arrested criminals, managed the jailhouse, oversaw Kyoto's communities of outcasts (*eta* and *hinin*) and policed places of entertainment, temple markets and other events that attracted crowds. The *zōshiki* had semi-warrior status. They received modest fiefs (defined as taxable lands, but paid out in rice, or rice bills) from the Kyoto governor, while also retaining the right to collect levies directly from commoner house owners.

For Kyoto's commoners, Hideyoshi's rule brought great changes. The new hegemon transformed not only the city's physical infrastructure but also its underlying structure of overlord privileges and property rights. On Hideyoshi's orders, cadastral surveys (*kenchi*) mapped productivity across the country in terms of a hypothetical 'assessed yield'. Hideyoshi took direct possession of all surveyed lands and redistributed them to new holders as he saw fit. This applied not only to agricultural land but also to urban blocks. In medieval Kyoto, both temples and noble houses had held land rights in many parts of the city and collected rents (*jishi*) from the inhabitants. After having surveyed villages around Kyoto, Hideyoshi annulled all land rights within the city and compensated owners – if he found them deserving – with substitute lands in the surrounding countryside. This affected also the Gionsha; in 1586, the shrine submitted a letter of gratitude over the substitute lands it had received, accepting conditions concerning the use of future proceeds from those lands. Hideyoshi confirmed Gionsha's rights to those lands in a so-called vermilion-seal document (*shuinjō*), dated 13.9.1591.[4] In that same year, he exempted Kyoto's inhabitants from *jishi* rents in all eternity.[5] With this, another medieval bond that had tied city merchants to temple overlords was broken. The commoners of Lower Kyoto were no longer tied to the Gionsha through such legal structures as *jinin* guilds or land rents. Only faith and custom could now make the shrine relevant to their lives.

In extending his rule to commoners, Hideyoshi built on the pre-existing structures of streets and streets' associations (*chō* and *chōgumi*) and adapted them to his own purposes. The streets became administrative units with their own rules and regulations, and with collective assets and obligations. Hideyoshi, like Nobunaga before him, introduced a system of collective punishments where neighbours could be penalized, and even executed, for the crimes of others in their 'ten household group' (*jūningumi*). This strengthened the need for effective social control among the street inhabitants, so as to avoid heavy fines or worse. The Tokugawa regime continued the same policy, reducing these mutual surveillance groups to 'five households' (*goningumi*). In the early 1600s, Kyoto governors threatened streets with collective punishment if they failed to report Christians or suspicious masterless warriors (*rōnin*). They also imposed citywide rules for the closing and opening of street gates. Such measures gave streets a new reason to organize themselves. Only a system of tight social control could reduce the risk that trouble caused by one inhabitant would expose all to the wrath of the warrior authorities.

The military situation stabilized in the first decades of the seventeenth century, allowing Kyoto's governors to transition to a more civilian mode of governance. While harsh collective punishments became rare, the governors took an ever more detailed interest in commoner affairs. The *chō* streets now became a vital channel for the promulgation and implementation of warrior laws and regulations.

As we have seen, streets already had their own infrastructure, going back to the time when Kyoto's inhabitants had to defend themselves against a host of enemies. The oldest extant 'street laws' in Kyoto date from the time of Hideyoshi's rule, the 1580s and 1590s. In 1596 the inhabitants of Niwatori-hoko's street signed an oath vowing to follow seven street laws or be reported to the warrior authorities and suffer divine punishment. The people of this street pledged to abide by the decisions of the street 'aldermen' (*toshiyori-shū*) and to attend monthly 'stew gatherings' (*oshiru*) in the street's meetinghouse (*kaisho*).[6] Presumably, these aldermen were the successors of the 'monthly representatives' (*gachi gyōji*) whom we met in 1533. Stew gatherings were originally a custom of the nobility. Participants were expected to bring ingredients, which were then cooked up to make a stew. These monthly gatherings were occasions to pass down orders and decisions from higher authorities, discuss and decide on communal matters, and mingle over a hot meal.

It would appear that the Niwatori-hoko street was ahead of most other streets. In a situation where the population was relatively fluid and rapidly growing, not all streets had effective systems of administration. This bothered the Kyoto governors, who needed a functioning street infrastructure to communicate new laws and regulations. In 1655, the newly appointed governor Makino Chikashige (1607–77) made it obligatory for all streets to hold stew gatherings on the second day of every month. A follow-up order in 1656 established a standard model for street management. Henceforth every street was to select one alderman and two or three associates, confusingly known as *goningumi* (five household group) officials, in spite of the fact that they were quite unrelated to those collective surveillance groups. The alderman and his associates had to be senior house owners (*kamochi*) of good birth, with an excellent economy and good business connections. Streets were to report the names of their street officials to the governor's office promptly.[7]

Initially, most streets held their gatherings in the houses of the alderman or other house owners, often by rotation. More and more streets, however, followed the example of Niwatori-hoko's street and set up *kaisho* meetinghouses. Circumstances varied, but in many streets such houses were rented out to street administrators, men who were hired by the street to assist the officials. These administrators were on permanent duty in the meetinghouse, sleeping upstairs or in the back. In addition to a largish meeting room, many *kaisho* had a storehouse in the yard behind the house, and often also a small shrine or Buddhist chapel. In the float streets, the materials used to assemble the floats were stored in these fire-resistant storehouses, while the divine figurines of the float might be installed in the *kaisho* shrine. By the latter half of the Edo period, street administrators (or their assistants, *tedai*) often doubled as barbers. The *kaisho*, then, were the best place to hear the last rumours, get a shave or find help with one's outfit for formal occasions.[8]

In the course of the Edo period the street laws gradually changed character. In the early 1600s, they were geared towards avoiding collisions with the warrior authorities in an atmosphere of lingering insecurity. Streets continued to serve as channels for warrior control throughout the Edo period, but as peace settled ever more conclusively, internal matters gradually took more space. Dues paid by the street's house owners covered the maintenance of the *kaisho*, the wooden gates and guard house, and other street infrastructure; the costs of gatherings and communal events; the salaries of the street's administrative staff and the hired guards manning the gates; congratulatory gifts in celebration of weddings, adoptions and coming of age ceremonies; communal outings for the street's house owners and, in the Lower City, the Gion festival. Street administration grew ever more extensive and detailed. When a house was sold or inherited, street permission had to be secured in advance, and fees were to be paid into the street coffers. Conflicts between neighbours, or even within households, were at times arbitrated by the street's aldermen. In the case of fire or other hardships, victims could expect financial aid from their street. Streets also guarded the comfort and business interests of their inhabitants by banning the establishment of noisy and smelly trades, of competitors to already established businesses and of fire hazards like bathhouses. Other streets took advantage of their neighbours' dislikes by allowing such trades, reaping the financial benefits. There were also some streets that allowed only craftsmen of a specified trade. In short, while Kyoto's streets were diverse, they all served as a regulatory force that gave stability to their inhabitants – at the cost of many detailed regulations, time-consuming communal labour, hefty monetary contributions and intense social control.

Full membership of streets was limited to house owners. Renters and servants were excluded from decisions about street affairs. Most houses facing the street were shops and businesses, selling wares in their shopfronts that were produced in workshops in the rear. Behind those shopfronts, workshops and plastered warehouses vied for space with rental shacks. The street's businesses employed indented workers, servants and maids, many of whom worked for food and accommodation or received modest wages. Salaried labour gradually became more common in the second half of the Edo period. Renters, servants and salaried employees might be called upon to contribute their labour to street undertakings or to attend the monthly street gatherings, but they could be cast out of the street at their employer's or landlord's whim. The street was an exclusive club, run by and for an elite of house owners.

Streets were further organized in larger units, which derived from the *chōgumi* or streets' associations that had emerged in the troubled 1530s. As Kyoto grew, so did the number of these associations, and by the 1660s Lower Kyoto consisted of eight *chōgumi*. The city had expanded rapidly since the early 1600s. Newly developed streets were incorporated in existing streets' associations, and some such associations were split as they grew unmanageably large. In many cases, streets joined the association of the first inhabitants' street of origin, rather than the closest one. This resulted in a complicated pattern of scattered enclaves and exclaves. Obligations between 'parent streets' (*oyachō*) and 'branch streets' (*edachō*) were institutionalized and persisted throughout the Edo period. As we shall see later, such obligations became an important ingredient of the economic structure of the Gion festival.

Serving as an alderman was a cumbersome task; all the more so if one's duties extended to *chōgumi* affairs. As official business gradually increased, the *chōgumi* resorted to hiring professional administrators, as did many streets. These *chōgumi* administrators were known as 'aldermen's representatives' (*chōdai*). After the creation of the Kyoto magistracies in 1668, the *chōdai* were gradually absorbed into the warrior administration.[9] Starting out as salaried aids of the aldermen of a streets' association, they evolved into hereditary supervisors of those aldermen, working for the warrior magistracy as much as for the townspeople who paid them. While the *chōdai* retained commoner (townsman) status, their duties included not only *chōgumi* business but also a range of policing tasks, such as reporting on incidents, summoning and accompanying suspects to the magistracy for investigation, and signing permits. At New Year, the *chōdai* led a delegation of aldermen to Edo to show their gratitude to the shogun. Fees that earlier had been payable to the street (for example, when a house was sold or inherited) now went to the *chōdai*. In this manner, the *chōgumi* evolved into a civilian extension of warrior authority, limiting the autonomy of Kyoto's streets.

When we compare seventeenth-century Kyoto with the same city a century earlier, the differences are immediately obvious. The new Kyoto was much larger, more urban, affluent and stable. Everyday life was less precarious, and the boundaries of status and privilege were more closely guarded. Warriors, nobles, monastics, house owners, renters and outcasts had their own life worlds, constrained by rules and systems of supervision that were less flexible than they had been a century earlier. Yet there was still a remarkable degree of flux. Kyoto was a city full of immigrants, a favoured destination for people in search of a livelihood and a better future. Systems of adoption and entrepreneurship could open new doors. Different social groups depended on each other and interacted in often unexpected ways. Recent immigrants found work at the compounds of nobles as scribes and exchanged poems with wealthy merchants. Warrior sons settled in commoner streets as doctors, storytellers or teachers. People of all classes mingled in the amusement quarters that were established on the city's outskirts, in such places as Shimabara in the west and Gion in the east.

One occasion where such interaction was particularly visible was the annual Gion festival. The festival involved commoners, warriors, priests, nobles and outcasts, engaging the entire city in a month of festivity. How did this festival adapt to the structures of the new Kyoto? The festival was among the most prominent events on Kyoto's annual calendar, and was treated accordingly by the city's warrior authorities. The new structure of streets radically changed the way both the float parades and the *mikoshi* processions were organized, funded and manned. At the same time, the festival was embellished with new events that increased its attractiveness both to locals and to outsiders. In this chapter, I will take a closer look at all of these festival elements, their changing significations and their social dynamics.

The early modern float parade and the *yorichō* system

The early modern Gion festival was performed on orders of the Kyoto governor.[10] Following the example of the Muromachi shoguns, the governor viewed both parades from two temples along the route.[11] As in medieval times, the festival was an event carried out by commoners in the name of the rulers, wooing the gods while casting glory over the benevolent government that maintained peace and allowed the city to prosper. The festival's prestige was such that doors with paintings of Gion floats were installed in the palace halls of Empress Tōfukumon'in.[12] The festival was not just a matter of commoners; it was an official rite, performed in the name of emperor and shogun.

To an even greater degree than before, administrative matters pertaining to the festival were delegated to the *zōshiki* watchmen. These watchmen passed on orders from the governor (or, from 1668 onwards, the city magistrates) to the Gionsha, the float streets and the streets that were responsible for the *mikoshi* processions. The watchmen coordinated these processions and paraded at their rear. They oversaw the drawing of lots that decided the order of the floats in both parades; the lots carried the seal of the governor and later of one of the city magistrates.[13] During the parades, the watchmen occupied a prominent location along the route where they stopped each float to check its lot and ascertain that there were no irregularities in the floats' decorations.[14] Kyoto's two magistracies and their warrior staff (senior *yoriki* and lesser *dōshin*) played no role in any of the festival proceedings. This created room for the traditional authority of the *zōshiki* watchmen and served as a legitimation for their historical right to impose charges on house owners in the Lower City.

What the warrior authorities did *not* do was covering any of the festival's costs in money or labour. Rather, the watchmen oversaw a new funding system designed to spread the burden of maintaining and parading the Gion floats. The float streets shared these costs with other streets called *yorichō* ('attendant streets'). The *yorichō* streets, of which there was a total of 258, were concentrated within the western half of the traditional territory (*shikichi*) or *ujiko* area of the Gionsha, between Nijō Street in the north and Matsubara Street in the south, Ōmiya Street in the west and Teramachi in the east – although a fair number of streets within this square did not serve as *yorichō*, and three streets further south did. The house owners in these streets paid a charge based on the width of their property along the street (*jinokuchi-mai*). This property charge was shared between the float street to which the *yorichō* 'attended' and the *zōshiki* watchmen. The watchmen, then, derived part of their income from the Gion festival. Their license to impose this charge on commoner house owners was a rare remnant of a medieval pattern of overlordship that survived into early modern times as a part of the festival system.

Not much is known about the origins of the *yorichō* system.[15] Tomii Yasuo (1971, 1996) distinguishes between two main types of *yorichō*: streets that bordered on the float streets within the medieval core of Lower Kyoto, and more distant streets in areas that were built up during or after Toyotomi Hideyoshi's reign. According to one of the lists in *Gion'e yamahoko no koto*, Hashi Benkei-yama was already in 1500 supported by a neighbouring *yorichō*, in addition to the float street itself.[16] *Yorichō* of this first type derived from the networks that had bound 'branch streets' to 'parent streets' since the days of Kyoto's reconstruction after the Ōnin war. The large majority of *yorichō*, however, belonged to the latter category of more distant streets. There was no obvious pattern in the distribution of this type of *yorichō*, nor are there any documents that shed light on their origins. Tomii calls the distant attendant streets 'new *yorichō*', and proposes that they may have been assigned by Kyoto's governors in the decades around 1600. This measure would have served the double purpose of securing *zōshiki* rights to property charges, while at the same time strengthening the financial basis of the Gion floats.

If this system was indeed a result of an official policy, it turned out rather haphazard. The number of *yorichō* per float street varied from one to nineteen; two float streets had none at all. The annual revenue that float streets with *yorichō* received was also unevenly distributed, varying from less than one *koku* to almost nine.[17] How much of this revenue was siphoned off by the *zōshiki* watchmen is not always clear. Maybe the seemingly arbitrary nature of *yorichō* distribution suggests that this system was not the result of a single act of top-down planning but, rather, an outcome of years of organic development, sanctioned 'as is' by the warrior authorities.

Tomii has conducted meticulous investigations of selected streets with relatively detailed records. His results show that the *yorichō* system functioned very differently between streets, and that informal arrangements were at least as important as the official system. Taka-yama, based in Koromo-no-tana Kita-chō (on Sanjō Street), is a particularly interesting example, although we must jump ahead to the latter half of the Edo period due to a lack of earlier sources.

In 1787, this street had fourteen houses but only five house owners, who rented out the remaining nine properties as landlords. Kita-chō was dominated by a single group of silk wholesalers, the Sengiriya, and the majority of its inhabitants were servants and employees who worked in the street's Sengiriya workshops and shops. Facing Kita-chō across Sanjō was Minami-chō; while most Kyoto *chō* consisted of the facing houses on both sides of a street, Koromo-no-tana was a rare exception. Minami-chō was an old *yorichō* of Kita-chō, and as such it played a privileged role in the Gion proceedings. The way in which the assembly of the Taka-yama float was organized exemplifies the interaction between these two facing *chō*. In the Bunka years (1804–18), Kita-chō asked Minami-chō for assistance in decorating the float on the day before the parade. The Minami-chō officials agreed and dispatched a group of renters. When the job was finished, Kita-chō invited the Minami-chō officials to a celebratory party at the *kaisho* meetinghouse. Minami-chō received a hundred *monme* in silver for its assistance, as well as fifty-two *chimaki* amulets. The Minami-chō officials would distribute most of these *chimaki* among their neighbours, walk down to the *otabisho* for worship and spend the hundred *monme* on food and drink in a Takasegawa fish restaurant.[18]

In 1787, Minami-chō's house owners paid a total of about 1.6 *koku* in property charges, while collecting another 1 *koku* from another street that served as an informal *yorichō* (perhaps a 'branch street') of Minami-chō. By the end of the eighteenth century, these payments were mostly made in coin rather than rice. Most of this sum (2.3 *koku*) was brought across the street to Kita-chō on the eleventh day of the sixth month, when the float was decorated and pulled along the street as a rehearsal for the parade a few days later. On this day, the two Minami-chō officials were received by one Kita-chō colleague in formal *kamishimo* attire, who feted them with an equally formal twelve-course meal.[19] In contrast, representatives from Kita-chō's 'new *yorichō*' delivered their *jinokuchi-mai* dues 'at the back door' (*ura*) on the morning of the twelfth, and were rewarded with a sip of rice wine from Kita-chō's altar.

Were these *yorichō* payments sufficient to cover the costs of staging a float in the Gion parade? In the case of the Taka-yama, they were not. Tomii supplies an overview of the income and expenditure of this float between 1739 and 1803. Even in normal years, the budget showed a considerable shortfall, mostly of several hundred *monme* (one *koku* corresponded to about sixty *monme*). The float needed extensive maintenance or new decorations fifteen times in the course of these sixty-five years. In such years, the deficit grew exponentially, to a thousand or, on one occasion, even three thousand *monme*. A particularly comprehensive set of repairs in 1782 cost more than eleven thousand *monme*, of which only about one thousand was covered by a combination of the annual *yorichō* payments and special donations. Deficits, then, were structural, and the float only kept going because the five house owners in Kita-chō continued to step in. When the float was badly damaged in the particularly rainy parade of 1826, it proved impossible to raise the funds to restore it. The float's figurines continued to be put on display in the *kaisho*, but the Taka-yama dropped out from the parade. Restoration efforts started only in 2014, and the finished float finally rejoined its parade in 2022.

Although few floats suffered Taka-yama's fate, it is clear that even with the help of their *yorichō*, the house owners in the float streets carried much of the financial burden of the parades. In normal years the costs were manageable, but serious damage due to fire or rain was more difficult to deal with. In such cases, the float street officials called on the business owners in their own street, their *yorichō* and anyone else to make special donations.

The biggest test in this regard was a disastrous fire that destroyed most of Kyoto in 1788. Not only the floats, but also the streets, the businesses and the *yorichō* that supported them suffered extensive damage. Recovery was slow. Even in 1790, the parade on the seventh featured only two floats (Hōka-hoko and Hakuga-yama), while the second parade had none. Over the next decade the parades were slowly restored at the cost of great financial sacrifices. Float streets started by exhibiting surviving or newly fashioned figurines and tapestries in the meetinghouse. After a few years, most partook in the parade again with smaller versions of their original float. Gradually, however, most streets recreated their original floats, often in an even larger and more flamboyant form than before. Most costly were the fabrics used to decorate the floats. Multiple floats used Gobelin tapestries from Europe; others displayed Central-Asian, Chinese, Indian, Persian or Korean carpets, imported at great cost.[20] Replacing a single such tapestry could easily cost a hundred *ryō* in gold or more – corresponding (roughly) to a hundred *koku* in rice or upwards of six thousand *monme* in silver. Repairs might amount to half that sum. A float needs numerous tapestries, at the price of at least half a century of annual *jinokuchi-mai* contributions each. This fact alone demonstrates the inadequacy of the *yorichō* system when it comes to providing the floats with a stable financial basis.

A float's renewal or revival, therefore, depended on substantial donations, not only from central actors and stakeholders but also from well-wishers further afield. The fact that this proved sustainable for centuries is truly remarkable. Clearly, the festival was valuable and important to many of the wealthier merchants in Lower Kyoto. Permission to rejoin the parade had to be granted by the magistracy via the *zōshiki* watchmen. A 1794 request for such permission has survived in the archives of Hakurakuten-yama. This document hints at numerous discussions in the street's meetinghouse, with a group of 'younger residents' pressing the aldermen and their *goningumi* assistants to attempt a full revival rather than a mere exhibition. Once the float was on the rails again, tapestries had to be repaired and newly acquired. Traces of a hectic search for sponsors can be found in the street's records, for example, in the form of a list of donors for a new brocade curtain (*mizuhiki maku*) ordered from a Nishijin merchant.[21]

The city's warrior authorities were not among the sponsors, and they offered no financial aid even after the 1788 fire. Neither did the *zōshiki* watchmen, who insisted on their right to collect their portion of the *jinokuchi-mai* property charge 'even if the rites of the Gion festival are delayed. The property charge is of the same character as a hereditary rice stipend (*chigyō-mai*). It is therefore collected at the same time every year, irrespective of the [Gion festival] rites'.[22] At the same time, there is also some evidence of pressure from the warrior authorities. Kanko-hoko was extremely slow to recover after 1788. This float street first exhibited its figurines again in 1806, and its house owners appeared less than eager to advance beyond that stage towards restoration of the float itself – until they were summoned to the magistracy in 1839 and given express orders to do so.[23] A new Kanko-hoko joined the parade in that very same year, suggesting that the long delay was due to a lack of interest as much as a lack of funds.

The floats, then, went through a cycle of constant repairs and embellishments, disrupted by periodical larger damage due to fire or rain. Even though the same streets continued to stage the same floats throughout the Edo period, the floats' design evolved in spurts, as periodical repairs inspired innovation within the limits of *zōshiki* approval. The Fune-hoko, for example, lost its mast at an unknown point in time, acquired a large bow figurehead in the form of gilded mythical bird (*geki*) in 1760, and was enlarged with a new roof in the 1780s. This roof was further embellished in the 1830s, when a gilt ceiling with paintings of twenty types of flowers of all seasons was added. In the same decade, the float was decked out with new tapestries, some with spectacular bas-relief embroidery, including glass inlays for dragon and crane eyes. More detailed ornamentation, such as an expanding range of finely crafted golden fittings (*kazari kanagu*), was added or replaced gradually throughout the period.[24] Clearly, the inadequacy of the *yorichō* system did not hold this float back.

Float street procedures

Most streets ran on similar schedules, starting with the assignment of tasks to street inhabitants in the fifth month and ending with the settling of bills right after the parade. For the float streets, key events were the twentieth day of the fifth month, when the *zōshiki* watchmen arrived with orders to start preparations, the day of the drawing of lots (on the sixth or the thirteenth of the sixth month) and the day of the parade itself (on the seventh or the fourteenth). In the course of the eighteenth century, many float streets compiled detailed procedures for easy reference. Such procedures concentrated on the allocation of tasks, the street officials' interaction with the watchmen and the *yorichō*, the contracting of outside specialists and budgetary matters. No doubt, much of the excitement – and, undoubtedly, frustration – of the festival occurred outside of this procedural framework. Yet, these documents are our best source on the festival's footprint in the life of the float streets. Here, I will take a closer look at the procedures of the last and first floats of the first parade, the Fune-hoko and the Naginata-hoko, both recorded in the late eighteenth century.[25]

The festival procedures of the Fune-hoko, titled *Gion'e shikirei* (Gion festival procedures), were compiled in 1778 by Nakamura Kihei, a street alderman, on the basis of older documents, of which 'there are so many that matters are easily confused'.[26] In this street, preparations began early in the fifth month. About a month before the festival, the street aldermen chose the year's two 'float organizers' (*hoko gyōji*) and two 'figurine wardens' (*ningyō-ban*) and informed them about their duties. These functions, the second more junior than the first, rotated among the street's house owners. The Fune-hoko street was divided into a northern and a southern section; both selected one organizer and one warden for the year's organizing team. On the twentieth day of this month the 'northern' float organizer was to dress up in formal *kamishimo* garb, including a *wakizashi* short sword. Accompanied by the street administrators, he was to stand near the western post of the gate at the northern end of the street and wait for the two *zōshiki* representatives to arrive. These brought a 'ticket' (*kippu*), containing orders for the street's float to participate in that year's parade. The atmosphere must have been tense; the procedures stress explicitly that 'special care must be taken to avoid any impoliteness or breach of protocol'.

On this same day, 20.5, the alderman of the southern section made a formal visit to his northern counterpart, while the northern alderman dispatched a street administrator to the meetinghouse in the southern section to report on the successful receipt of the *zōshiki* 'ticket'. The administrator also brought the drums and small cymbals (*kane*) for the *hayashi* music. In the evening, the youngsters and children of both sections gathered in the meetinghouse for the season's first practice session, while enjoying 'new sake', fish snacks (*ago*) and pickles. Practice continued on the following days. Here, as in most other streets, *hayashi* bands consisted of a rhythm section recruited among the street's youngsters, supplemented with professional flute players who were hired from elsewhere and joined later.[27]

The first day of the sixth month marked the start of the festival period (called *kippu-iri*, 'the start of the ticket'). On the morning of this day, representatives from all households gathered in the meetinghouse in formal garb (*hakama haori*). The southern and northern aldermen addressed the assembled street members. The float organizers were dispatched to the *yorichō* streets with another set of *kippu* tickets, issued by the street's aldermen. In the meetinghouse, sake, fish and pickles were offered to 'Tennō-sama' (a scroll marking the presence of Gozu Tennō) and shared among those present after the ritual had ended. Later on this day, representatives from the *yorichō* arrived with their *jinokuchi-mai* contributions. They were received by the float organizers and feted with more sake, fish and pickles. In return for their payments, the *yorichō* were rewarded with *chimaki* amulets.

On the fourth day of the sixth month, the two figurine wardens put the float's figurines on display in the meetinghouse (*ningyō kazari*). Most important was a figurine of Jingū Kōgō in armour; she was accompanied by the divine figures of Sumiyoshi Myōjin, Kashima Myōjin and Azumi no Isora. Again, a shared meal was held in celebration. The street aldermen sent written instructions to all households in preparation for the assembly of the float on the next day: beware of fire, no smoking on the float, no inappropriate dress or behaviour. On the fifth, hired carpenters arrived to raise the float,[28] while the figurines (*ningyō-sama*) were worshipped in the meetinghouse. When the float frame was ready, everyone was expected to help out with its decoration. The float was pulled through the street to make sure everything was in order (*hikizome*). Residents were to dress up in *kamishimo* for this occasion. The decoration work continued on the sixth.

On the seventh, the two wardens placed the figurines in the float. The two float organizers walked over to the Iwato-yama float street to greet and fetch their counterparts there. The Iwato-yama organizers needed to make sure that the Fune-hoko had been moved out of their way, so that their own float could pass. The Fune-hoko was among the floats that had a set place in the first parade; it brought up the rear every year (as it still does today). The parade started in the morning. When the Fune-hoko passed Daiun'in Temple at the intersection of Shijō and Teramachi Streets, it was to halt there for the sake of 'the governor's viewing'. At this point, once again 'special care must be taken to avoid any impoliteness or breach of protocol'. Lunch was served at Jōganji Temple, near the Teramachi-Bukkōji crossing. As soon as the float returned to its street, everyone was expected to assist with the removal of all the decorations and their storage. The wardens immediately returned the figurines to the meetinghouse.

On the eighth, the street's house owners were to meet up in the meetinghouse and hand over the year's property charge. The costs of the festival were calculated and shared out among the Northern and Southern sections of the street. Sake, fish and pickles were shared. After official business had been concluded, all youngsters and children were invited to enjoy a meal of stew and tea, offered by the two organizers.

Procedures from other streets follow roughly the same schedule, though with subtle differences. At the Naginata-hoko, matters were complicated by the scale of this float and its inclusion of a 'god child' (*chigo*), accompanied by two child assistants (*kamuro*). The *chigo* embodied the float deity, performing the same role as the figurines in most other floats. Flanked by the two *kamuro*, the *chigo* was seated at the front of the float platform during the procession, wearing white make-up and a crown and decked out in extravagant garb. During the parade, the *chigo* performed an elegant dance while hitting a small *kakko* drum. A document of street procedures (*Shikimoku narabi ni inkan, Naginata-hoko chō*, 1800)[29] stipulates that the duty to provide the *chigo* followed the row of houses along the street. In case there was no suitable child in the household on duty, such a child had to be 'hired' for the occasion (*yatoi-chigo*). All this involved costs that were only partly covered by charges on all house owners in this street.

In Naginata-chō, too, *kippu-iri* took place on the twentieth day of the fifth month. The street's house owners paid each other visits to offer congratulations, while the year's organizers (*shinji gyōji*) awaited the *zōshiki* to receive their ticket and supply them with a sheet that carried their names. After the *zōshiki* had left, all gathered in the meetinghouse in formal wear. In this street it was the *chigo* who took central stage. After worship at the altar and a shared meal, the dressed-up *chigo* practised his dance and was carried through the street on the shoulders of a male resident.

On the first day of the sixth month, the *chigo* was taken to the Gionsha for worship with an entourage of fifteen hired 'retainers', all carrying various objects but primarily serving to convey the *chigo*'s elevated status. The Naginata-hoko organizers also joined the *chigo*'s train. The shrine visit was followed by a meal at the nearby Nakamuraya restaurant; more festivities followed after the *chigo* and his entourage had returned home. The bill, including the wages of the retainers and the restaurant, was covered by the *chigo* household. This household was expected to pay for other treats and expenses as well, so the costs involved were quite extravagant, even with support from the other house owners in the street. On the other hand, due to the rotation system each household knew well in advance when it would be their turn, and had ample opportunity to plan for an impressive showing.

The float was set up on the first day of the sixth month and decorated over the following days. The *chigo* and the two *kamuro* were lifted onto the float platform on the third, and again on the fifth, this time in full costume. On that day, the float was pulled through the street by coolies (*ninsoku*) 'from the street'. The *zōshiki* arrived, demanding the full attention of the aldermen and the other street officials; they were offered a banquet and *chimaki* amulets, a pewter bowl of white sugar, and pine toothpicks. Representatives from the *yorichō* arrived to pay their dues and were rewarded with sake from the altar. Payments were made to the *zōshiki* and to the entrepreneur (*kurumaya*) who organized the pullers; the contract with this entrepreneur was signed on this day. On the sixth, residents took turns guarding the float through the night.

The Naginata-hoko led the parade, and was therefore the object of special attention from the *zōshiki* watchmen. These returned once more at dawn on the seventh, and they were once again feted by the street aldermen with sake and treats. The organizers from the year's first *yama* float (as decided by the drawing of lots on the sixth) arrived to receive orders from the *zōshiki* watchmen at the Naganata-chō meetinghouse. During the parade the float stopped at the Daiun'in so that the governor could enjoy the *chigo*'s dance.

As with the Fune-hoko, the float's decorations were removed as soon as it returned to the street. The wooden frame was disassembled and stored away on the following day. The *chigo* was carried to the *otabisho* for a final act of worship. On the eleventh, the costs of the year's festival were calculated and shared out; in this street, also renters had to contribute. Compared to the Fune-hoko, the Naginata-hoko was run on a much larger budget. The street contributed twelve *monme* in silver to the Gionsha for recitations of the *Daihannya-kyō*. Wages were paid not only to carpenters and flutists but also to helpers and coolies of various kinds. In contrast to the simple offerings of sake, fish and pickles at the Fune-hoko, the Naginata-hoko procedures included frequent offerings and distributions of *mochi* rice sweets, *kamaboko* fish cakes, *manjū* dumplings and other delicacies. The *chigo* (and, on a more modest scale, the *kamuro*) added more feasting and exchanges of gifts. The new procedures of 1800 were compiled in response to the lasting negative effects of the 1788 fire, and they included guarantees that there would be no interim outlays or additional charges for festivities or hospitality. Yet there were clear expectations that both house owners and renters made voluntary additional contributions, notably in the form of 'candle offerings' (*rōsoku kanjin*). Keeping up the prestige that came with heading the first parade remained a burdensome privilege.

The Gionsha and the *otabisho*

Reading the procedures of the float streets, one is struck by the almost total absence of the Gionsha and its priesthood. This was an effect of the loosening of ties between the inhabitants of Lower Kyoto, the Gionsha, and its old head temple, Enryakuji. The streets were still part of the Gionsha's 'territory' (*shikichi*), and their inhabitants were often described as its *ujiko* or 'parishioners'. Compared to medieval times, however, the bonds that held the different actors of the Gion festival together were now loose and abstract. To be sure, street representatives visited the Gionsha and the *otabisho* to do worship there, and some streets had rituals performed there – as exemplified by the Naginata-hoko's sponsoring of *Daihannya-kyō* recitations. Yet the festival in the streets was only tangentially concerned with the shrine, and the Gionsha had little influence over what other festival participants did.

Like the float streets, the Gionsha followed orders from the *zōshiki* watchmen. On the twentieth day of the fifth month, these watchmen gathered at the office of the Gionsha manager (*shigyō*) and passed on the governor's orders to 'perform the deity rites as in other years'. High-ranking 'senior *zōshiki*' then moved on to the Naginata-hoko and Kanko-hoko streets to pass down the same message, while pairs of 'junior *zōshiki*' did the same in the other float streets.[30] This was highly symbolic. In medieval times, the festival had lived its life under the authority of Enryakuji, which had the power to control not only the *mikoshi* but also most of the city's trade and finance. In the Edo period, that era was over. If the Gionsha priests were unhappy with the conduct of other actors, there was little they could do about it beyond sending a formal complaint to the city magistracy.

What, then, was the status of the Gionsha in the Edo period? The Gionsha had now attained full independence from Enryakuji. Also after Enryakuji had been rebuilt, the Gionsha remained a stand-alone institution without an official 'head temple' (*muhonji*).[31] It did not serve as a temple of registration under the system of compulsory temple registration that was introduced throughout the country in the 1660s. The Gionsha, therefore, had no *danka* members and no graves, and the inhabitants of its 'territory' were all members of other temples. The Gionsha had no formalized claim to their loyalty and depended on historical ties alone.

The Gionsha continued to be governed from the Hōjuin cloister, whose hereditary heads served as its priestly managers (*shigyō*). These managers, who were Buddhist monks (though not celibate), led the shrine's rituals and served as its outward face in the Gionsha's relations with the regime. As they had done in the Muromachi period, the *shigyō* also mediated between the shogun and the Gionsha gods as shogunal 'prayer masters' (*oshi*). Throughout the Edo period they made annual visits to Edo to thank the shogun for his worship and his support. Each successive Tokugawa shogun issued vermilion-seal documents to the Gionsha, confirming its full possession of 140 *koku* of lands, which were mostly concentrated around the shrine itself but included outposts in the nearby villages of Higashi Kujō and Saiin.[32]

In addition to the Hōjuin, there were a varying number of other cloisters at the Gionsha, all with their own hereditary lineages of 'shrine monks' (*shasō*). Eventually, the number stabilized at eight cloisters in total, including the Hōjuin and two Hōjuin branches who together constituted the leading 'three cloisters' (*san'in*) of the complex. The monks of the five lesser cloisters (*gobō*) staffed lower levels of the Gionsha's administration and shared both ritual tasks and shrine income between them. The shrine monks of the Gionsha, including the managers, dressed like monks and shaved their heads but married and passed on their positions to their sons.[33] There was no lineage of Shinto-type priests; the Gionsha remained a thoroughly Buddhist shrine.

The shrine complex was also home to a variety of lay retainers and ritualists. For the administration of the shrine and its possessions the Hōjuin hired lay administrators (*shadai*). Lay 'kagura performers' (*kagura-yaku*) and 'procurers of offerings' (*shinsen-yaku*) performed menial tasks at the shrine, gaining the right to offer specified services to worshippers in return. The *kagura-yaku*, for example, sold various amulets, provided propitious names for new-born babies, ran lotteries (*tomi*) and even made rounds of patron believers in the provinces.[34] The main shrine hall was surrounded by more than thirty small sub-shrines that were managed by lay priestly figures called *tanamori* or 'shopkeepers', many of whom doubled as *kagura-yaku*. There was also a group of 'fundraisers' (*hongan* and *dōshuku*) who collected donations for the maintenance of the Gionsha both in Kyoto and in the surrounding countryside.[35] The *shadai* administrator oversaw all these communities (referred to as *shachū*, 'the shrine collective'), and also the *inu jinin* group of guards.

The Gionsha grounds looked quite similar to today. The south-facing main shrine hall dominated a central courtyard, entered by the main gate to the south or the side gate to the west (today, the western gate on Shijō serves as the main gate for visitors, but the *mikoshi* continue to use the south gate). In front of the main hall stood the roofed stage that is today called the 'hall for dances' (*maiden*); in the Edo period it was known as the shrine's worship hall (*haiden*). In addition

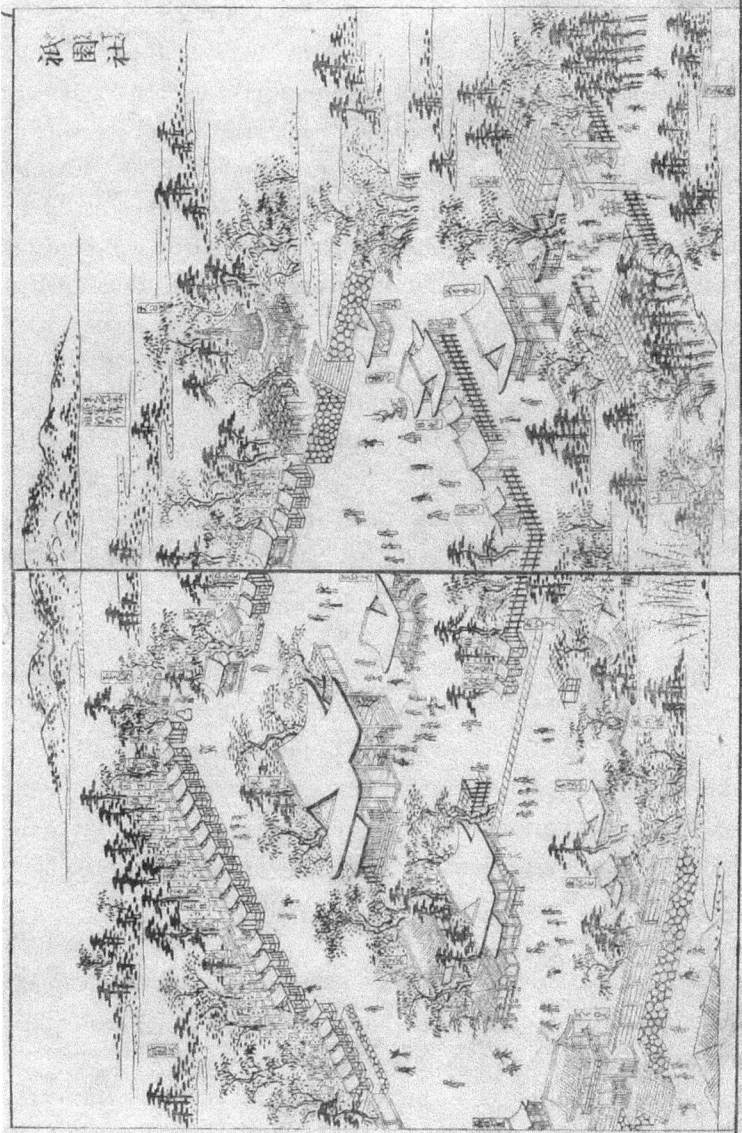

Figure 14 The Gionsha grounds, as depicted in *Miyako meisho zue* (1786). The Eastern Gate is on the bottom left and the (main) Southern Gate on the right. The largest building at the centre of the courtyard is the main hall; south of the main hall is the worship hall. The shrine between the Eastern Gate and the Main Hall contains the *honjidō* and the *daishidō*. A stupa dedicated to Dainichi Nyorai (*Dainichi-tō*) lies to the west of the main hall. National Diet Library digital collection.

to the sub-shrines around the main hall, there was a hall that enshrined the Buddhist 'originals' of the Gionsha deities (*honjidō*), also known as the Yakushi hall after the buddha from whom Gozu Tennō was believed to emanate. Another site of popular worship was the *daishidō* dedicated to Ganzan Daishi (aka Tsuno Daishi, the 'horned master'), the deified Tendai monk Ryōgen (912–85) who featured on potent amulets that ward off evil spirits. The *honjidō* and *daishidō* stood on the western flank of the main hall, on both sides of an open pavilion for the display of *ema*, votive boards donated by worshippers. East of the worship hall stood a two-storeyed stupa (*tahōtō, Dainichi-tō*), rebuilt in 1590.[36] A *kagura* hall and a storehouse for the *mikoshi* stood in the south-eastern corner of the shrine grounds. The cloisters of the shrine monks were lined up behind the stone wall that surrounded the central precincts, chiefly in the western half of the complex. The Hōjuin, however, was located east of the shrine, in what is today Maruyama Park.

More dramatic were the changes at the two *otabisho*. These shrines had had their own priests and *miko* until the 1440s. The medieval *otabisho* functioned as semi-independent shrines, albeit under Gionsha overlordship. The priestship of the Ōmandokoro *otabisho* was originally held by priests (*kannushi*) from the lineage of Sukemasa, but, as we have already seen, the Hōjuin fought a protracted battle, lasting from 1397 until 1443, to oust these priests and take full control of the site. At the Shōshōi, the position of *otabisho* priest with appurtenances was bought up by the financier Zenjūbō, a famous merchant house with close links to Enryakuji, in 1441.[37] The business of the Shōshōi *miko* was also sold at some time before 1500, to a more successful *miko* group based at nearby Goryō Shrine. Both *otabisho*, then, lost their independence already before the Ōnin war. Although we know little about the role of the *otabisho* priests in the medieval festival, it appears likely that these institutions were more prominent arenas of communal and ritual activity than in later times.

Some of the Kyoto screens of the sixteenth century help us imagine how both of the *otabisho* may have looked at that time – although the screens' artists may well have taken great freedoms in the way they depicted these places, since their main point was to acknowledge their existence while leaving space for more important scenes and buildings. The Ōmandokoro looks very different on the Rekihaku-A and Uesugi screens, perhaps reflecting the fact that this *otabisho* was burned and rebuilt multiple times. Both screens show it as a smallish square plot dominated by a bark-roofed shrine hall, a plank-roofed *mikoshi* stage and a large tree. The entrance is marked by a red *torii* gate along Karasuma Street, and the *otabisho* is surrounded by houses on all sides.

Figure 15 The *otabisho* before 1591. *Gionsha Ōmandokoro ezu*, courtesy of Nishiki Tenmangū.

A two-panelled screen from the same period that is dedicated solely to the Ōmandokoro (*Gionsha Ōmandokoro ezu*) follows the same pattern but gives a much more spacious impression and shows more details.[38] In addition to the shrine hall and *mikoshi* stage, we see multiple small shrines and a white stupa, a booth where donations are solicited with long-handled ladles, a roofed stage for performances, a well and a house that perhaps accommodated the shrine's staff. On this screen the *otabisho* is a hub of activity. The two *mikoshi* of Gozu Tennō and Hachiōji are placed on their stage, indicating that we are witnessing events that took place in the festival week. Temporary tea shops line the *otabisho* fence along Karasuma Street. At the *torii* gate two *miko* purify visitors with wands. In the yard in front of the main shrine, ten *miko* of both sexes, the women in red and the men in white, are performing *yudate kagura* around a large kettle of boiling water in front of an audience of worshippers.[39] More *miko* sit on the roofed stage on the other side of the yard.

Above the shrine, in a white cloud, hover the three buddhas who were known as the 'original grounds' (*honji*) from which the Gionsha gods emanate. Yakushi in the middle is easily recognizable, while the others are less clear.[40] A motley group of red and white demons riding a black cloud appears to waft up from the *mikoshi* and drift in the direction of the buddhas above the *otabisho* hall. The pestilence spirits that have been 'caught' by the *mikoshi* seem to be at the verge of getting sucked into the shrine, where they will be absorbed in the tranquil realm of Yakushi. This image offers a rare hint not only about festival events at this central site but perhaps also about their intended meaning and purpose.

The Rekihaku-A and Uesugi screens also show the Shōshōi *otabisho*. On both these screens this *otabisho* is located in the area of fields and shrubbery that separated the Lower from the Upper City at this time. Like the Ōmandokoro, this *otabisho* consists of a bark-roofed shrine fronted by a red *torii* gate; on the Rekihaku-A screen it is enclosed by a square wall. A few worshippers are welcomed by white-clad priests (or perhaps they are male *miko*), but otherwise no activity is shown. Yet we know that here too, *miko* must have been doing a brisk business. In 1500, when the festival was revived, a violent conflict arose between the old *miko* of the Shōshōi and their new masters at the Goryō Shrine. The leader of the latter, a woman called Shiba, called upon the Gionsha manager to enforce the compliance of the former. The Goryō *miko* also oversaw a group of 'walking *miko*' (*aruki miko*), who paid the Goryō *miko* for permission to carry out their trade around the city.[41] All this suggests that the Shōshōi, too, was a thriving hub of ritual activity both before and after 1500.

Both these *otabisho*, however, fell victim to Hideyoshi's reordering of Kyoto's spatial outlay. In 1591 Hideyoshi abolished the Shōshōi *otabisho* and moved the Ōmandokoro *otabisho* to a new location. At this time Shijō Street was closed off by Hideyoshi's embankment along the Kamo River. The new *otabisho* was placed in a dead-end alley between Teramachi Street and the bamboo grove that had been planted along the embankment; perhaps, this location was chosen because it was close to the site where millet was offered to the *mikoshi* during the procession on the fourteenth.[42] Some of this grove was later cleared and built up. By the 1630s, the *otabisho* consisted of a precinct containing a number of small shrines, a stage for the *mikoshi*, a small house

Figure 16 The new *otabisho*. *Gionè goryōe saiki* (1757), ARC Kotenseki Portal Database, Ritsumeikan University.

for the *otabisho* 'shrine-keeper' (*miyamori*), and, further back, a street called Otabi-chō, whose inhabitants struggled to keep charges and duties imposed on them by the Gionsha to a minimum.[43]

The whole of the *otabisho* was Gionsha land. Its shrine-keepers were now appointed by the Gionsha manager and ran the shrine under the authority of the *shadai* administrator. In 1595, the new combined *otabisho* was run by a Shijō shop owner who sold homemade medicines and fans. From 1672 onwards the position of *otabisho* shrine-keeper became hereditary within the Fujii family, a lay offshoot of a lineage of Gionsha shrine monks.[44] Unlike the medieval *otabisho* priests, the shrine-keepers of the Edo period were little more than caretakers, comparable to the 'shopkeepers' (*tanamori*) who exploited the small sub-shrines within the Gionsha grounds. There was no more *yudate kagura*, although a small *kagura* stage was still part of the new *otabisho*. Besides a shrine that housed the Gionsha gods, a smaller Shōshōi shrine and the *mikoshi* stage, much of the site was taken up by a shrine called Kajadono-sha, which was probably already there before the *otabisho* moved in. This shrine, of unknown provenance, specialized in helping merchants escape divine punishment when they broke oaths or used lies in their business. There is no better way to illustrate the social setting of the new *otabisho* than this little shrine.[45]

The early guidebook *Gion goryōe saiki* (A detailed record of the Gion festival, 1757) contains an image of the *otabisho* during the festival as it presented itself in the mid-Edo period.[46] Six high bamboo poles were set up at different places in the *otabisho*; each of these poles was the responsibility of a different street. Ropes hung with streamers ran from one bamboo to its neighbour, forming temporary 'gates' that led the visitor from the street into the presence of the *mikoshi*. On this image each of the three *mikoshi* is installed in its own hall, manned by monk-like figures in black robes. There are three small buildings where *kagura* dances are offered, one for each *mikoshi*; but no *kagura* performers are visible on the image. Men, women and children in festive clothing are seen praying in small and larger groups, while street sellers hawk their wares (food, drink, books) from small stalls.

The contrast between the sixteenth-century Ōmandokoro screen and the eighteenth-century guidebook picture is striking. The screen shows a site where demons are tamed, while the guidebook depicts the *otabisho* as a place to pray but also to see the sights, admire the *mikoshi*'s artwork and buy sweets. The atmosphere of precarious exorcism that – quite literally – hangs over the Ōmandokoro screen as a dark cloud has been replaced by a lighter ambiance of 'prayer and play', with even a touch of touristic sightseeing.[47]

The mikoshi

Part of this transition was due to a similar change in the perception of the *mikoshi*. The medieval *mikoshi* had been a formidable presence. The threat that the *mikoshi* might be held back by Enryakuji, that violence might follow in their wake or that they might even be abandoned along the route gave the festival an edge of danger. People averted their eyes as the *mikoshi* approached, in fear both of the gods and of the rods carried by six *inu jinin* who headed the processions (*bō no mono*). Nobles reminded themselves in their diaries to avoid the roads where the *mikoshi* passed and abstained from foods that might trigger the gods' anger.[48] In the medieval festival, the floats had been a spectacle to be enjoyed, while the *mikoshi* were an ambiguous presence at best. In the Edo period, however, this contrast became much less clear. The processions of the *mikoshi* developed into a spectacle that one might watch for the entertainment and excitement that they offered, while at the same time (as we shall see later in this chapter) the floats took on the status of shrines that carried their own deities.

The *mikoshi* were carried from their storehouse at the Gionsha to the *otabisho* by designated groups of people known as *kayochō* or 'palanquin bearers'. Each of the three *mikoshi* had its own group of bearers. Carrying the *mikoshi* of Gozu Tennō, known as the Ōmiya *mikoshi*, had been the privilege of a guild of clam sellers from the village of Imamiya, located where the Yodo River reached the Inland Sea, since the mid-fourteenth century at the latest. This practice continued also after 1500, and there is ample evidence that in the sixteenth century, the guild members sought to bargain for extended trading rights in return for their services in the festival. It would appear, however, that either Nobunaga or Hideyoshi put an end to these ambitions. From 1613 onwards, the Imamiya *kayochō* annually received orders from the Kyoto governor (and, later, the Kyoto magistrates) to fulfil their 'duty to the gods' without any mention of exclusive trading rights. This continued until 1868, when such orders ceased. At this point in time, the *mikoshi* passed into other hands.[49]

The other two *mikoshi*, Harisainyo's 'Shōshōi *mikoshi*' and the 'Hachiōji *mikoshi*', were the responsibility of designated streets, in a manner comparable to the floats. The early history of this arrangement is not well documented, but the Gionsha archives contain a pledge (dated 1427) signed by the '*kayochō* of sixteen streets' associated with the Hachiōji *mikoshi*, in which they swear to perform their duties without fighting or abandoning the *mikoshi* along the route.[50] This pledge reveals much about the nature of medieval *kayochō* and their communities. The task of bearing palanquins, whether they carried members of the imperial family, gods or goods, allowed *kayochō* groups to claim certain privileges. By refusing to perform their task, sometimes mid-route, *kayochō* were able to exert the kind of pressure that was needed to pursue lawsuits in defence of those privileges.[51] In medieval times, *kayochō* was not a mere profession but a status designation. This fact strengthened the hand of striking *kayochō*: they were not easily replaced by persons of a different status. The 'sixteen streets' of the Shōshōi were likely a *kayochō* community of this kind.

The Ōnin war, the revival of the Gion festival and the reordering of Kyoto by Nobunaga and Hideyoshi brought great changes also to this part of the festival. The *mikoshi* now became the responsibility of particular streets in the same manner as the floats. While the *mikoshi* were kept at the Gionsha, these streets kept the long beams (*nagae*) used to carry them. Reflecting this fact, they were collectively known as 'beam streets' (*nagae-chō*); I will call them *mikoshi* streets. The streets in charge of the Hachiōji *mikoshi* were clustered around the pre-1591 Ōmandokoro *otabisho*, south of Shijō Street. The Shōshōi streets, in contrast, were scattered around the Lower City, though most were located between Nijō and Sanjō Streets further north.[52] These arrangements remained in place throughout the Edo period, which implies that the system of *kayochō* outlasted the old *otabisho* by many centuries.

Like the float streets, the *mikoshi* streets had their own networks and procedures related to the festival. Nishiyama Tsuyoshi has analysed the case of one such street, Ishi Izutsu-chō, on the basis of a street record from 1725 with the straightforward title *Gion'e sadame* (Rules for the Gion festival). This street supplied bearers for the Shōshōi *mikoshi*. It was located just south of Shijō, neighbouring on the westernmost float street, and had four *yorichō* stretching further westwards along Shijō. This street's Gion schedule shows many similarities with that of float streets. Five 'organizers' (*gyōji*) were appointed in the fifth month. On the first day of the sixth month, offerings were made in front of the street's treasures, including the *nagae* beams, and a delegation of *zōshiki* watchmen arrived with orders to start preparations. On the third, both the street's members and the *yorichō* paid their *jinokuchi-mai* property charges, amounting to a total of about 2.5 *koku*; a portion of this was passed on to the watchmen on the fifth.

Street members no longer carried the *mikoshi* themselves. Instead, groups of bearers were organized by bosses who collected wages on the eighteenth. Only two street members participated in the processions, one holding a parasol and the other a bamboo stick. Among the bearers were also people who volunteered, or perhaps even paid to be allowed to carry the *mikoshi*. These devotees were called 'vow bearers' (*gankaki*), a name that suggests that the bearing was meant to add force to a personal prayer. In 1703, when a *mikoshi* caused some damage by crashing into a building along the route, this practice was banned.[53] The ban against *gankaki* was repeated eighteen times between 1744 and 1834, suggesting that this attempt at regulation was ineffectual.

In depictions of the *mikoshi*, Nishiyama notices a change in the dress of the bearers. On the sixteenth-century Rekihaku-A and Uesugi screens, bearers wear uniform white clothing, but seventeenth-century screens such as the Funaki and Hayashihara versions show bearers in mixed colours.[54] Likely, this reflects a transition from the use of street members as bearers to the new practice of hiring bearers, mixed with *gankaki*. Even more striking is the contrasting behaviour of bystanders. In the early screens people are shown praying with downcast eyes, while in the later versions the *mikoshi* bearers are surrounded by excited crowds, with onlookers enjoying the spectacle with stretched necks, raised eyebrows and open mouths. Little remains of the awe that permeated the scene in pre-Edo depictions.

This change was not approved by all. Nishiyama introduces a complaint, submitted by the Gionsha manager to the Kyoto magistrates in 1695. The manager writes:

> Ten streets in this city (along Karasuma, Muromachi, Nishi-no-Tōin, Sanjō, and Aburakōji Streets) and their *yorichō* are tasked with providing bearers for two of the three Gion'e *mikoshi*. The people of these ten streets hire people to do the bearing, while they themselves wait for the *mikoshi* at places of their liking along the route. These people pride themselves on the fact that they are entrusted with this ritual duty (*shinji no yaku*). They sit in shop fronts at those places or stand around along the route in a manner that is most disrespectful, apparently unaffected by the fact that the *mikoshi* procession is passing in front of their eyes. To be sure, not all ten streets behave like this; but two or three among them do. Since these are parishioners (*ujiko*) of our shrine charged with special duties, we would prefer to be lenient, but if others were to emulate this behaviour, this situation will deteriorate year by year.[55]

The Gionsha manager's complaint reveals how much the processions had changed. The *mikoshi* now moved from one 'waiting place' to another, where the bearers were encouraged to show off their prowess in front of an audience that included their paymasters. The spectacular lifting and shaking of the *mikoshi* that forms the processions' highlight today may well have originated in this setting. On pre-Edo screens the bearers look solemn and the progress dignified.

In contrast, the ten *mikoshi* streets turned their duty to the gods into a spectacle that both provided entertainment and added glamour to their community. Just like the float streets, the *mikoshi* streets succeeded in fashioning their role in the Gion festival as an expression of street identity and a source of pride. Needless to say, the Gionsha's complaint proved utterly powerless in the face of this trend.

The Gion pageant

While most streets in the Gion area had some role in the festival, whether as float streets or as *mikoshi* streets, there was also a considerable number of newer streets that were merely involved as *yorichō*, or not at all. This was particularly the case for the area east of the Kamo River, which developed rapidly after the construction of a new embankment along the eastern side of the river in 1669– 70. While the new bank did not necessarily stop flooding, it served to narrow the river and open up the area west of the Gionsha for development. In the following few decades, Gion (Gion-chō), 'New Gion' (Gion Shinchi, including Tominaga-chō) and Miyagawa-chō became hotspots of entertainment, filled with theatres, teahouses and brothels.[56] Prostitution in this area was legalized only in 1790, but Gion already outshone its main rival, Shimabara on the city's western edge, half a century earlier. The new amusement district on the doorstep of the Gionsha soon puts its mark on the Gion festival.

There was no space for new participants in the *mikoshi* processions or the float parades, but the festival offered other opportunities. Among them was the 'washing of the *mikoshi*' (*mikoshi arai*), which took place on the last day of the fifth month (today, 10 July).[57] On this day, a week before the procession, the three *mikoshi* were taken out of storage and placed on the stage of the worship hall (today's *maiden* or hall for dances). In the evening, a large flaming torch was carried from the Gionsha towards the river. It was followed by the Shōshōi *mikoshi*, which passed through the streets of Gion to the Shijō-Nawate crossing near the river. There it was purified ('washed') with water taken from the river in buckets. A second *mikoshi arai* took place on the eighteenth day of the sixth month (today, 28 July), some days after the *mikoshi* had returned to the Gionsha from the *otabisho*.

For those who lived east of the river, *mikoshi arai* was their closest encounter with the festival, and this ritual offered the new district that sprung up in this area a stage for involvement and embellishment. According to *Hinami kiji* (Notes to the Calendar, 1676), written less than a decade after the new embankment was built, 'actors from the theatres along [the eastern end of] Shijō' accompanied the *mikoshi* [from the river to the Gionsha], holding up large paper lanterns inscribed with their names and 'showing off their vigour'.[58] This new lantern parade attracted crowds of onlookers, who must have cheered for their favourite actors as much as for the *mikoshi*.

The idea of 'welcoming the *mikoshi* with lanterns' (*omukae chōchin*), as it was called by the end of the eighteenth century, caught on. If it was indeed Shijō theatre actors who started it, they were soon joined by many others. It would appear that by the 1710s, most of the lanterns in the welcoming parade came from streets within the Gionsha territory, both east and west of the river. These lanterns, many fashioned in imaginative ways, numbered in the hundreds when the weather and the circumstances were favourable. The parade soon diversified as the lanterns were joined by all kinds of portable contraptions, including dolls. The lantern carriers were accompanied by musicians and dancers, making for a merry display that added a playful atmosphere to the *mikoshi* progress.

This parade belonged to the genre of *nerimono*, 'walking pageants', a form of public festivity that became popular throughout Japan from the late seventeenth century onwards. The verb *neru* here means 'strut, flaunt, walk in a flashy manner'. *Nerimono* pageants featured costumes, music and artful objects designed to surprise and delight. In contrast to the float parades, the *nerimono* pageant of Gion was fashioned anew every year, providing an outlet for the creativity of the participants. It also offered a stage to performers who showed their comical acts (*niwaka*), either in the pageant itself or in the streets, for coins. The shops and restaurants of Gion, of course, also did a roaring trade on the *mikoshi arai* days.

The lantern pageant was not necessarily welcomed by the city authorities, who saw it as a source of chaos and a deplorable example of excessive consumption. The Gion *nerimono* fell outside of the authority of the *zōshiki* watchmen, leaving the coordination to the aldermen's representatives (*chōdai*) of the *chōgumi* city districts. This made the Kyoto magistracy even more suspicious, and in 1726 the magistrates decided to instigate a clampdown.[59] A month after the pageant had taken place, street officials in the Lower City were ordered to report whether their street had participated in that year's lantern parade, and if so, whether this was an established custom or a novelty in their street. The magistracy also wanted to know whether each street joined the lantern parade as an act of prayer (*kigan*), or simply because the street 'happened to be located in the Gion area'.

After these reports had been submitted, street aldermen were summoned to the magistracy and pressed with more pertinent questions. Had they paid bribes to their *chōdai* in connection with the lantern parade or, for that matter, for other festivities, such as New Year or the Tanabata star festival? It soon came to light that some streets had indeed done so. Both the *chōdai* who had taken these bribes and the aldermen of the streets who had paid them were punished. In the meantime, restrictions had already been imposed on the number and size of the lanterns; *tsukurimono* objects were banned outright.

Of course, these regulations were soon ignored. This episode is significant first and foremost because it reveals the logic of the Kyoto magistracy in its policy towards festivals. The magistracy distinguished between 'prayer' on one hand and what it saw as wasteful and inappropriate displays of splendour on the other. Prayer was a matter of a patron's free choice, but unmotivated splendour was frowned upon and restricted, especially in times of want. This logic inspired efforts to cast all aspects of the festival as expressions of prayer.

A particular striking example of this dynamic was the development of brothel district pageants. These, too, were carefully staged as offerings of prayers. Such pageants emerged in the eighteenth century in many Japanese towns. In Kyoto, the first pageant of this kind took place at Kami Shichiken, the city's oldest 'teahouse' area located next to Kitano Tenmangū in the Upper City. The dancing girls of Kami Shichiken held pageants both to Imamiya Shrine further north

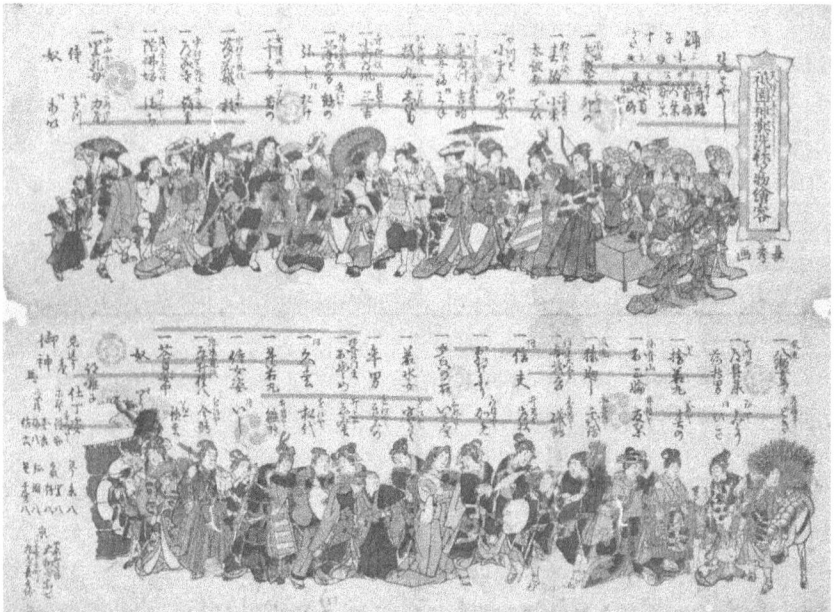

Figure 17 The Gion pageant. *Gion mikoshi arai nerimono eyō* (1835), Kyoto City Library of Historical Documents.

and to Kitano Tenmangū. The Imamiya pageant, which appears to have been the oldest, may well date back to the first half of the seventeenth century. The girls dressed up in fanciful costumes; paraded a 2.5-kilometre course to Imamiya accompanied by lanterns, *tsukurimono* objects, *hayashi* music and carts; entered the shrine precincts and performed song and dance on a stage there for a large and generous crowd, mainly from the nearby Nishijin area of textile merchants.[60] In their conception these performances were offerings (*hōnō*) to the gods, presented in an ambiance of prayer in the context of the ongoing Imamiya festival. In practice, one imagines, both the mood and the motivations behind the pageant were likely of a more worldly kind.

Similar pageants also became part of the Gion festival. They took place in the Gion district of teahouses and brothels, on the occasions of the *mikoshi arai* of 29 or 30.5 and 18.6. The most detailed early source on this part of the festival is *Getsudō kenmonshū* (Motojima Getsudō's collection of matters seen and heard), a miscellany covering the years 1697-1734. Getsudō's notes on the Gion festival relate almost exclusively to the *mikoshi arai*, while the float parades hardly get a mention. In 1721 Getsudō noted that the pageant on the last day of the fifth month was unusually subdued. Yet there were 'four *nerimono* groups', two from the teahouse streets of Gion-chō and Miyagawa-chō, and two more from the area along Sanjō Street west of the river. The costumes and performances of each group had a theme: the Gion-chō group impersonated the famous 'seven pieces of Ono no Komachi' (the ninth-century poetess who personified female beauty and passionate love), while Miyagawa-chō drew its inspiration from one particular piece about Komachi, *Amagoi* (Praying for rain).[61] Both these themes were derived from the repertoire of songs and dances that were performed in Gion's houses of entertainment.

The addition of such themed pageants helped the *mikoshi arai* to develop further into an immensely popular spectacle. As the amusement district around Gion expanded, so did the pageant. There are many descriptions of it in diaries and travelogues, all paying tribute to its cultured refinement and excitement. One of the most striking accounts comes from the Kyoto diary of the young Motoori Norinaga (1730–1801), who witnessed the *nerimono* in 1756 and 1757 when he was in Kyoto to study. In 1756, Norinaga noted that the Gion pageant filed through the crowds 'in such a dignified manner that people fell silent as it passed'.[62] His account from 1757 does a better job at conveying the excitement of the occasion.

On the eighteenth day [of the sixth month], it looked like the weather wouldn't be too good in the morning, but it cleared up in the course of the day. I left after the eighth hour in the afternoon [around 3 PM], excited to see the *mikoshi arai*. Not only Shijō but also all the other streets, large and small, were full of people heading east. From the *otabisho* to the Shijō Bridge, and further towards Gion-chō, the crowds were so dense that it was impossible to pass. (. . .) The route of the *nerimono* was lined with seating stands on both sides, full to the brim with people impatiently waiting for the pageant to begin. We planned to watch it at the Twin Teahouses [in front of the Gionsha's southern gate], but here too, lots of benches lined the road. We went inside and had some sake while we were waiting; needless to say, the Twin Teahouses were full of people as well.

After we had waited a good while, the *nerimono* of [Gion] Shinchi passed first, followed by Gion-chō some time later. Although the pageant is not that different from year to year, it was stunningly beautiful and full of amusing ideas. The girls looked indescribably gorgeous.

Those who were drinking inside heard people call out that the pageant had arrived, and they came running out. The benches at the front were all rented out, so people jostled to find some space behind them, standing on their toes to catch a glimpse. When the pageant had passed [through the Gionsha gate], the crowd became noisy and chaotic. We left and searched for a place to have some tea, but all the shops were full. Booths displaying paper artwork filled the streets, and small groups of street performers (*niwaka*) came and went. When night fell we decided to return, but Gion-chō was still so crowded that it was impossible to move. If you surrendered yourself to the pushing and shoving in the hope of getting through, you would soon be crushed to death. (. . .)

[When we finally reached the river], we saw that the riverbed was brimming with people sitting on wooden platforms, drinking and eating. It was now very late. The moon was high in the sky, the light clear, and the air cool. We wanted to go around all the booths to see the shows before going home. (. . .) Tea stalls and show booths filled the riverbed almost all the way up to the Sanjō Bridge. We ended up wearing ourselves out as we walked over the uneven riverbed, ignoring all cries to 'come in and see the show'.[63]

The fair along the riverbed lasted from the eighth until the eighteenth day of the sixth month, so Norinaga and his friends caught it on the final day of the season. It is mentioned for the first time in 1662, before even the 1670 embankment was built.[64] As examples of the kind of 'shows' that were on offer here, a guidebook from 1806 lists freak shows (*kibutsu*), *jōruri* songs and storytelling, pantomimes, horse tricks, acrobats, monkeys, talking parrots and more.[65]

Like Getsudō, Norinaga treated the Gion pageant as the main event of the Gion festival. In spite of his antiquarian interests, Norinaga hardly mentions the *mikoshi*,[66] and he shows no particular interest in the floats. This suggests that

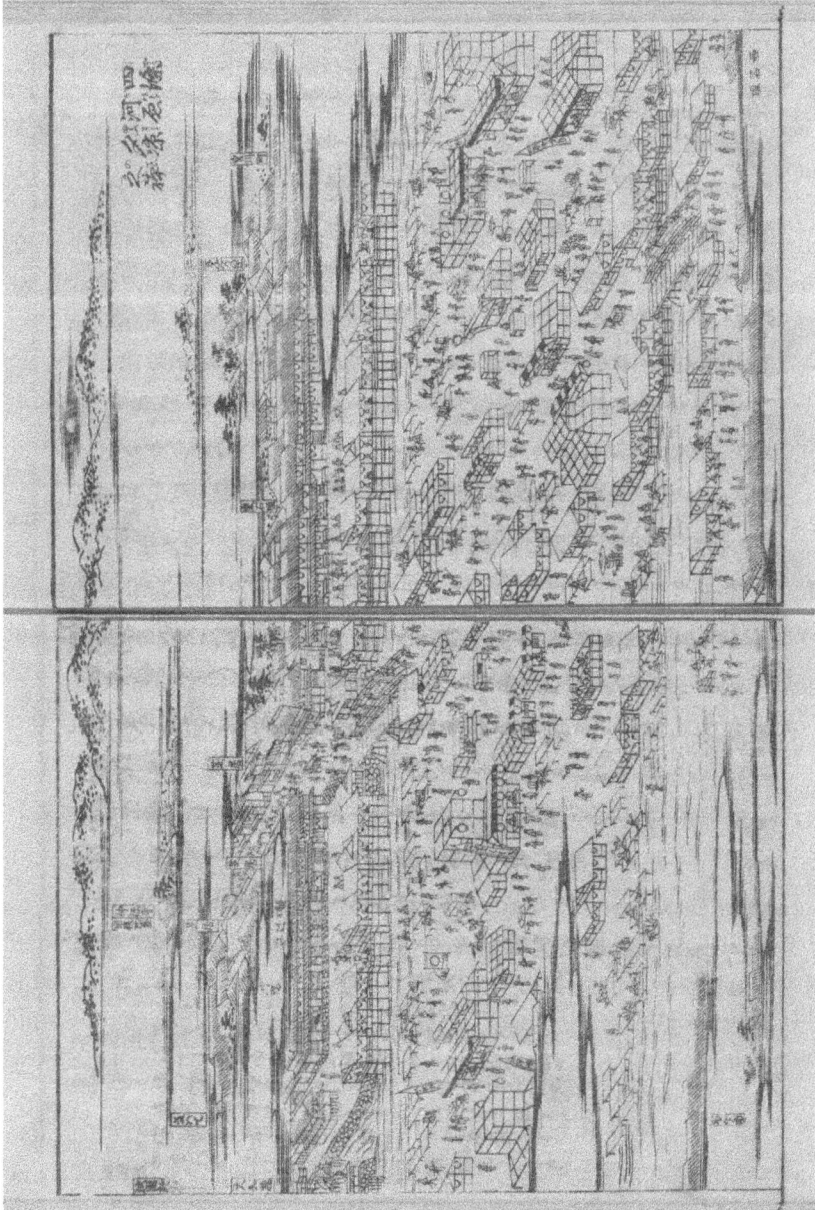

Figure 18 The fair along the Kamo riverbank. *Miyako meisho zue* (1786), National Diet Library digital collection.

for many others, too, the evenings in the lively streets of Gion and along the riverbank must have been the highlight of the festival. Within decades after their emergence, the Gion pageants had transformed the popular perception of the festival.

This popularity is also reflected in new publications by Kyoto's booksellers. The mid-eighteenth century saw the appearance of illustrated booklets dedicated solely to the Gion *nerimono* of a particular year. The costumed girls parade across the pages, labelled to explain the meaning of their attire.[67] By the end of the eighteenth century the *mikoshi arai* began to feature in illustrated guidebooks about the Gion festival, contributing further to its fame. In the 1830s printers started to sell sheets explaining the order of the upcoming pageant, specifying the names of the girls and the houses that employed them as well as their roles in the parade. There was even a market for flyers that reviewed the pageant after it had ended, grading the entries in the manner of sumo ranking sheets (*banzuke*).[68]

The *nerimono* survived a range of setbacks, in the form of fires, famines and restrictions. The so-called Tenpō reforms (1841–3) included a clampdown that almost put an end to the Gion pageant. In 1842 the Kyoto magistracy issued orders to close all brothel districts except for Shimabara.[69] Even though it soon proved impossible to enforce this policy, this was a severe blow to Gion. It was now best to lay low, and the Gion pageants were discontinued for more than a decade. They were restarted in 1860, interrupted once again by the chaos of the Bakumatsu years and given a new lease of life in 1871.[70]

The sacralization of floats

The logic that 'prayer is commendable' while 'empty extravagance is immoral' had an impact also on other parts of the festival. Most obviously, it affected the status of the floats and their rituals. In the course of the Edo period, the *hoko* and *yama* floats took on the character of temporary shrines that carried deities who were the object of worship.[71]

It is not at all clear that this was the case in earlier periods. As we saw in Chapter 3, the floats started as 'contraptions' (*tsukurimono*) designed for the enjoyment of the viewing crowds, and in particular the shogun. The themes of the floats' decorations were unrelated to the gods of the Gionsha; most referred to warrior lore, Noh plays or episodes from classical Chinese and Japanese literature. The Kyoto screens of the sixteenth century depicted people pointing, laughing and talking to friends while viewing the parade of floats. Some of the floats were directly humorous, displaying figures that hardly invited veneration.

Yet from the early eighteenth century onwards, the figurines of most floats began to be regarded as street deities. They were treated as deity objects and surrounded by tales of both miracles and *tatari* curses. The *hoko* floats carried small dolls on a tiny shelf (*shingidana, tennōdai*) high up the float's central pole. At some point in the eighteenth century it became customary to make these dolls accessible to people's prayers in the *hoko* streets' meetinghouses on the day before the *hoko* were assembled.[72] The same soon happened with the larger figurines that featured on the *yama* floats. As we saw already, some streets annually appointed 'figurine wardens', underlining their special status. The figurines were displayed in the meetinghouses on temporary altars with their faces hidden behind short curtains in the manner of deity statues; offertory boxes were set out in front of them. By the early nineteenth century many floats had begun to sell amulets for specific purposes, linked to the float's theme.[73]

The Fune-hoko was a particularly striking example of this trend. Jingū Kōgō, the main figure of this float, had once conquered Korea while pregnant, and she had not only succeeded in postponing delivery with the help of a stone but also given birth to an august child that would grow into the divine Emperor Ōjin, also known as Hachiman. On this basis the float advertised its figurine of Jingū Kōgō, and also a mask (dating from the 1440s), as deity objects that granted women an easy delivery.

The Fune-hoko street actively sought to enhance the divine aura of this figurine and mask by quite remarkable means. In 1758, when Emperor Momozono's wife Ichijō Tomiko was pregnant, a street official found a way to approach the court and arrange for the Jingū Kōgō mask and an auspicious *obi* belt to be delivered to Tomiko's quarters, where the mask was installed on an altar. Tomiko gave birth to a son who grew up to become Emperor Go-Momozono. Among the many gifts that the Fune-hoko received for its assistance during Tomiko's pregnancy was a box for the mask, decorated with the imperial chrysanthemum. This event became a precedent, and the mask would be lent to pregnant court ladies eleven more times before Meiji.

Murakami Tadayoshi traces the 'sacralization' of the floats in the pictorial record. He points out two changes in the design of floats that may be interpreted as expressions of their transition from *tsukurimono* into mobile shrines. The first is the replacement of 'old pines' with 'young pines' on the many *yama* that feature a 'hill' (made of woven bamboo strips covered with fabric) topped with a tree. In the sixteenth century, all such *yama* were depicted with old, gnarly pine trees of the kind one often finds in Japanese gardens. In the eighteenth century, these old pines were gradually replaced with young branches identical to those still used on today's floats. The second is the appearance of red parasols to cover the dolls on floats that don't include roofs. Such parasols became part of most *yama* in the course of the eighteenth century, roughly at the same time as the young pines.[74]

No Edo-period sources comment on these changes, and the motivations behind them are open to interpretation. I would argue that the parasols, in particular, offer proof of the changing status of the float figurines. They interfere with the narratives presented on these floats: the parasols look out of place especially in the more dynamic scenes depicted on floats like Jōmyō-yama, and the poverty of Ashikari-yama's reed-cutter would have been more poignant without the parasol. If the figurines on these floats were seen as deity bodies, however, the parasols had a clear function as sacralizing canopies.

The success of the lantern parade suggests that the exhibition of float figurines and the sale of amulets on the day before the parade was not *only* a response to popular piety. Today the days before the parade, when the floats are already assembled in the streets, are the busiest of the festival. Crowds of up to a million people mill around the float streets in the evenings, admiring the floats, offering a coin to the float dolls, listening to the *hayashi* music, and enjoying drinks and snacks as the night air cools. These *yoiyama* evenings, as they are currently called, came about in the course of the eighteenth century; at that time, they were called *yoimiya* or *yomiya*.[75] The first description of something similar can be found in the 1757 *Gion goryōe saiki*:

> The sixth day of the sixth month:
> The festival streets light countless lanterns on the day before the parade. [House owners] hang up curtains and compete with each other in decorating [their front rooms] with screens trimmed with gold and silver and tapestries of felted wool. In those rooms they then receive guests. Kyoto is never as splendorous as at this time.
> A fence is set up along the route of the float parade. In the *hoko* streets, the floats are lighted up with many lanterns, and *hayashi* is played from the hour of the rooster until the hour of the boar (c. 6-10 PM). The spectacle is incomparable. In the *yama* streets, people exhibit the figurines and treasures from the hour of the monkey (c. 4 PM) and allow people to view and worship them. All the streets are filled with people, high and low.[76]

This short passage describes three concurrent events, all designed to draw crowds to the float streets on the day before the parade. First, there is the lighting-up of the entire area with lanterns. In a time when street lights did not yet exist, and when candles were costly, the sight of thousands of lanterns burning late into the night was a spectacular extravagance, worth viewing in its own right.

Second, there were the exhibitions of *byōbu* screens, family treasures and *ikebana* arrangements in private houses. House owners removed the wooden lattices from their front windows and transformed part of their homes into a public space, where not only friends but also strangers could enter to savour their collection of artworks. Maids and servants were on duty in their best garb to serve visitors tea and sweets. It appears that this tradition drew on an earlier practice of viewing the float parades and *mikoshi* processions from similarly opened front rooms, decorated with screens for the occasion. Depictions of such scenes can be found on Kyoto screens from around the 1620s onwards. In the mid-eighteenth century, this practice appears to have inspired the development of the so-called *byōbu matsuri* or 'screen exhibitions' described in this passage.[77] In most float streets, only one or two houses opened their doors in this manner. These houses were typically owned by elite merchants, who also used the opportunity to enhance their reputation as dealers in exquisite merchandise.

Finally, there was the decoration of the street meetinghouses. Here, people could pray and offer coins to the float figurines, purchase amulets and enjoy *hayashi* music. The meetinghouses exhibited the street's treasures, including the tapestries, gilt float decorations and other ornaments that would only be attached to the float on the day of the parade – as well as spares, discarded objects used in the past and other heirlooms that added to the street's cultural prestige. The money spent by visitors covered some of the costs of the festival, and in the early nineteenth century the *yoiyama* were expanded to two or even three days.[78]

Like the *mikoshi arai* with its lantern parade and *nerimono* pageant, the *yoiyama* in the float streets added a new event to the Gion festival that catered to outside visitors. These events clearly belonged to a different category from the *mikoshi* processions and the float parades. While the latter were strictly regulated and overseen by the *zōshiki* watchmen and the city magistracy, the lantern parade and the pageant were free from such control and open to creative improvisation. The *mikoshi* processions and the float parades were all but identical from one year to the next, while the new events around *mikoshi arai* and *yoiyama* were more dynamic. In the context of the Sannō and Kanda festivals in Edo, similar 'additional events' were called *tsukematsuri*, a term that I am tempted to translate as 'the festival fringe'.

These events allowed new groups of people to make the festival their own. The streets and groups that participated in the lantern parade and the brothels and teahouses that organized the Gion pageant expanded the festival into new areas of the city. Even more striking is the development of the festival as a spectacle for outsiders – people from outside the Gionsha *ujiko* area, who had no role in any of the festival's rituals, parades or performances. The crowds at *mikoshi arai* and *yoiyama* included locals but also attracted many visitors from elsewhere.

As the publication of a steady stream of printed guides indicates, the Gion festival was rapidly becoming a tourist attraction. These tourists came from all layers of the population, and various new arrangements enabled people without much money to make their way to Kyoto during the festival period. Trips to see the Gion festival became part of the agenda of 'pious associations' (*kō*) even in quite distant places. Such associations pooled money to allow members to go on pilgrimages to famous shrines and temples such as Ise, Konpira, Zenkōji and many others. Almost every village or city neighbourhood had a selection of *kō*, which served a range of social and also financial functions beyond 'piety' alone. Multi-day tours to Kyoto at the time of the Gion festival were, for example, part of the annual calendar of an Ise *kō* in Higashi Futami, a village located about a hundred kilometres west of Kyoto along the Inland Sea coast.[79] In this, Higashi Futami followed the example of neighbouring villages and towns. The *kō* members from this village joined a veritable flood of sightseers from near and far. These tourists filled the city's inns and no doubt spent varying amounts of time at the Gionsha, some of the float streets, the show booths on the Kamo riverbank and other city attractions.

Conclusion

Kawashima Masao proposes to divide the history of the Gion festival in the Edo period into three periods, separated by two phases of transition. In his periodization, the first transition was completed in the 1680s and the second in the 1780s.[80]

In the period up to the 1680s, Kawashima argues, the Gion festival was brought under the control of the Kyoto governor and magistrates by way of the *zōshiki* watchmen. The calendar of festival events was set in stone, and any changes became subject to approval from the city authorities. The culmination of this development was an order issued by the magistracy in 1683, restricting the use of weapons and armour in all Kyoto festivals, including Gion.[81] In negotiations with the Gionsha, the number of cuirasses and helmets, swords and spears used in the *mikoshi* processions was reduced by about a third. Any swords worn by townspeople in the float parade were to be replaced with wooden copies.

Kawashima's second period, until the 1780s, was marked by the development of happenings 'for and by the townspeople' on the fringe of traditional festival events: the lantern parade and Gion pageant at *mikoshi arai*, the *yoiyama* in the float streets and the fair along the Kamo River. Finally, Kawashima proposes that the large fire of 1788 that destroyed much of the Lower City marked the beginning of a third period. While most streets succeeded in reviving their floats in the course of a few years, some struggled with the economic consequences for decades. This period ended in 1864, when, as we shall soon see, an even larger fire laid Kyoto waste once again, destroying almost all the float streets and their floats. After 1788 many of the floats were subtly redesigned; the post-1788 floats are today canonized as models for preservation and reconstruction.

Looking back on the changes that occurred in the course of the Edo period, I would propose to slice the cake somewhat differently. Warrior control over the festival, stressed by Kawashima as the main new development of the period up to the 1680s, was evident already in 1500 when Hosokawa Masamoto decided that the festival was to be revived. The new structure, where the *zōshiki* watchmen oversaw the festival as representatives of the Kyoto governors and magistrates, was a continuation of earlier systems of warrior control.

In comparison with the revolutionary changes in the sixteenth century – Enryakuji's demise as the overlord of the Gionsha and its festival, the emergence of the system of float streets and 'attendant streets' (*yorichō*), and the transformation of the *otabisho* – the transition into the Edo period was marked by continuity rather than change. The viewing shoguns were replaced by the Kyoto governors, and even the *zōshiki* of the Muromachi period were retained. The festival calendar remained unchanged, the main difference being that the festival now ran like clockwork, without any of the postponements that had marked the previous century.

The changes that occurred from the 1670s onwards, however, were truly revolutionary. The festival expanded into new parts of the Gionsha's *ujiko* area as novel events engaged the inhabitants of newly built-up areas, notably on the eastern side of the Kamo River. The festival of the eighteenth century, with its growing 'fringe', offered many more opportunities for both townspeople and tourists to simply have a good time. As the festival attracted more visitors from far and near, there was more space for new initiatives. The days before the parades (*yoiyama*) grew into popular events. Increased interest from outsiders inspired the inhabitants of the float streets to cater to their tastes and needs.

Lanterns appeared everywhere to light up the Lower City, the Kamo riverbank and the Gion district. The crowds attracted stalls, street performers and pickpockets. More people generated more events, which drew more people to the festival. As this dynamic rolled on, the festival as an experience was utterly transformed.

The 1788 fire was the largest among multiple crises that disrupted this dynamic. It was particularly noteworthy because it briefly brought the float parades to a full stop. The newer events, such as the lantern parades and the Gion pageants, were particularly sensitive to adversity. In years of failed harvests, scarcity and economic downturns they were much reduced or cancelled altogether.[82] Even rainy weather affected them badly. Their status, as 'fringe events', was markedly different from the *mikoshi* processions and the float parades. While the these processions and parades were performed on orders of the Kyoto magistrates, conveyed and enforced by the *zōshiki* watchmen, the lantern parade and the Gion pageant were overseen by the aldermen's representatives (*chōdai*) and regarded with some suspicion by the magistracy. They were not banned, but there were regular attempts to restrict and reduce them, especially in times of national or local sumptuary clamp-downs. The disruption of the Gion pageant from 1842 until 1859 as a result of the so-called Tenpō reforms was the most dramatic example.

Reforms of this kind were triggered by concrete financial crises. Warrior administrators tended to blame such crises on collapsing morals, corruption caused by greed, extravagant consumption by 'idlers' and crumbling status boundaries, notably between warriors and commoners. Their solution was ultimately based on a restoration of public morality, a renewed stress on duty and honour over greed, a reduction of consumption and a stricter adherence to status distinctions. The city festivals of the Edo period occupied an ambiguous position in this world view. On one hand, they symbolized peace and prosperity and thus cast glory over the rulers of the land. As a bestselling guidebook from 1787 put it, 'The bustle of Gion . . . is a reflection of the virtuous powers of the gods, a cry of celebration, a *banzai* befitting this age of order and peace throughout the realm.'[83] On the other hand, not all were impressed. The disgruntled warrior and social critic Buyō Inshi, writing in 1816, found the extravagance of festival parades in Edo 'shocking to behold'. Not only did townspeople deck out their children as 'great generals', crashing through the status boundary that separated commoners from warriors; they would also hire 'whole groups of prostitutes [. . . and] pay musicians' to accompany them in the parade. The cost, Buyō estimates, amounted to 'the same sum that an elite warrior with a stipend of 2,000 or

4,000 *koku* will receive for a whole year' – all for one day's magnificence.[84] In Buyō's eyes, festivals were places for louts who, 'crazed by their hot blood, think dissipation second to none to be a great deed'.[85]

Stressing the festival's connection to the gods was one strategy to dodge this kind of moral indignation. In 1726, as we saw earlier, the Kyoto magistracy checked whether the first fringe event – the lantern parade – was a form of 'prayer'. The implication was that the parade would be acceptable if participants were prepared to label it as a form of worship. In this, the magistracy followed a train of thought that also manifested itself elsewhere. As festivals around the country were growing larger and more extravagant, administrators sought to find a balance between austerity and splendour. They tended to find fault with human partying but allow splendorous worship.

A striking example of this in another context is cited by Ueki Yukinobu, writing about the Sannō festival in Edo. This festival was famous for the fact that its *mikoshi* procession and float parade were allowed to pass through Edo castle, where they were viewed by the shogun himself. As Edo grew more populous and prosperous the Sannō parades became ever more extravagant, and soon they were subjected to restrictive regulation. In 1721, for example, richly decorated carts (*yatai*) that served as moving stages for all kinds of performers were banned and the number of participants allowed per block (Edo's equivalent of the Kyoto street) was limited. Participants were ordered to use costumes and effects that were already in their possession, rather than spending a fortune on new ones designed for the occasion. All forms of 'splendour' (*kekkō*) were banned; the parade was meant to be simple but solemn.[86]

In 1750s, the parade was again growing too colourful for the taste of the city authorities. In 1759, a city regulation (*machibure*) elaborated on the authorities' thinking:

> Rituals for the deities (*shinji*), which are inspired by the shared faith (*shinkō*) of the townspeople, are growing ever more elaborate as the city blocks become more prosperous, and the number of people participating in them is increasing. Yet this is not a cause for censure. Henceforth, standing regulations must be followed, and neither *yatai* carts nor similar contraptions are allowed. Beyond that, however, these are rituals for the deities, and therefore they must be allowed to blossom.[87]

The ideal of 'blossoming' (*nigiwai*) sanctioned or even required the use of ornate costumes, drums and samisen music, and anything else that wasn't categorized as *yatai*, because this parade was not mere amusement for people but an offering to the gods. Strikingly, this regulation included even 'fringe' elements in the category of *shinji* ritual and allowed extravagance (within the limits of minimal decency) also for them. The block aldermen must have picked up the message: putting up a good show is allowed, and even appreciated; but make sure it is camouflaged as worship and prayer.

What happened in Edo resonated around the country and had an influence also in Kyoto. The distinction between mere human partying and honourable displays of reverence for the gods contributed to a subtle redefinition of both the Gion float parades and the fringe events, emphasizing aspects of worship where before there had been none. At the same time, the *mikoshi* processions appear to have lost some of the awe that they had inspired earlier, and people now viewed the processions as a spectacle much in the same way as they watched the float parades, or even the Gion pageant.

The effect was ambiguous: in Handelman's terms, the distinction between 'events that model' and 'events that mirror' became less clear. The *mikoshi* and float rites became street rituals that engaged and created street communities within the larger context of the Gion festival. In the process, the gods of the festival multiplied as the Gionsha deities were joined by the deified figurines of the floats. The *mikoshi* processions acquired a stronger element of 'mirroring' power and prestige, as symbolized by the members of *mikoshi* streets who posted themselves proudly along the route. Even the *mikoshi arai* acquired its 'mirroring' parade and pageant: these events were designed to reflect the standing of their participants or patrons and please human onlookers, rather than to sway the gods. The float parades, on the other hand, took on a new aspect of 'modelling' as the float figurines became objects of worship. There was an increased sense that the floats contained gods, and that the procedure of parading those gods would affect some positive change on the city.

The logic of prayer and 'blossoming' conflated Handelman's categories in a similar manner. The festival addressed the gods and sought to harness their divine powers to bring blessings; but at the same time, the festival reflected human prosperity and cast glory over the rulers who made this prosperity possible. The warrior regime regarded the festival as a public matter and saw its successful management as an important government responsibility. The festival both modelled (transformed) and mirrored (reflected) the state of the realm, and therefore it needed strict supervision. This was to change radically as the festival entered modernity; as a result, it would come close to 'flopping' once again.

1864–1952

The problems of modernity

The fall of the Tokugawa shogunate and the Meiji Restoration was a shocking experience for the city of Kyoto and its street communities. The instability of the Bakumatsu years was acutely felt already in 1862 when the shogunate loosened up the system of alternate attendance (*sankin kōtai*) that had forced daimyo to keep residences in Edo and spend much of their time there. The imperial court soon became a rallying point for those who opposed the opening of the country. In 1862 and 1863, many daimyos built new residences in Kyoto. Samurai from around the country fought a low-key guerrilla war in the streets of the city, marked by intrigue, murder and arson. Disaster struck in the seventh month of 1864. Rebels from Chōshū domain waged a full-scale attack on Aizu and Satsuma forces who guarded the Imperial Palace (the Kinmon or Hamaguri Gomon incident). The rebellion failed, but fires started by both parties raged out of control and burned for two days. Almost all of the Lower City went up in flames. According to one eyewitness, Kyoto

> entirely disappeared in one morning in the smoke of the flames of a war-fire, which was assisted in the work of destruction by a violent wind; and nothing was left of it, but a burnt and scorched desert. Alas! The loss most to be regretted was that of the triumphal cars used in that most splendid of all festivals of the Blossom-capital, the festival of Gion, which were almost entirely destroyed by the flames.[1]

This was only the start of Kyoto's troubles. For a moment, it looked as if Kyoto's Nijōjō Palace might become the seat of the new national government. That dream ended in 1869 when the emperor and his court were permanently moved to Tokyo, leaving a gaping hole in the heart of the city. The Imperial Palace, the villas of the nobility and also the compounds of numerous daimyo were left standing empty and were soon reduced to ruins. Kyoto's traditional

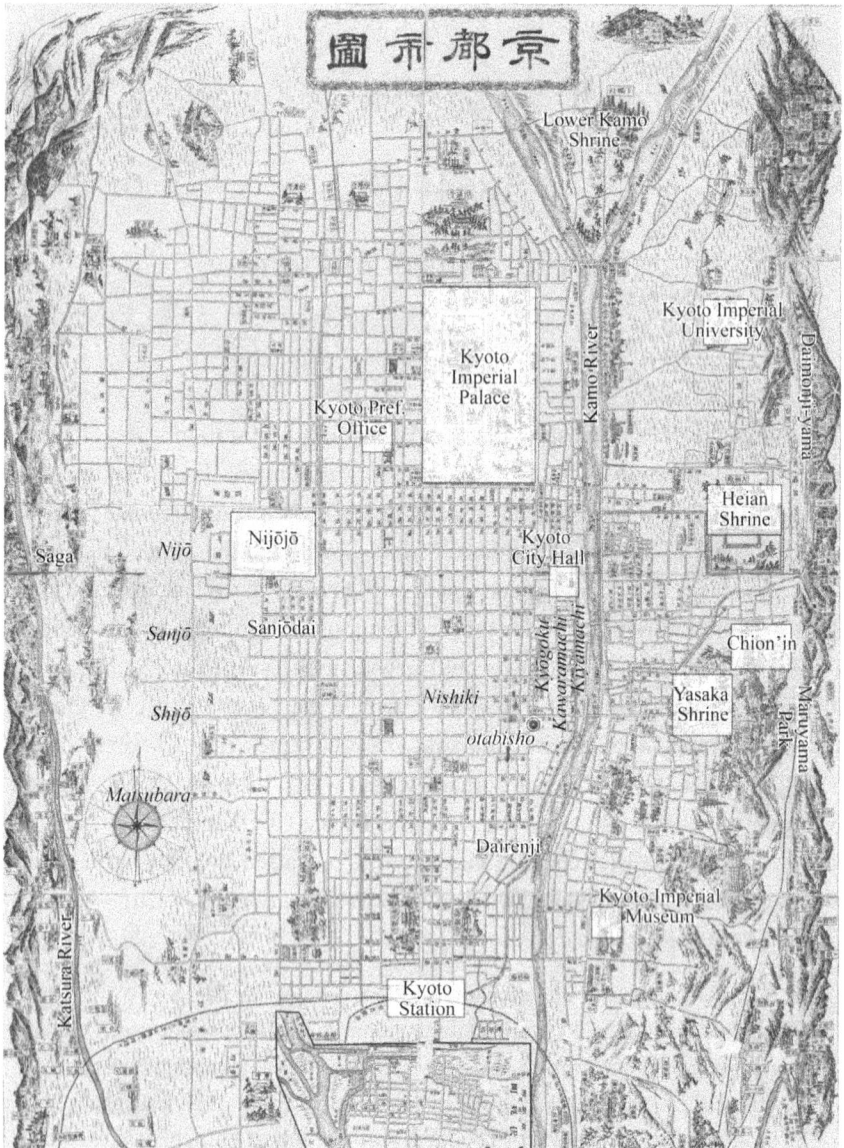

Map 6 Kyoto in the Meiji period. *Kyōto-shi zu* (1895), International Research Center for Japanese Studies.

industries, with their focus on luxury goods, lost many of their most valuable customers. Kyoto became markedly poorer, at a time when reconstruction after the 1864 disaster was still underway. The city's population dwindled from well over 300,000 to fewer than 250,000 inhabitants.

The new city government, now called Kyoto Prefecture (*Kyōto-fu*), sought to break out of this negative spiral by aggressive modernization, aiming to develop Kyoto into a centre of modern manufacturing, education and culture. Its package of 'Kyoto measures' (*Kyōto saku*) proved successful in setting the city on the track to recovery. This success is often attributed to the leadership of Makimura Masanao (1834–96), a Chōshū domain official who rose in the ranks of Kyoto Prefecture's bureaucracy to become the city's second prefectural governor in 1875. Economic development was now coordinated by a prefectural government with almost unlimited authority. French Jacquard machines revolutionized the weaving industry of Nishijin, and the country's first industrial fairs (some held in the partly cleared area of the old imperial court) stimulated new industries and opened new markets. The boundaries of the *chōgumi* districts were redrawn, dividing the city into sixty-six wards. Each ward was ordered to establish a primary school; by the end of 1869, sixty-four schools were already up and running. Various forms of higher education followed soon, making Kyoto a frontrunner in this field.

The rush to modernize came with a disdain for many of the traditions that had been central to the identity of Kyoto's *chō* streets. In the revolutionary mood of these extraordinary times, there was no looking back. A striking example of the rush to sweep the slate clean is the following order, issued in 1872:

> *Many of the people's old practices around Urabon'e [Obon, Jizō-bon] are both nonsensical and harmful. Henceforth such deleterious practices will cease within our district.*
>
> Based on old custom, people celebrate what they call Urabon'e around the fifteenth day of the seventh month. They invite the spirits of the dead (*tamamatsuri*), offer half-ripened fruits and grains to the buddhas, and serve their fellows drinks that soon go putrid. They 'send off the spirits' with fires, creating unnecessary hazards. (. . .) These customs are all based on absurd tales and bastard theories conceived, so to say, out of wedlock. They cause resources to be wasted, squandering the gifts of heaven for empty display. For the benefit of the children who are progressing towards civilization [thanks to the new schools], these practices will now be stopped.[2]

This ordinance sought to put an end to the Jizō-bon festivities in Kyoto's neighbourhoods and also to the *okuribi* fires on the hillsides around the city, including the famous Daimonji fire. While it is unlikely that this and similar orders were successfully enforced, they convey the attitude of the prefectural government towards the 'backward traditions' of Kyoto's streets. Such measures had very real consequences. In the same year, 1872, the streets were ordered to demolish their gates, dismantle the guard houses next to them, clear away the street latrines and rubbish heaps – and, to sanitize the people's customs, remove the small Jizō alters that came into focus during Jizō-bon. While repeated onslaughts of cholera justify the age's obsession with hygiene, these policies also struck at the foundations of street communities by removing their boundaries and dismantling their physical and mental infrastructure.

In spite of such measures, however, Kyoto's *chō* streets proved remarkably resilient. After the conflagration of 1864, Kyoto's narrow streets lined with traditional *machiya* shops and houses were rebuilt much as they had been before. Attempts to widen some streets into modern thoroughfares failed.[3] Compared to other Japanese cities, Kyoto's cityscape changed little in the course of the Meiji period. Wards (*bangumi*, later *gakku* or 'school wards') replaced the previous *chōgumi*, but the streets that made up these wards survived as community units without much change. The streets' meetinghouses continued to serve as centres of street administration and arenas for social interaction. Street aldermen became 'street representatives' (*chō sōdai*), chosen by the streets' house owners from among their number for a year at the time. The stew gatherings of the Edo period were now called 'street meetings' (*chō kaigi*); the new name brought little substantial change. Streets temporarily disappeared from the official structure of city management (from 1874), but they continued to function informally. They regained administrative status in 1897 with the introduction of street-based 'communal associations' (*kōdō kumiai*). These associations, unique to Kyoto, were 'added onto the roof' (in the words of one researcher) of the existing street structures as communication channels between the city authorities and street communities.[4]

In the Meiji years, streets updated their regulations as they were faced with new tasks. Chief among those tasks were the running of ward schools and the improvement of hygiene. As in the Edo period, street regulations continued to put limitations on the freedom of street inhabitants, while at the same time guaranteeing mutual assistance. House owners paid considerable contributions into the streets' coffers. They were expected to attend street meetings and perform street duties; if they absented themselves, the street imposed fines. In return, they received street assistance for weddings and funerals, and could even expect their street to offer them financial aid when their businesses incurred unmanageable debts. Within these close-knit communities one inhabitant's misdemeanour could easily have grave consequences for all, and streets organized communal events and outings to foster street solidarity. It was particularly important to prevent properties from passing into the hands of outsiders who might resist the burdens of communal life. Those who wanted to sell their property had to offer it to their neighbours first, and prospective buyers from elsewhere had to be approved in a street meeting before contracts could be finalized. Renters still had little influence on street affairs, although they were expected to contribute fees and labour within the bounds of their street's regulations.[5]

The power of street elites was gradually curbed by the emergence of a modern legal system, but street regulations retained their grip on social life. The 'communal associations' collected contributions among residents not only for local services (the hygiene committee, school maintenance, the night watch) but also for all kinds of broader agendas: in support of the armed forces (*shōbugikai*), to make street donations to the Ise Shrines, and to add lustre to large-scale celebrations in connection with imperial visits to Kyoto. How such funds were used was not always transparent, and as mobility increased with industrialization, so did pressure on the old system.[6] There were conflicts and reforms. In some streets, renters fought hard battles to be included in street management, while in other places, where there were many sales, residents and absentee landlords lost interest in communal affairs and street events dwindled away. A few streets abolished their communal associations altogether. In general, however, most streets weathered the storm of modernity at least until the end of the Meiji years, and managed to continue functioning as the social fabric that made the survival of an event as large as the Gion festival possible.

A striking example of the strength of street-based identity and pride can be found in the old community of *inu jinin*, who since the early Edo period were settled in Yumiya-chō Street, at the bottom of the slope that leads up to Kiyomizudera. At least in the first half of the Edo period, this was a stigmatized area. From 1668 until 1871, an enclosed colony of lepers with begging rights (Monoyoshi-mura) bordered on Yumiya-chō at its western end. Until the early Edo period, the inhabitants of Yumiya-chō had made their living as producers and peddlers of bows, bowstrings, arrows and leather goods, including monks' shoes and hats. At New Year they made rounds of the city twanging their bows to attract and dispel evil spirits, while chanting the phrase *tsuru meso*, 'please ride (or buy) the bowstring'; for this, they were sometimes called by the denigrating name *tsurumeso*. At some time in the mid-Edo period, however, Yumiya-chō lost its special status. By the turn of the nineteenth century, there were few traces of the bowyers, fletchers and leatherworkers of previous centuries.[7] In the 1870s this street was lined with family-run shops, mostly dealing in everyday necessities, while the backyards were filled with rental shacks. Not a single business in the street dealt in bows, arrows or bowstrings.[8]

Figure 19 The warriors of Yumiya-chō, 1936. Courtesy of the Kyūsenkaku and the Ritsumeikan University Art Research Center.

As we have seen, six *inu jinin* wielding metal rods (*bō no mono*) led the Gion *mikoshi* processions from the sixteenth century onwards. In the 1870s, however, this practice was no longer enforced by the city authorities and became a voluntary 'shrine duty' of Yasaka Shrine. The *zōshiki* watchmen had now been disbanded and the *mikoshi* were no longer a public concern. In these circumstances, the people of Yumiya-chō did not discard this duty but, rather, embraced and found pride in their old connection with the processions. The rod bearers were abandoned, but instead, street members donned helmets and padded cuirasses to impersonate the now-defunct *zōshiki*. The street staged a group of about thirty impressive-looking warriors, led by a 'general' who directed his troops on horseback.[9] In 1931, the inhabitants of Yumiya-chō joined forces to build a stylish new meetinghouse named the Pavilion of Bows and Arrows (Kyūsenkaku), which still stands today. The meetinghouse had its own plastered warehouse, where the helmets, cuirasses and other paraphernalia used in the *mikoshi* processions were kept – as they are to this day. Yumiya-chō is perhaps the best example of a street community that used its role in the Gion festival to build a strong identity, successfully overcoming the stigma that was one attached to the *inu jinin* and *tsurumeso*.

The Gionsha becomes Yasaka Shrine

The survival of street communities was all the more important because the Gion festival suffered a significant loss of status in the first heady years of revolutionary modernization. In the Edo period, the warrior authorities had treated the festival as an official event that honoured both the gods and the rulers. As we have seen, strictly choreographed ceremony underlined the fact that the festival was carried out on orders from the Kyoto governor, who was personally present to inspect the parades. After the Meiji Restoration, however, the festival was 'disestablished'. Not only did it lose its government patronage; it was in serious danger of ending up in the same category as the Jizō-bon: a superstitious, unhygienic and backward practice that was tolerated at best. Was this costly and ideologically dubious festival in tune with the modern need for civilization and enlightenment?

Between 1868 and 1882, the new government actively sought to engage the people in a purified Shinto teaching and practice that would lay the foundation for the new imperial state.[10] In this state, now under the direct rule of an imperial dynasty of divine origins, ritual and government would once more be united. The young emperor would lead the people in ritual worship of the Japanese gods, inspiring sentiments of loyalty and filial piety that would once again unite the people of the realm. These ideas drew on Edo-period teachings that promoted Shinto as Japan's original Way of loyalty and filial piety, pitted against 'foreign' Buddhism and Christianity, which were denounced as teachings that undermined those virtues. Christianity, which threatened to transfer the loyalties of converts to foreign powers, was seen as a particularly grave danger, but especially in the years up to 1872, government policy also had strong anti-Buddhist overtones. The Japanese gods needed to be disentangled from Buddhism so that their shrines could once more serve as sites for the performance of 'imperial state ritual' (*kokka no sōshi*). Most exposed to government interference were institutions and practices that were seen as syncretic 'bastards', defiling both traditions. The mix of ancestor worship, Buddhist street altars and 'unhygienic' consumption at Kyoto's Jizō-bon was a perfect example of the kind of unenlightened superstitions that, in the eyes of the modernizers, held the country back.

One such a 'bastard' institution was the Gionsha. The Gionsha was neither a shrine nor a temple; it was a *miyadera*, a shrine where deities were worshipped by Buddhist priests. As we have seen, the Gionsha was a stand-alone institution that had broken free from Enryakuji in the sixteenth century. Its priests shaved their heads but married and passed on their positions to their sons, so they were neither 'proper' Buddhist monks nor Shinto priests. Its deities, too, were syncretic. Gozu Tennō, for example, was also in the Edo period an important figure in rites related to calendrical taboos, in addition to being closely associated with Yakushi Nyorai, who had his own hall within the Gionsha grounds. The tale about Gozu Tennō's protection of Somin Shōrai and his revenge against Kotan Shōrai in India lacked canonical basis both in the chronicles of the Japanese court and in Buddhist scripture; it was primarily associated with the sale of dubious amulets.

In the eyes of Confucian and Kokugaku ('nativist') scholars, all this cast suspicion over the Gionsha and its deities. Representative of their scepticism was the (retired) Hie Shrine priest and Confucian scholar Umetsuji Shunshō (1776–1857), who wrote 'Expanded notes on the *Detailed record of the Gion Goryōe*' (*Zōho Gion goryōe saiki*, 1820), a comprehensive commentary on one of the most popular guidebooks about the festival.[11] In the opening section on the founding of the Gionsha and its deities, Shunshō notes:

> The Gionsha has three deities, enshrined in three sanctuaries [within its main hall]:
> In the centre: Susanoo no Mikoto.
>> Teiei says:[12] Gozu Tennō is the name of a buddha from India, not the name of a *kami* deity of our country.
> In the east: Hachiōji.
>> Today called Wakamiya. These are the children of Susanoo, three daughters and five sons.
> In the west: [Kushi-]inada-hime.
>> Today called Shōshōi.[13]

Shunshō quotes two passages from the *Nihon shoki* as ancient 'transmissions about the deities' of the Gionsha, while completely ignoring the popular legend about Gozu Tennō and Somin Shōrai. The first passage tells how Susanoo produced three daughters and five sons,[14] and the second relates how Susanoo married Kushi-inada-hime in the land of Izumo. As we saw in Chapter 1, Gozu Tennō was identified with Susanoo already in the thirteenth-century *Shaku Nihongi*. There, Urabe Kanekata cited his father's teaching that the Somin Shōrai episode transmits ancient deeds of this Japanese *kami*. Shunshō did not even mention the passage that Kanekata had used to link Susanoo to Gozu Tennō, and he added the claim that the Hachiōji 'princes' are Susanoo's sons and daughters.

The Susanoo postulate was not merely a pet theory of townsman intellectuals. In 1825, the Kokugaku scholar Hirata Atsutane (1776–1843) published a

'Refutation of the theory that Gozu Tennō is a calendrical deity' (*Gozu Tennō rekishin ben*), likewise arguing that Gozu Tennō is none other than Susanoo.[15] Atsutane's text was countersigned by the Gionsha manager (Edo Tameyuki, 1785–1830) before printing. At the time, Atsutane served as the Edo-based 'scholar-teacher' (*gakushi*) of the Yoshida house, the court family charged with overseeing Shinto affairs. His refutation, then, gave official status to the Susanoo theory already half a century before Meiji.

In the Bakumatsu years, Susanoo's persona was developed in new directions. In his 'Treatise on Gozu Tennō' (*Kanjin'in Gozu Tennō kō*, 1863), Atsutane's student Matsuura Michisuke (1801–66) argued that this deity was brought to Yasaka from Korea, rather than India. In the first years of Meiji, the head priest of the Gionsha, Ki Shigetsugu, endorsed this view in his 'Compilation of Yasaka Shrine's Ancient Records' (*Yasaka-sha kyūki shūroku*, 1870); thereafter it became the new official legend of the Shintoized Gionsha. The new theory identified Gozu Tennō/Susanoo with Korea's mythical first king, Tangun. This connection would later serve as proof of the colonial notion that Japan and Korea share a common ancestry, while associating Japan with the Heavenly Realm of Amaterasu and Korea with the Nether Realm (*ne no kuni*) of Susanoo.[16]

In addition to these new theories, the notion that the Gionsha was in fact a Shinto shrine rested on its inclusion in the system of twenty-two shrines in the eleventh century. In the run-up to the Meiji Restoration the court acted on this classical status, and the Gionsha was rapidly transformed into an imperial shrine with proper Shinto *kami*. At first, this transformation appeared to benefit the shrine. It is worth noting that in 1863, the first predecessor of Tokyo's Yasukuni Shrine (today's Motomiya) was stealthily erected within the precincts of the Gionsha by a group of imperial loyalists from Tsuwano domain. Then, in 1865, the *rinjisai* of classical times was revived, more than four centuries after it had perished in the Ōnin war. A court statement announced that the emperor had decided to restore this ancient rite as a response to 'the barbarians' designs on our Imperial Land'.[17] In the Meiji years, however, policies changed, and as we shall soon see, the *rinjisai* ceased in 1878.

The Shintoization of the Gionsha changed gear in the first year of Meiji, 1868. In the third month a directive from the Council of State banned the use of Buddhist deity names in Shinto shrines, mentioning 'Gozu Tennō' explicitly as an unacceptable example of syncretism. Gion ('Jetavana'), too, was a Buddhist name, and in the fifth month the Gionsha was renamed Yasaka Shrine, after the ancient name of its location. A few weeks earlier orders had arrived to remove all Buddhist statues and ritual objects from Shinto shrines. At the Gionsha, the hall enshrining the Buddhist 'original grounds' of the shrine's deities (*honjidō*) and the bell tower were identified as offensive and soon taken apart, sold off and moved elsewhere. The main image in the *honjidō* was an eleventh-century statue of Yakushi Nyorai, flanked by his customary attendants, two bodhisattvas symbolizing the light of the sun and the moon (Nikkō and Gakkō Bosatsu). These and other Buddhist statues were transferred to the nearby temple Dairenji and remain there to this day.[18] Other Buddhist effects were scattered around the city and beyond. A small statue of Gozu Tennō, for example, was evacuated to Kichimonji-chō, a street in the Lower City, where it has been put on display and worshipped as part of the local Gion festival procedures until recently.[19] Yasaka Shrine was no longer the home of the Medicine Buddha in the guise of an Indian deva-king and his family; it was now the residence of a *kami* household headed by Amaterasu's brother, the (Korean) 'uncle' of the imperial dynasty.

Also in the intercalary fourth month, all shrine monks (*shasō*) were ordered to give up their monastic status, let their hair grow and adopt lay names. The *shigyō* became *shamushoku* ('shrine manager') and took on the lay family name of Takeuchi. The heads of the various cloisters received the title of *shakan*, 'shrine officials' and some adopted the names of their original cloisters as their family names: Take, Nishiume and Higashiume. Lesser positions were found for other groups at the shrine as well, and for a while the reforms were more symbolic than substantial. In 1870 Yasaka Shrine was home to twenty-three households consisting of seventy-three people, thirty-five men and thirty-eight women: the shrine officials, their wives, children, grandparents and even the occasional uncle or aunt. Then, in 1871, the shrine was incorporated in the new hierarchy of national shrines as a *kanpei chūsha* – a 'shrine entitled to state offerings, middle rank'; at the time, there were only thirty-five shrines in this category. This elevated rank implied full nationalization. In the first month of 1872, the old community of hereditary Gionsha shrine monks and lay personnel (including the aforementioned Ki Shigetsugu) were replaced with new staff appointed from Tokyo. The cloisters that they had called their home were pulled down; the garden of the Hōjuin, with its famous weeping cherry trees, was eventually incorporated in Maruyama Park (created in 1886). With this, Yasaka Shrine lost much of its network of relations with the inhabitants of Lower Kyoto, built up by the Gionsha priesthood over centuries.[20]

In the third month of 1872, the Meiji government replaced its Shinto Missionary Office (Senkyōshi) with a joint Shinto-Buddhist Ministry of Edification (Kyōbushō), which launched the so-called Great Promulgation Campaign. This Campaign aimed to install in the population a spirit of 'reverence for the gods', patriotism, moral uprightness and imperial loyalty through a network of 'teaching institutes' (*kyōin*) and 'instructors' (*kyōdōshoku*). Under this system, which existed until 1884, Buddhist temples and Shinto shrines were designated as sites of such popular instruction. In 1873 Yasaka's head priest participated in a large preaching event held at the nearby Chion'in Temple, reportedly addressing a crowd of 2,000 'Yasaka parishioners'. Two years later, Yasaka Shrine established its own 'Minor Teaching Institute' where students received daily lessons; there were also monthly 'lectures' and 'preaching sessions'. Some of the shrine staff who had been dismissed in 1872 served as instructors in this institute.[21]

Linked to the institute was a new 'parishioners' association' called the *Seisei kōsha* or Purity Association. This association was formally authorized by the Ministry of Edification in 1875. The Purity Association sought to enrol family heads within the Yasaka *ujiko* area as its members. Its main goals were listed in a founding manifesto, which starts by pointing out man's dependence on the blessings of the gods, both in this life and after death. The Great Kami of Yasaka, the manifesto states, is none other than the brother of the imperial ancestress Amaterasu, who governs the visible realm of the living. He is also the father of Ōkuninushi, who rules over the invisible realm of gods and spirits.

> Because this Great Kami is closely linked to both the visible and the invisible realm (*ken'yū*), you must have profound faith in him and learn his divine teachings about the principles of life and death. Without erring, you must adhere to the principle of unity of ritual and government by obeying the emperor; embrace the teachings of this association; and advance the prosperity of both the state and your own household by exerting yourself in your family occupation.[22]

Members pledged to abide by the doctrines taught in the Great Promulgation Campaign, stay away from 'pernicious teachings' (i.e. Christianity) and partake in the association's rites in spring and autumn. Members were also encouraged to adopt Shinto funerals.

By the mid-1870s, then, Yasaka Shrine had become a very different place from the old Gionsha. It was now a site where the Meiji state propagated modern civil values through entirely new forms of ritual and teaching. The old gods had gone, as had the old shrine monks. The Buddhist rituals that had dominated the Gionsha's calendar had been exchanged for imperial ceremonies adapted from the *Engi shiki* (Procedures of the Engi period, 927) or fashioned anew: *kinensai* in spring and *niiname-sai* in autumn, both addressing Amaterasu to pray or say thanks for the harvest; *genshisai* in early January, in celebration of the origins of the imperial line; and *kigensetsu* in February, commemorating the reign of the first emperor of that line, the legendary Jinmu. It was these classical and modern imperial rites that occasioned the dispatch of offerings from public coffers. The Bakumatsu revival of the Gionè *rinjisai* was at odds with this new focus on strictly imperial ritual, and as we saw, it was soon demoted and abolished. The offensively named Gionè itself was henceforth referred to as the 'private festival of Yasaka' (*Yasaka shisai*). The Gion festival, with its eclectic mix of deities, actors and fringe events, was now on its own.

Festival reforms

In the meantime the festival was gradually recovering from the heavy blow it had suffered in the inferno of 1864. Even in the few streets where the floats had survived, most of the houses, shops and workshops had not, and for years it was impossible to stage a proper parade. In 1865, the first parade on the seventh had to be cancelled. The second, on the fourteenth, had only two *yama* and one 'chest' (*karahitsu*), which served as a statement marking the street's resolve to restore its float. Such chests became a dominant feature of the parades in the following decade: the first parade of 1866 consisted of three *yama* and twenty chests. The *hoko*, in particular, took a long time to rebuild. Kanko-hoko returned in 1869; Naginata-hoko, Tsuki-hoko and Niwatori-hoko in 1870; and Hōka-hoko in 1872. A few floats, including Kikusui-hoko and Tōrō-yama, were not revived until the post-war period. Yet, progress was being made. In 1871 the Gion pageant was also restarted. The festival was now set to regain some of its former glory.[23]

In those same years, however, many of the political and social structures that had supported the festival in the Edo period had either faded away or been actively discontinued by the new government. After the 1864 fire many of the 'attendant streets' (*yorichō*) demanded reductions or simply stopped paying their annual *jinokuchi-mai* contributions. The *zōshiki* watchmen were abolished in the first month of 1868. Although the new government took over some of their more practical functions, the richly ritualized presence of the city authorities in many parts of the festival disappeared with these watchmen. At the same time, the Gionsha was rapidly converted into an institution that appeared more distant from people's lives, and that even seemed to disapprove of many aspects of the 'private' festival. The streets, moreover, were reorganized into new wards whose most arduous task in these years was the founding and running of primary schools. Setting aside resources for the ailing Gion festival was not always a priority for ward officials.

The brewing crisis came to a head in 1872. In that year, as we have just seen, the old Gionsha priesthood was replaced by a much smaller team of new appointees. This created an unexpected problem. For a number of years prior to this, the responsibility for carrying the *mikoshi* had been transferred to a group of low-ranking employees (*shinjin*) of Yasaka Shrine, relieving – or depriving – the villagers of Imamiya (now renamed Naniwa Village) and the *mikoshi* streets spread around Kyoto of this task. In 1872, however, the *shinjin* bearers were dismissed together with the rest of the old Gionsha staff. No arrangements were made to replace them. Even as summer was approaching, it remained unclear who was to organize bearers for the *mikoshi* processions.

Tsuchida Sakubei (1822–99) was a central member of the Tsuki-hoko float who served as vice administrator of a ward that included ten float streets, today known as the Seitoku school ward.[24] In 1872, he stood up as one of the main initiators of bottom-up reforms, triggered by the sudden lack of *mikoshi* bearers. His personal account (*shuki*) of the process that made this possible is our main source on these reforms.[25] Tsuchida set out by summing up the problems that were threatening to plunge the festival of 1872 into chaos. The *mikoshi* streets were no longer functioning, and now the shrine's *shinjin* bearers had been dismissed. The Naniwa villagers had petitioned to be allowed to resume their practice of carrying the Ōmiya *mikoshi*, but as residents of a different prefecture they had not succeeded in gaining the ear of the Kyoto Prefectural Office. Speaking to elders of the old *mikoshi* streets, it became clear to Tsuchida that no one had a plan. In addition, Tsuchida was not at all confident that the floats could even be set up, now that the *yorichō* system had collapsed. Yet, he wrote, 'if this unrivalled festival were to wither away, people will no longer flood into Kyoto to see it. If that happens, the *ujiko* area, the entire city, and even the surrounding villages will lose their vigour'.

Tsuchida decided to push forward with a novel idea. Rather than trying to restore the outdated *yorichō* system, he argued, it would be more reasonable and sustainable over time to spread the costs among all the streets within Yasaka Shrine's *ujiko* area. After several meetings with ward administrators and labour-intensive lobbying in each and every one of the streets, his plan was finally adopted in the final days of the fifth month. The total costs of the festival were estimated at about 500 yen, in the new currency that had been introduced only a year earlier. The 435 streets in the *ujiko* area were found willing to contribute one yen each. Every year, two wards would serve as 'festival organizers' (*shinji tōban*); the streets promised to deliver their contributions at the primary schools of those wards by the twentieth day of the fifth month. The collected funds would then be distributed among the *mikoshi* organizers and the floats. If a float street felt that its float was in danger, the street leaders were obliged to take up the matter with the wards of the Yasaka *ujiko* area, or at least with their own ward. On the understanding that the parades were of essential importance to the city's 'vigour', some form of financial aid would then be considered. Days before the beginning of the festival, a formal petition from the assembled ward officials was issued to Kyoto's Prefectural Office and promptly approved, making the new arrangements binding.

The immediate problem of organizing bearers for the *mikoshi* was solved by hiring them through channels established in the Edo period. Young men from Sanjōdai Village, located a few streets south of the Nijōjō Palace, had supplied the *mikoshi* streets with ready-made teams of bearers already in the eighteenth century. This group had established its own meetinghouse in 1832, marking its development into a professional agency that not only dispatched local youth but also recruited workers from elsewhere.[26] Initially these were mostly tenants who worked lands owned by the agency's leaders; later these tenants were gradually replaced by longshoremen (*hamanakashi*) from the Saga area along the Katsura River. In 1872, the 'young men of Sanjōdai' (*Sanjōdai wakashū*, or *Sanwaka-gumi*) stepped in and took responsibility for all three *mikoshi*. A few years later, responsibility for the Shōshōi *mikoshi* was delegated to a similar group of workers from the lumberyards of Kiyamachi along the Takasegawa River. This group became known as the *Shiwaka-gumi*, named after Shijō Street.[27]

The success of Tsuchida's initiative shows that in spite of the relentless onslaught of modernizing reforms, the *chō* streets remained a strong feature of Kyoto life. The new system of street contributions was rooted in older networks. It was an initiative of the old class of street aldermen, conceived and implemented without any involvement of Yasaka Shrine or the Kyoto Prefectural Office other than the granting of post facto permission. It was a creative way to preserve the festival in a modern setting by building on the social structures of the Edo period.

It was perhaps a logical outcome that this system was soon absorbed into an institution with more solidly modern foundations: Yasaka Shrine's Purity Association. As we saw earlier, the 'private festival of Yasaka' did not originally feature on the official ritual agenda of the Purity Association. Yet the system of designating two streets as 'festival organizers' soon ceased, and instead, the streets took their contributions to the headquarters of the Purity Association within the grounds of Yasaka Shrine. Perhaps this change occurred already in 1875; we cannot be sure because the earliest preserved accounts of the Purity Association date to the mid-1880s.[28] By that time, the annual contributions from and subsidies (*hozonkin*) to the float streets had already become the largest post on the Purity Association's budget. In 1894, membership of this association was made obligatory for 'all residents of the *ujiko* area of Yasaka Shrine', and membership fees took on the character of a local tax.[29]

Although the Purity Association also gave some support to the *mikoshi*, the main recipients of its subsidies were the float streets. In these streets, the floats were communal street property, like the street meetinghouses; as such, their maintenance was the shared responsibility of all house owners. Staging a float was a source of pride but also a relentless burden. As had been the case with the *jinokuchi-mai* of the Edo period, the subsidies from the Purity Association covered only a fraction of the costs of maintaining and parading the floats, leaving two thirds or even three quarters of the bill to be covered by the residents of the float streets themselves.[30] Analysing the 1911 accounts of Hashi Benkei-yama, Satō Hirotaka finds that the 30 yen contributed by the Purity Association covered about a third of the expenses (86.40 yen). The rest was covered by a modest 'candle charge' paid by all house owners; much more substantial 'sake offerings' (*omikiryō*), partly supplied in kind and partly paid in cash by individual house owners based on their status; and fines from absentees. Ex-residents and even family members living elsewhere also donated money as sake offerings. Yet even after all this, there remained a deficit of 9.05 yen. Income from renting out rooms in the street meetinghouse was the most common way to cover such deficits; but some streets were forced to take up loans.[31]

Duties related to the Gion festival were spelled out in the modern street regulations of float streets. In Tenjin-yama Street, for example, articles 16 through 20 of the 1890 street regulations dealt with this matter. This street had its own association (*Tenjin-yama hozon tsumitate kō*) dedicated to the preservation of its float, Arare Tenjin-yama. The task of overseeing the finances of this association rotated among house owners. Contributions were determined by property size. While most matters were run by the house owners, two persons from the group of renters were responsible for the lanterns that lighted up the float and the meetinghouse during the festival period; this bill was footed by 'lantern contributions' collected from the street's renters. All residents, including the renters, were obliged to participate in the setting up and decoration of the float and to accompany the float in formal dress during the parade.[32]

In the late Meiji period, many streets suffered the kind of financial difficulties that Tsuchida had already foreseen. Particularly hard hit were streets that in the past had relied more heavily on income from *yorichō*, but that now had to make do with the same subsidies from the Purity Association as others in their category. In 1888, Niwatori-hoko's street announced that a debt of more than 8,000 yen left it no other choice but to sell its common property: the meetinghouse, the float and the float's decorations. Last-minute financial assistance from the Purity Association avoided this dramatic outcome. The Purity Association 'bought' the meetinghouse and the float, and the street members returned the money over the course of sixteen years. Tsuchida's own float, Tsuki-hoko, had a similar debt of about 10,000 yen, partly caused by expensive repairs. In 1889 the float's debtors announced their intention to take the matter to court. The 68 yen that this float received in subsidies counted for little in this situation. Following Niwatori-hoko's example, the float street appealed to the leadership of the Purity Association for help. In their appeal, the street representatives gave many reasons why their cause was worthy of support:

> Originally, our float joined the parade as a means to appease the gods of Yasaka Shrine. If we must liquidate it now for the sake of our debtors, it will be hard to know how the *kami* will react. Also, such a measure will surely affect the vigour of this city. Treasures that are unique in our country and celebrated for their beauty even in foreign lands will be scattered. Such a result will sadden not only our small group, but all the citizens of Kyoto. What is more, it will draw a sigh of despair both from the imperial dynasty and from the people of our country.[33]

Tsuki-hoko's appeal plays on all registers: the float's bankruptcy would anger the gods, damage the economic well-being of the city, lead to the loss of artworks that enjoy global fame and insult the honour of emperor and nation. This document is of interest because it puts words to the modern value and significance not only of this particular float but of the entire festival. Speaking to the Purity Association, naturally the gods must come first; but after this, the argument becomes more secular in tone. As in Tsuchiya's 1872 appeal, the economic effects on the city as a whole are underlined. The reference to the imperial house was credible because members of collateral branches of the imperial family (Fushimi-no-miya, Kuni-no-miya, Arisugawa-no-miya) viewed the first parade in 1880, 1881, 1883 and 1888.[34] In addition, the Tsuki-hoko float and, by implication, the festival as a whole are here presented as a flagship of Japanese culture, 'celebrated even in foreign lands'. The festival was entering a new context of nation states, competing not only for spheres of economic and military dominance but also for cultural repute.

No doubt partly thanks to Tsuchida, who sat on the board of the Purity Association, the situation was defused. Yet it took Tsuki-hoko's street until 1905 to clear its debt. This street was in good company: other floats, too, were accumulating debts.[35] Matters came to a head when nine of the largest floats refused to participate in the 1894 parade unless subsidies from the Purity

Association were raised. Again a compromise was reached at the last minute, but the financial situation of many float streets remained strained.

The emperor and the city tram

In 1877 Emperor Meiji was back in Kyoto. The occasion was the tenth anniversary of the death of his father, Emperor Kōmei (1831–67), whose mausoleum lies in Kyoto. The outbreak of the Satsuma rebellion (January–September 1877) caused the emperor's stay in Kyoto to be extended to all of six months. In those six months he visited both sites of modernity (schools, factories, courthouses, exhibitions) and places that pointed back at the country's and the dynasty's ancient roots: the mausoleum of Emperor Jinmu and the newly refurbished Shōsōin Repository of Imperial Treasures in Nara, the Byōdōin in Uji and the Kamo Shrines in Kyoto. Not all was well, however. The emperor found the palace in a dilapidated state, surrounded by empty plots where shrubs and weeds had replaced the old villas of the nobility. Takagi Hiroshi argues that this lengthy imperial sojourn in Kyoto served as 'the prompt for a new recognition of the value of Kyoto's history and traditions'.[36]

The 1877 progress laid the foundation for a new policy to develop Kyoto not only as a modern hub of manufacturing and Western-style education but also as Japan's ancient cultural and ceremonial capital. At the initiative of Iwakura Tomomi (1825–83), the nobleman-turned-oligarch who had led the Iwakura mission to the United States and Europe (1871–3), Kyoto Prefecture returned the old palace grounds to the Imperial Household in 1883. Refurbishment of the site as a stage for national ceremonies began in the same year.[37] This was a time when European monarchies sought to outdo each other with displays of national-romantic pomp. It struck Japanese diplomats that tradition was an integral element of modernity, and there was a rising awareness that Japan too needed to invest in such matters. In this scheme of things, there was a place for Kyoto as the cultural capital of the new nation. The cornerstone of this new identity was a proposal, presented by Iwakura, to move the most important imperial ceremonies (the accession ceremonies of *sokui* and *daijōsai*, and imperial marriages) back to Kyoto;[38] the 1871 *daijōsai* of Emperor Meiji had taken place in Tokyo. Iwakura's plan turned Kyoto into a capital once again, albeit for rare ceremonial purposes only. His model was czarist Russia, where Moscow played a similar role while Saint Petersburg served as the practical seat of government.[39] The accession ceremonies of the Taishō and Shōwa emperors (in 1915 and 1928) were indeed held in Kyoto. They served as milestones in Kyoto's modern history, triggering both cultural initiatives and infrastructural construction projects.[40]

What was the place of the Gion festival in this new environment? It was certainly nowhere near the top of the list of new imperial projects. In his 1883 proposal, Iwakura had expressed his regret at the demise of the parade that had once been the highlight of the Kamo (Aoi) festival. Whereas in the past, this parade had been a splendorous event that attracted visitors from near and far, the modern rite that had replaced it was a simple, standard affair of no interest to outsiders. He also argued for a revival of the imperial rites at Iwashimizu Hachimangū (*rinjisai*, *hōjōe*) and various annual court ceremonies at the palace itself. Finally, he proposed to build a new 'Heian Shrine' (*Heian jingū*) within the palace area in honour of Emperor Kanmu, the founder of ancient Kyoto, and all subsequent Kyoto emperors.[41] No other shrines or temples are mentioned in the proposal.

In spite of Iwakura's death that same summer, his plan carried weight. The Kamo festival parade was promptly resuscitated in grand style already in the following year (1884). The day of the parade (15 May) was declared an official holiday, and it soon grew into one of the largest crowd-drawing events of the city.[42] In that same year, the *hōjōe* was revived as an imperially sponsored ritual at Iwashimizu Hachimangū, now with the non-Buddhist name of the 'Iwashimizu festival' (*Iwashimizu-sai*). Heian Shrine took longer to realize. It was inaugurated in 1895 in its present location in the form of a replica of a part of the classical Imperial Palace.[43] This new shrine celebrated Kyoto's thousand-year anniversary, added cachet to Japan's Fourth National Industrial Exhibition held on a neighbouring site, and also happened to coincide with Japan's victory in the Sino-Japanese war (1894–5). The highlight of the inauguration was an entirely new festival called the 'festival of the ages' (*jidai matsuri*). A historical pageant of 800 men made its way from Kyoto City Hall to the new shrine, where the participants offered prayers to the newly enshrined Kanmu before turning back. This pageant, featuring hundreds of meticulously designed historical costumes, surveyed 'a millennium of history retold as an unbroken sequence of loyal acts' in the name of an equally unbroken imperial dynasty.[44]

The 1877 imperial progress and Iwakura's 1883 proposal did not turn the tide of modernization, but they gave the city an additional, unique dimension: as the realm's repository of imperial history and tradition. Yasaka Shrine and its 'private festival' were not part of Iwakura's plans because they did not belong to the inner sphere of imperial culture. This is not to say that the city authorities were oblivious to the festival. Already in 1876, curators of Kyoto's first museum (called simply Hakubutsukan, 'The Museum'), which had been founded a year earlier within the palace grounds, carried out a survey of all float streets. When Kyoto's first railway station was opened in February 1877 in the presence of the emperor and foreign diplomats, the foreign visitors were invited to an exhibition of tapestries from Naganata-hoko and Hōshō-yama. In 1888, the float streets hosted the art historian Ernest Fenollosa (1853–1908), then director of Tokyo's Imperial Museum, and Kuki Ryūichi (1852–1931), a politician and diplomat who at the time served as the president of a 'national survey of treasures'. Clearly, the paraphernalia of the festival already enjoyed public recognition as precious artworks that added to Japan's cultural prestige.

The Gion festival itself, however, retained its ambiguous status as a 'private' affair – as did most other city festivals. The gods in the *mikoshi* had been Shintoized, but from the viewpoint of Shinto orthodoxy, the festival floats remained a mess. They could be fitted into the narrative of Japanese civilization as a cultural display but not as an expression of legitimate Shinto ritual. By keeping the festival 'private', it was shielded from pressure to reform in accordance with its new Shinto status; but on the other hand, this cut the festival off from public support. The sudden abolition of traditional arrangements of *mikoshi* bearers and the financial crises of multiple floats were matters of no concern for the authorities. Yet, the fact remained that the festival contributed to the city economy by attracting large numbers of visitors to Kyoto. In tacit recognition of this fact, a 1907 guidebook to 'Kyoto's attractions' published by the Kyoto City Office (with English text!) advertised the 'Aoi Festival of the Kamo Temples', the 'Heianjingu Festival' and the 'Gion Festival' as the city's 'Three Great Festivals' (*san dai-matsuri*).[45]

The floats and the tram

The festival's struggle for public space in the modern city came to a head in 1912. Kyoto's infrastructure was finally brought up-to-date after the end of the Russo-Japanese war in 1905; one key element of the modernization programme was the enlargement of key roads and the construction of tramlines. As in many other Japanese cities, these years also saw the appearance of electrical and telephone lines, hung from poles placed in the middle of the road. These trappings of modernity presented physical barriers for the towering festival floats of many urban festivals. This was the case also in Kyoto. In 1912, Kyoto celebrated the completion of 'Three Great Ventures' (*san dai-jigyō*) that would bring the city into the modern age: a water tunnel from Lake Biwa to Kyoto, a new system of water supply within the city and the broadening of main thoroughfares, including the opening of municipal tramlines. In the midst of these festivities, the leading Kyoto newspaper *Hinode shinbun* (later renamed *Kyōto shinbun*) reported that 'Kyoto Prefectural Office will not permit a temporary suspension of tram traffic and bans the parade of floats' (11 June 1912).

Hinode shinbun announced its opposition to this plan in a long article on its front page, titled 'The Gion'e in Crisis'. Although it is reasonable to give weight to public transportation, the newspaper contended, the Prefectural Office's stand on this matter is stubborn beyond reason. While not all 'old things' (*furuki mono*) deserve our respect, human nature naturally values at least some old things more than new things. The Gion festival is known as one of Kyoto's Three Great Festivals, and its fame is so great that it attracts not only citizens of Kyoto but even foreigners. Its main attraction lies in the float parades, whose 'artistic glory' is acknowledged in the Orient as well as the Occident.

> Police! Stop denigrating the Gion'e as 'childish tomfoolery' (*jigi*)! Lay aside the arrogant argument that city transportation cannot be stopped for the sake of 'tomfoolery'! With this kind of reasoning, *all* human affairs are mere tomfoolery. (. . .) The Gion'e is a form of social play (*shakaiteki yūgi*). One cannot understand the essence of human affairs, the true meaning of society, without appreciating the importance of social play. If we were to take away social play from human beings, claiming that it is 'useless', people would no longer be able to face the melancholy of everyday life, and all 'useful' human affairs would suffer as a result.

The newspaper refers to suggestions that the parade might be replaced by a 'sitting exhibition' (*imatsuri*) and protests that such a solution would please no one. In fact, it reports, some float streets are arguing that if the parade were to be banned, it would be best to abandon the whole enterprise, keep the floats safely locked away in their storehouses and save a lot of money in that manner. This would surely mean the end of the entire festival – all for the sake of a few hours of tram traffic.

On the next day (12 June), the newspaper interviewed Tanaka Yohei of the Purity Association. If the Prefecture were to ban the parades, Tanaka stated, the floats would become useless for ever. In that case there will be a need to determine who 'owns' the floats, so that they can be sold. The float treasures might be transferred to a museum, or they might simply be liquidated. The money could then be put to good use in various ways. It might serve as a preservation fund of Yasaka Shrine; or it could be shared and distributed among the *ujiko*. It would suffice to pay for a good portion of the city's Three Great Ventures. While there is a note of angry sarcasm to this article, the collective determination of the float streets not to agree to a sitting exhibition was real.

Meanwhile, the head of the Prefectural Police assured the newspaper that it was technically impossible to remove electricity lines for the duration of the parades (13 June). This is a structural problem that will not go away, and it will force the festival to yield sooner or later. Perhaps the floats might be kept in storage near Yasaka Shrine and be assembled in Maruyama Park for visitors to admire at their ease. 'In the end', the head of police said, 'what is more important, public transportation or festival bedlam (*omatsuri sawagi*)?' He pointed at Tokyo, where many festivals had shown flexibility in adapting to the appearance of tramways; perhaps he was thinking of the Kanda and Sannō festivals, which had already given up their soaring floats by this time due to the proliferation of electricity, telegraph and telephone lines. In Kyoto, too, the advent of modern infrastructure would necessitate changes in the interest of progress.

Meanwhile, Tanaka of the Purity Association urged the members of Kyoto's Chamber of Commerce and Industry to support the protests against the ban, arguing that the demise of the festival would do untold damage to the business of inn-keepers, retailers and textile merchants. To put pressure on the prefectural governor, it was decided that the shrine visit of the *chigo* on 1 July, which was the first highlight of the festival, would be cancelled. Work started to lobby among members of the City and Prefectural Assemblies and to prepare a broad-based petition to the Prefectural Office.

In the following days, *Hinode shinbun* published a variety of pieces in support of the parades. These pieces are of interest because they put new ideas about the value of the festival into words. Ichimura Mitsue (1875–1928), a professor of law at Kyoto Imperial University,[46] pointed out that surely no one would ever consider visiting Kyoto in the oppressive heat of summer if it were not for the Gion festival. The demise of the festival, therefore, would spell the demise of Kyoto itself (14 June). He mocked the short-sightedness of bureaucrats who failed to see that tradition is an essential ingredient of modernity. In Munich, he pointed out, trams were routinely stopped to allow the Carnival parade to take over the streets. Westerners (*seiyōjin*) would certainly deride the provincialism of Kyoto's administrators.

Next (16 June) was another professor from the same university, the historian Miura Hiroyuki (1871–1931). Miura gave the festival a historical significance that fitted the age:

> When the Tokugawa era closed the Japan's borders, even the dauntless Japanese were confined to their own country. Before that era, however, in the age of Warring States, the Japanese race sought progress across the sea, and many engaged in free trade. The *yama* and *hoko* floats are decked out with materials that were imported and exported in that age, and they tell us about the heroic exploits of that time. The rhythms of Gion's *hayashi* music are like an alarm clock that wakes up our slumbering nation. We must not underestimate the educative impact that it has on the people.

By 1912, Japan had acquired a colonial empire that included Taiwan, Korea and southern Sakhalin. The Gion floats, decorated with Chinese, Korean and even Persian and European tapestries, served to remind the nation of the fact that before the unfortunate slumber of the Edo period, the Japanese had not hesitated to pursue their interests on the world stage. Together with the Aoi festival, which symbolized classical imperial rule in the Nara and Heian periods, the Gion festival now found its place in the national historical narrative as an expression of Japan's medieval vitality and boldness.

In the end, formal petitions submitted to the Kyoto mayor by the Purity Association, Yasaka Shrine and the Chamber of Commerce and Industry turned the tide. None other than Kyoto's first mayor, Naiki Jinzaburō (1848–1926, in office 1898–1904) agreed to submit the petition as the representative of Yasaka's parishioners (19 June). The current mayor and the prefectural governor now agreed that it had all been a misunderstanding. They diverted the blame to the engineers who had given the impression that removing electricity lines was 'technically impossible' rather than merely 'bothersome' (21 June). One day later the newspaper announced that the problem had been solved. The parade would be carried out as usual, and a committee of experts would advise the governor on the best way to ensure that the Gion festival would be preserved 'in all eternity' (22 June).

On 18 July, *Hinode shinbun* offered a long and colourful account of the parade of the seventeenth, which had attracted unprecedented crowds. Special mention was made of the presence of Prince Kuni-no-miya Kuniyoshi and a number of foreign dignitaries, including a London professor, a nephew of the Chilean ambassador, an educator from New York, a merchant from Berlin and more 'gentlemen' from the United States. These foreigners all impressed on

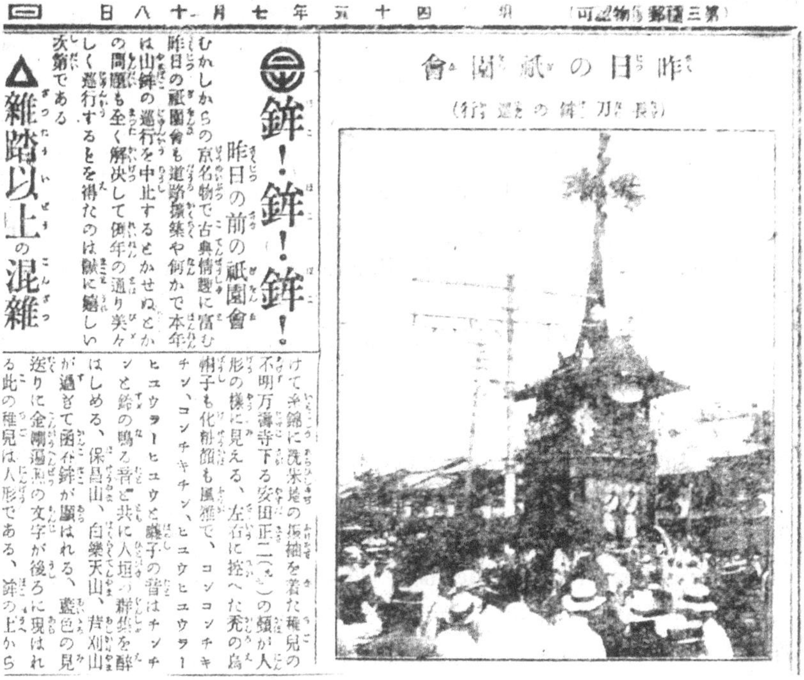

鉾！鉾！鉾！

昨日の前の祇園會

むかしからの京名物で古典情趣に富む昨日の祇園會も道路擴築や何かで本年は山鉾の巡行を中止するとかせぬとかの問題も全く解決して例年の通り美々しく巡行するを得たのは誠に嬉しい次第である

△雑踏以上の混雑

けて糸錦に洗朱地の振袖を着た稚兒の不明万壽寺下る安田正二（　）の顔が人形の様に見える、左右に控へた禿の烏帽子も化粧顔も風雅で、コンコンチキチン、コンチキチン、ヒユウヒユウラーヒユウと囃子の音はチンチンと鈴の鳴る音と共に人垣の群集を酔はしめる、保昌山、白樂天山、芦刈山が過ぎて函谷鉾が顯はれる、藍色の見送りに金剛遍照の文字が後ろに現はれる此の稚兒は人形である、鉾の上から

Figure 20 *Hinode shibun*, 18 July 1912: Celebrating the victory of the float parade. The photo shows the Naginata-hoko. The headings on the left read '*Hoko! Hoko! Hoko!*' and 'Crowded beyond jam-packed'.

the reporter that the floats were renowned monuments of Kyoto's history that should be preserved for ever. 'Truly', the newspaper concluded in large type, 'the excitement of these foreigners upon seeing the parade of floats, which they praise as one of the most famous sights of Japan, is beyond the bounds of our imagination as natives of this country.' Their praise, of course, further underlined the festival's value. The float parade on the twenty-fourth, however, was cancelled due to a critical deterioration of Emperor Meiji's health; the emperor died a week later, on the thirtieth.

Arguably, the successful 1912 campaign to save the Gion festival marked the end of its discursive exile from public life. Within two weeks' time, the festival went from being an impediment to modernization to a priceless monument of Japanese civilization. The festival retained its official status as a private event, but by agreeing to stop the tram and disconnect the electricity lines along the parade route, the city and prefectural authorities had now officially acknowledged its right to occupy public space in the modern city of Kyoto. The festival won that right for two reasons: its economic value for the city and prefecture of Kyoto, and its artistic and historic value for the Japanese nation.

Strikingly, in this campaign there was not a single gesture towards the possible religious or spiritual value of the festival. Rather than as an expression of faith or reverence, it was characterized as an occasion for 'social play'. The 'private festival' kept its distance from the discourse of public Shinto, in spite of the prominence of that discourse at Yasaka Shrine and within the Purity Association. This meant that the festival was exempt from the systematic Shintoization that had taken place at the shrine, and yet escaped condemnation as vulgar superstition. The shrine and the festival drifted into two diverging narratives of value: the shrine as a ceremonial stage for imperial rites of loyalty and filial piety, and the festival as a flamboyant display of national art and culture.

In 1916 Yasaka Shrine was promoted to the elite status of *kanpei taisha*, a 'shrine entitled to state offerings, highest rank'. The solemn rites led by imperial envoys were covered in much detail in *Hinode shinbun* (2 and 3 May). The newspaper also featured a page-long piece arguing that although shrine worship is a patriotic duty that transcends personal religious beliefs, this does not mean that Shinto is not a religion: 'This Land of the Gods is a suzerain state in the world, and Shinto is a religion in the world; therefore, the shrine system is the religious system of our nation.'[47] The Gion festival is not mentioned with a single word in connection with the shrine's promotion, confirming the distance between the private festival and public Shinto. Vice versa, Yasaka Shrine's new status was not part of the narrative in the extensive coverage of the Gion festival two months later. Reporting on the first parade, a reporter writes (18 July): 'Of course, the trams were stopped on Shijō Street. Thanks to the float parade, for just one day, material civilization was wrestled to the ground by outdated custom (*inshū*). This is the true value and pride of the Gion'e.' In this newspaper's reporting, the contrast between shrine worship as a modern practice and the festival as a temporary relief from modernity is palpable.

Public subsidies

In the meantime, the financial situation of the float streets continued to deteriorate. Kanko-hoko, in particular, was in need of extensive repairs, but did not have the means. In December 1922, leaders of this float reached the conclusion that the contributions of the Purity Association were no longer sufficient; only additional public subsidies from Kyoto City could secure the floats' survival. At the initiative of Shimizu Ryōsuke of the Fune-hoko, representatives of the nine *hoko* drew up a petition, notified the Purity Association and submitted their request to Kyoto City. The *hoko* leaders pledged that until some solution was found, they would collectively refuse to set up their floats. In the petition they pointed out that contributions from the Purity Association covered only half of the total festival costs (5,000 out of 10,000 yen). To make matters worse, many of the festival's nine *hoko* and twenty-nine *yama* were in need of major repairs that street inhabitants were unable to cover. 'If this classical event of unrivalled beauty were to break down, the gloom of summer in this city will not bear imagining. This would put an end to the festival's great contribution to the prosperity of this city and the preservation of ancient art.'[48] Annual subsidies of 500 yen per *hoko* and 100 yen per *yama* would be sufficient to prevent such an outcome.

Four decades had passed since the last wave of financial trouble in the 1880s. Clearly, the structural problems that had caused that earlier crisis had not been resolved. A likely reason behind this new impasse was the increasing mobility of residents in the float streets. The historical geographer Satō Hirotaka has mapped sales of properties in the float streets between 1888 and 1940, using public records. He found that between 1888 and 1912, 61 per cent of properties had changed hands. This trend continued after 1912. In the course of the period 1912–40, 68 per cent of properties were sold.[49] About half of the new owners lived elsewhere and were not fully part of community life. In the first half of this period, Shijō and Karasuma Streets were widened as part of the Three Great Ventures project. This affected many properties negatively, leading to a wave of sales. This is the area where most large *hoko* floats are based. Keeping costly street traditions going under these circumstances was a difficult task.

With the 1912 crisis fresh in everyone's memory, the 1922 petition found the sympathy of the city administration. From 1923 onwards Kyoto City supported the floats annually with 200 (rather than the requested 500) yen per *hoko* and 100 yen per *yama* for repairs (*shūzenhi*). This subsidy was channelled through a new coordinating body, the Gion Festival Floats Association (*Gion'e yamahoko rengōkai*), which was run from Shimizu's modest home in the Fune-hoko street. Most of this money was deposited in a bank account; its payment ceased in 1944. In the meantime, however, the Floats Association had successfully appealed for a new subsidy to 'encourage the organization of events during the Yasaka private festival' (*gyōji shōreihi hojokin* or *shisai shōreikin*). Disbursement of this subsidy began in 1939. At a total of 2,000 yen, it covered about a tenth of festival costs for the float streets. The float streets also received about 7,000 yen from the

Purity Association; taken together, these contributions paid for almost half of the festival's expenses.[50]

This new willingness to support the festival shows that in the course of a few decades, the attitude of both Kyoto City and Kyoto Prefecture had changed radically. The float parades, once seen as an impediment to modernization, were once again a matter of public concern, supported with tax money. The main motivation behind this support was the increasing importance of tourism. The years 1915 and 1928 brought huge crowds to Kyoto when the city hosted the *daijōsai* enthronement ceremonies of the Taishō and Shōwa emperors. The new identity of Kyoto as the hub of imperial culture, first envisioned by Iwakura Tomomi in 1883, was now played out in real life, with overwhelming success. In preparation for the 1928 'Grand Ceremony' (*gotaiten*), Kyoto City set up its first Tourist Information Office in front of Kyoto station (in 1927). In 1930, when the visitor boom was fading away, Kyoto became the first Japanese city to establish a Tourism Division (*Kankōka*). The Gion festival emerged as one of the main touristic events on the annual calendar of this office. By the late 1930s, the Tourism Division produced thousands of posters and pamphlets about Kyoto events, including the Gion festival, in Japanese and English to attract visitors from near and far. In a booklet about the Division's activities, the Floats Association is mentioned as one of its partner institutions.[51]

As the main touristic 'events' (*gyōji*) of Kyoto, the Tourism Division listed 'Four Great Festivals', adding to the established three a recent 'Dyeing festival' (*senshokusai*) that included a pageant of 'ladies' (*fujin*) dressed in exquisite costumes 'in the manner of the beautiful girls of this city's amusement establishments'.[52] The others were the Aoi and Gion festivals and Heian Jingū's 'festival of the ages'. The Division described the Gion festival as Kyoto's 'most colourful' event, 'luxurious and extravagant (*gōka kenran*) beyond compare'.[53] Besides these four 'greats', the Division highlighted the Daimonji fire of Urabon'e (the same rites that were banned in 1872), and public dance performances by the assembled *geiko* (geishas) of Gion, called *miyako odori* and *Kamogawa odori*. It is no coincidence that the Gion pageant was briefly revived as a showcase of *miyako odori* in these same years – although in the end, it was actually performed only once, in 1936.[54]

The Gion festival, in short, became part of the city's agenda to promote tourism in the 1930s. In that context the festival functioned as a spectacle of the same nature as geisha dance shows and pageants paying tribute to Kyoto's history and industry. The festival became part of Kyoto's profile as a 'city of tourism', characterized by its rich 'history, spiritual culture, arts and crafts, and overall beauty'.[55] In this context, the main events of the Gion festival were the two parades and the Gion pageant. The Tourism Division followed the general trend of separating the festival from both shrine and Shinto and propagating it to a broad audience as a grand show of historical and artistic culture. This was also the narrative that legitimized the allocation of public subsidies. Aspects of the festival that were not related to tourism were excluded from such subsidies; this included the *mikoshi* processions.

For the shrine streets, the introduction of these subsidies necessitated new arrangements to ensure that bureaucratic requirements were fulfilled. In the 1920s and 1930s, three floats formed preservation associations (*hozonkai*), with formalized boards, statutes and a new juridical framework.[56] The twenty-eight float streets paid an annual membership fee of 10 yen each to the Floats Association, which was divided into of a *hoko* and a *yama* group. From its beginning in 1923 until the end of 1948, this association was run singlehandedly by Shimizu Ryōsuke, who was also the coordinator of the *hoko* group. Shimizu took care of all the negotiations and paperwork in the Floats Association's dealings with Kyoto City, Kyoto Prefecture, the Tourism Division, the Prefectural Police and the Purity Association.

The 280 yen in memberships fees were topped up by the Purity Association with 30 yen,[57] bringing the annual budget of the Floats Association to just over 300 yen. A small portion of this sum was used to pay for complementary *chimaki* amulets and decorated fans for key contacts at City Hall and in the Purity Association, offerings presented at ceremonies, and other lesser expenses; but apart from such modest outlays, almost the entire budget was spent on an annual post-festival party (*konshinkai*) at a restaurant, attended by some forty-five float street leaders. The Floats Association also gave awards to 'persons of distinguished service' (*kōrōsha*) from the float streets, which contributed both to the streets' sense of common purpose and to the association's budget – awardees (or their streets) paid a fee for this honour. The association, then, not only coordinated the distribution of subsidies but also added a layer of social interaction between street representatives.

The Floats Association may have remained inconspicuous in street proceedings for all but a few insiders, but its appearance marked the beginning of a gradual change in the institutional structure behind the festival. The Purity Association, which had saved the festival in the Meiji period and still contributed a much larger proportion of the floats' budget than the city did, lacked the close contacts with public administrators that the Floats Association was now developing. Over time, floats would come to depend more on Kyoto

City and less on the Purity Association, which increasingly concentrated its efforts on the *mikoshi* processions and events that involved Yasaka Shrine. The Floats and Purity Associations came to represent two aspects of the festival that were increasingly regarded as separate. The float parades and *yoiyama* evenings were the outward face of the festival, supported by the Tourism Division, while the *mikoshi* processions and shrine rites formed the festival's inner core, sacred to insiders but of less interest to visitors. In the post-war period, as we shall soon see, this separation would become a defining fault line in the festival's structure.

War

The outbreak of the second Sino-Japanese war in 1937 put a stop to festive events across the country. Citizens were to exercise self-restraint in solidarity with the sacrifices of Japan's soldiers. In Kyoto, the Gion pageant that was restarted in 1936 turned out to be a one-time event, and the Dyeing Festival entered a period of temporary suspension from which it never recovered. On the other hand, festivals were also seen as occasions to raise people's spirit and convince the world that Japan was taking the war in its stride. Festivals could be dedicated to victory and turned into mass manifestations of support for the Imperial Army and Navy. Vice versa, cancellation could be interpreted as an admission that the country was struggling, weakening people's morale in a critical time. Also, festivals like Gion added a much-needed boost to the local economy. There were good reasons to stop festivals as a waste of critical resources; but also to keep them going as physical proof that the country was doing well.

In what follows, I will primarily rely on unpublished records of the Floats Association, written in numbered, but unpaginated, notebooks by its chairman Shimizu, titled *Gion yamahoko rengōkai kiroku* (Records of the Gion Floats Association).[58] In two notebooks labelled as numbers 4 and 5, Shimizu recorded all duties he performed as president of the association in great detail, and in thankfully clear handwriting. Notebook nr. 4 starts on 7 June 1941, and nr. 5 runs to 28 December 1948. The next Floats Association record, titled simply *Kirokuchō* (Records), starts on 11 January 1951 under a new president, leaving a gap of two years. Shimizu occasionally added cuttings from newspapers to his record, which therefore combines perspectives from the inside of the organization with outside reports from the media. I will here follow Shimizu's record to the end of the war and, beyond that, to the restoration of the float parades that began in 1947.

In the wartime economy, access to resources soon became a serious problem. Already in 1937, Kyoto City subsidies for the Gion parades had been slashed substantially; the initial 200 yen per *hoko* and 100 yen per *yama* (for repair costs, *shūzenhi*) had dwindled to 89 and 29 yen by 1941. The subsidy for festival costs (*gyōji shōreihi*) was cut back from a total of 2,000 to 1,700 yen in 1942. More and more necessities became subject to rationing, and Shimizu spent much of his time filing applications for such necessities as matches, rice, oil and sake. Even worse was the fact that the streets of Kyoto were emptied of young men. In June 1942, the Hōka-hoko representative voiced his doubts at a preparatory meeting of the Floats Association. Were the other streets really prepared to set up their floats, now that the lack of manpower had made it impossible to stage the festival properly? Shimizu reacted with scorn to this 'absurd question':

> In this Divine Land of Japan, the victory of the Imperial Army depends to no small measure on the will of the gods. Therefore we must carry out the divine rituals (*shinji*) with even greater pomp and solemnity than usual. By doing so we will demonstrate that our victorious Empire is unperturbed even by this Great War. Also, it will bring our soldiers solace to know that all is well at the home front.[59]

By this time, however, the United States had executed its first bombing raid on Japan. The 'Doolittle Raid' of 18 April 1942 hit targets not only around Tokyo but also in Osaka and Kobe. Although there was little physical damage, this raid put Japanese cities on edge. On 3 July, when preparations for the first float parade were already in full swing, a preliminary alert was issued in Kyoto; it was lifted only on the sixth. Shimizu visited the Gojō police station multiple times to discuss whether the festival should go ahead, and if so, what should be done if American bombers disrupted the parade. During *yoiyama* lights and lanterns were banned, and Shimizu noted that the atmosphere was rather desolate. This sense of gloom was absent, however, from the report that Shimizu cut from *Mainichi shinbun*'s Kyoto edition of 17 July:

> Also in the *hayashi*, a note of prayer:
> Today, the *yamahoko* floats will parade through Kyoto

> Today, in the midst of the Great Asian War, the float parade, the pride of Kyoto and one of Japan's Three Great Festivals,[60] will progress through the avenues of the capital in prayer for the eternal victory of the Imperial Army. As always, the festival streets will be graced with crested draperies, lantern-lit gilt screens, and flowery tapestries, but there are no *chimaki* amulets to distribute among the

ujiko, nor any newly-tailored costumes for participants to wear. Yet each beat of the Gion-*bayashi* music is filled with prayers for final victory in this Sacred War; it is as though one hears the drums call out, 'we will fight to the end!' – 'we will emerge victorious!'[61]

Slogans dedicating the parade to military victory were printed on lanterns and hung from some of the floats on large banners.

Also in 1943, pressure was exerted on the Floats Association to stage the parades in defiance of the circumstances. Yasaka Shrine, the Purity Association and also Kyoto City's Culture Division (as the Tourism Division was now called) all made it clear to Shimizu that they expected a similar performance as in the previous year. The *mikoshi* processions went ahead as usual. In the float streets there was some music and decoration, but all things considered, it was no longer practically possible to set up the floats, let alone parade them. In a general meeting, representatives discussed how a suspension of the parades could be phrased in a manner that 'would not give rise to the misunderstanding that we lack the determination to revere the gods, or that we are allowing our morale to wilt due to the war' (23 June 1943). After the meeting, Shimizu composed a document addressed to the Kyoto mayor where he explained that 'only in this year', the lack of manpower and resources and the impending danger of bombing raids forced the Floats Association to cancel the assembly of the floats and the parades. The association expressed the hope that this decision would free hands to strengthen the city's defences against such raids and help raise awareness of the demands of the war among the general public. Instead, the gods would be worshipped indoors with the greatest solemnity, so as to 'foster reverence for the gods and the imperial ancestors (*keishin sūso*) and raise the national spirit'.

In 1944, even the Purity Association had to throw in the towel. The *mikoshi* processions were now also cancelled. Air raids had become a frequent occurrence. Though Kyoto had suffered only smaller attacks so far, measures were taken to prepare the city for the inevitable horror of American firebombing. On 17 July 1944, the day of the cancelled first parade, a first wave of forced evacuations and demolitions was set in motion.[62] Houses were cleared to improve access for the fire brigade, to create empty plots where survivors could find shelter, and to protect important buildings with firebreaks. This was to be the first of four waves of demolition, of which the third and largest affected much of Lower Kyoto. In March 1945, Shimizu received requests from Kyoto City and the police to lend out the floats' pulling ropes; those ropes were now used to pull down the houses and businesses of street residents. In that same month, the head of the Culture Division called upon the float streets to move their treasures into storage at the Kyoto Museum (today's National Museum), but most streets lacked the manpower and the carts necessary to take up this offer. In July the representative of the Niwatori-hoko float contacted Shimizu in desperation. The storehouse that held the float and its treasures was scheduled for removal. There was no alternative storage site, nor a feasible method to transport the valuable load. In the end, houses around the storehouse were cleared to protect it from spreading flames. The float survived the ordeal in its barricaded shell, surrounded by the ruins of the community that had once supported it. The *otabisho* was likewise scheduled for demolition in August; in an emergency meeting, Yasaka Shrine and the Purity Association decided to refrain from making an appeal to save it, in fear of appearing insensitive to the losses of others.[63]

When the war ended on 15 August 1945 there was little prospect for a revival of the festival. Kyoto had escaped the firebombing that had destroyed most Japanese cities. As by a miracle, the floats had been spared. Even so, most street communities had been dispersed, bankrupted or, at the very least, demoralized. The festival had been all but cancelled for three years; the country was under foreign occupation; there were severe shortages of food, fuel and almost everything else; and galloping inflation forced many to sell their last belongings. New occupants in the float streets were hardly in the mood to make sacrifices for the sake of a tradition that had never been theirs, and also the old residents who remained had more pressing worries. To make matters even worse, many participants with special skills, from carpenters to musicians, had disappeared.

Meanwhile, Yasaka Shrine fell afoul of the so-called Shinto Directive, issued by the Occupation authorities on 15 December 1945. As indicated by its full name, this directive banned 'governmental sponsorship, support, perpetuation, control, and dissemination of State and Shrine Shinto', even while allowing shrines to reinvent themselves as private religious institutions. Abruptly, the priests lost their state salaries, and funding for maintenance and official rites ceased. The Purity Association could no longer depend on obligatory contributions from all inhabitants within the shrine's *ujiko* area. City subsidies for the floats had been discontinued in 1943 and 1944; it seemed unlikely that they would be resumed. In short, all sections of the festival were in crisis at the same time. Surely, this would finally spell its end?

Post-war revival

Yet there were signs that the festival was still wanted. Different groups of people showed that they missed it, or that they had use for it. In short, the festival was started up again with a single parade (along a much shortened route) of just two floats in 1947 and 1948. The *mikoshi* procession was likewise revived in 1947. In 1949 the number of floats increased to nine, 1950 saw the restoration of the second parade and in 1952, two months after Japan had regained its sovereignty, all twenty-nine floats were back on course. The lantern parade for *mikoshi arai* was also revived in 1952. The year 1953 even saw the reappearance of a float that been lost in the fire of 1864 and never rebuilt since: the Kikusui-hoko.[64] How was this possible?

Insider sources from the period are rare, making Shimizu's record particularly valuable. From 1945 onwards, Shimizu was not only the chairman of the Floats Association but also a member of the board of the Purity Association, so he had first-hand access to information from many quarters. Shimizu must have been among the most knowledgeable and influential figures in this association as well, and his words carried weight.

Shimizu reveals that the Purity Association and Yasaka Shrine sought for possibilities to restart the festival already in 1946. In a meeting on 1 June 1946, Shimizu expressed his honest opinion about this idea:

> Let us assume that prices have risen fifteen-fold since the wartime. The parades cost 20,000 yen at that time; that means that today, the cost will be around 300,000 yen. The float streets can't come up with that kind of sum, nor is there any method for the Purity Association to collect enough contributions.

Yet Shimizu found some encouragement, too. On 15 and 16 July 1946, lanterns were lit in the streets and *hayashi* music was played. Shimizu noted: 'The festival atmosphere filled the city and attracted lots of people. It almost felt like the *yoiyama* of the past.' Different streets took turns performing *hayashi* at the shrine, too. Large crowds gathered around the worship hall every day.

No doubt, the public response in 1946 inspired higher hopes for the following year. In early June of 1947, the main goal of the Purity Association was to restore the *mikoshi* procession to the *otabisho*. Their main partners in realizing this were the shopping streets (*shōtengai*) of Lower Kyoto. Representatives from four shopping streets[65] attended meetings at Yasaka Shrine and reacted with enthusiasm to the news that revival was an option. More importantly, they accepted the challenge of raising funds to cover the costs. It turned out that the

Mibu group of *mikoshi* bearers was defunct, and the young men's association of the Nishiki shopping street agreed to step in. The *mikoshi* would be back in action if only the businesses of Lower Kyoto could be persuaded to make donations totalling 70,000 yen.

This effort exhausted the ambitions of the Purity Association for 1947, and nothing more would have happened if hadn't been for Kyoto City's Tourism Division, which had been restored only in April of this same year. In June, the head of this Division met with representatives from the shopping streets and the Purity Association to discuss 'Kyoto City's wish' that at least one float would be set up during the festival period. Shimizu pointed out that the mere assembly of a single float now cost 120,000 yen, or 200,000 yen if the float was to be paraded. This money would have to be raised 'by the city or the shrine', because the float streets could offer little more than voluntary labour.[66] In a subsequent meeting of the *hoko* group, it was agreed that 200,000 yen would suffice to pay for the assembly of two floats, and hopes were expressed that this might be possible if donations were collected from Kyoto's department stores, train and tram companies, banks, geisha houses (*yūkaku*), restaurants and stall owners.

This sounded unlikely, but now Kyoto City showed that it meant business. Once again, the shopping streets and the Purity Association were summoned to Yasaka Shrine, this time to meet a leading figure within the so-called Tourism Alliance (*Kankō renmei*), the veteran politician, administrator and entrepreneur Suzuki Kichinosuke (1887–1951). This alliance, founded at the initiative of Kyoto City in October 1946, functioned as a bridge between the Tourism Division and private enterprise. Suzuki proposed to feature the Gion festival as the main event on the alliance's programme of 'touristic festival events' (*kankōsai gyōji*) of 1947, which included the Daimonji fires, a 'tourism sports festival', an 'international dance party', a 'national *karuta* competition' and an 'international grand tea ceremony'.[67] Suzuki offered to support both the float parades and the *mikoshi* processions in this manner; but there was no more discussion about the processions because the *mikoshi* costs were already covered. If the organizers of the Gion festival agreed to join this programme, they would gain access to funds raised by the Tourism Alliance as well as resumed city subsidies, totalling, in Suzuki's estimation, about 210,000 yen. In the evening, Shimizu joined the head of the Mayor's Office, four senior staff of the Tourism Division and Suzuki of the Tourism Alliance for dinner in an exclusive restaurant. At this point in his records, we witness a decisive shift of agency within the festival. On 24 June 1947, the festival passed into the portfolio of Kyoto City 'events', and the city authorities gained decisive leverage over the proceedings.

A few months earlier, on 3 May 1947, Japan's new constitution had come into force. It included articles stipulating that 'no religious organization shall receive any privileges from the State' (Article 20) and that 'no public money . . . shall be expended or appropriated for the use, benefit or maintenance of a religious institution or association' (Article 89). These articles, drafted by American advisers, reflected a narrative that staged the occupiers as liberators who brought democratic rights to Japan – including freedom of religion.[68] In practice, these articles supported measures that 'gave preferential treatment to Christian missionaries and subjected Shinto shrines and priests to special scrutiny'.[69] The implications of this strict separation of state and religion, and particularly of Shinto from the state, were still being worked out in 1947. Was the Purity Association, with its close ties to Yasaka Shrine, a 'religious association'? Could Kyoto City subsidize the Gion festival with public money, in spite of its obvious ties with a Shinto institution?

In contrast to the pre-war and wartime years, the problem in 1947 was no longer that the Gion festival was defined as a 'private rite' (*shisai*), but rather that the festival was intertwined with a shrine that had been heavily tainted by 'State Shinto' and that was now banned from public life. Under the old regime, the lack of coherence between the private festival and public Shinto ideology had been a sensitive issue that needed to be navigated with care. Now, however, there was a fear that the Occupation authorities would associate the festival with Shintoism, militarism and emperor worship. In the float streets, there were rumours that the floats and their treasures would be confiscated and the festival banned outright.[70] Float treasures were hidden away, and in these desperate times they were not always retrieved.

The 1949 propaganda film *Japan and Democracy*, which includes footage of the revived Gion festival, illustrates the climate that gave rise to such fears. This seventeen-minute newsreel, from the series *The March of Time*, celebrates the role of Christian churches in spreading 'Western ideas of right and wrong among the Japanese people'. The revival of 'Shintoist festivals', exemplified visually by the Gion parade, is presented as an ominous sign that the work of inculcating Western virtues in Japan is still incomplete. After all, the narrator warns, these festivals prove the continued 'existence of this religion, which made it possible for the military to establish the perverted cult of State Shintoism, fostering the belief that all mankind must be brought under the rule of the emperor'. Scenes from the parade are followed by shots of Hirohito surrounded by cheering crowds. The narrator observes gravely that the emperor, though no longer worshipped as a god, 'still receives the adulation of millions of his people'. This newsreel sums up the dominant Allied narrative of the time: only Christian values can save Japan from dangerous Mikadoism.

Considering this ideological backdrop, negotiations with the Occupation authorities in Kyoto turned out to be surprisingly smooth. In 1947, the initial plan was to set up the Naginata-hoko and Kanko-hoko floats. In a meeting at the headquarters of the Prefectural Police, an American officer of the Military Police informed the head of the Tourism Division and Shimizu (via an interpreter) that permission to set up the Naginata-hoko was unproblematic. The Kanko-hoko, however, would occupy parking space used by the Occupation forces. This matter was resolved by assembling the Tsuki-hoko instead. The negotiations were conducted by Kyoto City, which presented the parade to the Occupation authorities as a secular tourism event; a draft of the application sent to Shimizu by Suzuki stated only that the floats would be decorated with 'ancient works of art' and mentioned neither Yasaka Shrine nor even the Gion festival. Questions of 'Shintoism', as featured in the newsreel, were skilfully avoided in this manner. In the end, enough funds were available to pay pullers for the Naginata-hoko only; the Tsuki-hoko remained stationary. On 17 July the Naginata-hoko paraded along Shijō up to the Teramachi crossing and back. All necessities, from lubricant oil to candles and naphthalene, were procured with the help of the Tourism Division. Seating was set up for Occupation personnel and their families; remaining seats were sold to the general public. The tickets read: 'Organised by the Floats Association, with the support of the Tourism Alliance'.

The Naganata-hoko parade was a resounding success. According to the newspapers, the *yoiyama* evening on the sixteenth and the parade the following morning drew a 'killer crowd' of 400,000 people, by far the largest gathering since the end of the war. One journalist wrote: 'A reaction from soldiers of the Occupation army: 'We have no idea why so many people have come out!' – but they are smiling happily as they follow the festival spectators down the street.'[71] To celebrate the 1947 revival, Shimizu organized an extravagant 'tea party' on 23 July at the street meetinghouses of the Naginata-hoko and Tsuki-hoko floats. Tellingly, the guests of honour were representatives from the Tourism Division and the Tourism Alliance; they are mentioned ahead of the head priest Takahara of Yasaka Shrine.

These events in 1947 laid the foundation for the way the festival would be run in subsequent decades. In 1950, Mayor Takayama Gizō took further steps to develop Kyoto as an 'international city of culture and tourism', identifying the Gion parades as one of the city's major attractions. The fundraising operations of the Tourism Alliance were upgraded with the creation of a new half-public, half-private organization dedicated solely to the Gion festival: the Float Parades Support Association (Gion'e Yamahoko Junkō Kyōsankai). This association was headed by Naiki Seibei, one of Kyoto's leading industrialists and the son of Kyoto's first mayor Naiki Jinzaburō (who, as we saw, played a crucial role in the 1912 crisis). The increased effectiveness of this Support Association, combined with an upswing in economic activity (stimulated, among other things, by the outbreak of the Korean War), made the rapid return of the Gion festival feasible.

We saw that already before the war, there was a tendency to regard the *mikoshi* processions as a responsibility of the Purity Association, while the float parades were singled out for public sponsorship as tourism events by Kyoto City. Suzuki's offer to include the *mikoshi* in the programme of the Tourism Alliance was not repeated. Rather, it was decided that the administrative border between the secular and the religious spheres would run between the float parade and the *mikoshi* processions. Taking note of the success of Kyoto's support for the Gion festival, other cities wondered whether this was a model that they could emulate. In reply to a query from the mayor of Kagoshima City, which has its own Gion festival, Kyoto City explained why its support for the float parades did not impinge on the constitutional separation of state and religion:

> The rituals for the gods are organized by Yasaka Shrine, but the float parade, which is the main event of the festival, is organized by the Float Parades Support Association. The shrine rituals and the *mikoshi* processions are by nature religious events and Kyoto City does not touch them at all, but we regard the float parades as annual touristic events and are actively engaged with them.[72]

This official take on the festival was never challenged. It is difficult to determine whether this model for dealing with festivals was a Kyoto invention, but in view of that city's intense focus on tourism, this appears quite likely. Kagoshima City's enquiry is one example of the way in which this administrative 'Gion model' spread around the country.

The Gion model came to define the place of shrine festivals in the post-war social order, and it became immensely influential. It tied the float parades closely to city policy. This made the parades vulnerable to city pressure for 'improvements' that were in line with the goals of the Tourism Division. In 1956 the route of the float parades was changed to wider roads that could safely accommodate larger crowds of visitors. The initiative for this change was taken by Kyoto's mayor Takayama Gizō (1892–1974, in office 1950–66), overriding protests from Yasaka Shrine, the Purity Association and Matsubara Street, which was now no longer on the parade route. In 1966, the second parade was merged with the first, again according to Takayama's plan; the second parade was restored only in 2014. The separation of the 'secular' float parades from shrine ritual allowed the city authorities to override the concerns of 'religious' stakeholders and act with the consent of the float streets only.[73] For legal reasons, 'religious' and therefore private *mikoshi* processions and shrine rituals have been excluded from public support and subsidies. Needless to say, this causes tensions. Another legacy of the Gion model is the designation of float parades around the country as public cultural properties from the late 1970s onwards, and as UNESCO Intangible Cultural Heritage since 2009; the 'religious' *mikoshi* processions are separated out from these designations. It is my impression that while festival participants do their best to ignore such bureaucratic complications, many feel that the exclusion of the *mikoshi* and the shrine is wrong – even while they cherish the autonomy that their own group enjoys within the festival's decentralized structure.[74]

The modern Gion festival: Between private and public

The modern period (1868–1945) began and ended with a major crisis. In 1868, the festival lost its status as an official event performed on orders of the city's shogunal administrators. Instead, it became a 'private rite' (*shisai*) that was of no concern to the authorities. Social and economic structures that had supported the festival for centuries were no longer enforced, or even banned. The Gionsha, the groups of *mikoshi* bearers and the network of streets that supported the floats all changed beyond recognition. The individual float streets, too, were increasingly struggling to retain their relevance as social units. Under these circumstances, the festival might well have flopped.

Yet it did not. What saved the festival was first of all the commitment of leading figures from the street communities in Lower Kyoto. At great cost to themselves and their fellow street members, street leaders rebuilt, repaired and redecorated their floats. They were enabled to do so by voluntary donations collected by a new *ujiko* organization, the Purity Association, which had its roots in networks developed entirely at the initiative of community leaders. Others took responsibility for organizing *mikoshi* bearers as soon as the reformed 'Yasaka Shrine' dropped the ball. Even the official vanguard that had headed the procession before Meiji was replaced thanks to grassroots initiatives. As we have seen, the inhabitants of Yumiya-chō impersonated the *zōshiki* watchmen who had added gravity to the processions in the Edo period. The divine treasures that had been carried by priests of the *otabisho* were taken over by the leading branch of the Purity Association – the Miyamoto branch, based in the school ward of Yasaka in front of Yasaka Shrine. Members of this branch, many of whom owned shops and businesses along Shijō Street east of the Kamo River, also took over other ritual tasks that had once been performed by *otabisho* priests, most prominently during the 'washing' of the *mikoshi* and the transfer of the gods. All these arrangements, initiated through informal channels, were post facto recognized and confirmed by the city authorities and the shrine. The agency, however, was in the hands of private 'stakeholders'.

What was at stake for these community leaders? Of course, there was pride and prestige. This largest 'communal project' of the year was an occasion to create street identity and solidarity, enhance or (depending on the street) soften up the hierarchy between residents, and express the street's standing in front of the entire city, district and even nation. Religious faith was certainly important to some, notably those who were active members of the Purity Association, but perhaps less prominent in the general atmosphere of the festival. Business was another motivation; networks of sponsorship and obligation inspired many to make lavish contributions and donations, and as we have seen, the Chamber of Commerce and Industry was crucial to the festival's rescue in 1912. The fact that the Lower City was a hub of well-connected textile wholesalers goes a long way towards explaining the positive outcome of that particular crisis.

These motivating factors, however, were often offset by demotivating burdens. There is no doubt that many actors must have felt the temptation to opt out or give up. Talk of selling the floats as a way to escape from the self-imposed duties of the festival was more than mere rhetoric. When we ask ourselves what caused the festival to endure, we must give due weight to group pressure. All festival participants are dependent on the continued efforts of others. When a float street announced that it was planning to throw in the towel, mechanisms of aid and persuasion kicked in. In 1880, for example, the street of Minami Kannon-yama decided to stop participating in the festival until accumulated street debts had been paid off.[75] However, pressure from other streets in the ward, communicated in no uncertain terms by the ward officials, forced the street's hand. With help from the Purity Association, and at the cost of much hardship, this street finally cleared its debts in 1892. Without collective pressure, the outcome would have been different. Clearly it was practically impossible for struggling festival groups to quit, and none managed to make a clean escape.

While the value of the festival went largely unexplained in pre-Meiji times, modernity required explicit definitions of its significance. The 'logic of prayer and blossoming' that had motivated shogunal administrators to allow the festival to flourish in the Edo period no longer applied. The distance between the imperial rites and ideology of Shinto embodied by Yasaka Shrine on one hand and the syncretic chaos of the Gion festival on the other made it difficult to present the festival as an expression of the orthodox 'Japanese spirit'. To modern eyes, beliefs expressed in the festival looked more like superstition. When competition for public space hardened, the festival's defenders described its value in strictly secular terms: as culture, art and social play, or as a tourism resource that brought great economic benefits to Kyoto. It was primarily this last argument that eventually saved the festival. Public subsidies were justified on these same grounds: the 1923 subsidy for 'repairs' sought to preserve the floats as monuments of historical and cultural value, and the 1939 subsidy for 'event costs' was predicated on the festival's value as a tourism event. In addition to the Purity Association, Kyoto City's Tourism Division now became a central patron of the festival – but only of those parts of the festival that attracted tourists.

The outbreak of the war changed the rhetoric about the festival. Now that tourism had disappeared, it was defined as a 'ritual dedicated to the gods' (*shinji*) in prayer for victory. On 9 June 1943, the head of Kyoto City's Culture Division told Shimizu: 'Because [the float parade] is a *shinji*, it is our wish that it will be performed as usual in as far as this is possible. We ask you to carry out this event even if some unavoidable changes must be made.'[76] The festival now served as proof of the government's ability to sustain normalcy even as the war escalated, and its continuation was seen as a valuable contribution to maintaining morale at the home front. In this time of crisis, the 'logic of prayer and blossoming' made a comeback: once again the festival was staged as a rite that addressed the gods, while at the same time reflecting human prospering and casting glory over the rulers and the nation. In the context of total war, the distinction between public and private was no longer relevant. In this setting the festival once again drifted into the position of a 'modelling event' (an event that harnesses the power of the gods) that simultaneously 'mirrored' state power.

The collapse of that power, however, changed everything. In 1945, the festival had become both impossible and meaningless. Street communities were scattered, the country was suffering under hyperinflation and shortages of food and many other essential goods, Yasaka Shrine was struggling to adapt to the new regime, the Purity Association had lost the capacity to collect compulsory contributions from *ujiko*, and permission from the Allied Occupation needed to be arranged. Could the festival be revived, and, if so, how and by whom? Shimizu gave a succinct answer to this question in June 1947: with the streets in disarray, only Kyoto City or Yasaka Shrine could possibly pick up the pieces. In the end, both did: Kyoto City and the Float Parade Support Association took on the float parades, while Yasaka Shrine and the Purity Association went on to support the *mikoshi* processions and shrine rituals.

In my account, I have given too little credit to the efforts and sacrifices of the many people who have kept the festival alive under these new circumstances. Also today, floats raise most of their income on their own. In 2015, dependence on subsidies ranged between 8 and 44 per cent.[77] All festival participants are volunteers; none get paid for their time. Private contributions to the Support Association, the Floats Association or to individual floats are primarily inspired by a genuine wish to see the festival flourish. The festival depends on the continued dedication of thousands of people, including craftsmen and musicians, elders and school children, *mikoshi* bearers and float pullers, bento cooks and street sweepers.

Yet it is clear that unless the festival is facilitated by local, regional and even national authorities, it must fail. To argue that this distracts from the festival's authenticity would be most unreasonable. In all stages of its history, the festival has required both active patronage from above and sustained commitment from below. In the post-war period, the festival has won an unassailable position in local and national politics as a valuable asset for the city of Kyoto as well as a cultural treasure of Japan, and it receives both organizational and financial assistance from the authorities. Subsidies are only one aspect of this; the festival organizers readily receive permission to use public space, and they enjoy the cooperation of the police, the fire brigade and other public services for such mundane matters as traffic control, the handling of electricity cables, rubbish removal, first aid posts and much more.

Old social structures, such as the street communities, have long since eroded away, but new networks have formed of people who find joy and meaning in the many events that make up the festival. One researcher describes these new networks as 'hybrid collectives' and 'communities of practice', pointing out that the members of these groups interact at the time of the festival but have little or no connection with each other outside of the festival setting.[78] Many live elsewhere and participate as volunteers, sometimes contributing with special skills, but in other cases (including my own volunteering) merely doing whatever needs to be done out of curiosity and interest in the sheer 'experience'.

It is essential that there are stable core groups of dedicated organizers; beyond that, reliance on fluid 'actor networks' has proved to be a feasible alternative to older structures of participation. Even this is perhaps not such an unprecedented state of affairs; both the guilds of the Muromachi period and float and *mikoshi* streets in the Edo period likewise employed outsiders to do much of the labour involved in the festival – although in contrast to today's students and volunteers, those outsiders usually had to be paid. It appears that once again, drastic social changes that could have pushed the festival into a situation where it might well 'flop' are being handled in a creative manner, as new groups of participants are helping the festival to adapt and flourish in new ways.

Conclusion

Mirroring by modelling

In the introduction to their volume *Ritual Matters* (2010), Christiane Brosius and Ute Hüsken point out the need for a more dynamic approach to the study of ritual. Central to their agenda is the understanding that 'a notion of "stability" of rituals is highly questionable'. To bring out the contingent nature of ritual, Brosius and Hüsken focus on the historical, social and structural dynamics of ritual traditions. Such dynamics, they argue, are revealed when the development of a ritual is examined in the *longue durée*. Rather than regarding the persistence of a ritual tradition as a sign of stability, Brosius and Hüsken call attention to frequent instances of 'ritual transfer' – the active translation of rituals for reuse in a new context. Ritual transfer can refer to both place and time. A ritual can be moved to a new site of practice and a new community, or it can be renewed or reinvented in its original location, adapted to the needs of a new age. The concept of ritual transfer helps us to break out of the myth that traditions propagate themselves, seemingly unaffected by historical change. When we think about ritual in terms of ritual transfer, we are forced to focus on the agency of real people, reacting to real historical circumstances. The history of the Gion festival, too, was never stable. It included many moments of ritual transfer, when the festival was restarted and redesigned in a new social and political setting by participants and patrons with many different motivations.[1]

This perspective forms a striking counterpoint to the 'cultural epidemiology' approach of Olivier Morin (2016) referred to in the introduction to this volume. Morin looks for stable traditions in human behaviour and examines the conditions that must apply for cultural practices to persist in the face of historical change. Morin is interested in the problems of accurate transmission, which is constantly undermined by the 'wear and tear' that, over time, erodes and corrupts such practices. He points out, however, that once a practice has become established, there are mechanisms that allow it to withstand or repair such erosion: a lost tradition may be reintroduced from another site where it has been preserved, or it may have been recorded so that it can be reconstructed across time. More lethal than wear and tear is what Morin calls 'flopping': the demise of a tradition due to a loss of relevance under new conditions. While Brosius and Hüsken may disagree with Morin about the very possibility of stability over time, the implications of both perspectives are similar. No traditional (or ritual) practice remains unaffected by historical change, and unless such a practice is regularly transferred, translated and reconstructed, it will soon disappear. The precondition for such an active restoration of eroding traditions is relevance. For a practice to survive, it must retain relevance in ever new ways in constantly changing contexts.

What, however, does relevance mean in this context? Brosius and Hüsken stress that 'rituals, like other modes of human action, are performed with a certain aim'.[2] Rituals are expected to have efficacy; to be seen as successful, they must produce an effect. Don Handelman, too, emphasizes this point: 'My premise is that "rituals" were invented in order to act on the world, on the cosmos, in predicted ways.'[3] What, however, does the Gion festival 'do'? Can we talk about the festival as having ritual efficacy, and if so, in what sense? And, in light of the unlikelihood of stability, must we assume that the festival has catered to the same notions of efficacy over time, or was that notion itself periodically translated to fit the circumstances of a new age?

Handelman offers us a few handles that are helpful in discussing the ways public events act on the world. In short, 'events that mirror' present the social order rather than seeking to effect a change, while 'events that model' do have the ambition to change something, in ways that may or may not be in line with the current social order. An event that mirrors typically displays (and thereby affirms) power, while an event that models seeks to heal, exorcize, influence the weather or transform somebody or something in other ways.[4] These two major types of events each have their own logic and follow characteristic 'meta-designs'. A typical event that mirrors 'organizes, displays, enunciates, and indexes lineaments of statehood, nationhood, history, and civic collectivity through march-pasts, assemblies, theatrics, mass performances of close-order coordination, and synchronization among performers'.[5] An event that models, on the other hand, follows a 'model' that reduces phenomena in the world to a ritual microcosm, and conducts a set procedure with the concrete aim to change something. A simple way to distinguish between these two meta-designs is to check whether the event might as well have been performed in the reverse order. An event that mirrors will still make sense, while an event that models will no longer work.

In the course of this book, I have tried out Handelman's conceptual scheme on the Gion festival in its different phases of development. Before tackling the question whether Handelman's scheme adds to our understanding of this festival, and whether the festival can be used to refine his concepts, it will be useful to briefly sum up some of the watersheds that we discovered in its history. This history can be cut up in different ways, depending on one's focus. Here, I will zoom in on two aspects of the festival: changes in its physical appearance and shifts in the composition of its actors.

The main changes in the festival's appearance

Including its initial formation in the 970s, the festival went through five metamorphoses in the period covered in this book – up to 1952.

970s:

The founding of the first *otabisho* (974?) marks the beginning of the festival. At this stage, the main events were the return of the *mikoshi* on the fourteenth day of the sixth month (*goryōe*), and court offering rites, Gagaku dances and horse races on the fifteenth (*rinjisai*). The *mikoshi* processions expanded in the eleventh and twelfth centuries but declined from the 1170s onwards. These processions featured costumed horse riders (*uma no osa*) and various dances, most prominently by *dengaku* groups. What happened at the *otabisho* during the time the *mikoshi* stayed here, we don't know.

1340s:

'*Yama* floats and other contraptions (*tsukurimono*)' get their first mention in a 1345 diary entry. This marks the origin of the float parades, which soon surpassed the *mikoshi* processions as the festival's main event. Perhaps the floats were paraded separately from the *mikoshi* already in the 1340s, as was the case with the '*hoko* groups' that appeared two decades earlier. It is also possible that the parades came into their own only after 1369, when the *mikoshi* were lost in fighting. The *uma no osa* and *dengaku* disappeared around 1350.

1500:

After a gap of more than three decades, caused by the outbreak of the Ōnin war in 1467, the festival was revived. The float parades, which before 1467 had included floats and 'contraptions' that varied from one year to the next, were now standardized and canonized. The *rinjisai*, which had already been reduced to an offering of Gagaku dances only, did not survive the war.

1670s:

The *mikoshi arai* (the 'washing of the *mikoshi*' a week before and after the processions) became the stage for new events in the emerging Gion district of theatres, teahouses and brothels. A new lantern parade and a pageant performed by girls from Gion's houses of amusement attracted large crowds, as did a popular fair along the Kamo riverbank.

1750s:

The floats were now set up one or two days before the parade. The float streets offered crowds of visitors the chance to stroll among thousands of glowing lanterns, take a good look at the floats, pray, buy amulets and enjoy the *hayashi* music. Exhibitions of heirlooms were staged in street meetinghouses, shops and merchants' homes. This was the beginning of the *yoiyama*, which soon grew into the most popular event of the festival.

Some further new rites were added in modern times (e.g. the *hanagasa* parade), while others (notably the Gion pageant) have disappeared, but in broad strokes, the festival format has changed little since the mid-eighteenth century.

Participants and patrons

Another way to trace the festival's development is by focusing on its changing actors. Who paid for, took responsibility for or participated in the festival in different periods of its history? This is more difficult to determine, but if we focus only on the most dominant groups, we can recognize seven main phases.

970s–1150s:
Commoner traders, the imperial court and Mt Hiei

The first *otabisho*, founded in the 970s, was the residence of a rich commoner. This man and his peers must have staged various rites there during the *mikoshi*'s week-long stay in the heart of the city's commoner district. In contrast, the *rinjisai* was a court event, and also the second *mikoshi* procession was the object of court patronage to the extent that commoner initiatives were actively suppressed. The Gionsha, meanwhile, was a branch of Enryakuji, the temple complex on Mt Hiei. In the eleventh century the Fujiwara and the retired emperors, who were vying for influence, invested heavily in festival displays. The subsequent decline of court involvement was due to the conflicts of the twelfth century and the subsequent rise of warrior power.

1150s–1370s:
Merchant guilds step in as the court loses interest

In the twelfth century, the rich commoners of the tenth century developed into guild merchants. Enryakuji and its branches, including the Gionsha, functioned as the overlords of Kyoto's guilds. This century also saw the beginning of a new system of festival funding: the *bajōyaku* levy (sanctioned by the court in 1157). A significant portion of the festival bill was now sent to selected merchants. It is possible that the *otabisho* priests played a role in this system, but soon, it was absorbed into the Enryakuji sphere of influence. As court involvement in the festival decreased, Enryakuji and the merchants in its guilds stepped in.

1370s–1467:
A new alliance between the Ashikaga shoguns and guild merchants

From the 1370s onwards, the Ashikaga shoguns challenged Enryakuji's control over both the guild merchants and the festival. Ashikaga Yoshimitsu extended shogunal jurisdiction and taxation to guild merchants, undermining Enryakuji's old prerogatives. Grand shogunal viewings of the Gion processions and parades offered merchants an opportunity to display their cultural and economic capital in front of the city's new masters; hence the floats drew heavily on shogunal culture. However, the start of the Ōnin war in 1467 destroyed most of the city and all of its festivals.

1500–1590s:
New warrior masters, the demise of Mt Hiei and the rise of 'street' communities

The festival's revival in 1500 was made possible by the city's new military leader: the shogunal deputy Hosokawa Masamoto. To make this happen, Masamoto first had to neutralize Enryakuji; he achieved this by burning Mt Hiei to the ground in 1499. Enryakuji recovered, but its power was finally broken by Oda Nobunaga, who reduced the entire monastic complex to ashes once more in 1571. In the meantime, the medieval guilds, with their close ties to Mt Hiei, had lost their hold over Kyoto's networks of trade. Instead, townspeople organized themselves in tight-knit street communities. The floats of the Gion festival now became identified with these streets. The *otabisho* had active communities of priests and *miko* but lost much of their vitality after Toyotomi Hideyoshi closed one and moved the other in 1591.

1600–1868:
Street house owners, shogunal overseers and new events for and by townspeople

In the Edo period the festival was performed on orders of the shogunal governor of Kyoto and overseen by a special force of 'watchmen' (*zōshiki*), who accompanied the *mikoshi* processions and inspected the float parades. Warrior supervision was strict but not very intrusive. In practice, the festival was run by a network of house owners in the streets of Lower Kyoto, who either staged their own floats or paid contributions to a float street as its 'attendant street' (*yorichō*). Streets developed their floats into flagships of street pride. A smaller number of *mikoshi* streets, responsible for moving the gods to the *otabisho* and back, did the same with the *mikoshi*. The emergence of 'fringe' events like the lantern parades and the Gion pageants was another expression of the growing dominance of townspeople over the festival.

1864–1912:
City abandonment and street resilience

The relative autonomy of these townspeople prepared the festival for the collapse of established festival structures (notably the *yorichō* system) after the fire of 1864, and of the shogunate in 1868. As the festival's main caretakers, street leaders managed to navigate the many reforms of the 1870s, which included the replacement of the Buddhist Gionsha with the Shinto Yasaka Shrine that was completely re-staffed in 1872. The city's new authorities now saw little merit in the festival, which struck them as a remnant of a deplorable past. It was tolerated as a 'private rite', even though it was a bad fit for the new, imperial Yasaka Shrine. The festival's caretakers, however, kept the festival going by developing new organizational structures: the Purity Association (1875), new *mikoshi* associations and such groups as the inhabitants of Yumiya-chō, who replaced the watchmen in the *mikoshi* processions.

1912–52
Kyoto City and the Tourism Alliance step in

In 1912, the city authorities tried to ban the float parades to prevent them from disrupting the newly introduced municipal tramline. After a month of intense protest and debate, however, the prefectural governor and the mayor backed down. The festival now found its place in modern Kyoto as a display of art and history, as well as a tourism resource that added 'vigour' to the city. When float streets ran into financial difficulties that were beyond the power of the Purity Association to fix, Kyoto City stepped in with subsidies (1923, 1939). The Tourism Division became a prominent actor in the festival's funding and organization; the Floats Association was created in 1923 to mediate between the city authorities and the float streets. This trend intensified after the war, when half-public and half-private organizations (the Tourism Alliance and the Float Parades Support Association) made the festival's revival possible. This revival was completed in 1952, to coincide with the end of the Allied Occupation.

These two attempts at periodization show that changes in the festival's networks of actors do not always coincide with changes in its appearance. At times, new actors perpetuate older practices, and new practices may be initiated by existing actors. Overall, the festival's appearance is more stable than its social base. The floats survived the demise of the medieval guilds, and today's float preservation associations (*hozonkai*) are filling in for the long-disappeared *chō* street communities of yesteryear. There are even reconstruction efforts that span centuries. The *hanagasa* parade, started in 1966 at the initiative of Yasaka Shrine, includes performances of *dengaku* dancing, heron dances (*sagi mai*) and even classical 'horse chiefs' (*uma no osa*) – now performed by a range of recent associations, including members of the shrine's Boy and Girl Scouts.[6] Behind an apparently timeless façade, new participants are constantly 'transferring' ritual forms into a new setting. Even rites that have long since 'flopped' remain available to the evolving festival, allowing it to be 'timeless' in a timely manner.

Mirroring and modelling

Can Handelman's theory of meta-designs help us to make sense of the festival's process of ritual transfer? And can the example of the Gion festival be used to enrich this theory?

Looking back on the *longue-durée* transformations sketched here, it is clear that the question whether this festival is an 'event that mirrors' or an 'event that models' has no easy answer. This is no surprise; Handelman finds the same in most of his case studies and concludes that 'the probability of a given, real event fitting neatly within one type is necessarily small'.[7] The usefulness of Handelman's concepts is not taxonomic but analytic: thinking through these concepts helps us to ask new questions about a particular public event.

Thinking about the Gion festival in these terms, it strikes me first of all that the question what the festival is designed to 'do' can be answered in many different ways, depending on the perspective of the many different participants and patrons involved. The shogun in his pavilion, the *mikoshi* bearer sweating under his load, the *hayashi* drummer on a float platform, the rod-wielding outcast at the head of the *mikoshi* procession, the public servant of the Tourism Division and the Gion dancing girl who has vowed to talk to no one while running to the *otabisho* to present her deepest wish – they must all have had very different answers to this question. On the level of individuals, it is plainly impossible to generalize about functions, meanings, motivations or emotive responses.

Perhaps this *is* possible, however, on the more abstract level of public discourse about the festival in different periods. The current consensus, conveyed in numerous official documents, brochures, guide books and also by many of the participants themselves, is that the festival serves to dispel illness from the city. This notion does indeed surface in different guises in all phases of the festival's long history, but has it consistently constituted what Handelman calls the 'teleological purpose' that informs its meta-design as a modelling event? Statements about purpose are rare in primary sources; even rarer are attempts at explaining how the festival 'works' as a means to achieve such purposes. Much more common are references to precedents, preferably citing an imperial or shogunal edict or order of some kind. By performing the festival in the correct way, the participants are recreating an ancient order, even if the epidemic that originally inspired the procedure has long since ended. Recreating an ancient order in the present is typically what a mirroring event does. Here, we already see that our categories are getting tangled up. Are the participants presenting power and prestige ('mirroring') by exorcizing pestilence spirits ('modelling')?

In the Edo period, the official view on festivals was that they combined prayer with displays of 'blossoming'. There was a distinction between rites addressing the gods (*shinji*) and displays of human blossoming (*nigiwai, tsukematsuri*).[8] Those displays escaped censure as wasteful splendour because they were understood as celebrations of peace and prosperity, and as such cast glory over the regime that made this blossoming possible. The gods, too, enjoy a beautiful spectacle and might well begrudge misplaced frugality. Again the boundary between modelling (following a procedure to influence the cosmic realm, or, in this case, the behaviour of the gods) and mirroring (reflecting and strengthening social structures of power) is difficult to draw. The gods, after all, are, by definition, on the side of the rulers. Presenting the social order (mirroring) through a display of prosperity pleases the gods and thus exorcizes evil influences (modelling). In this setting, the festival 'models' by way of 'mirroring' – or, depending on one's perspective, 'mirrors by modelling'.

In the absence of explicit statements of purpose, we can perhaps use Handelman's notion of meta-designs in our search for clues about the question what the Gion festival has been expected to 'do' in its different phases of development. In pre-Edo versions of the festival, the *mikoshi* processions were fraught with danger. Court nobles stayed away from the routes taken by the *mikoshi* and took measures to avoid the impurity swirled up by the processions. The processions often triggered violence, and on some occasions the *mikoshi* had to be abandoned mid-route. People made themselves small and averted their eyes when the *mikoshi* passed. In contrast, the float parades were designed to be watched and admired. The *mikoshi* processions served the purpose of bringing the gods to the *otabisho* and back; they went from A to B and from B to A in an irreversible order. The floats, on the other hand, circled the Lower City in an order that was determined simply by geography and lots. Clearly, the *mikoshi* processions followed a modelling design, in contrast to the mirroring 'march-past' that was the float parade.

Yet there were clear mirroring aspects to the *mikoshi* processions, too. In classical times, *uma no osa* horse chiefs and *dengaku* groups of dancers and musicians made up of or sponsored by court nobles paraded along with the *mikoshi*. At the same time, 'contraptions' offered by commoners were banned and intercepted. By acting in this manner, the imperial court (or the court of the retired emperor) used mirroring devices to claim credit for the festival's modelling efficacy. Much later, in the eighteenth century, the *mikoshi* processions developed into a spectacle to be enjoyed, while the floats came to be seen as vehicles of divine beings. If there was a sense that the *mikoshi* processions were qualitatively different from the float parades, this logic appears to have collapsed. Yet the festival continued to 'do' what people expected of it; there was no attempt to stop this development or return to earlier formats. Perhaps this smooth transition was facilitated by the notion that modelling was already a method of mirroring?

One would expect that in a modern setting, claims that the festival has modelling efficacy (in the sense of powers to exorcize) would be met with scepticism. The pre-war discourse that ascribed value to the festival primarily as historical culture or social play can be interpreted as evidence of such scepticism. Yet the notion that the festival moves the gods returned during the war, when the parades were construed as modelling *shinji*, performed as a prayer for victory in an atmosphere of great solemnity. Perhaps this was largely a matter of rhetoric, but the notion that rituals addressed to the gods contributed to the success of Japan as the Land of the Gods was certainly taken seriously, and this discourse spurred float and *mikoshi* organizers to make great efforts without direct coercion. Clearly, modern disenchantment was but a thin veneer.

What survives of the logic of mirroring by modelling in the festival's contemporary guise? In 2020, the festival was struck by the Covid-19 pandemic. Both the *mikoshi* processions and the float parades were cancelled. However, cancelling a disease-quelling festival because of an epidemic felt wrong. In the end, new ways were found to bring the gods to the *otabisho*, and from the *otabisho* to the Yasaka parishioners of Lower Kyoto.[9] In designing this procession, and also alternative parades without floats, there was much reflection on the 'true meaning' (*hongi*) of the festival. Both the festival's caretakers and the media agreed that this true meaning is to be found in prayer. The tenor of reporting was that the 2020 festival, with its complete absence of tourists, was more 'true' than ever and, therefore, particularly moving.

Stripped of its elements of show and display, the 2020 festival reverted to its original essence as a *shinji* – an event that addresses the gods, rather than an audience of human onlookers. Yet no one wants to keep the festival in this 'stripped down' state. The efficacy of a public event is measured in its ability to create *nigiwai*, 'human blossoming', as much as in its more abstract thaumaturgic effects. The crowds make the rituals work, and the rituals cause the crowds to gather. Without the *shinji* at its core, the festival is in danger of losing its feel of authenticity and appearing as a soulless show, propped up by external subsidies for the sake of tourism. Without the extravagant displays of human blossoming, the festival can't serve as a mirror of Kyoto's (or Japan's) sense of pride and tradition.

In Handelman's terminology, *shinji* are 'events that model', while *nigiwai* is expressed through 'events that mirror'. The Gion festival, then, is a public event where these two meta-designs are inherently intertwined. We might describe this intertwinement as 'mirroring by modelling'. The mirroring works because the festival is *both* a spectacle of human blossoming *and* a display of power that 'acts on the world' in the manner of a modelling event. Prestige is reflected upon the participants of the festival because the festival has the power to move the gods. And, vice versa, prestige is reflected upon the gods because the festival has the power to move its human participants. I am tempted to argue that it is this integration of mirroring and modelling that has made the festival so resilient in the face of historical change for more a millennium.

Notes

Introduction

1 There are, in fact, multiple ways to categorize the floats; also, there are *hoko* called *yama* and the other way around. For an overview, see Ueki 2001, chapter 1.

2 Naginata-hoko has one *chigo*, accompanied by two child 'assistants' (*kamuro*). The other *hoko* floats replaced their *chigo* with dolls (*ningyō chigo*) between 1839 (Kanko-hoko) and 1929 (Hōka-hoko). The two *kasa* floats, Ayagasa-hoko and Shijō Kasa-hoko, have six and two *chigo* respectively.

3 Ueki and Fukuhara 2016: 10.

4 In 2016, the Gion festival was withdrawn from this list and included as a sub-element of a serial nomination of thirty-three float festivals. The float parades, then, retained the status of Intangible Cultural Heritage.

5 https://ich.unesco.org/en/RL/yama-hoko-yatai-float-festivals-in-japan-01059. On these matters, see Teeuwen 2020a. The Gion festival began its career within Japan's heritage system in 1952, when it was listed as a national 'intangible cultural property'.

6 Matsudaira 2001 (first edition 1983): 1–2.

7 Morin 2016: 41.

8 Teeuwen and Breen 2017.

9 *Kyōto shinbun*, 16 July 1963; Teeuwen 2020a: 114–15.

10 Yasaka Jinja 1997: 156–60. This booklet was originally written in 1971 by head priest Takahara Yoshitada (1892–1989; head priest 1938–76) and later revised by Mayumi Tsunetada (1923–2019, head priest 1993–2002).

11 On 2011, see Porcu 2012: 95. On 2020, see Teeuwen 2021: 157–9.

12 Brumann 2009: 290.

13 For a condensed and updated version of Handelman's theory of the modes or meta-designs of public events, see Handelman 2006.

14 Schnell 1999: 32.

15 For example, Yoneyama 1974, 1986, Brumann 2012, Porcu 2020 and Teeuwen 2020a.

Chapter 1

1 Stavros (2014, chapter 1) gives a lower estimate, at 70,000. Urban historians Inoue Mitsurō and Kitō Hiroshi have given slightly higher numbers, on either side of 100,000. Around the year 800, Japan as a whole likely had between five and six million inhabitants. Stavros 2014 is the best English-language source on the urban history of Kyoto, from its eighth century beginnings until the age of Toyotomi Hideyoshi in the late sixteenth century.

2 The regent Fujiwara no Tadahira, for example, founded Hosshōji in 925, and Michinaga built Hōjōji in *c.* 1017.

3 For a brief account of the *jingi* cult and its relation to Shinto, see Breen and Teeuwen 2010: 24–41.

4 For an introduction to this system, see Grapard 1988.

5 Adolphson 2000: 85–6. Shirakawa's Hosshōji (法勝寺) is written differently from Tadahira's (法性寺).

6 On epidemics and their impact on daily life between 700 and 1150, see Farris 2009.

7 On these matters, see Philips 2018. Phillips analyses the Heian-period discourse on wrathful spirits through such terms as *mononoke, jaki, mokke* and *tatari* and explores its impact on the body politic.

8 *Honchō seiki*, entry 28.7.945.

9 *Honchō seiki*, entry 3.8.945.

10 This ritual was practised as an annual event since 821; the formula quoted here is recorded in *Gishiki* (872). Nakai 2013: 137. On the development of Japanese *tsuina* from Chinese exorcist court rites (*nuo*), see Suzuki 2000.

11 *Nihon koten bungaku taikei* 1, vol. *Kojiki norito*: 431–3. 'Underworld' translates *ne no kuni soko no kuni*.

12 For example, *Nihon shoki* (720), Aston 1972, I: 25.

13 Shibata 1984; Nishiyama 1995.

14 *Nihon sandai jitsuroku*, entry 20.5.863.

15 *Nihon sandai jitsuroku*, entry 14.6.865.

16 *Teishin kōki*, entry 23.i6.920. Only excerpts from this diary have survived.

17 *Yasaka jinja kiroku* 1: 577. Ennyo is mentioned as the Gionsha's founder also in *Iroha jiruishō*, a late-Kamakura dictionary, and in *Kyūrei zatsujiki*, a record compiled at Iwashimizu Hachimangū between 1367 and 1376. Jōjūji flourished until a fire destroyed the temple grounds in 884. Kubota Osamu (1974: 91) suggests that control over the Gion temple may have passed into the hands of Kōfukuji (in Nara) soon after this calamity. See also McMullin 1988.

18 *Yasaka jinja kiroku* 1: 574. Kubota 1974: 34; Nakai 2013: 129. McMullin 1987 lends credence to this account, and stresses Mototsune's activity in founding numerous temples and cloisters on Mt Hiei in this same period.

19 The authenticity of the 935 edict remains contested, but the fact that 'Gion Tenjindō' was among the temples and shrines called upon by the court at times of epidemics or earthquakes (e.g. in 938 and 958) in subsequent decades leaves no doubt that it had risen to a high status by that time. Nakai 2013: 131; Suzuki 2019: 90.

20 This edict is known only from a quotation in *Nijūnisha chūshiki*, a text from the Muromachi period (included in *Gunsho ruijū*). For discussions about its interpretation, see Kubota 1974: 38; Imahori 1999b; Nakai 2013; Suzuki 2019.

21 Nakai 1993, chapter 'Ekibyō to goryōe'. The name Kankeiji draws on the year periods Jō*gan* (859–77) and Gen*kei* (877–85).

22 *Rihō ōki*, entry 2.8.945. This diary was written by Prince Shigeakira, one of Emperor Daigo's sons. Yu 2003: 166.

23 *Chūgaishō* entry 19.7.1147; Moromoto's interlocutor was the imperial regent Fujiwara no Tadazane (1078–162). Suzuki 2019: 93.

24 *Honchō seiki*, entry 29.3.1148; Suzuki 2019: 94.

25 *Kakuzenshō* 1, *Yakushi-hō*; Suzuki 2019: 94. *Kakuzenshō* is a compendium of esoteric rituals and deities, compiled by Kakuzen around the year 1200.

26 *Asabashō* cites the no longer extant text *Sōshin hachi mandara shō* (attributed to the Tendai abbot Son'i, 866–940) in its section on Bishamon Tennō (Vaiśravaṇa). Misaki 1956: 218.

27 *Fusō ryakki*, entry 14.10.1070. Murayama 1991: 324. On the development of the Daishōgun cult (referring also to the Gionsha), see Faure 2012, 2021.

28 *Nijūnisha chūshiki* gives 972, *Shake jōjō kiroku* 974, and *Nihongi ryaku* and *Nenjū gyōji hishō* cite 975.

29 It is likely that before this time, Gionsha was for a while part of the Kōfukuji network, as was nearby Kiyomizudera. Kubota (1974, chapter 4) and McMullin (1988) offer different views on the circumstances around Enryakuji's takeover.

30 For a brief history of the Hie Shrines, see Breen and Teeuwen 2010, chapter 3.

31 The founding of an *otabisho* in 974 is first mentioned in shrine records from the late-Kamakura period (*Shake jōjō kiroku*, c. 1323). *Yasaka jinja kiroku* 1: 579.

32 *Nihongi ryaku*, entry 15.6.975; Okada 1994: 474.

33 Seta Katsuya relates this document, which is included in the Edo-period archival collection *Gionsha ki* (vol. 23, *Yasaka jinja kiroku* 1: 828), to a 1431 lawsuit in which two parties fought over the priestship of this *otabisho* (Seta 2009: 355–6) – a conflict to which we will return later. These documents use old materials as evidence in a new and very particular setting, and thus must be handled with care; it is likely that their contents have been slanted.

34 Seta 2009: 355; *Yasaka jinja kiroku* 1: 828.

35 Okada 1994; Seta 1979.

36 Fukuhara 1995: 14 and 70. Fukuhara refers to *yudate kagura* performances by *miko* shrine maidens at the *otabisho* during the period that the *mikoshi* were stalled

there; but the earliest source on such *kagura* dates from 1550 (p. 73, note 43), and
such rites are in my view more naturally explained in other ways. *Yudate kagura*
consisted of sprinkling water from a boiling kettle onto the spectators to convey
the blessings of the gods that are present at the *otabisho* only during the brief spell
between the two processions.

37 *Nihongi ryaku*, entry 27.6.994. The entry ends by noting that this was not a
    performance sanctioned by the court, but an event that started from 'street
    rumours'. This *goryōe* is adduced as the legendary origin of the Imamiya festival,
    referred to as the Murasakino *goryōe* in classical times. For an analysis of this
    festival, see Honda 2013.

38 There are many such entries in court diaries. For examples, see *Inokuma kanpaku
    ki*, entry 13.6.1197, and *Denryaku*, entry 14.6.1111.

39 *Shunki* entry 9.4.1040. According to this entry, the author 'secretly' viewed
    the Inari festival (*Inari-sai*) on this day from a 'small hut near the Shichijō-
    Horikawa intersection'. First mention of this festival dates back to 1006 (*Shōki
    mokuroku*: 'During the Inari festival there was fighting and rioting'; quoted in
    Ueki 2001: 35). The *otabisho* appears first in *Sankaiki*, entry 23.4.1167 (Okada
    1994: 461).

40 Okada 1994: 468. Matsunoo's festival is even more sparsely documented than that
    of Fushimi Inari, which makes it impossible to find conclusive evidence.

41 Okada 1994 discussed the origins and early history of six *mikoshi* festivals in Kyoto
    (Inari, Matsunoo, Gion, Kitano, Imamiya and Izumoji).

42 *Honchō seiki*, entry 14.6.999. Koyama 2013: 626. Ueki (2001: 49), however, reads
    mura 村 as *hashira* 柱, a 'pillar'.

43 Note, however, that *dengaku* troupes were also referred to as *mura*, in this case
    designating a troupe of performers.

44 Tōno 2004. The description of the *hyō* is from *Shoku Nihon kōki*, entry 16.11.833;
    the twenty pullers are mentioned in *Gishiki* 3.

45 Phillips 2018: 230–3.

46 *Ō-no-mai* ('dance of the king') was performed by a masked man carrying a halberd.
    The figure of Sarutahiko, which plays a role in many festivals and folk rituals until
    this day, developed from this dance.

47 *Sei-no-o* (or *sainō*) is a geometric dance performed by men with covered mouths,
    associated with *goryōe*.

48 Gomi Fumihiko interprets this scene differently, taking the disassembly of the
    otabisho as evidence that this sequence does not depict the Gion festival at all, but
    rather the Imamiya festival, another *goryōe* that started in 1001 in a site outside
    of the city to the north-west of the palace (Gomi 1984: 352). Interpreting this site
    as *rekke no tsuji* rather than the *otabisho* (which was a temporary structure for the
    Imamiya festival, but permanent for Gion) renders it possible to identify this scene

as a representation of the Gion festival. Either way, these two festivals appear to have been very similar, again reminding us of the fact that the Gion festival was part of a broader *goryōe* culture.

49 Gomi 1984, chapter 4; Wakita 2016: 43.
50 *Makura no sōshi*, section 80.
51 See Raz 1985; Plutschow 1983.
52 *Nihongi ryaku*, entry 10.4.998. *Zōnin* can either refer to commoners without rank, or to lowly servants or guards of courtiers or warriors. It is not always possible to determine what is meant in specific contexts.
53 Inoue 1972.
54 *Rakuyō dengaku ki*. For a slightly different translation, see Raz 1985: 297.
55 Toda 1971; Yu 2003.
56 *Shake jōjō kiroku* (*Yasaka jinja kiroku* 1: 587). *Hyakurenshō*, entry 14.6.1157, likewise reports the introduction of this system for the Gion festival. Yamaji 2009: 43; Wakita 2016: 58–9.
57 *Hyakurenshō*, entry 29.4.1138. Shimosaka 2001: 261, note 1.
58 *Hyakurenshō*, entry 14.5.1179; *Sankaiki*, same date.
59 Seta 2009: 370–6.
60 Reporting a fire, *Hyakurenshō* (entry 13.1.1117) describes this site as a detached shrine (*betsugū*) of the Gionsha already some decades earlier. *Shake jōjō kiroku* records that the Shōshōi plot, on the intersection of Reizei and Higashi-no-Tōin Streets, became shrine property in 1136 as the site of a new *otabisho* for 'Harime' (*Yasaka jinja kiroku* 1: 587). In 1134, *Chōshūki* (the diary of Minamoto no Morotoki, a courtier who served under Retired Emperors Shirakawa and Toba) notes that two *mikoshi* were swept away by the river waters on their way to the Ōmandokoro, suggesting that by that date, the third *mikoshi* was already destined for Shōshōi. Ueki 2001: 54, note 4.
61 *Hyakurenshō*, entry 7.6.1234, quoted in Gomi 1984: 353; Ueki 2001: 53; Seta 2009: 392; and others.
62 Seta 2009: 359.
63 In 996, the Gionsha was added as the twenty-first on a list of shrines that received regular and interim offerings from the court in reaction to epidemics in 994 and 995. This list was later finalized with the addition of the Hie Shrines in 1039, completing what has since been called the 'system of twenty-two shrines'.
64 *Nihongi ryaku*, entry 15.6.975; Okada 1994: 474.
65 Yasaka Jinja 1906: 85–6.
66 Gomi 1984: 352.
67 Gomi 1984: 356.
68 In a transitional phase, which stretched far into the Kamakura period, both court nobles and selected merchants were duty-bound to supply *uma no osa* for the Gion

procession. Among nobles, however, compliance with this duty proved impossible to enforce. Gomi 1984: 364–5.

69 *Sankaiki*, entries 12.4 and 6.5.1167; Okada 1994: 463–4.
70 Michael Como, for example, argues that the use of masks (in the Bugaku dances) and horses at the Kamo festival derived from Chinese rites and were intended to produce *yang* energies, thus diluting the *yin* miasmas that caused illness (Como 2009, chapter 5). Suzuki Masataka (2000) points out a similar rationale of boosting *yang* energies in the Chinese *nuo* rites that developed into *tsuina* rites of demon exorcism in Japan.

Chapter 2

1 Gay 2001, chapter 2.
2 This is a close parallel to the Ōtsu *jinin* of the Hie Shrines, who used a similar offering at the Sannō festival as an important public statement of their privileged status.
3 Tanaka 2011: 85. The number sixty-four pertains to the situation in 1343, when these guilds were embroiled in a long court case on trading rights. The newer guild (*shinza*) claimed to have been founded in 1201–4; in response, the older guild (*honza*) put its origins in 1135–41.
4 Watanabe 2011: 22; Kawauchi 2006b. First mention of the Imamiya *jinin* as bearers of the Ōmiya *mikoshi* is in *Gion shigyō nikki*, entry 14.6.1352.
5 On such attacks, see Adolphson 2000.
6 *Chūyūki*, entry 1.1.1105. See Kubota 1974: 110 and Adolphson 2000: 243.
7 *Hyakurenshō*, entries 18.7 and 12.9.1123; *Tendai zasu ki*, entry 4.7.1123. Breen and Teeuwen 2010: 82–3.
8 Noda 1959; Yamamoto 2006. An alternative interpretation of the term *inu jinin* is 'pseudo-*jinin*' or 'people performing a function similar to *jinin*, but without enjoying *jinin* status'. Either way, there is no doubt that this was a denigrating appellation.
9 *Meigetsu ki*, entries 1.4 and 16.7.1229.
10 This period included an intercalary second month in 1352.
11 Hanada 2014.
12 *Kenshun sōjō nikki*, entry 14.6.1355.
13 In 1129, for example, the retired emperor viewed the *goryōe* from a pavilion at the crossing of Sanjō and Karasuma Streets. *Chūyūki*, entry 14.6.1129.
14 Collcutt 1981: 120–1; Adolphson 1997: 248–52 and 2000: 307–15.
15 Documents related to these events are collected in vol. 10 of *Gionsha ki* (*Yasaka jinja kiroku* 1: 657–74).

16 Mieda 2001: 28.

17 Futaki 1985: 83. According to *Gogumai ki* (entry 7.6.1370), the problem in
    1370 was not so much that the Gionsha lacked *mikoshi*, but rather that the Gion
    mikoshi were not allowed to leave before the Hie *mikoshi* had been restored. On
    7.6.1378, however, the same author states explicitly that the Gion *mikoshi* are
    'not ready'. Seta Katsuya (2009: 408, note 99) writes that the Hachiōji *mikoshi* was
    finally nearing completion in 1392. See also Adolphson 1997: 251.

18 No diaries refer to the Gion festival between 1380 and 1399, with the exception of
    two entries in *Yoshida-ke hinami ki* in 1383 (noting merely that *hoko* were paraded
    on the seventh). *Gionsha ki* (vol. 11, *Yasaka jinja kiroku* 1: 677–80) includes lists
    of payments in connection with the festival for 1397 and 1398, suggesting that the
    festival was performed in some form during these years. Kawauchi 2006a: 17.

19 Kosugi 1970; Nochi 1998.

20 On these estates, see Nishiyama 1974.

21 Mieda 2001: 12–18; Kosugi 1971.

22 Gay 2001: 81.

23 Futaki 1985: 64–103.

24 *Gogumai ki*, entry 7.6.1378.

25 Varley 1990: 463.

26 *Moromori ki*, entries 7.6 and 14.6.1364. Goshima 2004: 208.

27 *Yoshida-ke hinami ki*, entries 7.6 and 13.6.1402.

28 *Yasutomi ki*, entries 7.6 and 14.6.1422. Goshima Kuniharu, however, relates the
    size of the float parades to the presence or absence of the *mikoshi*, rather than the
    shogun (Goshima 2004: 206).

29 Futaki 1985: 94. These manuals, titled *Nenjū teirei ki* and *Nenjū kōreiki*, are
    undated.

30 *Meigetsu ki*, entry 7.1231.

31 Seta 2009: 380–3.

32 However, Watanabe Ayumu (2011) shows that this decree (*jinin kuji chōjirei*) had
    a much more limited impact than previously thought, because it was never meant
    to cover the duties of *jinin* to their shrine or temple overlords. Watanabe does not
    refer to the *bajōyaku* ban (*bajōyaku chōjirei*) issued in 1324, which Seta regards
    as a further elaboration of the *jinin kuji chōjirei*. As Seta points out, however,
    the *bajōyaku* was often levied on non-*jinin*. In the light of Watanabe's findings,
    it appears more reasonable to surmise that the *bajōyaku* would have become the
    object of a ban as a case of shrine/temple overlords extracting levies beyond their
    recognized territory or sphere.

33 Wakita 2016: 68–9.

34 The merchant in question was called Dōzen Hōshi. *Hōshi* ('dharma masters'), originally
    referring to Buddhist instructors, was widely used to refer to all kinds of laypeople in a
    temple's service, including even outcasts and beggars who prayed for alms.

35 Gay 2001: 69.

36 Seta 2009: 388; Gay 2001: 80.

37 Gay 2001: 81–5.

38 *Zōho Yasaka jinja monjo* 1: 222–488.

39 *Bajō onhoko shidai no koto, Zōho Yasaka jinja monjo* 1: 224. This document, dated
   7.6.1409, is also included in *Gionsha ki* (vol. 17, *Yasaka jinja kiroku* 1: 772). *Shintō
   taikei* vol. *Gion*: 216–217. Wakita 2016: 62–3.

40 *Gyokuzui* (the diary of Kujō Kaneie), entry 14.4.1220. The number thirteen
   features already in an 1158 report submitted to the court bureaucracy by the
   Gionsha priesthood (*Kanjin'in shoshi gebumi*). Wakita 2016: 96–7.

41 *Zōho Yasaka jinja monjo* 1: 320–2 (document nr. 397, dated 1423) and 331–4
   (document nr. 410, dated 1431).

42 *Bajō sanbyaku kanmon dō gegyō no koto*, Wakita 2016: 66–7. *Shinpen Yasaka
   jinja kiroku*: 3–26 includes many similar budgets ranging from 1397 to 1441, but
   strikingly not these two.

43 *Eikyō sannen gegyōchō*, Seta 2009: 346–7.

44 Shimosaka 2001: 242–3.

45 This turnaround must have been related in some manner to Yoshinori's
   troublesome relationship with Enryakuji. Before his sudden rise to the position of
   shogun in 1429 (famously, through the drawing of lots), Yoshinori had held the
   position of Tendai abbot; when he became shogun he sent his younger brother
   as his replacement. Yet he became embroiled in fighting between Enryakuji and
   its rival Onjōji in 1433–5, on the side of the latter. This conflict ended with the
   decapitation of Enryakuji leaders, the burning of the mountain's central hall
   (Konponchūdō), and the appointment of a new, shogun-friendly leadership on Mt
   Hiei. How Yoshinori's decision to return the *otabisho* to Sukemasa's descendants
   was related to these grand political events is not at all clear. The timing, however,
   leaves little doubt that Yoshinori's relationship with Enryakuji must have loomed
   large in the background.

46 On these matters, see Shimosaka 2016: 844–50.

47 The Hōjuin regained control over the Ōmandokoro and its priestship in 1443.
   Shimosaka 2016: 849.

48 *Manzai jungō nikki*, entry 7.6.1415, quoted in Kawauchi 2006a: 31.

49 Kawauchi 2006a: 21–22. The postponement in 1458 is reported by Kamo Arimori
   in his diary *Arimori-kyō ki*; see Kawauchi 2006a: 39.

50 Kawauchi 2006a: 38.

51 By 1419, the route of the floats was more or less the same as in modern times
   (before the rerouting of 1956): along the Shijō and Gojō (Matsubara Street) on
   the seventh day, and along Sanjō and Shijō on the fourteenth day (*Yasutomi
   ki*, entries 7.7 and 14.7.1419. In contrast, the three *mikoshi* crossed the Kamo

River at Shijō; two then turned south to the Ōmandokoro *otabisho*, while the third headed north to the Shōshōi *otabisho*. A week later, the three *mikoshi* were carried to a meeting point a few block further west, at the crossing of Ōmiya Street and Sanjō, from where they headed east towards the Gionsha. Kawauchi 2015: 88–9.

52 Yamaji 2009: 32.
53 Goshima 2004: 206–8.
54 *Munekata-kyō ki* (by the noble Funahashi Munekata), entry 26.8.1471. Kawauchi 2015: 75.
55 Kawauchi (2011: 3–4) lists all 'spectacles' (*furyū*) that figure in court diaries between 1322 and 1465.
56 Honda 2010.
57 Honda 2010: 4.
58 *Hanazono Tennō shinki*, entry 24.7.1321. This section draws heavily on Ueki 2001: 57–65.
59 *Hanazono Tennō shinki*, entry 14.6.1323.
60 Ueki 2001: 59.
61 Honda 2010: 5–6.
62 A 2014 report (Bunkachō 2014) discusses nineteen festivals within the modern boundaries of Kyoto City that involve such *kenboko* (also known as *hoko sashi*).
63 Honda 2010: 10.
64 In *Moromori ki* (the diary of the court noble Nakahara Moromori), entries 14.6.1349 and 14.6.1351. See Kawauchi 2011: 3.
65 *Gogumai ki* (a diary of the court noble Sanjō Sanefusa), entry 14.6.1376.
66 *Moromori ki*, entry 8.6.1345. My description draws on Ueki 2001: 60.
67 Two of the floats in today's parades are *kasa* (Ayagasa-hoko and Shijō Kasa-hoko). These, however, are placed on top of wheeled platforms, rather than integrated in dances, as at the Yasuraibana festival.
68 Ueki 2001: 62.
69 *Yasutomi ki* (Nakahara Yasutomi's diary), entry 14.6.1422.
70 *Moromori ki*, entry 7.6.1345.
71 Yamaji 2009: 48.
72 Kawauchi 2011: 3–4 lists all *furyū* that figure in court diaries between 1322 and 1465.
73 *Moromori ki*, entry 14.6.1365. *Kasasagi* means 'magpie', and at times, the character for this bird (鵲) is used with reference to this *hoko*. The heron (*sagi*) costumes used for the dance, however, leave little doubt that this *hoko* played on the theme of *sagi*. *Kasa-sagi* ('parasolled heron; magpie') is a playful pun.
74 Yamaji 2006: 53. Other possible interpretations are that the *shōmoji* of Kitabatake were sponsored by the *ōdoneri* guild as musicians and dancers, and that the

ōdoneri hoko that followed the dancers was by some regarded as part of the same float, and by others as a separate entry to the parade.

75 For example, in *Kanmon gyoki* (the diary of Prince Fushimi-no-miya Sadafusa), entry 14.6.1436. Sadafusa lists the *kasasagi-hoko* and the *ōdoneri-hoko* as two separate entities (in this year, both entered the palace grounds in the early morning of the fourteenth to show their respective halberds and dances to the nobility, and receive rewards for their efforts). In subsequent entries (1437, 1438 and 1441), however, he mentions the *kasasagi-hoko* and the *ōtonoe-hoko* as a pair (*ōtonoe* is a variant of *ōdoneri*). How to interpret this is not clear to me.

76 Izumi 2017; Hattan 2018: 30–7. These copies are currently kept at the Tokyo National Museum. Copies of these images can already be found in *Shokoku zue nenjū gyōji taisei* (1806) and *Zōho Gion goryōe saiki* (1812), where they are identified as 'ancient depictions of the Gion festival' showing floats that are no longer extant. For *Zōho Gion goryōe saiki*, see *Shintō taikei*, vol. *Gion*: 434–8.

77 Kojima 2020. The Sanjōbōmon palace came to be known as the 'Lower Compound' from 1432, and was no longer the stage of grand rites of the kind depicted on these screens.

78 This is also suggested in *Zōho Gion goryōe saiki*, with a reference to *Sekiso ōrai* (*Shintō taikei*, vol. *Gion*: 435).

79 Kawauchi 2015: 60–3.

80 Izumi 2017. *Katsuraotoko* features in the Chinese miscellanary *Youyang zazu* (c. 860). Banished to the moon palace for his magical practices, he spends his days swinging his axe at a giant osmanthus tree (*katsura*). This tale was well known in Japan since classical times.

81 Yamaji 2009: 56.

82 This is based on the *furyū* list in Kawauchi 2011.

83 Fukuhara 2006, quoted in Yamaji 2009: 118–19.

84 On this point, see also Goshima 2017: 32–56.

85 Iwata 2017.

86 Goshima 2017: 35–6.

87 The festival of Fushimi Inari developed in parallel with and along the same lines as the Gion festival in a relationship of mutual inspiration and copying. The Inari festival, however, did not enjoy the same amount of attention from the imperial and shogunal courts, and its large medieval float parade was not revived after the Ōnin war. While the Gion festival developed into a symbol of the splendour of the capital, Fushimi Inari's early parade remained a local event. It was therefore less influential in spreading this festival format to other parts of the country.

88 Ueki and Fukuhara 2016: 114–15.

89 Nishida 1962; Suzuki 2010, 2019; Saitō 2012.

90 Aston 1972, I: 50.

91 McMullin (1988), however, does accept this *Fudoki* as authentic.

92 For a brief discussion, see Suzuki 2019: 227.

93 This phrase, which derives from Chinese decrees, translates as 'Urgent [action required], in accordance with the laws'.

94 According to *Hoki naiden*, the red and white *mochi* to be offered on 1.1 represent Kotan's flesh and bones, the green mugwort (*yomogi*) *mochi* on 3.3 his skin, the irises on 5.5 his hair and beard, the noodles on 7.7 his tendons and the chrysanthemum sake on 9.9 his blood.

95 Saitō 2021: 498.

96 Murayama 1991: 327. It must be noted that Murayama's hypothesis is unconfirmed. Saitō (2021) rather sees *Hoki naiden* as a 'folk' commentary on calendrical taboos, compiled by unknown diviners outside of court circles.

97 Imahori 1993.

98 Honda Ken'ichi (2016: 204) adduces sources on this offering rite (*awameshi kugo*) from the fifteenth century onwards. *Kyō warawa* (1658) notes: 'Even though Somin Shōrai was poor, he offered lodging to [Susanoo no] Mikoto and served him millet. This is why millet is offered at the crossing of Shijō and Kyōgoku Streets on the fourteenth day of the sixth month.' This rite is last mentioned in 1689, when it was performed in the new *otabisho* along Shijō; its practice likely ceased in the eighteenth century (2016: 210). It is worth noting, moreover, that an offering of millet (*Awazu no goku*) was equally central to the Sannō festival of the Hie Shrines.

99 Hayek 2008: 153; Suzuki 2018: 257–8; Saitō 2021.

100 Suzuki 2018: 247.

101 Kawamura 2021: 6–7.

102 *Kennaiki*, entry 14.6.1439.

103 This section draws on Fukuhara 2016.

104 Teeuwen and Breen 2017: 95–7.

Chapter 3

1 For a helpful overview of these events, see Berry 1994: 46–7.

2 For a chronological overview of Gion festival performances between 1321 and 1602, see Kawauchi 2012: 33–54.

3 *Daijōin jisha zōjiki*, entry 16.6.1470.

4 Shimosaka 2014, chapter 2.

5 Murayama 1994: 288.

6 Hayashiya 1950, 1953a, and 1953b.

7 Minshushugi Kagakusha Kyōkai Kyōto Shibu Rekishi Bukai, narrated by Hayashiya Tatsusaburō, *Gion matsuri*, Tōkyō Daigaku Shuppanbu, 1953. This volume also contains a long essay by Hayashiya on the early history of the Gion festival (Hayashiya 1953b).

8 *Kyōto shinbun*, 14 July 2018.

9 Kawauchi 2007: 19–42; 2008.

10 Goshima 2004, chapter 6.

11 Goshima 2004: 189.

12 Hayashiya 1950: 42.

13 For an overview, see Hayashima 2006, chapter 2.

14 Hayashima 2006, part 3.

15 Berry 1994: 158–67. There is much controversy around the role of the Lotus leagues. Hayashiya understood them as a *machishū* movement that marked the rise of commoner autonomy, while others (e.g. Nishio 1981) have argued that they served primarily as a militia in the service of warrior hegemons – notably, Hosokawa Harumoto (1514–63). Berry stresses the 'religious passion that "lent zeal" to the movement' (Berry 1994: 169).

16 On the development and culture of *kanjin*, see Goodman 1994.

17 Shimosaka 2014: 287–92.

18 Shimosaka 2014: 289.

19 *Gionsha ki* 16, entry 13.2.1496, *Yasaka jinja kiroku* 1: 751; Kawauchi 2007: 77. Hayashima Daisuke (2006: 271) suggests that the shogunate was responding to pressure from the Ōmandokoro priests in this matter.

20 For an account of these events, see Berry 1994: 49–52.

21 *Yasaka jinja monjo* 1: 266–7. The order is dated 26.5.1497. Kawauchi 2007: 80–2.

22 Goshima 2004: 202.

23 It is worth noting that this order refers to the Hie festival (*Hie sairei*) rather than the already-defunct Kosatsuki-e. The Hie or Sannō festival, performed in the fourth month, survived the Ōnin war and went on to flourish under Tokugawa patronage. It was not linked to the *bajōyaku*, however, and in medieval times it was never mentioned in conjunction with Enryakuji interference with the Gion *mikoshi*.

24 *Gionsha ki* 16, entry 1.6.1500, *Yasaka jinja kiroku* 1: 753; quoted in Kawauchi 2007: 83.

25 *Gojigen'in-dono gyoki*, entry 7.6.1500. On the 1500 revival, see Hayashima 2006: 272–4; Kawauchi 2007: 76–89.

26 *Gohōkōin ki*, entry 7.6.1500.

27 *Gohōkōin ki*, entry 14.6.1500

28 *Gojigen'in-dono gyoki*, entry 14.6.1500.

29 *Tokikuni-kyō ki* (by the court noble Yamashina Tokikuni), entry 14.6.1501; Kawauchi 2007: 93.

30 *Gohōjōji kanpaku ki* (the diary of Konoe Hisamichi, who was Hisatsune's brother) and *Sanetaka kō ki* (the diary of Sanjōnishi Sanetaka), entry 7.6.1506. Kawauchi 2007: 93.

31 *Gojigen'in-dono gyoki*, entry 14.8.1494. On these events and their possible connection to the revival of the Gion festival, see Hayashima 2006: 268–71; Kawauchi 2012: 199–219.

32 Hayashima 2006: 273.

33 Berry 1994: 51.

34 *Gohōjōji kanpaku ki*, entry 23.5.1512. Kawauchi 2007: 103.

35 *Nisuiki* (Washinoo Takayasu), entry 27.6.1522. Kawauchi 2007: 106.

36 *Gionsha ki* 16, *Yasaka jinja kiroku* 1: 768; Kawauchi 2007: 55. This order is dated 22.5.1533.

37 *Gion shigyō nikki*, entry 7.6.1533. Kawauchi 2017: 61.

38 Hayashima 2006: 296–7.

39 *Gionsha ki* 16, order dated 9.8.1533. *Yasaka jinja kiroku* 1: 767; Kawauchi 2007: 66.

40 *Gionsha ki* 15 (*Yasaka jinja kiroku* 1: 738–47); *Shinpen Yasaka Jinja kiroku*: 54–61. The oldest manuscript is a copy by Matsuda Yorisuke's grandson, Yoritaka, dated 1560; perhaps Yorisuke's list was compiled in this format at that juncture.

41 This explains why in 1533, shogun Yoshiharu decreed that the festival was to be carried out 'in accord with our orders as issued in 1500 and 1506'. *Gionsha ki* 16, 22.5.1533 (*Yasaka jinja kiroku* 1: 768). Kawauchi 2007: 55.

42 'To the Ōmandokoro: west along Shijō until Karasuma Street, and then south to the *otabisho*; returning westwards along Gojō (that is, Matsubara Street) until Ōmiya Street, and then north to Sanjō. To Shōshōi: likewise along Shijō until Higashi-no-Tōin Street, and then north to Reizei Street where the *otabisho* is located; returning westwards along Nijō until Ōmiya, and then south to Sanjō.' *Shinpen Yasaka jinja kiroku*: 54.

43 For an analysis, see Kawauchi 2006a: 150–1.

44 *Shinpen Yasaka jinja kiroku*: 63. On the origins and further development of this element of the festival, see Kawauchi 2006c.

45 Urade-yama is referred to as Ayutsuri Jingu Kōgu-yama and Hakuga-yama as Kotowari-yama in this list. No float with the name Michitsukuri-yama features elsewhere, and in *Gion'e yamahoku no shidai* the street in charge of this *yama* (Shijō, between Machi – the later Shinmachi – and Nishi-no-Tōin Streets) has no float at all.

46 The two Tenjin-yama may refer to Arare- and Abura Tenjin-yama.

47 Kubota 2016: 87.

48 McKelway 2006: 2–3.

49 Rekihaku-A translates Rekihaku kōhon. This set of screens was earlier known as the Machida-bon and is recently also referred to as the Sanjōke-bon or Sanjō version.

50 McKelway 2006: 86. McKelway recognizes in the screens 'a carefully mapped landscape of human networks [that] revolve around the young shogun' Yoshiharu (McKelway 2006: 97).
51 McKelway 2006: 128; Ozawa and Kawashima 1994.
52 Satō Yasuhiro 2006: 52; Hattan 2018: 323. Satō suggests that a priest-like figure seated in one of the boats depicted on the Hie screen may represent the sponsor.
53 Kamei 2003: 230–8.
54 *Kototsugu-kyō ki*, entry 15.4.1548.
55 Kawauchi 2015: 140–3. The source is *Chōkyō nengo Kinai heiran ki*, *Zoku gunsho ruijū* 20 *jō*.
56 Hattan 2018: 325. Kawauchi (2015: 158) argues that the screen mixes not only events on different dates but also from different years, perhaps combining memories from 1522 and 1548. The screen depicts a *torii* gate on the Shijō Bridge over the Kamo River that was washed away by a flood in 1544.
57 Kyōto-shi 1969: 100–4.
58 Letter, dated 17 August 1561. Ruiz de Medina 1995: 350–2. Translation from Cooper 1965: 361–2, slightly adapted with reference to the original. I thank Martin Nogueira Ramos for his help with this source.
59 Yamabushi-yama comes closest; it shows how the Hiei monk Jōzō Kisho (891–964) used his esoteric powers to save the Yasaka pagoda when it tilted. Even that pagoda, however, had nothing to do with the Gionsha, although it served as a Gion landmark.
60 Handelman 1990: 41–3.

Chapter 4

1 This number remained relatively stable in the seventeenth century but dwindled gradually in the latter half of the Edo period, dipping below 300,000 by the 1850s.
2 Sugimori 2008, chapter 1.
3 *Zōshiki* (literally 'miscellaneous goods') is a classical court title, originally referring to storehouse guards at court. The link between the medieval *zōshiki* families and these earlier low-ranking guards (also known as *kodoneri zōshiki*) remains unclear. Kyōto-shi 1969: 566–9.
4 *Shinshū Yasaka jinja monjo, chūsei hen*, documents nr. 175 and 181.
5 Kyōto-shi 1969: 391–5.
6 Tani and Masui 1994: 81–2.
7 Kyōto-shi 1972: 72–3.
8 Tani and Masui 1994: 85.
9 Kyōto-shi 1972: 76–80.

10 This section builds mainly on Tomii 1996.

11 On the seventh, the governor installed himself in Daiun'in on the Shijō-Teramachi intersection. On the seventeenth, his viewing pavilion was at Seiganji, further north along Teramachi Street. In contrast to the Muromachi shoguns, the governors did not show themselves openly to the public. In this, they followed the practice of the Tokugawa shoguns, who preferred to conceal their person while subjecting others to their gaze (Walthall 2006).

12 Lillehoj 2004, chapter 7. These doors were installed in 1677. In her interpretation of these paintings, Lillehoj assumes that the Gion festival was conceived as an expression of 'the vitality of Kyoto commoners' (188) and sees Tōfukumon'in's choice to decorate her quarters in this manner as a sign of her 'interest in commoners' (189). However, this ignores the public nature of the festival in the Edo period.

13 Lots were drawn at the Rokkakudō Temple, which also served as the main meeting hall for the townspeople of the Lower City, on the day before each parade. A number of floats had fixed positions in the parade; a complicated system ensured that *hoko* and *yama* floats were spread evenly through the first parade (with the *hoko* separated by three *yama*).

14 On the seventh, the *zōshiki*'s control post was at Shijō-Takakura; on the fourteenth, at the intersection of Sanjō and Higashi-no-Tōin Streets.

15 For another full overview, see Gion Matsuri Yamahoko Rengōkai 1974: 10–19.

16 *Shinpen Yasaka jinja kiroku*: 64 (list 4). Hashi Benkei-yama is here listed as 'Ushiwaka no yama'.

17 For a full overview, based on records from the late Edo period, see Tomii 1971: 239–46.

18 Tomii 1971: 216.

19 Koromo-no-tana Kita-chō had one other 'old *yorichō*' (Kamanza-chō, its neighbour to the west along Sanjō Street), which was treated with the same level of respect as Minami-chō.

20 For a complete overview, see Gion Matsuri Yamahoko Rengōkai 2012. Gion Matsuri Yamahoko Rengōkai 1994 includes images of all the highlights.

21 Kawashima 2010: 96–7; Hakurakuten-yama Hozonkai 1976.

22 *Zōshiki yōroku* (*Nihon shomin seikatsu shiryō* 14): 342; Tomii 1971: 209).

23 Wakahara 1982: 105; Kawashima 2010: 92.

24 Satō and Yano 2018: 27–40.

25 A similar set of procedures for the Ayagasa-hoko (*Gion'e teishiki*, 1858) can be found in *Shinpen Yasaka jinja kiroku*: 552–66.

26 On the Fune-hoko procedures, see Satō and Yano 2018: 163–78; Satō 2019: 20–8.

27 The flute used in *Gion-bayashi* is a traverse bamboo flute developed for Noh plays, called *nōkan*. This is an instrument that demands special skills.

28 To be more precise, there were three categories of such hired 'carpenters'. *Tettaigata* assembled the float's lower frame, and also directed the pullers during the parade. *Daikugata* added the upper stage, including the roof. *Kurumagata* were responsible for the wheels. Teams of pullers were also hired; most commonly, the *tettaigata* leader was responsible for arranging this. Satō 2019: 22–4.

29 Naginata-hoko Hozonkai 2016: 22–48; Takamaki 2000: 286–96.

30 Tomii 1996: 60.

31 Religious connections with Enryakuji survived, and many of the Gionsha shrine monks were initiated and ordained in imperial cloisters that were part of the Enryakuji complex (notably, the Shōren'in). Ishizu 2020.

32 The vermilion-seal document issued by Tokugawa Ieyasu lists these land grants; see *Gion hon'en zatsu jikki*, in *Shinpen Yasaka jinja kiroku*: 97.

33 This fact was widely known. In his defence of non-celibacy (*Nikujiki saitai ben*, c. 1669), for example, the Shin priest Chikū (1634–1718) listed examples of married monks outside of the Shin sect; the Gionsha shrine monks were the first that came to his mind.

34 Wakita 2016: 141–2.

35 Kitamura 2019, chapter 3.

36 This stupa was lost to fire in the Kansei years (1789–1801) and not rebuilt afterwards.

37 Teeuwen 2022. On the Ōmandokoro, see Shimosaka 2016: 844–50; on the sale of the Shōshōi priestship, see *Shinshū Yasaka jinja monjo, chūsei-hen*: 82.

38 This screen, dated to the sixteenth century, is in the possession of Nishiki Tenmangū in central Kyoto. A similar image, copied in the eighteenth century, is kept at the Naginata-hoko. Kawauchi 2015: 32.

39 *Zōho Yasaka jinja monjo* 1 (nr. 918–19) includes two undated documents in which a newly appointed '*yudate* master' (*oyudate dayū*) promises to perform his duties without fail.

40 While the *honji* of Gozu Tennō was generally identified as Yakushi Nyorai, opinions were divided on Harisainyo and Hachiōji. *Gion hon'en zatsu jikki* (dated to the 1670s, *Shinpen Yasaka Jinja kiroku*: 67) quotes Jūichimen Kannon or Batō Kannon for Hairisainyo, and Bishamon or Shō Kannon for Hachiōji; perhaps the scroll shows Jūichimen and Shō Kannon.

41 Wakita 2016: 138–9.

42 Honda 2016: 210.

43 Tsuchimoto 1994.

44 Shimosaka 2016: 852–9.

45 Tsuchimoto 1994: 230–1; Honda 2016: 209–10.

46 A digital version of this text, and many others, can be viewed in the ARC Kotenseki Portal Database of Ritsumeikan University.

47 On the 'amalgam of prayer and play' that was characteristic of Edo-period religion, see Hur 2000.

48 This is a common theme in late-classical noble diaries (Teeuwen 2022).

49 Kawauchi 2012: 190–1.

50 *Shinshū Yasaka jinja monjo chūsei-hen*: 61.

51 Nishiyama 2015: 45–164.

52 Nishiyama 2017: 22–41.

53 Tomii 1996: 66–7; Nishiyama 2017: 36.

54 Nishiyama 2013: 25–42. Both the Funaki and the Hayashihara versions are dated to the first half of the seventeenth century.

55 Nishiyama 2017: 35; Gion Matsuri Hensan Iinkai 1976: 25–6.

56 Teahouses (*chaya*) offered both tea and female company. 'Girls who serve tea' (*chakumi onna*) was a much-used code word for (illegal) prostitutes. Upscale teahouses summoned girls from nearby brothels (*okiya*). These girls, who were accomplished in music, dance and party games, lived in the *okiya* that had them under contract, but served their customers in the teahouses.

57 In the solilunar calendar the last day could either be the twenty-ninth or the thirtieth.

58 Tomii 1996: 71; Fukuhara and Hattan 2013: 40. *Hinami kiji* was written by the Kyoto physician and historian Kurokawa Dōyū (1623–91).

59 Tomii 1996: 73.

60 Fukuhara and Hattan 2013: 100–5.

61 This piece is based on a poem that, according to legend, was made by Ono no Komachi when she was praying for rain at the Shinsen'en.

62 *Zaikyō nikki* (Kyoto diary), entry 18.6.1756. *Motoori Norinaga zenshū* vol. 16: 75.

63 *Zaikyō nikki*, entry 18.6.1757. *Motoori Norinaga zenshū* vol. 16: 114–16.

64 Nakagawa Kiun, *Annaisha* (The guide, 1662). Quoted in Kawashima 2010: 173.

65 Hayami Shungyōsai's *Shokoku zue nenjū gyōji taisei* (Illustrated compendium of seasonal events in all provinces, 1806). Quoted in Kawashima 2010: 174.

66 Norinaga wonders whether *mikoshi arai* derived from an older *mikoshi harai* ('*mikoshi* purification'), but his interest is purely academic, and he does not offer a witness account of the *mikoshi* processions.

67 Hattan (2018: 685–710) introduces and analyses *Gion nerimono ezukushi* (A pictorial record of the Gion pageant, 1755).

68 Hattan 2018: 711–27.

69 Kyōto-shi 1974: 364.

70 Hattan 2018: 774.

71 Ueki and Fukuhara 2016: 72.

72 *Zōho Gion goryōe saiki* 1 (Umetsuji Shunshō, 1820), *Shintō taikei* vol. *Gion*: 307.

73 The earliest known example of such amulets is Arare Tenjin-yama, which distributed amulets for protection against fire in 1735. Murakami 2010: 301–2.

74 Murakami 2010: 292–9.

75 See, for example, *Zōho Gion goryōe saiki* 1, *Shintō taikei* vol. *Gion*: 321. Today, *yoimiya* refers to the transfer of the gods to the *mikoshi* at Yasaka Shrine on 15 July.

76 *Gion goryōe saiki*, folio 4b; quoted in Murakami 2010: 306–7.

77 Murakami 2006.

78 Murakami (2006: 109) notes that at Urade-yama, lanterns were lit on the fourth, fifth and sixth by 1818 at the latest.

79 Onodera 1995.

80 Gion Matsuri Hensan Iinkai 1976: 21–8; Kawashima 2010: 16.

81 Kawashima 2010: 57–60.

82 Tomii (1996: 72) mentions 1721 as an example of such an occurrence.

83 *Shūi miyako meisho zue* vol. 2 (1787), quoted in Fukuhara and Hattan 2013: 64.

84 Buyō Inshi, *Seji kenbunroku* (1816); translation from Teeuwen and Nakai 2014: 269–70.

85 Teeuwen and Nakai 2014: 100.

86 Ueki 2001: 220–1.

87 Ueki 2001: 222.

Chapter 5

1 Baba 1905: 237. Satow translates 'car' (and 'was') in the singular; I have corrected this to 'cars' (and 'were'). 'Blossom-capital' (*Karaku* or *Kakei*) is a poetic epithet of Kyoto.

2 Nakagawa 2015: 45.

3 Nakagawa 2015: 40–9.

4 Kobayashi 2014: 93.

5 For telling examples see Kobayashi 2007 on the street of Arare Tenjin-yama, and Nishimura and Okuda 2011 on Tearaimizu-chō, another street with close links to the Gion festival.

6 Okuda 2010: 72.

7 Shimosaka 2019: 9. This street was named Saka ('The Slope') or Saka-chō until the mid-Edo period, when it housed lepers, *inu jinin* and a cremation site. When the colony of lepers was enclosed and separated from the rest of this street, Saka was divided into Monoyoshi-mura and (Saka) Yumiya-chō; this occurred in the early 1700s at the latest.

8 Satō 2021b.

9 The cuirasses deteriorated over time, and since 1974 Yumiya-chō no longer participates in the processions. Instead, the remaining armour is displayed in houses along the street and the Kyūsenkaku is opened to the public during the festival period.

10 These developments are analysed most precisely in Maxey 2014. For my own take on these matters, see Teeuwen 2017.

11 Shunshō served as a priest at the Hie Shrines in Sakamoto, but retired in 1807 and settled in Kyoto where he founded a private academy. Detailed Record of the Gion *Goryōe* (*Gion goryōe saiki*), by the famous publisher Yamamoto Chōbei, first appeared in 1757.

12 Fujita Teiei, otherwise unknown, is the author of the preface to Shunshō's work.

13 *Shintō taikei* vol. *Gion*: 301. Cf. also Figure 6, showing an image of Gozu Tennō from the 1792 *Zōho shoshū butsuzō zui*. The note on the left of this image identifies the gods of the three shrines of the Gionsha as 'Gozu Tennō (another name for Susanoo), Inada-hime, and Hachiōji'.

14 When Susanoo travelled up to the Plain of High Heaven to bid his sister Amaterasu farewell, Amaterasu met him with distrust. To prove his good intentions, Susanoo proposed a trial. When Amaterasu chewed up Susanoo's sword and spit it out, it morphed into three goddesses. Then Susanoo did the same with Amaterasu's pearls, and five male gods appeared. This outcome delighted Susanoo and reassured Amaterasu. Amaterasu's pearls were gathered in a necklace that was 'eight feet' (*yasaka*) long; Shunshō wrote *yasaka* with the characters 八坂 rather than 八尺 to connect this tale to the Gionsha.

15 *Shinshū Hirata Atsutane zenshū*, vol. 7.

16 Weiss 2022: 145–73. Mayumi Tsunetada, head priest of Yasaka Shrine from 1993 until 2002, likewise found Susanoo's origins in Korea (Mayumi 2000: 36–46).

17 Takahara 1962: 261–2. From 1867, however, the *rinjisai* was limited to a performance of Gagaku dance only (*azuma asobi*).

18 Dairenji was originally located in the temple district on the Kamo riverbank at Gojō but was in 1945 moved to its present location near Nijō, a fifteen-minute walk north of Yasaka Shrine.

19 *Kyōto shinbun*, 11 December 2018, 'Gozu Tennō, wagaya ni azukarimasu.'

20 Takahara 1962: 279–86. At the same time, land reforms (*agechi rei*) deprived the shrine of much of it land. The 15,122 *tsubo* of the old Gionsha precincts were reduced to a mere 3,852 (Tomii 1979: 297). Much of the expropriated land is in today's Maruyama Park.

21 Takahara 1962: 291. The Yasaka Teaching Institute survived the 1882 reforms, which separated ritual from teaching and banned priests from serving as campaign instructors. The institute was renamed Preaching Station of the Yasaka Church (*Yasaka kyōkai sekkyōsho*) and continued to function as the religious arm of the now 'non-religious' shrine.

22 *Kessha yuji* (An appeal to join our association, 1875), quoted in Tomii 1979: 298. The reference to Amaterasu and Ōkuninushi as lords over the visible and invisible realms draws on the teachings of Hirata Atsutane (1776–1843), and was at the core of conflicting views on the meaning of Shinto in this period; this triggered a conflict known as the 'enshrinement debate' (*saijin ronsō*) that erupted in the same year 1875, and ran until 1881. See Zhong 2016, chapter 5.

23 Gion Matsuri Hensan Iinkai 1976: 29; Tomii 1979: 288. The three floats of
    1864 were Hashi Benkei-yama, En no Gyōja-yama, and Suzuka-yama (chests
    only).
24 Tsuchida cooperated closely with Murata Gorōbei, a member of the Hōka-hoko
    float street and official of a ward with thirteen floats. Tsuchida and Murata
    remained central figures in the organization of the float parade for many years after
    this episode. Itō 2017: 33 and 39 note 8. The old Seitoku Primary School serves
    today as the offices of the Floats Association.
25 Tsuchida's account is reproduced in full in Takahara 1962: 295–9 and Tomii 1979:
    283–6.
26 This meetinghouse, rebuilt in 1926, still functions as the headquarters of the
    Sanwaka *mikoshi* association at its original location.
27 Yoneyama 1986: 23–6. *Sanwaka-gumi* and *Shiwaka-gumi* are today known as the
    Sanwaka and Shiwaka *shin'yokai* or '*mikoshi* associations'.
28 Tomii 1979: 300–1.
29 Satō 2019: 32. Satō notes that this change was officially registered in 1899, but
    introduced already five years earlier.
30 Gion Matsuri Yamahoko Rengōkai 1974: 32.
31 Satō 2017: 67–8.
32 Kobayashi 2007: 7–9.
33 Gion Matsuri Yamahoko Rengōkai 1974: 33.
34 'Gion matsuri yamahoko gyōji kin-gendaishi nenpyō' (a timeline of major events in
    the history of the Gion festival, and the float parades in particular, up to 2010) in
    Kyōto-shi Bunkazai Hogoka 2011: 57–73.
35 In addition to Tsuki-hoko and Niwatori-hoko, Minami Kannon-yama,
    Hakurakuten-yama, Naginata-hoko, and Kanko-hoko were particularly hard-
    pressed. Itō 2017: 34–5; Satō 2019: 38–43; Hakurakuten-yama 1976: 39.
36 Takagi 2020: 24.
37 For a richly illustrated discussion of the redevelopment of the Imperial Palace and
    Heian Shrine, see Tseng 2018, chapter 1.
38 *Kyōto kōkyū hozon ni kanshi ikensho* (On the preservation of the Kyoto Imperial
    Palace, 1883), Iwakura-kō Kyūseki Hozonkai 1906: 2038–48.
39 Iwakura mentions Moscow as a model in *Kyōto kōkyū hozon ni kanshi ikensho*;
    Takagi 2020: 25.
40 Tseng 2018, chapter 3.
41 Iwakura-kō Kyūseki Hozonkai 1906: 2046.
42 Breen 2020: 45–8.
43 On the chaotic planning process of this monument/shrine, see Van Goethem 2018.
44 Breen 2020: 42.
45 Kyōto-shi Sanjikai 1907: 14.

46 Ichimura was elected as Kyoto mayor in 1927 but only served for a few months before health problems forced him to retire.

47 *Hinode shinbun*, 19 June 1916. This piece was written by the *haiku* poet Ōgama Kodō (1878–1958).

48 Kanko-hoko Hozonkai 2001: 28.

49 Satō 2021a. Satō published these numbers in connection with a lecture, delivered at the Ritsumeikan Research Society for Historical Geography on 18 July 2021. See also Satō 2019: 50–2.

50 Teeuwen 2020b: 225.

51 Kyōto-shi Sangyōbu Kankōka 1938: 10.

52 This festival started in 1931. The parade was suspended in 1937 due to the war in China and never revived, while the *shinji* part of the festival, with rites performed at Heian Jingū, continued until 1951.

53 Kyōto-shi Sangyōbu Kankōka 1938: 71–2. *Gōka kenran* is to this day the most used cliché phrase in descriptions of the float parades.

54 Hattan 2018, chapter 7.

55 Kyōto-shi Sangyōbu Kankōka 1938: 7–8.

56 Arare Tenjin-yama 1926; Hōshō-yama 1932; Suzuka-yama 1938.

57 This came on top of the much larger subsidies that the Purity Association paid to the float streets, via the Floats Association.

58 I gained access to these records thanks to the staff of the Floats Association office in Yamabushi-yama Street and the mediation of Murakami Tadayoshi, formerly of Kyoto City's Division for the Preservation of Cultural Properties (Bunkazai Hogoka). For more on this source, see Teeuwen 2020b.

59 Teeuwen 2020b: 227.

60 Usually, this phrase refers to the Kanda festival in Tokyo, the Gion festival in Kyoto, and the Tenjin festival in Osaka.

61 A cutting of this article is pasted into *Gion yamahoko rengōkai kiroku* 4.

62 Kawaguchi 2014.

63 *Gion yamahoko rengōkai kiroku* 4, entries 20–23 March, 12 July, 10 August, and 12 August 1945.

64 Kyōto-shi Bunkaka 1967 gives an outline of developments in the festival in the first two decades after the war. See also 'Gion matsuri no ayumi: Shōwa 20nen kara kyō made' in Gion Matsuri Yamahoko Rengōkai 1991: 170–6, and Gion Matsuri Hensan Iinkai 1976: 71–3.

65 These four shopping streets were Kawaramachi, Kyōgoku, Nishiki and Shijō.

66 *Gion yamahoko rengōkai kiroku* 4, entry 19 June 1947.

67 *Kyōto shinbun*, 9 July 1947. *Karuta* are cards carrying lines from a hundred famous *waka* poems. Players sit opposite each other and compete to find and collect the cards that complete the poems.

68 Thomas 2019.
69 Thomas 2014: 276.
70 Fukami 2018. Fukami Shigeru, who served as head of the Floats Association between 1996 and 2011, stems from a family that has lived in the Kuronushi-yama float street since the Edo period.
71 From an unidentified newspaper cutting in Shimizu's record.
72 Itō 2010: 2840; Teeuwen 2020a: 141. On Kyoto City policy related to the festival more generally, see Akimoto 2005.
73 Proposed changes in the float parades in the 1950s and 1960s were discussed at length with and among all float streets, and were finally decided by vote at general meetings of the Floats Association. Although a few floats dissented, a large majority supported the changes or at least acquiesced without much protest.
74 In the 1970s, the National Association of Shrines (Jinja Honchō) coordinated the Conference for Research on Folk Cultural Properties (*Minzoku bunkazai kenkyū kyōgikai*), an organization that lobbied for the inclusion of 'deity rituals' (*shinji*) in cultural properties. See Teeuwen 2020a: 147–9.
75 Satō 2019: 54–5.
76 *Gion yamahoko rengōkai kiroku* 4, entry 9 June 1943; Teeuwen 2020b: 228.
77 Satō 2019, figures 6.5 and 6.6.
78 Komatsu 2008.

Conclusion

1 Brosius and Hüsken 2010: ix–xi.
2 Brosius and Hüsken 2010: x.
3 Handelman 2006: 42.
4 In this scheme, carnivalesque play is seen as a sub-category of 'events that mirror', because the satire ultimately serves to draw attention to temporarily suspended social norms.
5 Handelman 2006: 45.
6 Yoneyama 1986: 133–57. This parade was started in response to the merger of the two float parades in 1966, with the aim of marking the *mikoshi*'s return in a different manner. *Sagi mai* disappeared from the Gion festival during the Ōnin war but was reintroduced from Tsuwano (*Tsuwano Yasaka jinja no sagi mai*) in 1956 as a shrine rite, performed on 16, 17 and 24 July within the grounds of Yasaka Shrine.
7 Handelman 1990: 60.
8 Morita 2015 elaborates on this model in his analysis of festivals in and around Kyoto and Osaka. Morita's preferred concepts are *matsuri* (i.e. *shinji*) versus *kami-nigiwai* ('festive events performed in the presence of the deities'). For the term *kami-nigiwai*, Morita draws on Orikuchi Shinobu (Morita 2015: 39).
9 Teeuwen 2021.

References

Adolphson, Mikael S. 1997. 'Enryakuji – An old power in a new era'. In *The origins of Japan's medieval world*, ed. Jeffrey P. Mass, Stanford University Press: 237–60.

Adolphson, Mikael S. 2000. *The gates of power: Monks, courtiers, and warriors in premodern Japan*. University of Hawai'i Press.

Akimoto, Seki 2005. 'Sengo fukkōki no Gion matsuri to Kyōto shisei'. *Kyōto shiseishi hensan tsūshin* 22: 6–8.

Aston, W. G. 1972. *Nihongi: Chronicles of Japan from the earliest times to A.D. 697*. Tuttle.

Baba, Bun'ei 1905. *Japan, 1853–64, or, Genji Yume Monogatari*. Tr. Ernest Mason Satow. Naigai Shuppan Kyōkai.

Berry, Mary E. 1994. *The culture of civil war in Kyoto*. Berkeley: University of California Press.

Breen, John, and Mark Teeuwen 2010. *A new history of Shinto*. Wiley-Blackwell.

Breen, John 2020. 'Performing history: Festivals and pageants in the making of modern Kyoto'. In *Kyoto's renaissance: Ancient capital for modern Japan*, ed. John Breen, Maruyama Hiroshi, and Takagi Hiroshi, Renaissance Books: 33–64.

Brosius, Christiane, and Ute Hüsken, ed. 2010. *Ritual matters: Dynamic dimensions in practice*. Routledge.

Brumann, Christoph 2009. 'Outside the glass case: The social life of urban heritage in Kyoto'. *American Enthnologist* 36–2, 276–99.

Brumann, Christoph 2012. *Tradition, democracy and the townscape of Kyoto: Claiming a right to a past*. Routledge.

Bunkachō 2014. *Kyōto kenboko no matsuri, chōsa hōkokusho, eizō-hen kaisatsusho*. Kyoto-bunkaisan.com/report/pdf/tyousa/02/kenboko_10.pdf.

Collcutt, Martin 1981. *Five Mountains: The Rinzai Zen monastic institution in medieval Japan*. Harvard University Press.

Como, Michael 2009. *Weaving and binding: Immigrant gods and female immortals in ancient Japan*. University of Hawai'i Press.

Cooper, Michael 1965. *They came to Japan: An anthology of European reports on Japan, 1543–1640*. University of California Press.

Farris, William Wayne 2009. *Daily life and demographics in ancient Japan*. University of Michigan Press.

Faure, Bernard 2012. 'The God Daishōgun: From Calendar to Cult'. *Cahiers D'Extrême-Asie* 21–1: 201–21.

Faure, Bernard 2021. 'Like an Evil Wind—Gozu Tennō'. In *Rage and ravage: Gods of medieval Japan*, University of Hawai'i Press: 107–49.

Fukami, Shigeru 2018. 'Shōnen ga kenbun shita shūsengo no Gion matsuri tenbyō: rejime ni mo nokosenai ohanashi'. Lecture hand-out, Miyako no Matsuri Bunka Kenkyūkai, 21 April 2018.

Fukuhara, Toshio 1995. *Sairei bunkashi no kenkyū*. Hōsei Daigaku Shuppankyoku.

Fukuhara, Toshio 2006. 'Sengoku Shokuhōki ni okeru shokoku Gion'e no kakko chigo mai'. In *Sengoku Shokuhōki no shakai to girei*, ed. Futaki Ken'ichi, Yoshikawa Kōbunkan: 149–74.

Fukuhara, Toshio 2016. 'Orikuchi Shinobu yorishiro-ron no genten – higeko to kasahoko'. In *Yama, hoko, yatai gyōji: matsuri o kazaru minzoku zōkei*, ed. Ueki Yukinobu and Fukuhara Toshio, Iwata Shoin: 141–96.

Fukuhara, Toshio and Hattan Yūtarō 2013. *Gion matsuri, kagai nerimono no rekishi*. Rinsen Shoten.

Futaki, Ken'ichi 1985. *Chūsei buke girei no kenkyū*. Yoshikawa Kōbunkan.

Gay, Suzanne 2001. *The moneylenders of late medieval Kyoto*. University of Hawai'i Press.

Gion Matsuri Hensan Iinkai, ed. 1976. *Gion matsuri*. Chikuma Shobō.

Gion Matsuri Yamahoko Rengōkai, ed. 1974. *Kaitei Kinsei Gion matsuri yamahoko junkōshi*. Private publication.

Gion Matsuri Yamahoko Rengōkai, ed. 1991. *Yama-chō hoko-chō: Tokubetsu kinengō*. Private publication.

Gion Matsuri Yamahoko Rengōkai, ed. 1994. *Gion matsuri daiten: Yamahoko meihō o chūshin ni*. Kyōto Shinbunsha.

Gion Matsuri Yamahoko Rengōkai, ed. 2012. *Gion matsuri yamahoko kenshōhin chōsa hōkokusho, torai senshokuhin no bu*. Private publication.

Gion yamahoko rengōkai kiroku 4 and 5. 1941–48. Unpublished manuscripts, kept at the offices of the Yamahoko Rengōkai.

Gomi, Fumihiko 1984. *Inseiki shakai no kenkyū*. Yamakawa Shuppansha.

Goodman, Janet R. 1994. *Alms and vagabonds: Buddhist temples and popular pilgrimage in medieval Japan*. University of Hawai'i Press.

Goshima, Kuniharu 2004. *Kyōto chō kyōdōtai seiritsushi no kenkyū*. Iwata Shoin.

Goshima, Kuniharu 2017. 'Gion goryōe yamahoko no kiban to shite no 'chōnin''. *Geinōshi kenkyū* 217: 32–56.

Grapard, Allan G. 1988. 'Institution, ritual, and ideology: The twenty-two shrine-temple multiplexes of Heian Japan'. *History of Religions* 27–3: 246–69.

Hakurakuten-yama Hozonkai 1976. *Hakurakuten-yama*. In-house publication.

Hanada, Takuji 2014. 'Nanbokuchō-ki ni okeru shōgunke oshi-shoku no igi: Kensen, Shōsei, Seishun no shigyō-shoku arasoi saikō'. *Ritsumeikan bungaku* 637: 42–59.

Handelman, Don 1990. *Models and mirrors: Towards an anthropology of public events*. Cambridge University Press.

Handelman, Don 2006. 'Conceptual alternatives to "ritual"'. In *Theorizing rituals: Issues, topics, approaches, concepts*, ed. Jens Kreinath, Jan Snoek, and Michael Stausberg, Brill: 37–49.

Hattan, Yūtarō 2018. *Egakareta Gion matsuri: Yamahoko junkō, nerimono no kenkyū.* Shibunkaku.

Hayashima, Daisuke 2006. *Shuto no keizai to Muromachi bakufu.* Yoshikawa Kōbunkan.

Hayashiya, Tatsusaburō 1950. 'Machishū no seiritsu'. *Shisō* 312: 34–49.

Hayashiya, Tatsusaburō 1953a. 'Gōsonsei seiritsuki ni okeru machishū bunka'. In *Chūsei bunka no kichō*, Tōkyō Daigaku Shuppan.

Hayashiya, Tatsuzaburō 1953b. 'Gion matsuri ni tsuite'. In *Gion matsuri*, ed. Minshushugi Kagakusha Kyōkai Kyōto Shibu Rekishi Bukai, Tōkyō Daigaku Shuppankai: 59–100.

Hayek, Matthias 2008. *Les mutations du yin et du yang: divination, société et représentations au Japon, du VIe siècle à la fin du XIXe siècle.* PhD thesis, Inalco.

Honda, Ken'ichi 2010. 'Chūsei Kyōto no sairei ni okeru hoko to sono hen'yō: hikaku sairei bunkashi no tame no kisoteki sankō'. *Geinōshi kenkyū* 189: 1–15.

Honda, Ken'ichi 2013. *Chūkinsei Kyōto no sairei to kūkan kōzō: goryōe, Imamiya-sai, rokusai nenbutsu.* Yoshikawa Kōbunkan.

Honda, Ken'ichi 2016. 'Gion matsuri ni okeru Shijō otabisho o megutte'. *Ritsumeikan bungaku* 645: 202–19.

Hur, Nam-lin 2000. *Prayer and play in late Tokugawa Japan: Asakusa Sensōji and Edo society.* Harvard University Asia Center.

Imahori, Taitsu 1993. 'Ekibyō to jingi shinkō no tenkai: Gozu Tennō to Somin Shōrai no shison'. *The Journal of the History of Buddhism* 36-2: 1–44.

Imahori, Taitsu 1999. 'Gozu Tennō to Somin Shōrai no shison'. In *Honji suijaku shinkō to nenbutsu: Nihon shomin bukkyōshi no kenkyū*, Hōzōkan.

Inoue, Mitsurō 1972. 'Eichō gannen no dengaku sōdō – insei shoki no bunka to sciji'. *Geinōshi kenkyū* 36: 1–18.

Ishizu, Hiroyuki 2020. 'Kinsei ni okeru jinja to monzeki no kankei: Gionsha to Shōren'in, Myōhōin o jirei to shite'. *Hisutoria* 278: 49–75.

Itō, Masayoshi 1980. 'Jidō setsuwa kō'. *Kokugo kokubun* 555: 1–32.

Itō, Setsuko 2010. '1956nen no Gion matsuri yamahoko junkōro no henkō ni kansuru kōsatsu: Kyōto-shi no seisaku dōkō ni chakumoku shite'. *Nihon Kenchiku Gakkai keikakukei ronbunshū* 75-658: 2837–43.

Itō, Setsuko 2017. 'Kindai ni okeru Gion matsuri yamahoko junkō no keizoku ni kansuru kōsatsu'. *Kankō kenkyū* 29-1: 29–41.

Iwakura-kō Kyūseki Hozonkai, ed. 1906. *Iwakura-kō jikki (ge)*, vol. 2. Iwakura-kō Kyūseki Hozonkai.

Iwata, Hideo 2017. 'Kyōgen ni miru Gion'e furyū: *Kuji zainin* o chūshin ni'. *Geinōshi kenkyū* 218: 42–56.

Izumi, Mari 2017. 'Egakareta furyū: 'Tsukinami sairei zu' no zuzō no keifu to sono saisei'. *Geinōshi kenkyū* 217: 3–19.

Kamei, Wakana 2003. *Hyōshō to shite no bijutsu, gensetsu to shite no bijutsushi: Muromachi shogun Ashikaga Yoshiharu to Tosa Mitsumochi no kaiga.* Buryuke.

Kanko-hoko Hozonkai 2001. *Kanko-hoko chō hyakunenshi: Meiji, Taishō soshite Shōwa.* Zaidanhōjin Kanko-hoko Hozonkai.

Kawaguchi, Tomoko 2014. *Tatemono sokai to toshi bōkū: 'hi-sensai toshi' Kyōto to senchū, sengo.* Kyōto Daigaku Gakujutsu Shuppankai.

Kawamura, Minato 2021. *Gozu Tennō to Somin Shōrai densetsu: kakusareta ijintachi* (expanded edition). Sakuhinsha.

Kawashima, Masao 2010. *Gion matsuri: shukugi no Kyōto.* Yoshikawa Kōbunkan.

Kawauchi, Masayoshi 2006a. *Chūsei Kyōto no toshi to shūkyō.* Shibunkaku.

Kawauchi, Masayoshi 2006b. 'Gion'e mikoshi kayochō to Imamiya jinin: Muromachi, Sengoku ki ni okeru'. *Ritsumeikan bungaku* 569: 115–36.

Kawauchi, Masayoshi 2006c. 'Gion'e yamahoko kujitori kō: sengoku jidai kara kinsei zenki ni kakete'. In *Toshi no kurashi no minzokugaku: toshi no hikari to yami*, ed. Shintani Takanori and Iwamoto Michiya, Yoshikawa Kōbunkan: 79–101.

Kawauchi, Masayoshi 2007. *Gion matsuri to sengoku Kyōto.* Kadokawa Sōsho.

Kawauchi, Masayoshi 2008. '*Sengoku jidai no Gion matsuri* ron: yutaka na imēji to shijitsu no kangeki'. *Geinōshi kenkyū* 183: 26–39.

Kawauchi, Masayoshi 2011. 'Gion'e o kenbutsu suru to iu koto: Muromachi-ki ni okeru'. *Ritsumeikan bungaku* 622: 1–15.

Kawauchi, Masayoshi 2012. *Gion matsuri no chūsei: Muromachi, Sengoku-ki o chūshin ni.* Shibunkaku.

Kawauchi, Masayoshi 2015. *Kaiga shiryō ga kataru Gion matsuri: Sengoku-ki Gion sairei no yōsō.* Tankōsha.

Kitamura, Norio 2019. *Kinsei Kyōto jisha no bunkashi.* Hōzōkan.

Kobayashi, Kei 2014. 'Kyōto-shi Kōdō kumiai no seiritsu to hensen: Shōwa no Tairei e no taiō o chūshin ni'. *Tōkyō Daigaku Nihonshigaku Kenkyūshitsu kiyō* 18: 91–120.

Kobayashi, Takehiro 2007. 'Kindai Kyōto no chō shikimoku o megutte: Tenjin Yama chō no baai'. *Shakai kagaku* 79: 1–15.

Kojima, Michihiro 2020. '*Tsukinami saireizu byōbu* ni egakareta bakufu to jinja'. In *Tsukinami saireizu byōbu no fukugen to kenkyū: yomigaeru Muromachi Kyōto no kagayaki*, ed. Iwanaga Terumi et al., Shibunkaku: 124–31.

Komatsu, Hideo 2008. 'Gion matsuri no yamahoko-chō no akutā nettowāku to jissen komyunitī'. In *Kyōto no 'machi' no shakaigaku*, ed. Ajisaka Manabu and Komatsu Hideo, Sekai Shisōsha: 58–77.

Kosugi, Satoshi 1970. 'Gionsha no shasō'. *Shintōshi kenkyū* 18-2: 33–48 and 18-3: 30–42.

Kosugi, Satoshi 1971. 'Gionsha no oshi'. *Shintōshi kenkyū* 19-1: 15–30.

Koyama, Toshihiko 2013. 'Gion goryōe to ōchō bungaku'. *Ritsumeikan bungaku* 630: 625–34.

Kubota, Osamu 1974. *Yasaka jinja no kenkyū.* Rinsen Shoten.

Kubota, Keisuke 2016. 'Gion matsuri, Ayagasa-hoko ni tsuite'. *Sairei no bi: Ishidori matsuri to Gion matsuri: Kuwana-shi Hakubutsukan Heisei 28nendo tokubetsuten UNESCO mukei bunka isan tōroku kinen tokubetsu tenji*, ed. Kuwana-shi Hakubutsukan, In-house publication: 82–100.

Kyōto-shi Bunkaka 1967. *Gion matsuri: sengo no ayumi*. In-house publication.

Kyōto-shi Bunkazai Hogoka, ed. 2011. *Shashin de tadoru Gion matsuri yamahoko gyōji no kindai*. Kyōto-shi Insatsubutsu.

Kyōto-shi Sanjikai 1907. *Kyōto meishochō*. Kyōto-shi.

Kyōto-shi Sanjikai, ed. 1969. *Kyōto no rekishi vol. 4, Momoyama no kaika*. Gakugei Shorin.

Kyōto-shi Sanjikai, ed. 1972. *Kyōto no rekishi vol. 5, Kinsei no tenkai*. Gakugei Shorin.

Kyōto-shi Sanjikai, ed. 1974. *Kyōto no rekishi vol. 7. Ishin no gekidō*. Gakugei Shorin.

Kyōto-shi Sangyōbu Kankōka, ed. 1938. *Kyōto-shi kankō jigyō yōran*. Kyōto-shi.

Lillehoj, Elizabeth 2004. *Critical perspectives on classicism in Japanese painting, 1600–1700*. University of Hawai'i Press.

Matsudaira, Makoto 2001. *Matsuri no bunka: Toshi ga tsukuru seikatsu bunka no katachi*, Yūhikaku (first edition 1983).

Maxey, Trent E. 2014. *The 'greatest problem': Religion and state formation in Meiji Japan*. Harvard University Asia Center.

Mayumi, Tsunetada 2000. *Gion shinkō: Shintō shinkō no tayōsei*. Toki Shobō.

McKelway, Matthew P. 2006. *Capitalscapes: Folding screens and political imagination in late medieval Kyoto*. University of Hawai'i Press.

McMullin, Neil 1987. 'The Enryaku-ji and the Gion shrine-temple complex in the mid-Heian period'. *Japanese Journal of Religious Studies* 14–2/3: 161–84.

McMullin, Neil 1988. 'On placating the gods and pacifying the populace; The case of the Gion *Goryō* cult'. *History of Religions* 27–3: 270–93.

Mieda, Akiko 2001. 'Nanbokuchōki Kyōto ni okeru ryōiki kakutei no kōzō: Gionsha o rei to shite'. *Nihonshi kenkyū* 469: 1–34.

Minshushugi Kagakusha Kyōkai, Kyōto Shibu Rekishi Bukai (narrated by Hayashiya Tatsusaburō) 1953. *Gion matsuri*. Tōkyō Daigaku Shuppanbu.

Misaki, Ryōshū 1956. 'Gozu Tennō no mikkyōteki yōso'. *Indogaku bukkyōgaku kenkyū* 4–1: 216–19.

Morin, Olivier 2016. *How traditions live and die*. Oxford University Press.

Morita, Akira 2015. *Nihon no matsuri to kami-nigiwai*. Sōgensha.

Motoori Norinaga zenshū. 20 vols. 1968–1975. Chikuma Shobō.

Murakami, Tadayoshi 2006. 'Byōbu matsuri no keifu'. In *Toshi no kurashi no minzokugaku: toshi no hikari to yami*, ed. Shintani Takanori and Iwamoto Michiya, Yoshikawa Kōbunkan: 96–124.

Murakami, Tadayoshi 2010. 'Shinsei o obiru yamahoko: kinsei Gion matsuri yamahoko no henka'. In *Nenjū gyōji ronsō: Hinami kiji kara no shuppatsu*, ed. Hinami Kiji Kenkyūkai, Iwata Shoin: 289–312.

Murayama, Shūichi 1991. *Nihon onmyōdō shi sōsetsu*. Hanawa Shobō.

Murayama, Shūichi 1994. *Hieizan shi: tatakai to inori no seiiki*. Tōkyō Bijutsu.

Naginata-hoko Hozonkai, ed. 2016. *Naginata-hoko zaidan hōjin 50nenshi*. Private publication.

Nakagawa, Osamu 2015. *Kyōto to kindai: Semegiau toshi kūkan no rekishi*. Kashima Shuppankai.

Nakai, Shinkō 1993. *Gyōki to kodai bukkyō*. Nagata Bunshōdō.

Nakai, Shinkō 2013. 'Gionsha no sōshi to Gozu Tennō: Imahori Taitsu-shi no shoron ni yosete'. In *Hōnen shōnin eden no kenkyū*, Shibunkaku: 121–47.

Nihon koten bungaku taikei 1, vol. Kojiki norito. 1958. Ed. Kurano Kenji and Takeda Yūkichi. Iwanami Shoten.

Nishimura, Takashi and Okuda Iari 2011. 'Kindai Kyōto ni okeru chō jichi to kiyaku: Tearaimizu-chō o jirei to shite'. *Keizaigaku ronsō* 62–4: 59–76.

Nishio, Kazumi 1981. 'Machishū ron saikentō no kokoromi: Tenmon hokke ikki o megutte'. *Nihonshi kenkyū* 229: 56–75.

Nishida, Nagao 1962. '*Gion Gozu Tennō engi* no shohon (jō-chū-ge)'. *Shintōshi kenkyū* 10–6: 135–170; 11–2: 41–55; and 11–3: 17–32.

Nishiyama, Masaru 1974. 'Inseiki ni okeru binpo no ho no keisei: Gionsha ryō yonkaho no seiritsu ni tsuite'. *Shintōshi kenkyū* 22: 29–45; 23: 27–47.

Nishiyama, Ryōhei 1995. *Goryō shinkō ron*. Iwanami Kōza Nihon tsūshi vol. 5. Iwanami.

Nishiyama, Tsuyoshi 2013. 'Kinseiki ni okeru Gion'e shin'yo kayochō no henka: Rakuchū rakugaizu byōbuhon o tegakari ni'. *Suzaku* 25: 25–42.

Nishiyama, Tsuyoshi 2015. 'Koshi o katsugu hitobito: rikisha, kayochō, Yase dōji'. In *Kōza: Jinken yukari no chi o tazunete, 2013nendo kōenroku*, Sekai Jinken Mondai Kenkyūjo: 145–64.

Nishiyama, Tsuyoshi 2017. 'Chūkinsei ni okeru Gion'e shin'yo o meguru hitobito: Gion'e shin'yo kayochō o megutte'. *Geinōshi kenkyū* 218: 23–41.

Nochi, Hidetoshi 1998. "Shasō" saikō: chūsei Gionsha ni okeru monbatsu keisei'. *Bukkyō Daigaku daigakuin kiyō* 26: 1–13.

Noda, Tadao 1959. 'Chūsei senmin no shakai-keizaiteki ichikōsatsu'. *Kyōto Gakugei Daigaku gakuhō* 14–3: 54–74.

Okada, Shōji 1994. 'Heian-kyō chū no sairei, otabisho saishi'. In *Heian jidai no kokka to saishi*, Zoku Gunsho Ruijū Kanseikai: 440–99.

Okuda, Iari 2010. 'Kindai Kyōto yamabokochō ni okeru funjō to jichi'. *Shakai keizai shigaku* 76–1: 65–80.

Onodera, Atsushi 1995. 'Higashi Harima ni okeru kinsei no Ise sangū: Akashi-shi Higashi Futami o jirei ni'. *Kōtsūshi kenkyū* 35: 85–95.

Ōtsuka, Katsumi 2001. 'Chūsei ni okeru Gion matsuri no chihō denpan'. *Suzaku* 13: 23–37.

Ozawa, Hiromu and Kawashima Masao 1994. *Zusetsu Uesugi-bon Rakuchū Rakugaizu byōbu o miru*. Kawade Shobō Shinsha.

Phillips, Nathalie 2018. *The epistemological significance of meta-physical beliefs within the socio-political context of Heian Japan*. PhD thesis, Edinburgh University.

Plutschow, Herbert 1983. 'The Fear of Evil Spirits in Japanese Culture'. *TASJ 3rd series* 18: 133–51.

Porcu, Elisabetta 2012. 'Observations on the blurring of the religious and the secular in a Japanese urban setting'. *Journal of Religion in Japan* 1: 83–106.

Porcu, Elisabetta 2020. 'Gion matsuri in Kyoto: A multi-layered religious phenomenon'. *Journal of Religion in Japan* 9: 37–77.

Raz, Jacob 1985. 'Popular entertainment and politics. The Great Dengaku of 1096'. *Monumenta Nipponica* 40–3: 283–98.

Ruiz de Medina, Juan G. 1995. *Documentos del Japón 1558–1562*. Instituto Histórico de la Compañía de Jesús.

Saitō, Hideki 2006. *Yomikaerareta Nihon shinwa*. Kōdansha Gendai Shinsho.

Saitō, Hideki 2012. *Araburu Susanoo, shichihenge: chūsei shinwa no sekai*. Yoshikawa Kōbunkan.

Saitō, Hideki 2021. 'Rekishin to shite no Gozu Tennō: rekichūsho, saimon, shinzō emaki o megutte'. In *Shin Onmyōdō sōsho vol. 4, Minzoku, setsuwa*, ed. Koike Jun'ichi, Meicho Shuppan: 491–514.

Satō, Hirotaka 2017. 'Kindai Kyōto no Gion matsuri ni okeru Hashi Benkei-yama no un'ei kiban: chiiki jūmin shudō no chō-monjo dejitaru ākaibu o katsuyō shite'. *Geinōshi kenkyū* 217: 57–74.

Satō, Hirotaka 2019, *Kyōto Gion matsuri no yamahoko gyōji no sonritsu shisutemu ni kansuru kenkyū: gendai toshi ni okeru sairei no keishō*. PhD thesis, Ritsumeikan Daigaku.

Satō, Hirotaka 2021a. 'Kindai Kyōto no toshinbu ni okeru mochiya-ritsu teika ni tomonau Gion matsuri yamahoko gyōji e no eikyō'. Lecture, Jinbun Chiri Gakkai Rekishi Chiri Kenkyū Bukai, 18 July 2021. https://www.bukkyo-u.ac.jp/news/uploads/202107/1de4e156ef160b7335c2cc2d4ba45ee2.pdf

Satō, Hirotaka 2021b. 'Kindai Kyōto ni okeru chō-monjo o mochiita chōnai keikan no fukugen: Kyōto-shi Higashiyama-ku *Yumiya-chō monjo* no seikaku to fukugen hōhō no kentō'. *Art Research* 21: 19–30.

Satō, Hirotaka and Yano Keiji, ed. 2018. *Fune-hoko, zaidan hōjin setsuritsu 50shūnen kinenshi*. Kōeki Zaidan Hōjin Gion Matsuri Funehoko Hozonkai.

Satō, Yasuhiro 2006. *Nihon no bijutsu 484 sairei zu*. Shibundō.

Schnell, Scott 1999. *The rousing drum: Ritual practice in a Japanese community*. University of Hawai'i Press.

Seta, Katsuya 1979. 'Chūsei Gion'e no ichikōsatsu: bajōyakusei o megutte'. *Nihonshi kenkyū* 200: 15–51.

Seta, Katsuya 2009. *Rakuchū Rakugai no gunzō: ushinawareta chūsei toshi e*. Heibonsha Library.

Shibata, Minoru 1984. *Goryō shinkō*. Yūzankaku Shuppan.

Shimosaka, Mamoru 2001. *Chūsei jiin shakai no kenkyū*. Shibunkaku.

Shimosaka, Mamoru 2014. *Chūsei jiin shakai to minshū: shuto to bashaku, jinin, kawaramono*. Shibunkaku.

Shimosaka, Mamoru 2016. 'Gionsha, dōsha otabisho no yakushoku rekidai'. In *Shinpen Yasaka jinja kiroku*, ed. Yasaka Jinja Monjo Hensan Iinkai, Rinsen Shoten: 825–66.

Shimosaka, Mamoru 2019. 'Chūkinsei no 'saka' no ryōiki to fūkei'. In *2018 nendo sabetsu no rekishi o kangaeru renzoku kōza kōenroku*, ed. Kyōto Buraku Mondai, Kenkyū Shiryō Sentā: 3–20.

Shinpen Yasaka jinja kiroku. Yasaka Jinja Monjo Hensan Iinkai, ed. 2016. Rinsen Shoten.

Shinpen Yasaka jinja monjo. Yasaka Jinja Monjo Hensan Iinkai, ed. 2014. Rinsen Shoten.

Shinshū Hirata Atsutane zenshū. 15 vols, 6 additional vols. Ed. Hirata Atsutane Zenshū Kankōkai, 1976–1981. Meicho Shuppan.

Shinshū Yasaka jinja monjo (chūsei-hen). Yasaka Jinja Monjo Hensan Iinkai, ed. 2002. Rinsen Shoten.

Shintō taikei, vol. *Jinja-hen 10, Gion.* Shintō Taikei Hensankai, ed. 1992. Shintō Taikei Hensankai.

Stavros, Matthew 2014. *Kyoto: An urban history of Japan's premodern capital.* University of Hawai'i Press.

Suzuki, Kōtarō 2010. 'Susanoo to Gionsha saijin: *Bingo fudoki* itsubun ni tan o hasshite'. *Ronkyū Nihon bungaku* 92: 55–72.

Suzuki, Kōtarō 2019. *Gozu Tennō shinkō no chūsei,* Hōzōkan.

Suzuki, Masataka 2000. 'Tsuina no keifu'. In *Oni to geinō,* ed. Matsuoka Shinpei, Shinwasha: 87–121.

Takagi, Hiroshi 2020. 'The Emperor system and Kyoto: Images from of the ancient capital'. In *Kyoto's renaissance: Ancient capital for modern Japan,* ed. John Breen, Maruyama Hiroshi, and Takagi Hiroshi, Renaissance Books: 3–32.

Takahara, Yoshitada 1962. 'Kaei igo no Yasaka jinja'. *Shintōshi kenkyū* 10–6: 259–321.

Takahara, Yoshitada 1972. *Yasaka jinja.* Gakuseisha.

Takamaki, Minoru 2000. *Kinsei no toshi to sairei.* Yoshikawa Kōbunkan.

Tanaka, Kaori 2011. '*Gion shigyō nikki* ni miru chūsei Gionsha no wata shōbai no jinin'. *Nihon bunkashi kenkyū* 42: 79–95.

Tani, Naoki and Masui Masaya, ed. 1994. *Machi Gion matsuri sumai: toshi sairei no gendai.* Shibunkaku.

Teeuwen, Mark and Kate Wildman Nakai, ed. 2014. *Lust, commerce, and corruption: An account of what I have seen and heard, by an Edo samurai.* Columbia University Press.

Teeuwen, Mark and John Breen 2017. *A social history of the Ise Shrines: Divine capital.* Bloomsbury.

Teeuwen, Mark 2017. 'Clashing models: Ritual unity vs religious diversity'. *Japan Review* 20: 39–62.

Teeuwen, Mark 2020a. 'Kyoto's Gion festival as heritage'. In *Sacred heritage in Japan,* ed. Aike P. Rots and Mark Teeuwen, Routledge: 134–58.

Teeuwen, Mark 2020b. '*Gion'e yamahoko rengōkai kiroku* ni miru senji-senryōki no Gion matsuri: hendōki ni okeru toshi sairei no igi to kachi o kangaeru'. *Jinbun gakuhō* 115: 223–37.

Teeuwen, Mark 2021. 'Faith as authenticity: Kyoto's Gion festival in 2020'. *Japanese Journal of Religious Studies* 48–1: 125–63.

Teeuwen, Mark 2022. 'Kyoto's Gion festival in late classical and medieval times: Actors, legends, and meanings,' *Religions* 13–6: 545.

Thomas, Jolyon B. 2014. 'Religious policies during the Occupation of Japan, 1945–52'. *Religion Compass* 8–9: 275–86.

Thomas, Jolyon B. 2019. *Faking liberties: Religious freedom in American-occupied Japan.* University of Chicago Press.

Toda, Yoshimi 1971. 'Shōen taisei kakuritsuki no shūkyōteki minshū undō: Eichō Dai-Dengaku ni tsuite'. *Rekishigaku kenkyū* 378: 8–15.

Tomii, Yasuo 1971. 'Gion matsuri no keizai kiban'. In *Kyōto shakaishi kenkyū*, ed. Dōshisha Daigaku Jinbunkagaku Kenkyūjo, Hōritsu Bunkasha: 189–246.

Tomii, Yasuo 1979. 'Ishinki no Gion matsuri no tsuite'. In *Kyōto chiikishi no kenkyū*, ed. Akiyama Kunizō Sensei Tsuitōkai, Kokusho Kankōkai: 279–305.

Tomii, Yasuo 1996. 'Kinsei Kyōto no shihai to shinji: *Kyōto machibure shūsei* ni miru Gion'e'. In *Kyōto machibure no kenkyū*, ed. Kyōto Machibure Kenkyūkai, Iwanami Shoten: 57–94.

Tōno, Haruyuki 2004. 'Daijōe no tsukurimono: hyō no yama no kigen to seikaku'. *Kokuritsu Rekishi Minzoku Hakubutsukan kenkyū hōkoku* 114: 21–32.

Tseng, Alice Y. 2018. *Modern Kyoto: Building for ceremony and commemoration, 1868-1940.* University of Hawai'i Press.

Tsuchimoto, Toshikazu 1994. 'Kinsei Kyōto ni okeru Gion otabisho no seiritsu to hensen: ryōshuteki tochi shoyū no kaitai to rinchi kyōkaisen no seisei'. *Nihon Kenchiku Gakkai keikakukei ronbunshū* 59–456: 227–35.

Ueki, Yukinobu. 2001. *Yama, hoko, yatai no matsuri: furyū no kaika.* Hakusuisha.

Van Goethem, Ellen 2018. 'Heian Jingū'. *Journal of Religion in Japan* 7–1: 1–26.

Varley, H. Paul 1990. 'Cultural life in medieval Japan'. In *The Cambridge history of Japan vol 3, Medieval Japan*, ed. Kozo Yamamura, Cambridge University Press: 447–99.

Wakahara, Shimei 1982. *Gion'e yamahoko taikan.* Yasaka Jinja.

Wakita, Haruko 2016. *Chūsei Kyōto to Gion matsuri: Ekijin to toshi no seikatsu.* Yoshikawa Kōbunkan.

Walthall, Anne 2006. 'Hiding the shoguns: Secrecy and the nature of political authority in Tokugawa Japan'. In *The culture of secrecy in Japanese religion*, ed. Bernhard Scheid and Mark Teeuwen, Routledge: 331–56.

Watanabe, Ayumu 2011. 'Go-Daigo shinsei shoki no jinin kuji chōjirei saikō'. *Ajia bunkashi kenkyū* 11: 17–32.

Weiss, David 2022. *The god Susanoo and Korea in Japan's cultural memory: Ancient myths and modern empire.* Bloomsbury.

Yamaji, Kōzō 1998. 'Gion-bayashi no genryū to hensen'. In *Kōza Gion-bayashi*, Gion Matsuri Yamahoko Rengōkai: 19–67.

Yamaji, Kōzō 2009. *Kyōto geinō to minzoku no bunkashi.* Shibunkaku.

Yamamoto, Hiroko 1998. *Chūsei shinwa.* Iwanami Shinsho.

Yamamoto, Naotomo 2006. 'Gionsha to inu jinin'. In *Kōza: Jinken yukari no chi o tazunete, 2004-nendo kōenroku.* Sekai Jinken Mondai Kenkyūjo: 45–71.

Yasaka Jinja, ed. 1906. *Yasaka shi.* Yasaka Jinja.

Yasaka Jinja 1997, *Yasaka jinja*, Gakuseisha.

Yasaka jinja kiroku, 2 vols. Yasaka Jinja Shamusho, ed. 1923. Yasaka Jinja Shamusho.

Yoneyama, Toshinao 1974. *Gion matsuri: toshi jinruigaku no kotohajime*. Chūō
   Kōronsha.
Yoneyama, Toshinao 1986. *Dokyumento Gion matsuri: toshi to matsuri to minshū to*.
   Nihon Hōsō Shuppan Kyōkai.
Yu, Zhenshun 2003. 'Eikyō Dai-Dengaku ni okeru kizoku to minshū'. *Gendai shakai
   bunka kenkyū* 27: 159–74.
Zhong, Yijiang 2016. *The origin of modern Shinto in Japan: The vanquished gods of
   Izumo*. Bloomsbury.
Zōho Yasaka jinja monjo, 3 vols. Yasaka Jinja Shamusho, ed. 1998 [1939 and 1940].
   Yasaka Jinja Shamusho.

Index

Page numbers in *italics* refer to figures.

www.ingramcontent.com/pod-product-compliance
Lightning Source LLC
Chambersburg PA
CBHW050412280326
41932CB00013BA/1827